Marriage and Cohabitation

POPULATION AND DEVELOPMENT
A SERIES EDITED BY RICHARD A. EASTERLIN

Marriage and Cohabitation

ARLAND THORNTON

WILLIAM G. AXINN

YU XIE

THE UNIVERSITY OF CHICAGO PRESS   CHICAGO AND LONDON

The University of Chicago Press, Chicago 60637
The University of Chicago Press, Ltd., London
© 2007 by The University of Chicago
Paperback edition 2010

Printed in the United States of America

19 18 17 16 15 14 13 12 11 10   3 4 5 6 7

ISBN-13: 978-0-226-79866-0 (cloth)
ISBN-13: 978-0-226-79867-7 (paper)
ISBN-10: 0-226-79866-6 (cloth)
ISBN-10: 0-226-79867-4 (paper)

Library of Congress Cataloging-in-Publication Data

Thornton, Arland.
    Marriage and cohabitation / Arland Thornton, William G. Axinn, Yu Xie.
        p.   cm.
    Includes bibliographical references and index.
    ISBN-13: 978-0-226-79866-0 (cloth : alk. paper)
    ISBN-10: 0-226-79866-6 (cloth : alk. paper)   1. Marriage—United States.   2. Unmarried
couples—United States.   3. Young adults—United States—Attitudes.   4. United
States—Social conditions—1945–   I. Axinn, William G.   II. Xie, Yu, 1959–   III. Title.
    HQ536 .T455 2007
    306.810973'09045—dc22

                                                                                2007003732

♾ The paper used in this publication meets the minimum requirements of the American
National Standard for Information Sciences—Permanence of Paper for Printed Library
Materials, ANSI Z39.48-1992.

Contents

Acknowledgments

We are indebted to many individuals and groups for their many valuable contributions to this book. We begin our expressions of appreciation with the approximately one thousand families who participated in our study from 1962 through 1993. The mothers in these families participated in eight interviews across these 31 years, while one child in each family participated in three interviews between 1980 and 1993. The data provided willingly—and often enthusiastically—by these families provide the foundation for most of the analyses and conclusions provided in this book.

The baseline data collection for this study was conducted as part of the Detroit Area Study, a training and research program of the Sociology Department of the University of Michigan. Subsequent interviews were conducted by the field staff of the Survey Research Center of the University of Michigan. The interviewing, coding, and computer staffs of the Survey Research Center provided the energy and commitment to complete the long-term panel data upon which this book is primarily based. The contributions of several members of the Detroit interviewing team—especially Elsie Bremen, Helen Flanagan, and Jackie Thorsby—were especially invaluable over many waves of the project.

The study was first based at the Population Studies Center and directed by Ronald Freedman, David Goldberg, and Lolagene Coombs. Since 1975 it has been located within the Survey Research Center and the Population Studies Center and directed by Arland Thornton, with Deborah Freedman as his research associate from 1975 through 1995. Many additional faculty members have contributed to the design, operationalization, and analysis of these data, including: Duane Alwin, William Axinn, Jennifer Barber, Frances Goldscheider, David Mann, Terri Orbuch, Paul Siegel, and Yu Xie. Judy Baughn, Donald Camburn, Julie de Jong,

Li-Shou Yang, and Linda Young-DeMarco have provided important administrative and research support to the collection and analysis of data.

The data collection, analysis, and reporting represented in this book have been greatly facilitated by our associations with the Family and Demography Program and the Quantitative Methodology Program, both located jointly within the Population Studies Center and the Survey Research Center at the Institute for Social Research of the University of Michigan. We are especially indebted to several of our program colleagues who collaborated in the analysis and writing of various chapters and appendices. These include Georgina Binstock, Kimberly Goyette, James Raymo, Li-Shou Yang, and Linda Young-DeMarco. The chapters and appendices on which they collaborated are noted in the text of the book. In addition to these individuals, comments, suggestions, and materials were provided by Jennifer Barber, Ron Lesthaeghe, Pamela Smock, and Scott Stanley.

Many other people have made significant contributions to the production of this volume. Judy Baughn has provided overall administrative support for the project. Jana Bruce and Julie de Jong also gave administrative assistance. Linda Young-DeMarco oversaw the management and processing of the data and provided many contributions to our conceptualization and execution of the analyses. Li-Shou Yang also provided data analysis assistance. The preparation and management of the manuscript was handled by Julie de Jong. Additional people providing computing and/or manuscript preparation assistance include Susan Brower, Susan Clemmer, Tera Freeman, Anu Gupta, Stephen McLandrich, Jennifer Richardson, Shirley Roe, and Rebecca Thornton. N. E. Barr provided editorial assistance in the preparation of the book. Assistance with library materials has been provided by Nika Bareket, Yan Fu, Pearl Johnson, Alberto Lares, Allison Purvis, Lee Ridley, and Jeff Zelinsky. We also appreciate the contribution of Ron Lesthaeghe and Lisa Neidert for permission to use a figure from their 2006 paper.

The preparation of this book has benefited from the comments, suggestions, and contributions of several people associated with the University of Chicago Press. These include the input of Richard Easterlin, who is the editor of the series of which this book is a part, Alex Schwartz, Parker Smathers, and the anonymous reviewers of the Press.

We express appreciation to the National Institute of Child Health and Human Development (NICHD) for its financial support for this project. NICHD has provided financial support for the data collection and processing for the project since the 1977 data collection. In addition, an

NICHD research grant (5 R01 HD19342, Intergenerational Effects on Marriage and Cohabitation) has provided financial support for the data analysis and manuscript preparation for this volume. We greatly appreciate the support of NICHD for this work.

Finally, and most importantly, we give special thanks to our wives and children: Arland to his wife, Shirley, and children, Richard, Blake, Rebecca, and Amy; Bill to his wife, Jennifer, and children, Elena and Noah; and Yu Xie to his wife, Yijun, and children, Raissa and Kevin. The loving support of each of these family members has been a substantial contribution to our scholarly careers and the production of this book.

PART I
Historical and Conceptual Issues

CHAPTER ONE

Introduction

Situating the Study

Throughout history, the family has been a central—some would argue *the* central—institution in human society. Historically, the family has been involved in almost all activities of human life, including, but not limited to, production, consumption, reproduction, parenting, social relations, governance, religion, and leisure. As a collective unit, the family has provided its members a common environment within which to interact, care for each other, and share resources. Although the precise role of the family in organizing specific social activities has changed over time, the centrality of the family to human society remains in place. Today, as has been true for thousands of years, the family is still a primary unit of human interaction, providing the basis for both generational renewal and individual linkage to the larger society.

Throughout most of the recorded history of the Western world, a family consisting of a wife, a husband, and children was the main social institution that structured the lives, activities, and relationships of women, men, and children. In the Western world, marriage governed the essential processes of mate selection and sexual expression; it was also the place for childbearing and childrearing. The marriage and family unit was the primary economic locus of society, being the main place of production, consumption, and the distribution of property within and between generations. Marriage defined womanhood, manhood, and adult status; it governed living arrangements; and it was also central in determining the division of labor and authority within the family and between the sexes.

Historically, the status of wife or husband was a central element of human identity and becoming a wife or husband was one of the most important transitions in people's lives. Marriage was also a central element in defining economic well-being, and physical and mental health.

For many, marriage also had religious significance. For some time in the Western world, the Catholic Church made marriage a sacrament and instituted a canon law governing marriage. Although this rigid link between marriage and religion was modified during the Reformation and weakened by a secularization trend in recent centuries, a close connection between religion and marriage at the level of personal beliefs and values remains strong to the present day.

Likewise, in recent centuries marriage has been significant to the state in Western societies. In fact, in most Western countries, the state has extensive legal systems to regulate marriage and related behaviors.

From another point of view, marriage is considered one of the fundamental characteristics that identifies our species as human. Along with large brains, language, culture, bipedal movement, and dexterous hands, the combination of features defining the human solution to mating, childbearing, and childrearing is unique in the animal kingdom. Among these features are concealed ovulation, private sexual expression, sexual expression independent of ovulation, internal gestation, maternal nursing, prolonged dependency of the young, and tremendous investment of parental time and resources in the rearing of children. The long-term bonding of women and men into family units and the investment of mothers and fathers in the bearing and rearing of children are important elements of human mating and reproduction.

One of the most important stories of the past several centuries of Western history is the transformation of the institution of marriage—in particular, the declining centrality of marriage in defining and guiding human behavior and relationships (Axinn and Thornton 2000; Cherlin 2004). Marriage has become less central in organizing economic production, consumption, and the transfer of property across generations. It has become less influential in delineating the relationships between men and women, the transition to adulthood, and the identity for men and women. It has also become less relevant as a context for sexual expression, living arrangements, and the bearing and rearing of children. In addition, marriage has become less sacred, being increasingly viewed as a secular rather than a religious institution.

Although many of these trends have existed for a long time, the pace of change in the last four decades has been especially rapid. Today, most people have extensive experience living apart from their parental families without being married—in dormitories, by themselves, or as housemates with other unmarried people. During the past 40 years both first marriage and remarriage rates have fallen dramatically; age at first marriage has risen sharply; and divorce has increased to a rate that suggests about half of all marriages in America will end via divorce rather than death. Rates of sexual activity, pregnancy, and childbearing have increased sharply among the unmarried, with about a third of all American children born to unmarried parents. Together, the high rates of divorce, low rates of marriage (including remarriage), and high rates of nonmarital childbearing mean that more than one-half of all American children live in a single-parent household at some point in their lives, with some experiencing multiple marital dissolutions and extensive periods of living with a single parent. In addition, many American couples—both young and old—choose to live in nonmarital unions as an alternative to marriage, as a step in the process leading to marriage, or simply as an alternative to living alone or with parents or housemates. Today, about half of all Americans cohabit before marriage, and many more will cohabit following the dissolution of their marriages.

Accompanying these many behavioral changes in recent decades have been equally dramatic changes in the norms, values, and beliefs underpinning the institution of marriage. This period has seen the relaxation of acceptable choices, in the areas of sex, marriage, living arrangements, divorce, childbearing, and childrearing. The normative imperative to marry, to stay married, and to refrain from sexual relations, cohabitation, and childbearing outside of marriage has weakened considerably in recent decades. Thus, many important behaviors previously restricted by prevailing norms have become accepted by large fractions of Americans. In addition, historically positive views about marriage have declined over the past several decades.

In fact, marriage has been transformed so dramatically in recent decades that it is no longer clearly understood by ordinary Americans—or for that matter, by scholars who specialize in studying it. As one important book stated, "the role of marriage itself in society has become blurred" (Waite and Gallagher 2000, 15). Similarly, two prominent sociologists have recently written that we are now living "in a culture that we understand poorly with respect to what intimate relationships of various types mean" (Bumpass and Sweet 2001, 297). The recent trends in marriage and family life have sparked intense controversy and conflict. In fact, one observer has suggested that marriage and family issues are at the center of a cultural confrontation currently engulfing American politics (Hunter 1991). The very definition of family is now contested. What are the essential elements of families—marriage ties, blood relations, living together, economic interdependencies, companionship, or mutual support? Are families permanent organic units or voluntary associations? Similarly, the definition of marriage and its place in society are being debated. What are the central components of marriage—love and affection, personal support, religious sanction, government licensure and approval, community endorsement, or individual consent and commitment? Is marriage just a piece of paper or is it an important part of human life? Is marriage the source of personal satisfaction and happiness or is it harmful to human beings, especially women? What is the role of government in regulating and encouraging marriage? What are the differences between cohabitation and marriage? All of these issues are now open to scrutiny and debate in both public and private forums.

Divorce, teenage sexuality and pregnancy, unmarried childbearing, single parenthood, and unmarried cohabitation are particularly high-profile dimensions of these larger issues in today's public discourse. Adding to this mix the closely related issues of women's rights, childcare, abortion, and homosexuality (including the possibility of homosexual marriage) produces a discourse of widely contrasting images of good and moral that can be intense, even explosive.

The recent changes in marriage raise (at least) three important scholarly and practical questions. First is the issue of the forces stimulating the transformation of marriage. What are the social, economic, cultural, religious, technical, and political forces that have changed the ways in which Americans organize their personal and intimate lives? Equally intriguing is the issue of consequences. What are the effects of the transformation of marriage and intimate relationships in the lives of individual women and men, for children, and for the larger society? Third is the issue of individual variation in personal relationships. What are the forces in the lives of individuals and their families that lead to different experiences, values, and beliefs concerning courtship, marriage, divorce, cohabitation, sex, and childbearing? Why is there such diversity in the attitudes and behaviors concerning these central dimensions of the human experience?

Each of these three sets of issues is large, complex, and difficult. Together, they are sufficiently challenging that they occupy the attention of scholars from an array of academic disciplines, including anthropology, economics, demography, psychology, biology, education, history, sociology, medicine, public health, and family science. Scholars in diverse fields have produced an extensive body of literature concerning these issues, and many studies are ongoing. Nevertheless, many important and interesting questions remain.

In this book our primary focus is on the third broad set of questions outlined previously: the ways in which the marriage and cohabitation decisions of young people are influenced by their personal circumstances, experiences, attitudes, and the larger family system. We investigate a wide range of these causal influences. A secondary goal focuses on the first set of issues previously outlined concerning social change. Although data limitations prevent us from investigating why the recent changes in union formation have occurred, we are ideally situated to evaluate the family and personal characteristics of individuals who participated in these changes. The second set of issues—the consequences of family change—is largely outside the scope of this book.

We focus our attention in this book on factors that predict young people's entrance into marital and cohabiting unions. We investigate the tempo of forming marital and cohabiting unions, the choice between cohabitation and marriage, and the transformation of cohabiting unions into marriage. Our aim is to provide a comprehensive analysis of forces shaping young people's decisions to enter marital and cohabiting relationships.

Because decisions to enter marital and cohabiting relationships have their roots quite early in adulthood, sometimes as early as in adolescence, our investigation begins by considering the influence of parents as well as that of the young adults on these decisions. In the following paragraphs, we outline our reasoning regarding the intergenerational influences on decisions to marry or cohabit. Then, we briefly review the chief overarching theoretical principles guiding our effort to establish a comprehensive analysis of the influences on entrances into marriage and cohabitation. Next we explain the main data source we use in our investigation. Finally, we briefly outline our analytical strategy, and the implications of this strategy for understanding social changes in marriage and cohabitation.

Influences on Marriage and Cohabitation

We address the individual and familial forces that influence the formation of marital and cohabiting unions in young adulthood—the factors that shape both the entrance into unions and the selection between cohabitation and marriage. Our research is motivated and guided by an appreciation of the breadth of the causal forces influencing the formation of marital and cohabiting unions. As noted earlier, we begin with the understanding that union formation is an intergenerational process that involves, in direct and indirect ways, a range of influences from both young adults and their parents. Our primary goal is to understand the many ways in which influences from both young people and their parents combine to affect young adults' transitions into marital and cohabiting unions. We construct a theoretical model that links together influences from two generations on marriage and cohabitation behaviors and then we evaluate empirically many of the propositions in this model using intergenerational panel data.

Although some starry-eyed young adults may believe they are marrying only their spouse, they usually marry into an entire family with attendant interactions, relationships, and responsibilities that extend far beyond the spouse (Le Masters 1957). Parental influence may come in many different forms and from multiple directions. In the very beginning parents bequeath their offspring a rich inheritance of genes and physical characteristics that may influence the children's own approach to courtship, cohabitation, marriage, and childbearing. Children also receive a cultural and religious inheritance from their parents that provides models for experiencing reality and living with reality—a complex of norms, values, attitudes, and beliefs that guide subsequent decisions and experience concerning union formation. In addition, parents come to the experiences of childbearing and childrearing with their own familial heritage and experiences that have shaped their behavior and views of life. As children grow and mature in the parental home, they have numerous opportunities to learn the values and attitudes of their parents. They also have front-row seats for observing the realities of marriage in one family—their own—and how parental marriage, divorce, remarriage, and childbearing influence all family members. We also know that parents have a strong influence on their children's educational, occupational, and financial aspirations and accomplishments, which, in turn, have historically been intricately related to union formation.

Although individuals can cohabit and marry without the consent, and even knowledge, of the older generation, historically parents have assumed important support roles in the production of love, courtship, cohabitation, and marriage in the younger generation. Parents have historically provided advice and consent in the courtship and marriage process—and many apparently still try to influence their children's marital choices today (Whyte 1990). Many parents still believe that they have a stake in their children's marriages, and it matters to the parents who, when, and under what circumstances their children marry (Michael et al. 1994). This happens because parents care how the marriage will affect their own lives, their relationships with children and grandchildren, and their standing in the community. Parents also understand the importance of marriage in affecting the quality of their children's lives. Similar considerations suggest that parents will try to influence the decisions of their children about cohabitation as well, although, as with marriage decisions, parents understand the ultimate power to make and break unions lies with their children (Gillis 1985; Leonard 1980).

It is also likely that most young people have positive relationships with their parents, care about their parents' feelings and well-being, and want to please their parents (Rossi and Rossi 1990; Thornton, Orbuch, and Axinn 1995). Given these ties, it is likely that most children will be motivated to take into account—at least to some extent—the beliefs, values, and aspirations of parents concerning love, sex, courtship, cohabitation, marriage, education, and employment (Ajzen 1988; Ajzen and Fishbein 1977, 1980; Barber 2000; Fishbein and Ajzen 1974, 1975). For example, a study in the Netherlands found that most young adults report that social approval is an important factor in their decisions, and in particular, that the perceived opinions of parents concerning union formation were strongly related to intentions to marry or cohabit (Liefbroer and de Jong Gierveld 1993). In addition, recent research concerning the process of children leaving home in America—a process that is frequently linked to union formation—suggests that parental expectations and ideas about this process are exceptionally influential in children's decisions. In fact, they may be more influential than the views of the children themselves (Goldscheider and Goldscheider 1993).

Although the avenues for parental influence on marriage and cohabitation experiences are numerous and broad, we also know that, in the United States, the actual decisions are made by the children. Marriage decisions—including when and whom to marry—have been controlled in many societies by the parents, but in the Western world primary responsibility for those decisions has long resided in the younger generation. The autonomy and authority of young adult children in this process has probably been enhanced in recent years. It is the young people—rather than their parents—who choose their dates, determine when to go steady, decide about cohabitation, make and accept proposals, pick out wedding rings, and exchange vows that turn girlfriends into wives and boyfriends into husbands. For this reason we conceptualize the second-generation participants as the primary decision makers in the intricate process leading to cohabitation and marriage.

Young people bring to these decisions their own religious commitments and values along with specific attitudes, values, and beliefs concerning sex, gender roles, marriage, cohabitation, divorce, and the bearing and rearing of children. Also, the courtship process has its roots in adolescence, as young people learn about male-female relationships through their experiences with dating, going steady, and initiating intimate relationships. Much evidence indicates that religiosity, a range of attitudinal and value factors, and individual experiences with dating and sex are associated with subsequent marriage and cohabitation experience.

We also know that historically marriage has been one of the central elements in the transition to adulthood—perhaps the period in the life course with the most personal and family transitions. During late adolescence and early adulthood today young men and women are making some of the most important decisions of their lives. They are deciding how much education to obtain, what occupations to pursue, where and with whom to live, when and with whom to marry or cohabit, and the number and timing of children. During this period in life, individuals make entrances into and exits out of schools, jobs, occupations, living arrangements, romantic involvements, and geographical locations. They are also involved in negotiating the transition from dependency in the parental home to fully independent adulthood. These life course decisions and transitions are interrelated in important ways within a complex and multidirectional nexus. The nature and timing of these choices undoubtedly influence subsequent life course decisions and experiences, including the entrance into marital and cohabiting unions.

Overarching Theoretical Principles

Our research concerning the influences on marriage and cohabitation is guided by five overarching theoretical principles. We use these general principles to formulate specific hypotheses regarding the factors that are likely to affect marital and cohabiting behavior. The five key principles that form the foundation of our theoretical framework are: 1) some combinations of social roles are compatible and others create role conflict; 2) individuals' attitudes and beliefs shape their behavioral choices; 3) the formation and dissolution of unions require interpersonal bargaining in a world of relative choices; 4) experiences early in the life course shape circumstances and decisions later in the life course; and 5) the organization of activities between family and nonfamily units has implications for the lives of individuals. Each of these ideas has a long and rich history in the social sciences.

Role Compatibility and Role Conflict

Starting with the idea that individuals take on social roles as they interact with others in their daily lives (Goffman 1959), many social scientists have argued that some combinations of roles tend to be more compatible than others (Barber, Axinn, and Thornton 2002; Blossfeld and Huinink 1991; Crimmins, Easterlin, and Saito 1991; Kasarda, Billy, and West 1986; Rindfuss 1991; Rindfuss, Swicegood, and Rosenfeld 1987). Closely related is the idea that when individuals attempt to occupy multiple social roles simultaneously, they may experience role conflict if those social roles are not highly compatible (Burr et al. 1979; Crimmins, Easterlin, and Saito 1991; Goode 1960). Such role conflict may motivate individuals to avoid roles whose demands conflict or compete with the demands of other roles they prefer or have already adopted.

At the foundation of these hypotheses is the idea that the finite nature of our time and resources limits behavioral choices (Barber, Axinn, and Thornton 2002). As young people make the transition to adulthood, they must choose among a variety of possible pathways and roles. Choosing one role may make it difficult to fulfill some other roles or may ease the transition to different roles (Rindfuss 1991; Rindfuss, Swicegood, and Rosenfeld 1987). With respect to marriage and cohabitation, these roles fall under two broad categories: those that *facilitate* family formation and those that *compete* with family formation (Barber, Axinn, and Thornton 2002). This categorization does not suggest that individuals cannot fulfill multiple roles simultaneously, but rather indicates that some combinations of roles are *more difficult* to fulfill simultaneously than others. We expect particularly difficult role combinations to lead to the postponement of one of the roles.

For example, some family roles are particularly difficult to fulfill in combination with schooling (Barber, Axinn, and Thornton 2002). The role of a student usually involves spending large amounts of time away from home and constrains the ability to achieve economic independence for cohabitation and marriage (Thornton, Axinn, and Teachman 1995). Other roles facilitate or encourage family formation. For instance, an early pregnancy may lead to union-formation decisions, particularly marriage (Manning 1993).

Values, Beliefs, and Decision Making

Following Fishbein and Ajzen's models of Reasoned Action and Planned Behavior, we posit that young people approach the courtship process with numerous beliefs and values relevant to cohabitation and marriage (Ajzen 1988; Ajzen and Fishbein 1977, 1980; Fishbein and Ajzen 1974, 1975). Fishbein and Ajzen's theories form the most widely used framework in the social sciences for studying links between attitudes and behavior (Barber 2000, 2001; Barber, Axinn, and Thornton 2002; Liefbroer and de Jong Gierveld 1993). In this framework, attitudes toward a particular behavior—along with subjective norms—predict intentions, and intentions predict behavior. Thus, in the case of marriage or cohabitation, positive attitudes toward marriage or cohabitation, coupled with social pressure or social support, increase the likelihood of marrying or cohabiting (Fishbein and Ajzen 1975; Liefbroer and de Jong Gierveld 1993; Vinokur-Kaplan 1978).

Beliefs and values concerning dating, sex, living arrangements, the roles of women and men, cohabitation, marriage, divorce, and childbearing are all of direct importance in the study of marriage and cohabitation. Somewhat less direct, but still important, are beliefs and values concerning education, consumption, and employment. Beliefs concerning the outcomes associated with behaviors such as cohabitation, marriage, education, and employment are combined with the evaluations of these outcomes to produce attitudes toward those behaviors. The historical connection of the spiritual and the physical in the realm of marriage also makes religious background—including religious affiliation, participation, and commitment—an important influence on marriage and cohabitation values, attitudes, and behavior.

Although theoretical and empirical research on attitude formation and stability suggest that young adulthood is a time of relatively unstable attitudes (Alwin 1994; Thornton and Binstock 2001), Barber, Axinn, and

Thornton (2002) argue that attitudes held during the transition to adulthood are particularly likely to have a substantial influence on family formation behavior for two reasons. First, the transition to adulthood is a period of relatively abundant opportunities, and thus individuals are likely
to form their attitudes and intentions about one particular activity in explicit comparisons to the alternatives to that activity (Barber 2001; Barber, Axinn, and Thornton 2002). For instance, attitudes and intentions
toward family formation at age 18 are likely to be heavily influenced by
attitudes toward pursuing a college education and establishing a career,
because educational and career opportunities are most abundant at these
ages. Second, decisions made during the transition to adulthood have
a particularly long-lasting influence on the remainder of the life course
because they set individuals on paths that are sometimes difficult to
change (Barber, Axinn, and Thornton 2002). For instance, individuals
who choose early family formation often find it difficult to complete college and establish careers (Hoffman 1998), and individuals who choose
educational attainment and careers tend to marry and have children later
(Thornton, Axinn, and Teachman 1995; Barber 2000, 2001).

Interpersonal Bargaining and Marriage Markets

Marriage and cohabitation are unions that bring together two individuals—
each with distinct characteristics, values, and aspirations—into complicated
interactions with extensive negotiation and bargaining (Lundberg and
Pollak 1993, 1996, 2001; Pollak 1994, 2000). The outcome of this courtship
and negotiation depends upon both individuals and the values and experiences they bring to the relationship. It may also depend on their perceptions of their own alternative partnering options, which some social scientists liken to the concept of a "marriage market" (Lichter, LeClere, and
McLaughlin 1991; Lundberg and Pollak 1993). Though we do not focus
on the choice set of potential partners in our examination of marriage and
cohabitation, we do recognize that couple-level interpersonal bargaining
takes place within a context of individual perceptions of other options.

The Life Course

The life course perspective (Elder 1977, 1998; Elder, Johnson, and Crosnoe
2003) posits that experiences and circumstances early in life—including
biological and social factors—affect later life. We consider this for both

the parental and the young-adult generations. Parents' experiences long before their own children are born may shape the ways they rear those children. In the young-adult generation, circumstances and experiences in childhood may influence subsequent decision making. So, young people come to decisions about marriage and cohabitation with their own bio-genetic make-ups and personal and family experiences that can be powerful forces in the choices they make.

The Organization of Social Activities

The modes of organization framework focuses on the social organization of the family and highlights the ways that families intersect with other institutions to organize the basic social activities of daily life. It places families on a continuum from those in which family social networks organize nearly all of life's daily activities to those in which family social networks organize practically none (Thornton and Fricke 1987; Thornton and Lin 1994). The extent of family organization affects the nature of individuals' social interactions with family and nonfamily members and can motivate differences in family formation behaviors. This framework has proved useful for understanding shifts in family formation behavior in Asian countries (Axinn and Yabiku 2001; Thornton and Lin 1994), but it has rarely been applied to the study of family formation processes in the United States. We believe, nevertheless, that it is also useful for understanding American family attitudes and behaviors, including entrance into marital and cohabiting unions.

A great deal of previous research indicates that young people's marital and cohabiting decisions vary across different racial and ethnic identities. Some scholars argue that these differences are produced by variations in the social and economic circumstances of different racial and ethnic groups, while others suggest that differences in values and beliefs across racial and ethnic groups produce differences in marital and cohabiting behaviors. We investigate in detail the consequences of variations both in social and economic circumstances and in values and beliefs, but we do not study the consequences of racial and ethnic identity itself.

Data Sources

Although we draw upon data from numerous sources, the primary data we use in this book is the Intergenerational Panel Study of Parents and

Children (IPS). The IPS is a long-term panel study of parents and children that began in 1962 with the selection of a sample of white couples in the Detroit Metropolitan area who had just given birth to their first, second, or fourth child in the summer of 1961. Approximately equal numbers of women from each parity group were selected for the study. The study extends over the 31-year period from 1962 through 1993—from just after the children were born in 1961 to when they were age 31 in 1993 (Thornton, Freedman, and Axinn 2002). The data were gathered in eight interviews with the mothers and three interviews with the children born in 1961. The mothers were interviewed twice in 1962, and once in 1963, 1966, 1977, 1980, 1985, and 1993. The children were interviewed in 1980, 1985, and 1993.

In 1962, 92 percent of the original families sampled (1,113 women) were interviewed during the first wave. Attrition throughout the entire 31-year study period was exceedingly light and at present the dataset contains the information necessary for studying the intergenerational determinants of family formation for 950 families, or 87 percent of the original families interviewed. IPS follow-up interviews were conducted regardless of the mother or child's geographical location, accommodating respondents' residential changes within and outside of the state of Michigan since 1961. Inasmuch as the attrition from the sample was small, the characteristics of the continuing sample were almost identical to those of the original sample.

The eight waves of data from the mothers that were collected across the lifetimes of the participating children contain a wealth of information about the personal, social, economic, marriage, divorce, childbearing, and religious experiences and circumstances of the parents. The mothers also provided information about their attitudes and values concerning a broad range of family issues, as well as information concerning their aspirations and plans for their young-adult children.

The data from the children of these mothers are also extensive, covering three interviews across the 13 years from ages 18 through 31. These three interviews contain wide-ranging information about the young people's attitudes, plans, and behavior. The children also provided extensive information about their relationships with their parents, religious participation, living arrangements, and dating and peer relationships. Monthly data are also available on a wide range of experiences, including cohabitation, marriage, childbearing, work, and education from ages 15 through 31. The extensive information from both parents and children extending across the entire lifetimes of the children makes the data set a valuable resource for studying intergenerational influences on marriage and co-habitation. More information concerning the data set, including a discussion of its advantages and limitations, is provided by Thornton, Freedman, and Axinn (2002).

Although our sample has many unique advantages for studying marriage and cohabitation, it also has disadvantages. Foremost is the limitation of the sample to children born to white women in the Detroit Metropolitan Area in 1961, with African Americans and Asian Americans being excluded from the sample. And with only a small Latin population in Detroit in the early 1960s, only a few Latin Americans were included in the study. This sampling limitation means that we can generalize our conclusions only to the majority White population. Consequently, we cannot make any conclusions about the increasingly important minority populations in the United States. Fortunately, a great deal of the research literature using other data sources focuses explicitly on racial and ethnic variations in cohabiting and marital behavior (Bennett, Bloom, and Craig 1989; Crissey 2005; Dunifon and Kowaleski-Jones 2002; East 1998; Lee 1998; Loomis and Landale 1994; McLoyd et al. 2000; Smock 2000; Taylor, Jackson, and Chatters 1997). This literature describes differences from the White population, as well as influences on marital and cohabiting behavior in the African, Latino, and Asian American populations. To place our findings from the White population in a broader comparative context, in each of the chapters presenting specific empirical results we also provide a brief summary of what is known about other racial and ethnic groups based on this literature. Nevertheless, this is a limitation of the study that should be remembered as we proceed.

In addition, we cannot generalize our results beyond children born in 1961 in the Detroit Metropolitan Area. Our concern about the limitation of geographic location, however, has been substantially ameliorated by the lack of theoretical models positing that underlying causal mechanisms of union-formation processes vary across geographical areas. Although it is sometimes hypothesized (and empirical evidence confirms) that local circumstances such as the economy may influence union formation, these models do not suggest that these causal relationships themselves interact with geographical area (Lichter, LeClere, and McLaughlin 1991; Lichter et al. 1992). In addition, we have made several comparisons of data and findings from this data set with those from nationally representative data from White Americans, and those comparisons have been very reassuring. We have found that when comparisons can be made across data sets, the results of our study are generally consistent with those from national studies (Thornton and Axinn 1996; Thornton, Freedman, and Axinn 2002). We note many of these comparisons throughout the book. Finally, we also note that Michigan itself appears to fall near the median of marital and cohabiting behaviors in the United States. As we describe in chapter 4, recent comparative research by Lesthaeghe and Neidert (2006) demonstrates that, although the populations of some states exhibit relatively unique patterns of marital and cohabiting behavior, the population of Michigan is not among these outliers, but instead exhibits marital and cohabiting behaviors quite similar to the national averages.

Using a sample of children born in 1961 limits the temporal generalizability of our study. Although, as we outline in the following paragraphs, the children born in 1961 represent a particularly interesting cohort because they grew up in a period of great change, this fact also makes it difficult to generally apply their experiences to young people born in earlier or later periods. Again, we use the research literature on change over time in cohabiting and marital behaviors to provide some comparative evidence throughout the book (Bumpass and Sweet 1989; Bumpass, Sweet, and Cherlin 1991; Bumpass and Lu 2000). Unfortunately, this literature is not as voluminous as the literature on race and ethnic differences in cohabitation and marriage, making it difficult to know just how the forces influencing families in our study might be different for other cohorts. As a result, additional research will have to be done with other cohorts to establish exactly how they are similar to or different from the young adults and families included in the IPS.

The limitation of the IPS to interviews with mothers and children also restricts the scope of our analyses and conclusions. Although we can analyze information about fathers from mothers and children, the fact that this information does not come from the fathers themselves limits what we can say about fathers and their influence on children. This is a significant limitation of the study as we know that fathers play important roles in most families.

With long-term intergenerational panel data we are able to investigate the influence of many dimensions of the parental family on the marriage and cohabitation behavior of young-adult children. Our examination of parental influence begins with explanatory factors from early in the lives of the parents, before the children are born. These factors include parental immigration status, farm background, family size, and religiosity during the parents' own childhood. We also examine family organization and the extent to which parents organize their activities and interests around family units or around institutions outside the family. Parental educational and financial circumstances are also considered, along with parental aspirations for children's educational and occupational achievements. We also investigate parental religious affiliation, participation, and commitment. Finally, we examine the influence of the parents' own experiences, values, and attitudes concerning marriage, cohabitation, childbearing, and divorce.

To these parental factors we add many dimensions of life among young-adult children and ask how they influence entrance into marriage and cohabitation. Of central importance here are the religious involvement and commitment of young adults. Of similar importance are the attitudes and values young adults have concerning important family and personal matters such as sexual expression, marriage, cohabitation, divorce, and appropriate roles for women and men. We also consider the ways in which young people coordinate and integrate their union-formation experiences with other aspects of life, including school and work, with educational and career aspirations being an important part of the story.

Using the intergenerational panel data we present a comprehensive examination of the intergenerational causal pathways operating to influence decisions concerning cohabitation and marriage. We theoretically formulate and empirically evaluate many causal pathways. We then integrate these complex and multifaceted causal pathways into a comprehensive picture of the intergenerational influences on union formation during young adulthood.

Estimating Total, Direct, and Indirect Influences

Courtship and family formation are subject to numerous intergenerational influences that have multiple mechanisms and operate over extensive periods in the lives of parents and children. Parental factors that might affect the decisions of children concerning marriage and cohabitation can arise early in the lives of the parents—their own childhoods and adolescence—and extend through midlife when their children are making the transition to adulthood. We expect that some of these factors influence the family formation decisions of young people directly while others operate indirectly by influencing subsequent parental experiences or values that, in turn, influence the children's behavior. Parental factors can also influence children's cohabitation and marriage indirectly by influencing other dimensions of the children's lives that are connected to union formation.

Of course, second-generation union formation is also influenced by the experiences and values of the children themselves. These explanatory factors extend across the life course—from childhood and adolescence through the years that the children are making the transition to adulthood. Again, many of these factors in the lives of children are likely to influence the family formation process directly, while others have indirect influences through other life dimensions.

One primary goal of this research is to evaluate overall or total effects for each of these parent and child explanatory factors on the marriage and cohabitation experiences of young adults. Our purpose in estimating total effects is to understand the overall influence of an explanatory factor without considering the direct and indirect causal mechanisms transmitting that effect. We estimate these total effects in the context of a model controlling factors exogenous to the factor being examined.

A second goal of this research is to understand and elaborate the direct and indirect mechanisms that transmit the total effects of these explanatory factors. We do this by introducing potential intervening factors into the analysis and estimating how much of the total effect of a factor operates independently of the intervening factors. That is, the effect of a factor from early in the lives of parents or children estimated with later factors controlled indicates the direct effect of the more exogenous factor that does not operate through the intervening factors added to the analysis.

Finally, we note that the indirect effect is the part of the total effect transmitted through the intervening factors. It is the difference between the total effect of an explanatory factor and the direct effect when a set of intervening factors is taken into account. We want to both identify those intervening factors that help transmit the total effect of an explanatory factor and to estimate the magnitudes of the indirect effects of a specific explanatory factor through each of the relevant intervening factors.

Our approach to evaluating the total, direct, and indirect effects of parent and child factors on children's behavior follows time-tested procedures used by many methodologists and empirical researchers (Alwin and Hauser 1975; Blalock 1971; Clogg, Petkova, and Shihadeh 1992; Clogg, Petkova, and Haritou 1995; Duncan 1966, 1975; Xie and Shauman 1998). That is, we specify appropriate models that estimate the total effect of a particular attribute of interest while trying to ensure that the effects of interest are not biased or spurious. And we elaborate the relationship between a behavior and its explanatory factors by introducing additional factors that are plausible intervening factors.[1]

Estimating total, direct, and indirect effects of first- and second-generation factors on children's entrance into marital and cohabiting unions requires the formulation and empirical estimation of properly specified models (Blalock 1971; Clogg, Petkova, and Haritou 1995; Duncan 1966, 1975; Xie and Shauman 1998). Proper model specification requires researchers to be aware of the factors influencing the outcome of interest, the appropriate causal ordering of these explanatory factors, and any reciprocal influences between the outcome of interest and the explanatory factors. Misspecification can produce biased results and faulty conclusions. In our case, the substantial number of explanatory factors potentially influencing any particular outcome and the complexity of the relationships among these explanatory factors make assumptions about causal ordering difficult.

Our approach to the specification problem has been to design a multi-wave prospective panel study that measures as many of the theoretically important influences on family formation as possible. By starting our data collection at the children's births and measuring a broad range of influences from both parents and children, we can include in our empirical models many factors that are frequently omitted from other analyses but considered significant sources of unobserved heterogeneity. Examples of these influences include religiosity, attitudes toward family issues, aptitude, and educational and career aspirations. We do not claim to have measured all of the relevant factors—for example, we do not include genetic attributes, physiological attributes, or community characteristics—but the breadth of our explanatory factors allows us to obtain many new insights while minimizing model misspecification bias.

We have relied upon theoretical reasoning and the intergenerational panel design of our data to deal with the issue of reciprocal causation and endogeneity bias. The lifetime of panel data about the children and their families provides the opportunity to construct models with plausible causal assumptions. However, although the causal ordering of influences in many of our models is uncontroversial, in other instances the complexity of the models requires more difficult assumptions. And, of course, without experimental data we cannot exclude the possibility that our estimates are biased. That is, our statistical estimates are dependent upon the quality of the data and assumptions.

Nevertheless, we believe that our estimates and conclusions are reasonable. Consequently, in the interest of ease of communication, we use the language of cause and effect to discuss the estimates that we obtain from our analytical models, acknowledging that our observational data are not sufficient to eliminate all sources of bias necessary to support definitive causal statements. Also, instead of repeating this caveat at each relevant point in our presentation, we provide only a general encompassing note of caution about the tentativeness of our causal inferences.

Implications of Our Study for Understanding Social Change

Because our data and analyses focus on the marriage and cohabitation decisions and behavior of a single cohort of young people, we cannot make comparisons across historical periods or birth cohorts while controlling for age. Thus, we cannot use these data to evaluate directly historical changes in behavior or to specify the kinds of forces that might have changed marriage and cohabitation behavior across different historical times. We also cannot determine the extent to which the intergenerational effects we observe in this cohort of young people would be observed in younger or older cohorts.

Nevertheless, the historical context of our study permits us to fulfill our second goal and make contributions to the understanding of historical changes in marriage and cohabitation in the last third of the twentieth century. The parents in this study were born primarily before the end of World War II and had reached adulthood, married, and begun childbearing by 1961. The children were all born in 1961, experienced childhood and adolescence in the 1960s and 1970s, and reached adulthood in the 1980s.

Although the children participating in the Intergenerational Panel Study were born into a world that had already experienced important changes in marriage and related institutions, marriage and family life in the early 1960s was very different than it was at the end of the century. In 1961, when the study children were born, America was still at the height of its postwar marriage and baby booms, the postwar acceleration in divorce was not yet apparent, divorce was still legally difficult, oral contraceptives were not widely used, and the Supreme Court had not legalized abortion. Similarly, premarital sex was still widely disapproved, although not uncommon, nonmarital cohabitation was still extremely rare, only 4 to

5 percent of children were born outside of marriage, relatively few never-married people maintained their own households, most mothers of young children were not employed outside the home, the women's movement was relatively dormant, and the dramatic late-twentieth-century movement toward egalitarian sex-role attitudes was still in the future. We now know, of course, that all of these dimensions of marriage and family life were transformed in fundamental ways by the end of the century. Thus, the families participating in this study, both parents and children, were among the cohorts of Americans that produced and lived through the dramatic changes from the 1960s through the end of the century—perhaps the period of the most rapid changes in marriage and family life in American history.

Our examination of the factors related to these children's entrance into marital and cohabiting unions provides insights into the characteristics of the people who participated in the upward trajectory of cohabitation. It provides insights into the types of parental families that reared children who would later cohabit and/or postpone marriage, as well as the kinds of experiences, values, and aspirations possessed by the young people who would subsequently postpone marriage and/or decide to cohabit. This information is valuable in helping us to understand more fully the dynamics of the tremendous changes that occurred in marriage and cohabitation during the latter part of the twentieth century.

Of course, just as the families participating in the Intergenerational Panel Study provide an excellent group to study how the changes in marriage and cohabitation were experienced by young people born in the early 1960s and reaching maturity in the late 1970s and 1980s, they provide no information concerning the experiences of later cohorts of young people. Furthermore, we expect that the continuing trends in union formation will result in the experiences of later cohorts being different. Research on later cohorts of young people will be necessary to document the continuing changes in marriage and cohabitation experience.

Organization of the Book

We have organized the book into four parts with twelve chapters. The remainder of Part I (chapters 2–4) is devoted to historical and conceptual issues, presenting information about the meaning of marriage and cohabitation, and discussing the experience of young people with union formation. In Part II of the book (chapters 5–6) we analyze the roots of marriage and cohabitation experience in the parental generation, beginning with the experience of the parents from early childhood and extending into the middle teenage years of the study child. The book shifts in Part III (chapters 7–11) from a focus on parental influences during the years of childhood and adolescence to the influences of both generations during the years when the young adults begin to experience union formation. Part IV (chapter 12) integrates and summarizes the findings of the earlier sections of the book, with particular emphasis on synthesizing the central conclusions of the project.

CHAPTER TWO

Historical Perspectives on Marriage

This study of marriage and cohabitation begins with the understanding that the institutions of marriage and family have their roots in the ancient unrecorded histories of numerous cultures and societies. Perhaps the dominant source of family and marriage culture in the United States today lies in the historic patterns of marriage, living arrangements, childbearing, childrearing, and economic production of northwestern Europe. Merging with the family and marriage systems of northwestern Europe were the traditions of Judaism and early Christianity as popularized and evangelized by the Roman Catholic Church. Also relevant were the institutional roots of marriage and family life in the cultures of Greece and Rome. All of these systems blended into an amalgam in northwestern European societies—with considerable variance across these societies—that was ultimately exported when people from this region began migrating to North America in the 1600s. In addition to these influxes from northwestern Europe, America's population grew and changed via forced slave migrations from Africa and later migrations from Asia, Latin America, and eastern and southern Europe. Also, of course, some Americans trace their roots back to the cultures and histories of the native people of America.

This chapter is based on the premise that understanding the forces underlying marriage and cohabitation in the United States today is facilitated by knowledge of the historical roots of family life. Many features of the institutions of marriage and family in America today can be traced back hundreds and even thousands of years to the northwestern European past—and appear often in remarkably similar form. Other features of personal and family life in America today have changed dramatically over the centuries—often in surprising and little understood ways. Knowledge of trends over the centuries helps us to understand current patterns of marriage and cohabitation and the way they are evolving today.

It is important to note that we are *not* historians. We are family sociologists with a strong appreciation for the view that a careful understanding of the historical roots of current behavioral patterns is essential to our interpretation and understanding of those patterns. To obtain an understanding of these historical roots we must rely upon the accomplishments of scores of historians who have done the painstaking work of documenting the histories of marriage, family, and related dimensions of social life. Thus our objective in this chapter is to provide a secondary summary of the primary research of other scholars in order to establish the historical context for the research on more recent dimensions of marital and family behaviors we present later in the book.

We break our historical overview into two sections, divided roughly by the American Revolution and the establishment of the new republic at the end of the 1700s and beginning of the 1800s. In the first section, we discuss in general terms the role of families and marriage in social organization, the marriage and household system, parental involvement in courtship and marriage, sex and childbearing, and marital dissolution. Here we consider the historical roots of marriage and family life in the northwest-European past, with particular emphasis on England, and in the English colonies of North America. There were, of course, important differences across time, space, and society in marriage and family life, with especially significant differences between the aristocracy and people lower in the social hierarchy (Stoertz 2001). Our focus in this chapter is on the lives of the ordinary people who made up the majority of those in northwest Europe and the English colonies in North America. We also draw from multiple countries in the northwest-European region, choosing to emphasize commonalities rather than differences across countries. We set as our baseline the period at the turn of the eighteenth century, but we also provide information from previous periods when particularly relevant. Even in a relatively long historical chapter we cannot do justice to the many differences across time and space, but instead describe patterns in broad terms. One particularly important limitation of this account is our focus on our European roots, with little attention paid to the people and

family heritages of Africans, Asians, and Native Americans. Our time ref-
erent does not extend past the 1300s, where the historical record becomes
very sketchy and before which some scholars speculate that there has
been substantial family change (for example, see Duby 1983/1981; Goody
1983).

In the second section of the chapter, we shift our emphasis to the 1800s
and 1900s. We outline trends across both centuries, but place particular
emphasis on the second half of the 1900s—an emphasis dictated both by
the availability of data and by the setting of our detailed analyses in subsequent chapters in this period. Continuity and change in a number of
dimensions of social and economic life are traced across these two centuries: the place of the family in society, the institution of religion, and
the culture of liberty and equality. We also trace trends in marital status,
marital dissolution, the process of contracting marriages, courtship, sexual experience, childbearing, and unmarried cohabitation. Although our
primary focus in this period is the United States, we also look secondarily
at northwestern Europe to provide a comparative perspective. Again, we
describe general trends without providing a full picture of counter trends
and differences across societies.

Our historical review is limited to the past several hundred years, but
we note that humans were mating and rearing children long before we had
historical documents to record that experience. In fact, evolutionary scholars
suggest that the patterns of human mating and reproduction observed
during the past several hundred years coevolved with many other features of the human condition over a very extensive period of time (Broude
1994; Buss 1994; Daly and Wilson 2000; Diamond 1992; Hrdy 1999).

Although human marriage and family life both have strong biological
foundations and appear to be universal, different world cultures exhibit
an extensive array of family and marriage forms (Broude 1994). This vari-
ability among different societies, and the complexity of translating meaning across languages and cultures, has made it very difficult to define in
any universal way the concepts of marriage and family. Among the central
and unique features of the northwestern-European family, marriage, and
household formation systems were: households primarily consisting of
mother, father, and dependent children; a relatively late age at marriage;
significant numbers of people never marrying; and an extensive involvement of young people in the mate-selection process. Although a comparative analysis of cross-cultural family differences is beyond the scope of this
book, we note some of these unique features in our following discussion.

Marriage and Family before the Nineteenth Century

Family Mode of Organization

Immigrants who moved from northwestern Europe to the new world of America in the 1600s and 1700s brought with them the fundamental cultures and social structures of their old world. Key among these was reliance on the family as the fundamental institution providing meaning and structure to human relationships (Hanawalt 1986; Herlihy 1985; Ogburn and Tibbitts 1933; Parsons and Bales 1955; Thornton and Fricke 1987). And even while the family mode of social organization varied in precise features among these societies, it was manifest in many broadly common ways. Individual lives were primarily experienced and structured within families rather than nonfamilial institutions. Substantial fractions of life activities were conducted within family contexts and with relatives. Babies were born into families and were socialized by relatives. Protection, information, and the necessities of life were largely obtained through family members. Family authority was very important in the lives of both children and adults. Finally, family units were the primary locus of economic activity (Coleman 1990; Demos 1970; Hanawalt 1986; Laslett 1984; Lesthaeghe 1980; Shahar 1983; Thornton and Fricke 1987; Tilly and Scott 1978).

There were also *nonfamilial* organizations and institutions that helped structure the social lives of the English colonies in America. These included the state, the church, military organizations, and economic markets (Hajnal 1982; Kussmaul 1981; R. M. Smith 1979, 1981, 1984; Tadmor 2001).

Place of Marriage in Society

Just as the family was a primary institution organizing social life in northwestern Europe and its overseas colonial populations prior to the 1800s, marriage was the central institution structuring family life (Gillis 1985; Hanawalt 1986; Hufton 1995; Phillips 1988; Shahar 1983). The primary residential units in these populations were usually composed of a married man and woman and their dependent children, or what we commonly call the nuclear family. Although some older parents lived with their adult children, few households included multiple married siblings.[1] In fact, it was marriage that usually created a household (Gillis 1985; Hajnal 1982; Laslett 1984; Phillips 1988; Seccombe 1992; R. M. Smith 1979, 1981).

These nuclear households formed the central economic units of northwestern-European societies in this period, as both production and consumption occurred primarily within them (Demos 1970; Hajnal 1982; Laslett 1984). Within these households the husband and wife were the master and mistress in directing and organizing household activities (Gillis 1985; Macfarlane 1986). Both sex and childbearing were discouraged among the unmarried, while expected for married couples (Davis 1985; d'Avray and Tausche 1981; Macfarlane 1986; Nock 1998; Rothman 1984). In addition, manhood, womanhood, and full membership in adult society were associated with marriage (Chambers-Schiller 1984; Hanawalt 1986; Hufton 1995; Nock 1998; Perkin 1989; Rothman 1984; Shahar 1983).

Marriage has also been closely linked with love, social support, and companionship for many centuries in northwestern Europe and its overseas populations.[2] People understood that marriage was based on love, companionship, and a deep bond between husband and wife. Love was viewed as the essential element of marriage, either as a prerequisite to or growing out of marriage (Brundage 1987; d'Avray 1985; d'Avary and Tausche 1981; Davies 1981; Gillis 1985; Leclercq 1982; Macfarlane 1986; Morgan 1966; Noonan 1967; Norton 1980; Olsen 2001; Ozment 1983; Riley 1991; Rothman 1984; Sarsby 1983). In fact, love may have been more important in the choice of a mate in the 1700s than economic prospects, religious affiliations, or family connections (Rothman 1984; also see Ingram 1985). It was in courtship that young people found and nurtured love and affection, and it was in marriage that they promised to love, cherish, and honor each other throughout life (Book of Common Prayer 1552).[3]

Marriage as a Privileged Status

Because of the association of marriage with an independent household, economic production and consumption, love and companionship, social support, manhood and womanhood, and sexual expression and childbearing, it is not surprising that marriage was viewed as an honorable and privileged status (d'Avray 1985; d'Avray and Tausche 1981; Gillis 1985; Wrightson 1982). Before the 1800s, marriage was seen as the route from the subordinate dependent status of singlehood to the good life of independent and mature adulthood (Chambers-Schiller 1984; Demos 1970; Flandrin 1980; Gillis 1985; Greven 1970; Hufton 1995; Kett 1977; Koehler 1980; Rothman 1984; Shahar 1983). Marriage was viewed as the single most important event between birth and death and the natural progression of the life course for both women and men (Hanawalt 1986; Hufton 1995; Perkin 1989; Rothman 1984). Benjamin Franklin gave expression to this viewpoint in the mid-1700s, asserting that marriage is the "most natural State of Man, and therefore the State in which [people] are most likely to find solid Happiness"; that it is "Man and Woman united that make the compleat [*sic*] human Being"; and that man without marriage "resembles the odd Half of a Pair of Scissars [*sic*]" (Franklin 1961, 30).

People who did not marry maintained a juvenile status (and the designation of "lad" or "maid") throughout their lives (Gillis 1985). Most unmarried adults were expected to live as dependents and subordinates in the households of parents, siblings, or other married families, although living arrangements were somewhat more flexible for single men than for single women (Chambers-Schiller 1984; Norton 1980).[4] As dependents in these families, the unmarried often found their situations difficult, particularly because they generally were obliged to trade domestic or economic services for room and board (Chambers-Schiller, 1984; Norton, 1980). The limitations on single adults were so strict in colonial New England that some communities either legally mandated that unmarried individuals live in a family household or taxed single men who lived outside a family unit (Chambers-Schiller 1984; Howard 1904; Seeman 1999). Such legislation may have indicated not only that public sentiment opposing independent singlehood was very strong, but also that the number of singles living (or wanting to live) independently was large enough to motivate a policy response.

In some places, particularly the New England colonies, being single was not only seen as juvenile and dependent but for older unmarried people was often viewed with disdain and suspicion. In fact, in America the clergy condemned celibacy outside of religious orders as inevitably leading to sexual sins, as sinful and evil itself, and as representing "the antithesis of all social, religious, and familial order" (Seeman 1999, 405; also Chambers-Schiller 1984; Howard 1904; Koehler 1980). Single women were variously called thornbacks, spinsters, and old maids—all terms with negative connotations (Chambers-Schiller, 1984; Koehler, 1980), and they were subject in both fiction and real life to pity, ridicule, and even charges of witchcraft (Deegan 1951; Howard 1904; Hufton 1995; Phillips 1988).

Given the centrality of marriage as an economic, social, and psychological unit, it is not surprising that the institution was important not only to individuals, but to families, friends, communities, religious groups, and governments. Parents and other relatives played significant roles in the marriages of young people, although they did not arrange marriages in the ways that occurred in many other societies such as China and India. Communities were concerned about the formation of marriages, the proper functioning of marriages, and the behavior of single men and women.

Both the church and state—two central nonfamilial institutions in Western societies—also played large roles in marriage and family life. The Roman Catholic Church took an interest in marriage very early in its history and, by the beginning of the second millennium, it had formulated a religious endorsement of marriage, teaching that it was a divine institution ordained and honored by God (d'Avray 1985; d'Avray and Tausche 1981; Glendon 1977; Herlihy 1985). In fact, Catholicism made marriage a sacrament—a relationship involving God as well as the husband and wife. Although the Protestant reformers of the 1500s said that marriage was not a sacrament, they continued to teach that "marriage was ordained by God" (Phillips 1988, 195; also, see Brundage 1987; Witte 1997), and they often described it as a covenant with God or as a commonwealth with the Church (Witte, 1997). Between the 1100s and 1500s—and longer in some places—the doctrines and policies of the church formed the law of marriage;[5] in later centuries they were reflected in secular laws governing marriage and family life (Ammons 1999; Brundage 1987; Engdahl 1967; Glendon 1977; Howard 1904; Pollock and Maitland 1968; Witte 1997).

The state's relatively minor role in marriage in Europe until the 1500s expanded in subsequent centuries. The state increasingly became involved with legislating, administering, and adjudicating marriage, including the formation and dissolution of marriages (Gillis 1985; Glendon 1977; Hufton 1995; Ozment 1983; Phillips 1988). In this regulation of marriage and divorce the state also helped define marriage and the fulfillment of marital obligations (Regan 1999).

The Marriage and Household System

For centuries prior to the American Revolution, marriage was a deeply gendered institution religiously, socially, and legally—a characteristic that would form the basis for substantial controversy and battle in the coming centuries (Ammons 1999; Davies 1981; Flexner 1975; Glendon 1977; Hanawalt 1986; Koehler 1980; Nock 1998; Norton 1980; Ozment 1983; Pollock and Maitland 1968; Schama 1997; Seccombe 1992; Shahar 1983; Ulrich 1982; Weitzman 1981, 1985). The merger of wife and husband into one family unit through marriage was accomplished before the 1800s primarily by the incorporation of the wife's interests and identity into those of the husband (Ammons 1999; Flexner 1975; Glendon 1977; Norton 1980; O'Donnell and Jones 1982; Shahar 1983; Weitzman 1981, 1985). The husband was considered to be the head of the family, with the authority to represent the family and wife in the larger community. Although practices varied in different locations, women frequently lost their legal ability to control property, to make contracts, and to sue and be sued. The subordinate status of the wife was manifest in many marriage ceremonies with the bride's promise to obey as well as love and cherish her husband (*Book of Common Prayer* 1552; Glendon 1977; Koehler 1980; Pollock and Maitland 1968; Whitelock 1952). Although both husband and wife were typically involved in a wide range of productive activities, the husband was generally seen as having financial responsibility for family affairs while the wife had responsibility for the care of home and children (Glendon 1977; Hanawalt 1986; Norton 1980; Pinchbeck 1969; Seccombe 1992; Weitzman 1981). In her care of the home and family, the wife was a junior partner who had considerable authority as she directed children and other workers in her household (Hanawalt 1986; Morgan 1966; Norton 1980; Ozment 1983; Seccombe 1992; Ulrich 1982; Wrightson 1982). Although most of the wife's work took place in or near the home, her contributions to the household were essential economically as well as domestically (Hanawalt 1986; Pinchbeck 1969; Seccombe 1992; Shahar 1983; Ulrich 1982).

The family system of northwestern Europe and the European diaspora in North America also meant that most couples did not enter marriage until they had arranged or built an independent economic and household unit, for although men and women married for love and companionship, marriage required the means for the necessities of life (Berkner 1972; Flandrin 1980; Franklin 1961; Gillis 1985; Hajnal 1965, 1982; Hanawalt 1986; Herlihy 1985; Howell 1998; Lynch 2003; Macfarlane 1986; Rothman 1984; Seccombe 1992; R. Smith 1979, 1981, 1984). The establishment of an independent home and economic unit was usually a formidable and time-consuming project, making youthful marriages difficult. In addition, early marriage was seen as harmful to the health of both the marital partners and their offspring (Macfarlane, 1986). The prerequisites of marriage were frequently not met for women until they were in their early twenties and not for men until they were in their late twenties (Carr-Saunders 1922; Flandrin 1980; Hajnal 1965, 1982; Hanawalt 1986; Herlihy 1985; Macfarlane 1986; Myrdal 1941; Seccombe 1992; R. Smith 1979, 1981, 1999). By international standards, northwestern Europeans not only married at a late age, but they had a high incidence of remaining unmarried—a proportion reaching one-fifth of some societies (Carr-Saunders 1922; Hajnal 1965, 1982; Laslett 1984; Myrdal 1941).

Because the state of the economy was a factor in the ability of young couples to establish homes, both the timing of marriage and the number ever marrying fluctuated historically and across geographical areas (Carr-Saunders 1922; Franklin 1961; Herlihy 1985; Lynch 2003; Schofield 1985; Weir 1984; Wrigley 1981; Wrigley and Schofield 1981). In particular, the greater availability of economic opportunities in colonial America contributed to the earlier and more universal marriage there[6] (Franklin 1961; Haines 1996; Modell 1985; Smith 1993).

Another unique feature of the northwestern-European family system with important implications for marriage was the institution of "lifecourse servanthood" (Berkner 1972; Carr-Saunders 1922; Gillis 1974; Hajnal 1982; Hanawalt 1986, 1993; Herlihy 1985; Kussmaul 1981; Pinchbeck 1969; R. Smith 1979, 1981, 1984; Tadmor 2001). Before entrance into marriage in their twenties, large fractions of young people left their parental families—frequently before or during their teenage years—to live and work in the homes and economic units of other families. This pattern of lifecourse servanthood operated to transfer young people from a family with surplus labor to a household with a labor deficit. In any household, fluctuations in the need for and supply of labor depended in important ways on the number and ages of children. A couple with young children might take in working-age children from other households until their own children reached working age, at which time they might send out one or more to work in other households. Many young people in cities also left their parental homes for the households of others to participate in apprenticeships, during which they learned trades and prepared for entrance into guilds (Hanawalt 1993). Because lifecourse servanthood and apprenticeship were common experiences, many young people experienced living apart from parents in the households of other families prior to marriage (Boswell 1988; Gillis 1974; Hajnal 1982; Kussmaul 1981; R. Smith 1981).

Parental Families

The central position of marriage in family, economic, and community life before the 1800s meant that the creation of new households and economic units had extensive implications for parents and for the community more generally (Berkner 1972; Bourdieu 1976; Chaytor 1980; Foyster

2001; Gillis 1985; Hanawalt 1986, 1993; O'Hara 1991; Seccombe 1992; Shahar 1983; Wrightson 1982). In many instances parents assisted young couples in obtaining the economic resources they needed to marry, including a house and work place, with implications for both the new couple and their parents. Ties between parents and their married children often remained strong, with frequent interactions and interchanges (Ben-Amos 2000). The well-being of elderly parents undoubtedly depended, at least to some extent, on their relationships with their married children (Foyster 2001). The behavior and success of children could also affect their parents' standing in the community. Children who broke the rules of courtship and marriage or entered a union with a partner of lower socioeconomic status or of ill repute could bring embarrassment and loss of status to parents. Bearing a baby out of wedlock had implications not only for the unmarried parents but also for the grandparents of the child. These considerations made parents and the larger community direct stakeholders in the courtship and marriages of maturing children.

Most parents were motivated to have their children do well, not only because of the impact on their own well-being and social standing, but because of their affection and commitment to their children[7] (Ben-Amos 2000; Foyster 2001; Gies and Gies 1987; Gillis 1985; Hanawalt 1986, 1993; Herlihy 1985; Ozment 1983; Pollock 1985; Shahar 1983, 1990; Taglia 1998; Wilson 1984; Wrightson 1982). They often helped their children transition to adulthood—arranging servanthood and apprenticeship programs, contributing resources needed for children to establish themselves as independent householders, and providing economic assistance.

In many societies the crucial importance of marriage to the family and community has been associated with the parental generation having the responsibility and authority for when and whom to marry (Broude 1994; Thornton and Fricke 1987; Thornton and Lin 1994). In these societies marital decisions were made almost entirely by the parents, and contact between marrying couples was often extremely limited before the marriage was contracted. Despite the tremendous importance of marriage in northwestern-European populations, this kind of arranged marriage system did not predominate among them. Rather, free consent of the marrying couple was an essential element in the contract of marriage (Brooke 1981; Brundage 1987; Chaytor 1980; Donahue 1976, 1983; Glendon 1977; Gottlieb 1980; Helmholz 1974; Herlihy 1985; Hufton 1995; Ingram 1981, 1985; McSheffrey 1998; Noonan 1973; O'Hara 1991; Olsen 2001; Outhwaite 1995; Ozment 1983; Pollock and Maitland 1968; Schama 1997;

Seccombe 1992; Sheehan 1971, 1978, 1991b; Smith 1979, 1986; Smout 1981; Wrightson 1982). Young people in these societies had remarkable freedom in courtship and mate selection. Despite parental interest and influence, marriage in these populations can be characterized as "youth-run" or "participant-run," particularly in contrast to the arranged marriage systems in other parts of the world. By and large, young people mingled together, fell in love, courted, and proposed and accepted matrimony on their own. Although this autonomy was probably less pronounced among the privileged classes and varied across both time and place, it was particularly marked among the common folks (Brooke 1981; Burguière 1987; Donahue 1983; Gillis 1985; Glendon 1977; Herlihy 1985; Hufton 1995; Ingram 1981, 1985; Macfarlane 1970, 1986; McSheffrey 1998; Myrdal 1941; Rothman 1984; Schama 1997; Shahar 1983; Sheehan 1971, 1978; Smith 1986; Zumthor 1994).

The autonomy of courtship in northwestern Europe was probably related to many other features of the larger family and social system in the region (Ingram 1985; Smith 1979, 1986). Lifecourse servanthood separated the generations before marriage, and nuclear households separated them after marriage. Late marriage also meant that it was relatively mature adults instead of adolescents who made courtship and marriage decisions. And high mortality meant that many young people lost one or both parents before they married. In addition, the historical record suggests that children in northwestern-European societies, especially relative to children elsewhere, had substantial autonomy and freedom in a range of matters besides marriage. Parents provided supervision and guidance to their children, but gave them extensive latitude for decision making and action in many dimensions of life (Koehler 1980; Macfarlane 1970, 1979, 1986; Outhwaite 1995; Rothman 1984; Wrightson 1982).

The participant-run courtship and marriage system of northwestern Europe was also buttressed—and even encouraged—by the strong support given to the principle of individual consent by the Catholic Church (Brundage 1987, 1993; Donahue 1976, 1983; Engdahl 1967; Gottlieb 1980; Helmholz 1974; Herlihy 1985; Murray 1998; Noonan 1973; Olsen 2001; Outhwaite 1995; Ozment 1983; Seccombe 1992; Sheehan 1971, 1978, 1991a, 1991b; Witte 1997). As we outline in the following, the Church not only insisted on the necessity of individual consent in marriage, but made such consent the essential and defining ingredient for the contraction of marriage itself. Given the importance of ecclesiastical authority, law, and jurisprudence in family matters in Europe, this religious principle provided strong support to the youth-run system.

Because the marriage of offspring held great significance for parents and yet was largely controlled by children, it tended to be an inter-generational process. Parents influenced their children's decisions about courtship and marriage through their guidance and support, and influenced their children's choice of potential mates through their geographical location, economic status, religious affiliation, and other attributes. The young people who lived and worked as lifecourse servants and apprentices in households apart from their own parents were also liable to influence from the masters and mistresses of these households.

Parents and parental figures also had many opportunities to be directly involved in their children's courtships and marriages (Berkner 1972; Brundage 1987; Chaytor 1980; Donahue 1976; Foyster 2001; Gillis 1985; Gottlieb 1980; Hanawalt 1986, 1993; Haskell 1973; Ingram 1981, 1985; McSheffrey 1998; Nicholas 1985; O'Hara 1991; Rothman 1984; Seccombe 1992; Shahar 1983; Smith 1978; Smout 1981; Wrightson 1982). They frequently provided advice and consultation in the process—sometimes making introductions and offering encouragement or discouragement concerning particular potential partners. Parents also played important roles in monitoring courtship, negotiating economic and social arrangements, and planning the wedding itself. Because the provision of a home and economic unit often involved the assistance of both sets of parents, and sometimes included the transfer of a home and farm, the parental families had significant influence on both the feasibility and timing of marriage. The involvement of two generations from two families in the marriage process often necessitated considerable premarital negotiation and inter-action.

The transfer of family resources—including the means of production—that often allowed young adults to marry had important implications for the older generation. In fact, the same transfer of resources that allowed young people to marry often initiated the retirement of the parents. So the marriage decision was often linked to decisions and arrangements regarding the economic needs of the parents. In some places in Europe this marital and retirement transaction was implemented through an explicit agreement between parents and children in which the younger generation legally contracted to take care of the needs of the older generation (Berkner 1972; also see Howell 1998 on marriage contracts).

In addition, children were generally expected to ask their parents for permission to marry—a step that was generally taken seriously by both generations although it was legally and socially recognized that mature young people could marry without the consent of their parents (Brundage

1987; Chaytor 1980; Donahue 1976, 1983; Glendon 1977; Gottlieb 1980; Haskell 1973; Helmholz 1974; Herlihy 1985; Ingram 1981, 1985; McSheffrey 1998; Noonan 1973; O'Hara 1991; Ozment 1983; Pollock and Maitland 1968; Schama 1997; Sheehan 1971, 1978, 1991b; Smout 1981; Wrightson 1982). Consequently, parental opposition might slow down some marriages or result in family discord, but it only infrequently prevented marriage of a determined couple (Brundage 1987; Burguière 1987; Chaytor 1980; Donahue 1976, 1983; Gillis 1985; Haskell 1973; Helmholz 1974; Hufton 1995; Ingram 1985; Macfarlane 1986; McSheffrey 1998; Noonan 1973; O'Hara 1991; Ozment 1983; Rothman 1984; Shahar 1983; Sheehan 1971; Smout 1981; Wrightson 1982).

Courtship

Mate selection and entrance into marriage in northwest Europe and colonial America were social processes that varied significantly across individual couples, communities, and historical circumstances. Robert McCaa (1994) described these varied processes and pathways to marriage in Mexico and Spain as "marriageways" to signify their plurality, their occurrence as processes rather than events, and the dominance of social interaction over legal ceremony. The primary way to marriage in the Western past involved the collaboration of women and men in what we now call courtship (Gillis 1985; Hanawalt 1986; Leeuwen and Maas 2002; Macfarlane 1986; Rothman 1984; Schama 1997). Courtship apparently occurred primarily at the local level, as most brides and grooms were from the same or nearby communities (Snell 2002). Unmarried people had numerous opportunities to meet and interact with one another in church, at markets, at festivals, at dances, in work groups, in fields and farmsteads, in the houses of relatives and neighbors, or more generally in the community. Introductions were also made through parents, siblings, and friends. Young people mingled in groups and as twosomes. Courtship involved spending time together in numerous settings and activities—visiting with others and going on walks or rides together. As the couple became more serious, they saw each other more frequently, often at the woman's residence. When these visits involved long distances, the man might be invited to spend the night at her house. Because of the general shortage of household space, the young man and woman might spend the night on the bed of the young woman—a practice known as bundling—which was supposed to occur with clothing on, the bedroom doors open, and within the bounds of sexual restraint (Burguière 1987; Flandrin 1980; Gillis 1985;

Howard 1904; Leeuwen and Maas 2002; Rothman 1984; Schama 1997; Stiles 1934). Although courtship was conducted within the general structure and surveillance of the family and community, parental oversight was relatively relaxed, providing young people considerable privacy (Gillis 1985; Macfarlane 1986; Rothman 1984).

This love-based, youth-directed courtship system clearly involved sexual attraction and the physical expression of affection, including kissing and fondling. Yet the norms of courtship and marriage drew significant boundaries around sexual expressiveness and discouraged sexual intercourse outside of marriage (Davies 1981; Flandrin 1980; Ingram 1985; Macfarlane 1986; Rothman 1984; Shorter 1977). Evidence indicates that the normative restrictions on nonmarital intercourse were quite effective, although there were certainly deviations from the norms (Ingram 1985; Laslett 1984; Morgan 1978; Shorter 1977; Smith and Hindus 1975). Apparently, this adherence to the sexual mores was based more on the internalization of the norms in young people and their exercise of self-control than on the control of the parents and society. Yet, we also know that parents acted to reinforce normative restrictions (Rothman 1984), and in many settings the penalties for violation of the norms against sexual intercourse for the unmarried were very severe, including the use of fines and whippings (Brundage 1987; Hanawalt 1986; Ingram 1985; Laslett 1984; Morgan 1978; Smith and Hindus 1975). That some violations occurred in the face of parental oversight and public sanctions indicates the difficulty of totally controlling a marriage system based on love and youthful autonomy.

Given the centrality of marriage for determining one's well-being economically, socially, and psychologically, decisions about marriage were made with substantial gravity. Young people were keenly aware of the difficulties that could occur within marriage, knew of marriages that had gone awry, and believed that they had to choose carefully (Chambers-Schiller 1984; Koehler 1980; Riley 1991; Rothman 1984). Because husbands served as the heads of their families, it is not surprising that prospective grooms initiated marriage proposals (Rothman 1984). Engagement periods were sometimes lengthy, allowing the couple to make the economic and residential preparations necessary for establishing their new family (Gillis 1985; Rothman 1984).

Becoming Wife and Husband

The essential marriageways in the Western past were astonishingly simple, although often elaborated by ritual and ceremony. At the turn of the twenty-first century, when the form and meaning of marriage have become so interwoven with the authority and ritual of church and state, it is easy to forget that people were making marriages in Western populations long before the church and state became involved (Brundage 1987; Buss 1994; Diamond 1992; Glendon 1977; Helmholz 1974; Hrdy 1999). Spiritual, religious, and community factors and considerations were probably important elements in marriage, but not in the form of a bureaucratically institutionalized church or state. Although the historical record is fuzzy and ultimately disappears into the unknown past, the authority for marriage and divorce in medieval Britain, as well as in much of the rest of Europe, apparently came from individuals, communities, families, and the social conventions that had emerged over centuries (Björnsson 1971; Brundage 1987; Gillis 1985; Glendon 1977; Helmholz 1974; Howard 1904; Hufton 1995; O'Hara 1991; Pollock and Maitland 1968; Rheinstein 1972; Trost 1979; Whitelock 1952). Marriages were frequently family and community events that included elaborate rituals, but the central act that joined husband and wife in matrimony was the simple exchange of vows pledging themselves to each other (Björnsson 1971; Gillis 1985; Glendon 1977; Helmholz 1974; Howard 1904; Ingram 1985; Jeaffreson 1872; Pollock and Maitland 1968; Rheinstein 1972; Whitelock 1952). The authority was vested neither in church nor state, but in the couple themselves.

Marriage was an important concern for the Catholic Church, and the church slowly became involved in the principles and practices of marriage in Europe. By about 1200 the Church had a sophisticated marriage theology that was reflected both in its own canon law and in the marriage law of Europe's Catholic populations. Jurisdiction for the administration and adjudication of family law also rested with church courts during this period[8] (Ammons 1999; Brundage 1987; Donahue 1983; Engdahl 1967; Glendon 1977; Gottlieb 1980; Helmholz 1974; Ingram 1981; Noonan 1967; Pollock and Maitland 1968; Rheinstein 1972; Witte 1997).

From about 1200 onward the Church increasingly intervened in the practice, administration, and control of marriage in northwestern European countries, even while it adopted into canon law and practice many of the features and rituals that characterized marriage in the era before Christianity (Brundage 1987; Burguière 1976; Gillis 1985; Glendon 1977; Gottlieb 1980; Helmholz 1974; Jeaffreson 1872; Koegel 1922; Macfarlane 1986; Pollock and Maitland 1968). Very important was the church's endorsement and support of the system that vested individuals with authority over their own courtship and marriage (Brundage 1987, 1993; Davies

1981; Donahue 1976, 1983; Glendon 1977; Helmholz 1974; Herlihy 1985; Ingram 1981; Murray 1998; Noonan 1967; Sheehan 1971, 1978, 1991a, 1991b). The power to form a marital union remained in the words, commitment, and behavior of the couple (Donahue 1983; Gillis 1985; Helmholz 1974; Ingram 1981, 1985; Jeaffreson 1872; Koegel 1922; Murray 1998; Noonan 1967; Ozment 1983; Pollock and Maitland 1968; Rheinstein 1972; Sheehan 1971, 1978; Witte 1997). In religious terms, this meant that the sacrament of marriage was administered by the prospective wife and husband (Burguière 1976, 1987; Glendon 1977; Murray 1998; Rheinstein 1972; Shahar 1983; Sheehan 1971; Smout 1981; Witte 1997).

Even with widespread consensus on the essentials that joined wife and husband in Britain and the rest of Catholic Europe, the rituals and practices surrounding entrance into marriage varied among groups and across time (Björnsson 1971; Gillis 1985; Ingram 1981; Laslett 1980, 1984; Pollock and Maitland 1968; Sheehan 1978). Although the Church endorsed and encouraged the use of marital ceremonies and rituals, preferably in a religious setting, the diversity of existing customs apparently inhibited the Church from specifying any particular marital ritual as essential (Glendon 1977; Ingram 1981; Pollock and Maitland 1968; Sheehan 1978). The best-known pattern of marriage, associated most fully with agriculturalists and artisans, was an extended process that in its most elaborate form involved four steps: betrothal; publication of banns or announcement; the wedding; and sexual consummation (Gillis 1985; Gottlieb 1980; Hanawalt 1986, 1993; Ingram 1981, 1985; Macfarlane 1986; Morgan 1966; Olsen 2001; Sheehan 1971, 1978; Smith 1986; Smout 1981).

The concept of *betrothal* was complex and somewhat variable. In many places, including England, Scotland, and the English colonies in America, betrothal or *spousels* constituted the first and crucial step that transformed an unmarried man and woman into husband and wife (Brundage 1987; Gillis 1985; Gottlieb 1980; Howard 1904; Jeaffreson 1872; Macfarlane 1986; Morgan 1966; Schama 1997; Smith 1986; Smout 1981; Witte 1997; Zumthor 1994). In fact, it was during betrothal that the couple clasped hands and exchanged the crucial vows that committed them to a lifetime of marriage as husband and wife (Gillis 1985; Jeaffreson 1872; Smout 1981). Although this ritualistic joining in the clasping of hands and the exchange of vows required no authoritative officiator, it often had someone who helped the couple in making their vows. The betrothal was usually, if not always, guaranteed by witnesses whose word could be very helpful if the existence of the marriage was later challenged (Brundage

1987; Ingram 1981; O'Hara 1991; Sheehan 1971, 1978; Smith 1986). Frequently gifts and rings were exchanged, the latter either at betrothal or at the subsequent wedding (Brundage 1987; Gottlieb 1980; Gillis 1985; Jeaffreson 1872).

The betrothal or marriage became public with the proclamation of banns—the announcement of the marriage to the larger community (Gillis 1985; Jeaffreson 1872; Morgan 1966; Sheehan 1971, 1978; Zumthor 1994). This was usually done through multiple oral announcements at church services or by the posting of a written notice at the church. At this time, the community could express its approval and support of the marriage or disapprove of the wedding. In some cases public disapproval was strong enough to terminate the marriage process. Public consent to the marriage could also take the form of a marriage license rather than the publication of banns.

The publication of banns in this marriage system was followed by a wedding, usually a large and public event held at the church with the participation of the clergy (Gillis 1985; Hanawalt 1993; Morgan 1966; Sheehan 1971, 1978, 1991b; Zumthor 1994). Marital endogamy meant that the wedding usually occurred in the home community of both the groom and bride, but when they came from different communities the wedding occurred more often in the bride's community, suggesting that the preponderance of the bride's family in hosting the marriage festivities is an old pattern (Snell 2002). The vows taken at betrothal were repeated, and the community joined in extensive ritual and celebration to bless and support the newlyweds in their lives together. The celebration was often accompanied by the ritualistic transfer of the bride and groom from their individual homes to their home together, followed by feasting, dancing, and the giving of gifts to the newlyweds (Gillis 1985; Smout 1981; Zumthor 1994).

The final step in the contraction of marriage was consummation through sexual intercourse, although the necessity of consummation for a legal marriage was an area of dispute. Apparently, most common people saw sexual consummation as an essential component in the finalization of the marriage process (Brundage 1987; Howard 1904; Macfarlane 1986; Morgan 1966; Pollock and Maitland 1968; Trost 1979). However, the official position of the church that was enforced by the ecclesiastical courts was that the exchange of vows in the present tense was sufficient to establish a valid marriage. In addition, the exchange of vows for a future marriage followed by sexual consummation constituted marriage (Brundage

1993; Helmholz 1974; Herlihy 1985; Ingram 1981, 1985; Noonan 1972; Ozment 1983).

Although the marriage system of betrothal, banns, and a church wedding with a religious officiator was the most highly sanctioned and prestigious route to marriage in Britain and many other northwestern-European populations, there were socially, religiously, and legally valid alternatives. For instance, couples could omit the proclamation of banns and the wedding itself with its associated rituals and celebrations. They could also hold a wedding without a clergyman, who was considered a "helper" rather than the required authority in the process (Björnsson 1971; Brundage 1987; Burguière 1987; Glendon 1977; Howard 1904; Jeaffreson 1872; Koegel 1922; Murray 1998; Noonan 1967; Sheehan 1978; Smout 1981; Witte 1997).

Another deviation from the large wedding involving extensive community and religious ritual occurred with the rise of Puritan power in the middle of the seventeenth century. During a brief period in England, the Puritans advocated against religious weddings and instituted purely civil proceedings (Gillis 1985)—a policy that Puritan New England also adopted and followed until the end of the 1600s (Morgan 1966). Even after that period, however, large portions of northern American marriages were contracted in the home of the bride rather than at church, although religious weddings became exceptionally popular in later years (Howard 1904; Rothman 1984).

The contraction of a legally and socially legitimate marriage could take many different forms—elaborate or simple, religious or civil, with or without religious or governmental authority—because all that was ultimately required was the exchange of vows, either publicly or privately, and sexual consummation (Brown 1981; Brundage 1987; Gillis 1985; Glendon 1977; Gottlieb 1980; Helmholz 1974; Howard 1904; Ingram 1981, 1985; Laslett 1984; Macfarlane 1986; Morgan 1966; Murray 1998; Noonan 1967, 1973; Olsen 2001; Outhwaite 1995; Ozment 1983; Pollock and Maitland 1968; Sheehan 1971, 1978; Smout 1981; Witte 1997). Although witnesses could be helpful in demonstrating that a marriage occurred, marriages could be, and sometimes were, exceptionally private, even clandestine (Brown 1981; Brundage 1987; Donahue 1976, 1983; Gillis 1985; Gottlieb 1980; Helmholz 1974; Howard 1904; Hufton 1995; Ingram 1981, 1985; Jeaffreson 1872; Kelly 1973; Lasch 1974; Shahar 1983; Sheehan 1971, 1978; Smith 1986; Smout 1981). These private marriages functioned like informal betrothals and, while they engendered less community status and church

support—and sometimes even negative sanctions from church officials—
they were nevertheless recognized as valid (Brown 1981; Brundage 1987;
Donahue 1976; Engdahl 1967; Gillis 1985; Gottlieb 1980; Helmholz 1974;
Ingram 1981; Kelly 1973; Koegel 1922; Pollock and Maitland 1968; Sheehan 1978; Smith 1986). Evidence indicates that significant numbers of
marriages were private or departed in significant ways from the church-
sanctioned marriage pattern of betrothal, banns, and wedding.

The combination of the growing authority of the church in defining and
administering marriage, the diversity of marriage forms, and the acceptance of private marriage led to extensive debate and litigation concerning
marriage contracts before the 1800s (Helmholz 1974; Ingram 1981, 1985;
Ozment 1983). In fact, the ecclesiastical courts heard numerous disputes
over the existence of particular marriages. Had the exchange of vows been
handled properly? Were the vows present or future tense? Was sexual
consummation necessary or not? These disputes, which suggest considerable disagreement over what constituted marriage, apparently dissipated
as the church slowly gained more authority and consensus for its definition of marriage and as marriage contraction became more formal and
public, a topic to which we return in the following (Helmholz 1974).

Sex, Pregnancy, and Childbearing

Because the exchange of vows and sexual consummation were the essential ingredients turning a man and woman into a husband and wife before the 1800s, the betrothal gave at least some legitimacy to prewedding
sex, pregnancy, and even cohabitation throughout much of northwest-
European history. The result was a significant number of pregnancies
occurring between betrothal and the public and ritualistic wedding
(Björnsson 1971; Ingram 1985; Gillis 1985; Laslett 1984, 1980, 1978; Macfarlane 1986; Rothman 1984; Seccombe 1992; Shorter, Knodel, and van
de Walle 1971; Smith 1986; Smith and Hindus 1975). In addition, if something occurred after betrothal that postponed or cancelled the wedding,
a postbetrothal pregnancy could become a prewedding ceremony birth.
Even the meanings of "bridal pregnancy" and "illegitimate child" become
fuzzy in the context of a complex marriage process that can extend over
a substantial period of time with multiple ceremonies and rituals (Laslett
1984, 1980, 1978). Nevertheless, although pregnancies and births sometimes occurred outside the context of marriage, evidence suggests they
tended to occur within the courtship and marriage process[9] (Brundage

1987; Depauw 1976; Gillis 1985; Haigh 1975; Hanawalt 1993; Hufton 1995; Laslett 1978, 1980; Norton 1980; Smith 1986; Viazzo 1986).

Documentation of nonmarital cohabitation during this period is very difficult because, given the marriage system, the primary difference between marriage and nonmarital cohabitation is the subjective definition and presentation of the couple. Unfortunately, very little data are available connecting together behavior, commitment, and presentation at this level during these years. However, given the strong control over prebetrothal sexual union, it does not seem likely that many northwestern Europeans in this era flouted community and familial standards by living together without having exchanged marriage vows. However, in some times and places—such as in Scandinavia—unmarried cohabitation may have been more accepted and more frequent (Bracher and Santow 1998; Trost 1978, 1988; also, see Depauw 1976; Laslett 1980).

In western Europe before the 1800s, the bearing and rearing of children were expected within the bounds of marriage (Hufton 1995). In fact, evolutionary scholars frequently view childbearing and childrearing as inseparably connected to the institution of marriage, given that all known societies have formalized mating alliances between men and women and that children have constituted essential outcomes of the mating element of marriage (Buss 1994; Daly and Wilson 2000; Diamond 1992). Birth control techniques were known among some in Western societies for many centuries prior to the 1800s, but they were used infrequently because knowledge about them was limited, because they were considered to be unacceptable, or because the desire to restrict childbearing was not extensive (Himes 1970; Knodel and van de Walle 1979; Shahar 1990; van de Walle and Knodel 1980).

Marital Dissolution

Marriage was apparently viewed as dissoluble in many areas of northwestern Europe, including England, before the Christian era (Howard, 1904; Phillips, 1988; Pollock and Maitland, 1968; Rheinstein, 1972b; Whitelock, 1952). As with marriage, the authority for the dissolution of unions apparently rested with the individuals themselves. One of the central reforms of popular practice suggested by the Catholic Church and some civil authorities was the idea that a valid marriage could not be dissolved through divorce. The implementation of indissoluble marriage came slowly, apparently formalized into religious and civil practice by about

1200 and into canon law with the Council of Trent in the 1500s (Glendon 1977; Hanawalt 1986; Helmholz 1974; Howard 1904; Mount 1982; Phillips 1988; Pollock and Maitland 1968; Rheinstein 1972; Whitelock 1952). Formal separation was permitted but normally not legal divorce and remarriage. During the Protestant Reformation, divorce was accepted by most reformers, but the grounds legitimizing it were exceptionally limited (Phillips, 1988; Witte, 1997). Marriage continued to be viewed socially, religiously, and legally as a lifetime contract (Glendon 1977; Helmholz 1974; Howard 1904; Mount 1982; Phillips 1988; Weitzman 1981; Witte 1997).

The social view of voluntary marriage dissolution was very negative (Phillips 1988; Riley 1991; Weitzman 1981) and, because marriage was the primary economic and residential unit of society, divorce was very difficult financially and logistically (Phillips, 1988). Consequently, couples generally followed in practice the ideal of lifetime marriage (exceptionally few legal divorces were granted), although many married couples undoubtedly experienced serious discord and some chose voluntary separation (Gillis 1985; Helmholz 1974; Norton 1980; Phillips 1988; Riley 1991; Shahar 1983).

Many marriages were short-lived, however, because of the relatively early death of the husband or wife. Consequently, there were large numbers of widowed individuals, orphans, and single-parent families. In addition, there were many reconstituted families created from the remarriages of widowed individuals.

Two Centuries of Change and Continuity in Social and Economic Life

The 1800s and 1900s in northwestern Europe and North America witnessed dramatic economic, social, demographic, and family change, accompanied by substantial continuities. Here we outline many of these, with emphasis on the last part of the 1900s when certain changes were particularly dramatic. We begin with three sections documenting some of the central trends in social and economic structures, including the place of family life in the larger society, the content and authority of religious groups, and the growing emphasis on freedom and equality associated with the Enlightenment. Then come several sections devoted to continuity and change in marriage and personal life. In these sections we discuss, in turn, trends in the status of marriage and single life, marital dissolution, the process of contracting marriages, courtship practices, sexual experience, childbearing, and unmarried cohabitation. The breadth of these topics means our discussion provides only an overview. We do not attempt to cover all of the ups and downs in the trend lines or the many differences in various geographical areas.

Changing Modes of Social Organization

A key change during the 1800s and 1900s was the shift of social organization from its primary locus within families to a broader arena that included many nonkinship-based organizations and relationships (Coleman 1990; Durkheim 1984; Seccombe 1992; Thornton and Fricke 1987). The activities of individuals in these societies were increasingly conducted within schools, factories, and other bureaucratic nonfamilial organizations. In addition, individuals increasingly depended upon such nonfamilial entities as the government, medical organizations, schools, businesses, the mass media, commercialized entertainment, and the police for information, sustenance, and direction. Over these two centuries improvements in transportation and communication—including the advent of the automobile, airplane, telephone, radio, computer, and television—dramatically improved both the speed of interaction and the range of people, institutions, and ideas with whom people could interact. Today, these other institutions increasingly organize human life, although families continue to be important organizations.

Particularly important in this shift to nonfamilial institutions is industrialization and paid employment. Whereas economic production was previously centered primarily within families and households, industrialization in the 1800s and 1900s moved many of the work activities of family members outside the home to factories, offices, and other bureaucratic organizations. In the beginning, this movement away from the home for economic production was concentrated among men and unmarried women (Davis 1984; Hochschild 1989; Tilly and Scott 1978). With their primary commitment to home and family during this period, married women were increasingly cut off from many of their previous economic activities and became more focused on taking care of home and children. Consequently, as recently as the years immediately prior to World War II, relatively few married women participated in the paid labor force (Oppenheimer 1970; Spain and Bianchi 1996). This situation changed dramatically during

World War II as numerous women were pulled into the war industries. In the last several decades of the 1900s, married women—including mothers of young children—continued to increase their participation in the paid labor force while retaining primary responsibility for home and children (Davis 1984; Goldscheider and Waite 1991; Hochschild 1989; Spain and Bianchi 1996).

The movement of economic production and the livelihoods of families to factories and offices fractured the historic link between economic production and marriage and households. Whereas in the past, economic production was largely coterminous with the family and its married master and mistress, husbands and wives no longer produced their means of sustenance in their marital and family roles but as individuals interacting with nonfamilial institutions. Paid employment outside the home also shattered the historical integration of women's economic activities with their care of home and children. Married women, especially mothers, increasingly have demanding dual careers in which they simultaneously hold jobs outside their families while maintaining primary care of the household (Goldscheider and Waite, 1991; Hochschild, 1989; Spain and Bianchi, 1996). Women's growing involvement in paid employment has greatly diminished their economic reliance on their husbands' paychecks and provided important economic options to marriage. In fact, today's women may find that marriage and motherhood are impediments to reaching their full career aspirations. The employment of both spouses in the labor market has also decreased the specialization of roles associated with marriage (Becker 1991; Goldscheider and Waite 1991)

Over the past two centuries, industrialization and paid employment outside the home have also affected the living arrangements of adolescents and young adults in Western societies (Goldscheider and DaVanzo 1985; Goldscheider and Goldscheider 1993, 1994; Kobrin 1976; Modell and Hareven 1973). As noted in the previous section, adolescents and young adults in northwest-European societies frequently worked and lived in the homes of other people as part of apprenticeships or lifecourse servanthood. Industrialization and paid employment brought to an end the need for young people to leave their parents' home for the households and economic units of other families. However, because new economic opportunities were more geographically concentrated, often in cities, young people in the 1800s and early decades of the 1900s frequently migrated from their farm homes to cities where they obtained room and board in private homes or factory-owned dormitories. In the later decades of the 1900s, with a very large proportion of the population living in cities, this kind of boarding and lodging virtually disappeared in the societies of northwestern Europe and North America (Modell and Hareven 1973). Today, substantial fractions of young people leave their parental homes for college, for military service, or to live independently (either alone or with unrelated housemates) in apartments or houses. This means that many young adults live as independent householders between the time they leave the parental home and the time they enter a marital or cohabiting union (Goldscheider and Goldscheider 1994; Goldscheider, Thornton, and Young-DeMarco 1993).

The growth of school attendance and the increasing reliance on educational attainment for occupational achievement has also modified the transition to adulthood and the possibilities of entrance into courtship and marriage. As the duration of school enrollment has extended, with virtually all Americans now attending school into their late teenage years and many continuing into the twenties and even thirties, education has assumed an increasing fraction of the life course. This typically increases the time of economic dependency and investment in human capital for young people, and thereby delays their entry into independent adult roles. It also affects living arrangements, since many young people who attend college live away from home in dormitories or apartments, either by themselves or with housemates. Of course, the usual presumption is that college will lead to a well-paying job that will facilitate a higher standard of living and the ability to support a family.

The implications of these shifts in social organization for marriage and family relations are dramatic and far-reaching. Of central importance is the toppling of the privileged position of marriage in structuring and defining adult life (Axinn and Thornton 2000; Gillis 1985). In the past, marriage was closely associated with household headship, independent living, and co-directorship of a unit of economic production, but it has become straightforward for a young person to attain independent living, household headship, and a good job without being married. In addition, as we discuss in the following, it has become increasingly acceptable and common for unmarried people to bear and rear children, activities previously associated with both adulthood and marriage. Marriage is, thus, no longer automatically and directly integrated with the other markers of independent-adult status in Western societies (Axinn and Thornton 2000; Goldscheider and Waite 1991; Mead 1949; Rothman 1984; Thornton and Freedman 1982).

The establishment of work outside the home severed economic production from marriage, but it did not disconnect marriage from economic independence or household headship. Self-sufficiency before marriage and nuclear households remained standard features of family life[10] (Gillis 1985; Franklin and Remmers 1961; Rothman 1984). In the United States today, the idea of economic independence as a prerequisite for marriage still predominates. In 2001, about five out of six never-married Americans in their twenties agreed that "it is extremely important to be economically set before you get married," and four-fifths agreed that "educational pursuits or career development come before marriage at this time in your life" (Whitehead and Popenoe 2001, 11).

Men served as the primary breadwinner for families throughout most of the past two centuries, and prospective grooms were expected to hold jobs that earned a family wage (Oppenheimer 2000; Franklin and Remmers 1961; Rothman 1984). As women have increased their participation in the paid labor force, they are increasingly able to contribute to the establishment of independent married households and to postmarriage family economics. Nevertheless, the historical pattern of a couple depending more on the man's earning capacity to marry continues to prevail (Oppenheimer 2000; Oppenheimer and Lew 1995; Smock and Manning 1997).

Changes in Religion

Important cultural and ideological forces have affected marriage and family life in the United States and other Western societies. We noted earlier the central role of religious institutions in defining the nature of marriage and the processes of marital formation and dissolution in Western societies. An important change in religion in western Europe in the 1500s was the division of the Western Church into Catholic and Protestant branches and the formulation of differing views on several dimensions of marriage, including its sacramentality, its dissolubility, and where it should be performed. The Protestant Reformation, however, was only the beginning of religious pluralism in the western-European world. Over the centuries the number of religious organizations and viewpoints has proliferated, resulting in many different centers of religious authority and views concerning family forms. This proliferation, which increased steeply in recent decades with immigration from many places outside the orbit of Christianity and Europe, has acted to diminish the sense of shared morality and expand the latitude for diverse opinions and behavior (Hunter 1991). Particularly important is the increased acceptance of the authenticity of the faith and values of other religions and the decline of the belief that one's own religion and morals are necessary for others (Bellah, Madsen, Sullivan, Swidler, and Tipton 1985; Caplow, Bahr, and Chadwick 1983; Roof and McKinney 1987; Wuthnow 1998).

Other societal changes have acted to alter the moral authority of churches and relationships between the churches and individuals. Science has expanded its domain; the notion of individual autonomy has grown; and many technological innovations have occurred (Greeley 1972; Phillips 1988). In particular, significant authority has been transferred from the churches to other institutions, such as schools, the state, and bureaucratic economic enterprises, and the mass media has increasingly conveyed secular messages and messages about new family forms (Bailey 1988; Phillips 1988).

Recent research indicates that the last half of the 1900s witnessed a significant decline in the authority of religious institutions and leaders in the United States. In particular, there has been a decline in the Bible's use as a literal guide to life and in the authority of religious pronouncements (Caplow, Bahr, and Chadwick 1983; Glenn 1987; Greeley, McCready, and McCourt 1976; Hout and Greeley 1987; Niemi, Mueller, and Smith 1989; Roof 1999; Wuthnow 1998). Americans have become less confident of finding religious answers for today's problems (Glenn 1987). Although religious identification and attendance at religious services had been on the rise prior to 1960 (Caplow et al. 1983), since 1960 Americans have decreased their identification with religion, membership in churches or synagogues, attendance at religious services, belief in the importance of religion, and frequency of prayer (Glenn 1987; Niemi et al. 1989).

In recent decades religious commitments and beliefs have increasingly been interpreted—by both the clergy and lay people—in individualistic terms and less in terms of institutional loyalty and obligation (Browning et al. 1997; Bellah et al. 1985; Roof 1999; Roof and McKinney 1987; Wuthnow 1998). Religion has become more voluntaristic, less oriented toward obedience, and less condemning and punitive toward deviations from community morals (Caplow, Bahr, and Chadwick 1983; Roof 1999; Roof and McKinney 1987; Wuthnow 1998). In fact, some observers note the development of a norm of tolerance that has increased the importance of personal choice (Caplow, Bahr, and Chadwick 1983; Roof and McKinney 1987).

Although religious relativism and the norm of tolerance have become especially powerful in recent decades, they have not entirely captured public and private beliefs and values. Substantial numbers of people maintain

historically orthodox views that emphasize the revealed and nonnego-
tiable nature of truth and the norms of marriage and family life. These
individuals take a much more literalistic view of religious scriptures and
the norms they derive from them for both private and public morality.
Interestingly, most major religious denominations include both the liter-
alistically and historically orthodox as well as individuals with more rela-
tivistic and pluralistic points of view (Hunter 1991).

In addition to religious relativism, the past several decades have also
seen a rise in the quest for an inner spirituality that is controlled by the
individual rather than the community (Roof 1999; Wuthnow 1998). This
trend encompasses a legitimization of doubt and uncertainty and skepti-
cism about absolute truth and hierarchical authority. Given the historical
connection between the realms of religion and family, these trends have
important implications for family behavior, including marriage and cohabitation.

The Enlightenment and Developmental Idealism

One of the most important and powerful ideational forces of the last
five hundred years has been the developmental paradigm (Mandelbaum
1971; Nisbet 1975; Thornton 2001, 2005). It can be traced back to Greece
and Rome and through the early Christian theologians, and it became
particularly dominant in Western societies in the 1700s and 1800s. This
paradigm was a model of social change that viewed the human condition
as progressing through a series of uniform stages of growth and development. Northwestern-European societies, including England, France, and
the United States, were seen at the pinnacle of this developmental trajectory and other societies around the globe were viewed at different points
along the ladder of progress. Although this model of social change has
been largely discredited in recent years, it had a powerful effect on both
scholarly theories and the behavior of ordinary people for the subsequent
centuries. Out of these ideas of progress and the association of northwestern Europe with the heights of development emerged developmental idealism, a set of ideas that became an important source of political, social,
cultural, economic, and familial change during the Enlightenment of the
1700s, and continues to be powerful through the present time (Thornton
2001, 2005).

Among other things, developmental idealism identified individualism,
nuclear households, youthful autonomy, older ages at marriage, high status

of women, family planning, and low fertility as positive personal and familial attributes associated with modern societies characterized by high levels of education, income, and health (Thornton 2001, 2005). Thus, these dimensions of family life became associated with some of the most powerful words in the English language—progress, enlightenment, development, civilization, and modernity—and their opposites became associated with traditionality, backwardness, and lack of development. In addition, developmental idealism declared that individuals were created with freedom and equality, with social relationships based on consent (Thornton 2001, 2005). These rights of freedom, equality, and consent, declared to be inalienable, were applied to social, political, and familial matters.

In recent centuries, and especially in recent decades, the ideas of developmental idealism and its emphasis on freedom, equality, and consent have been disseminated widely. These ideals have been promulgated through the educational system and by the increasingly effective mass media, including magazines, newspapers, television, and the Internet. In politics, developmental idealism has been influential in increasing the rights of individuals and bringing about governments based on the consent of the people (Ashcraft 1987; Bailyn 1967; Schochet 1975; Traer 1980). Equality, freedom, and consent were important ideological forces in the American and French revolutions and for the legitimization of democratic institutions. They were important forces in the movement to eliminate slavery and to bring about racial equality and freedom. They were essential in legitimizing the drive for equal rights and status for women and men (Abray 1975; Hole and Levine 1984; Rendall 1985). And, in many ways, they have come to be seen by some as essential elements of marriage (Shanley 2004).

The women's movement became an important and influential social force within the United States and other Western countries in the 1800s (Berg 1978; Flexner 1975; Hole and Levine 1971; Howard 1904). Although this movement eventually focused its energy primarily on women's suffrage, it also advocated for greater female rights in education, the work force, the law, and the family. The gender hierarchy within families was attacked as unfair and in violation of the basic human rights of freedom and equal treatment (Berg 1978; Flexner 1975; Hole and Levine 1971). Some observers predicted that the idea of equality was becoming so accepted and important that family relationships would either have to become more egalitarian or the family would disappear, a theme that would be continued in later decades (Goldscheider and Waite 1991; Howard 1904).

With the achievement of women's suffrage in the early 1900s, the social movement for women's rights subsided, only to reemerge in the United States in the 1960s with considerable energy and emotion (Flexner 1975; Hole and Levine 1971, 1984). Many of the earlier themes were emphasized—equal rights in both the public and domestic spheres—and many substantial changes resulted (Glendon 1976).

In addition, the institutions of marriage and family were challenged in new ways in the 1960s and 1970s. Some people in the women's movement of the late 1900s saw marriage not only as in need of reform, but as a negative institution that was destructive to many individuals, especially women (Berger and Berger 1984; Bernard 1982; England 2000; Hart 1972; Hole and Levine 1971; Wilson 2002). This viewpoint has been promulgated widely in the United States and elsewhere and has only recently received substantial serious challenge in the research literature[11] (Crittenden 1999; England 2000; Glenn 1997; Trost 1981; Waite and Gallagher 2000).

The Enlightenment and developmental idealism also shifted attention from families and communities as organic entities to individuals as independent from the communities and families in which they were embedded (Bellah et al. 1985; Berger and Berger 1984; Carmichael 1995; Chester 1977; Lesthaeghe 1983, 1995; Regan 1999; Roof 1999; Wilson 2002; Witte 1997; Wuthnow 1998). Although marriage had been seen by many as an institution that permanently fused the couple into a single organic social unit with common interests and identities (O'Donnell and Jones 1982; Weitzman 1981), developmental idealism emphasized the individual and the freedom of individuals to operate independently of the family unit. Increasingly across time, the family and marriage were defined in social, legal, and judicial systems as a voluntary association of interacting actors rather than as an organic whole (Berger and Berger 1984; Regan 1999; Schneider 1985; Wilson 2002; Witte 1997). Many of these changes were particularly dramatic during the last few decades of the 1900s, with the emergence of what Cherlin calls the *individualized marriage* (Cherlin 2004; Lesthaeghe 1995; Roof 1999; Thornton and Young-DeMarco 2001; Wuthnow 1998).

Although young people in northwestern-European societies, especially in England and its overseas populations, have always had extensive autonomy, the freedom of children relative to their parents has become even more valued and extensive. Although it is difficult to document such trends systematically before the 1900s, substantial evidence suggests dramatic changes in childrearing values between the 1920s and the 1980s in the United States. Increasingly, parents have encouraged their children to be tolerant, autonomous, and independent thinkers and to place less value on conformity, loyalty to church, and obedience (Alwin 1984, 1986, 1988; Bahr et al. 2004; Niemi, Mueller, and Smith 1989).

Changing Status of Marriage and Being Single

We believe that these substantial changes in social and ideological structures have been important forces changing the ways in which people view and approach marriage and family life (Axinn and Thornton 2000). They have probably been especially powerful because, despite marriage being privileged structurally, Western culture and Christian traditions have long had an ambivalent attitude toward celibacy (Chambers-Schiller 1984; Seeman 1999; Shahar 1990). Roman Catholicism—basing its views on Saint Paul in the Bible—has a history extending back into the first millennium valorizing the celibate role that denies marriage and sexual relations (Brundage 1987b; Chambers-Schiller 1984; Seeman 1999). In fact, this history suggests that true celibacy and the devotion of service to God and the church is superior to marriage itself—a belief that has spawned a substantial celibate clergy within Catholicism. Without this kind of service and commitment to abstinence, however, remaining single was viewed as both inferior to marriage and possessive of the potential for spiritual damnation.

Despite the negative connotations surrounding celibacy in America, several non-Catholic religious groups formed in the 1700s and 1800s to renounce sexuality and marriage and to advocate celibacy as a superior way for ordinary people to serve God (Chambers-Schiller 1984; Kitch 1989; Seeman 1999). The Shakers were probably the best known of these groups. Other groups also questioned the historic pattern of marriage and advocated communitarian forms of life that did not rest on the marriage patterns of the past (Gillis 1985). Although none of these groups accumulated many followers, they did offer a challenge to the idea that marriage was necessarily the best state for women and men.

The 1800s in America also witnessed a new movement outside of Catholicism that suggested that although marriage and motherhood were valued professions, they were not the only ways to happiness and fulfillment of one's destiny (Chambers-Schiller 1984; Norton 1980). By forgoing marriage, young women in this new movement would have the freedom and flexibility to pursue self-fulfillment and the noble vocations of nursing the sick, helping the poor, and assisting the oppressed. A small, but significant, number of women followed this route, but most were disappointed in the rewards of remaining single as they found that they were never able to outgrow the dependent status of daughter and enjoy independent household headship.

Despite these movements, many of the old views concerning marriage and single life continued into the first several decades of the 1900s. Marriage continued to be viewed by many, both in popular opinion and literature, as the natural and desirable condition of adult life (Ehrenreich 1983; Hurlock 1968; Kuhn 1955a; Mead 1949; Rothman 1984). Mature unmarried men and women were still portrayed in literature in unflattering and negative ways (Cargan and Melko 1982; Deegan 1951; Ehrenreich 1983; Gillis 1985; Mead 1949; Ruitenbeek 1966).

The systematic survey data that became available after World War II demonstrate that a substantial number of people continued to hold negative views of remaining single, but that such views were far from universal during this period. In a 1957 national survey of adults in the United States, slightly more than half reported negative (sometimes very negative) views of people who did not want to marry, while nearly one-half were neutral or positive (Thornton and Freedman 1982; Veroff, Douvan, and Kulka 1981). The same study asked people how they thought marriage changed a person's life, and two-fifths suggested a positive influence, meaning that three-fifths thought the changes were neutral or even negative.[12] Despite some of the ambivalences about marriage and single life, young Americans in the 1960s clearly envisioned marriage in their futures. Only 8 percent of female and 3 percent of male high-school students in the United States in 1960 said that they did not expect to marry (Thornton and Freedman 1982).

The marriage behavior of young people in northwestern Europe and the United States in the years immediately after World War II showed little ambivalence about the relative merits of marriage and remaining single. Although marriage timing and prevalence had fluctuated significantly in the United States and elsewhere, the marriage boom following World War II was probably the most prominent change throughout the 1800s and 1900s (Fitch and Ruggles 2000; Gillis 1985; Haines 1996). During this period the rate of marrying increased dramatically and the age at marriage dropped (Cherlin 1992; Fitch and Ruggles 2000; Kiernan 2000; Rodgers and Thornton 1985). This marriage boom also helped to fuel the postwar baby boom that reversed, at least temporarily, the long-term decline in fertility that was occurring throughout the Western world (Morgan 1996).

Although the marriage boom continued in most of the countries of northwestern Europe and North America through the 1950s and most of the 1960s, these years were immediately followed by substantial and rapid declines in marriage rates and increases in ages at marriage (Carmichael 1995; Casper and Bianchi 2002; Cherlin 1992; Eldridge and Kiernan 1985; Kiernan 2000; Kuijsten 1996; Lesthaeghe 1995; Prinz 1995; Rodgers and Thornton 1985; Trost 1978; van de Kaa 1987, 1994). In fact, the age at marriage is now higher in the United States than at any previous time in our history (Fitch and Ruggles 2000).

Accompanying these changes in marital behavior of the last few decades have been similarly dramatic changes in attitudes and values concerning marriage and single life. Although marriage remains a central element in the transition to adulthood, as Nock (1998) has recently argued, it plays a smaller role in determining adult femininity and masculinity, and it is no longer viewed as the only mainstream course to happiness and fulfillment. Negative stereotyping of singles has declined sharply. A 1976 replication of the aforementioned 1957 American study found that the fraction of respondents who reported negative views on a person who did not want to marry declined from about one-half to one-third (Thornton and Freedman 1982; Veroff, Douvan, and Kulka 1981); and the proportion who thought that marriage changed a person's life for the better declined from 43 to 30 percent. Similar trends occurred in several western-European countries (de Boer 1981; Thornton and Freedman 1982; van de Kaa 1987).

In the United States in the 1980s, only about one-third of respondents in a national study agreed that "it's better for a person to get married than to go through life being single" (Bumpass, Sweet, and Cherlin 1991, 924; Thornton and Freedman 1982). Furthermore, only about one-third of the eighteen-year-olds in the Intergenerational Panel Study (IPS) in 1980 said that they would be bothered a great deal if they did not marry, while an equal number would be bothered only a little or not at all[13] (Thornton and Freedman 1982). The mothers of these young people expressed even less concern about the possibility of their children remaining single (Thornton and Freedman 1982).

Among some people, the rejection of the necessity of marriage to achieve a satisfactory life has been accompanied by positive endorsement of forgoing marriage and remaining single. The percentage of adult

Americans positively evaluating a person who did not want to marry increased from 10 to 15 percent between 1957 and 1976, and the fraction evaluating marriage as altering a person's life negatively increased from 23 to 28 percent. Furthermore, in the IPS survey of eighteen-year-olds in 1980, about 30 percent endorsed the idea that "all in all, there are more advantages to being single than to being married," a proportion that declined as they grew older and entered marriage (Thornton 1989, 879; Thornton and Young-DeMarco 2001). Yet, most Americans continue to believe that a good marriage and family life are very important and plan and expect to marry. For example, among adults under 35 in the United States in the late 1980s, all but 5 percent had married or expected to marry (Sweet and Bumpass, 1992). Similarly, in recent decades, less than 10 percent of high-school seniors in the United States reported that they do not expect to marry (Thornton 1989; Thornton and Freedman 1982; Thornton and Young-DeMarco 2001; also see Axinn and Thornton 2000; Glenn 1996). In fact, the importance of marriage is high enough today that more than four-fifths of all college women participating in a national survey in the United States in 2000 agreed that "being married is a very important goal for me" (Glenn and Marquardt 2001, 4). In addition, even in economically poor communities where marriage often is postponed for many years, people express a high value for marriage, even giving it such importance that it should be postponed until after the achievement of economic success and stability (Cherlin 2004; Edin and Kefalas 2005; Smock 2004).

Changes in Marital Dissolution

The principle of marital indissolubility was breached, albeit only minimally, by the Protestant Reformation in the 1500s (Rheinstein 1972b). Although the Protestant reformers generally believed that divorce should be very difficult, they accepted its legitimacy in some very limited circumstances. The laws remained very restrictive for centuries, but were gradually amended to make divorce generally easier (Chester 1977; Phillips 1988; Rheinstein 1972b; Riley 1991; Weitzman 1985). Big changes in divorce laws occurred in the 1960s and 1970s as no-fault divorce laws were adopted in almost every state, making it very easy to end a marriage (Freed and Foster 1980; Glendon 1976; Weitzman 1985). These no-fault divorce laws also represented a long-term movement of the government away from its previous support of marriage as a lifetime commitment and toward support of individual autonomy and freedom (Weitzman 1985).

In addition, negative attitudes toward divorce have softened in the United States (Thornton 1989; also see van de Kaa 1987 and Lesthaeghe 1995 for the Netherlands). In 1962, about half of the mothers participating in our IPS survey disagreed that "when there are children in the family, parents should stay together even if they don't get along" (Thornton 1989, 880). In 1980, 80 percent of these same women disagreed with the proposition.

The overall trajectory of divorce in the United States has been generally upward for at least as long as we have had reasonably good records—back to about 1860 (Jacobson 1959; Preston and McDonald 1979; Riley 1991; Thornton and Freedman 1983). In fact, this trajectory has been so persistent that demographers in the 1890s accurately predicted the divorce rate nearly 100 years later in the 1980s (Willcox 1897/1891). With some fluctuations associated with depressions and wars, the American divorce rate increased slowly but steadily throughout the century from 1860 to 1960. Prior to 1960, this increase in divorce was countered by the steady decline in the mortality rate, which kept the overall marital dissolution rate relatively constant (Thornton and Freedman 1983). However, in the two decades after 1960, the divorce rate more than doubled, so that·by the beginning of the 1980s approximately one-half of all marriages would end in divorce. The rate remained high throughout the 1980s and 1990s (Bramlett and Mosher 2001; Bumpass 1990; Casper and Bianchi 2002; Ventura et al. 1995; Whitehead and Popenoe 2001). The level of divorce in northwestern Europe, while lower, also increased dramatically during the same period (Ahlburg and De Vita 1992; Kuijsten 1996; Prinz 1995; van de Kaa 1987, 1994).

The rising divorce rate has undoubtedly reinforced the historical concerns of young people about forming a bad marriage. However, now these concerns are not centered as much on having to endure a bad marriage as having to deal with the social, personal, and economic dislocation and trauma that can be associated with a marital dissolution. In fact, about one-half of young single adults (in their twenties in 2001) indicated that one of their biggest concerns about marriage was the possibility that it would not last (Whitehead and Popenoe 2001). This concern over the fragility of marriage has very likely contributed to the increase in unmarried cohabitation, as three-fifths of all unmarried young Americans believe that a period of living together prior to marriage will facilitate marital stability (Whitehead and Popenoe 2001). It is interesting to note that this belief persists despite many studies showing that marital stability is actually *lower* among those who cohabit before marriage (Axinn and Thornton 1992b).

This concern over divorce is also reflected in the recent finding that nearly 90 percent of young Americans believe the divorce rate is too high and should be lowered (Whitehead and Popenoe 2001). In fact, nearly one-half of Americans believe that laws need to be changed so that divorce is more difficult to obtain (Thornton and Young-DeMarco 2001; Whitehead and Popenoe 2001). Modifications to no-fault divorce laws have been suggested in many states, and covenant marriage—a new form of marriage contract involving premarital counseling and more difficult divorce—is now available in at least three states with a large fraction of Americans wanting to make it more widely available (Feld, Rosier, and Manning 2002; Thornton and Young-DeMarco 2001; Wardle 1999). However, the number of couples actually choosing covenant marriage is still very small (Nock et al. forthcoming).

Formalization of the Marriage Process

In Europe, the substantial number of private unions that were recognized but not performed by either church or state caused considerable concern for the reform of the marriage process among civil and religious leaders since at least the 1500s (Brundage 1987; Burguière 1976, 1987; Donahue 1983; Flandrin 1980; Gillis 1985; Glendon 1977; Howard 1904; Ingram 1981, 1985; Jeaffreson 1872; Kelly 1973; Koegel 1922; Lasch 1974; Outhwaite 1995; Ozment 1983; Pollock and Maitland 1968; Smout 1981; Witte 1997). At the time of the Protestant Reformation in the 1500s both the main Protestant reformers and the Catholic Church advocated a number of marriage reforms whose major thrusts were to formalize marriage and make it a public rather than a private event; to remove the authority of individual couples to, in essence, marry themselves; and to require many of the previously optional elements of marriage. These elements included the announcement of marriage through banns or a marriage license; the presence of at least two witnesses; the performance of the wedding by, or at least in the presence of, a religious or government official; and the registration of the marriage. These reforms suggested that sex and cohabitation could no longer be legitimated by betrothal but must be postponed until after the wedding.

Beginning in the 1500s, the essentials of many of these reforms were adopted in Catholic canon law and gained increasing acceptance in many

European legal systems (Björnsson 1971; Brundage 1987; Glendon 1977; Helmholz 1974; Ingram 1981, 1985; Koegel 1922; McCaa 1994; Witte 1997). The new Catholic canon law said that a priest should be involved in the marriage, and the law even suggested it was priestly authority that joined the couple together. However, the new canon law also said that a marriage did not have to be performed by a priest but only required its contraction in his presence, thereby leaving ultimate authority to the couple themselves (Brundage 1987; Glendon 1977; Koegel, 1922).

In England, an attempted reform of the marriage system along these lines failed in the middle of the 1500s, but ultimately triumphed in the middle 1700s when a law was passed requiring that a legal marriage be performed by a church officiator after thrice-called banns or the purchase of a license (Brown 1981; Gillis 1985; Glendon 1977; Howard 1904; Ingram 1985; Jeaffreson 1872; Lasch 1974; Macfarlane 1986; O'Donnell and Jones 1982; Outhwaite 1995; Witte 1997). This new law also declared betrothal ineffectual. As written, this law, and similar ones in other jurisdictions, transformed marriage from a personal contract to a contract relying on the authority of the church and state. This restrictive English law was repealed early in the next century and was replaced with one allowing much more latitude—including having a civil marriage as well as a religious one. The law did not explicitly allow private or self-marriages; but over the years, legislative, judicial, and administrative decisions have extended the old principles of consent to many of the circumstances of its earlier application (Bowman 1996; Gillis 1985; Howard 1904; Koegel 1922). And, despite the efforts to eliminate such marriages, they continued to be used by couples long after they were declared legally invalid (Gillis 1985). In fact, in some ways the new legal and religious efforts to formalize marriage helped create a two-tier marriage system—one recognized by the church and state and the other existing without religious and governmental legitimacy—with both being socially legitimate.[14]

The laws governing marriage in English America varied with colony and historical time. Interestingly, the English legal reform of the 1700s excluded from its jurisdiction both Scotland and overseas populations, including America (Koegel 1922; Smout 1981). At some times and places the law and practice followed the English system in place before the legislative action of the middle 1700s (Bowman 1996; Howard 1904; Koegel 1922; O'Donnell and Jones 1982). In other settings, such as Puritan New England and Virginia, the marriage laws were sometimes more restrictive and resembled English law after the reforms of the middle 1700s

(Bowman 1996; Howard 1904; Koegel 1922). In Puritan New England, for example, full marriage was presumed to occur only at the time of the wedding, and betrothed couples who joined in sexual union were subject to fines, although only at one-fourth the level of unbetrothed couples with similar behavior (Demos 1970b; Howard 1904). However, it appears that in colonial New England, marriages contracted without formal ceremony and authority external to the couple were still considered valid (Howard 1904).

Marriage laws and practices in the United States after independence were complicated. Although the primary jurisdiction for the legislation and administration of marriage law was vested in the states, the various state-level systems rested ultimately on federal principles and interpretations. In addition, English common law and the marriage principles and practices of England proved to be remarkably persistent and influential in the new country (Clark 1968; Howard 1904; Landis and Landis 1948; O'Donnell and Jones 1982; Vernier 1931). The combination of multiple levels of government, the continuation of English common law, and the influence of both judicial and legislative branches of government has made American family law—as one observer described it—a source of bewilderment and confusion (Vernier 1931; also see Bowman 1996; Weyrauch 1965).

Nevertheless, it appears that the essentials of marriage in the United States for most of the 1800s and 1900s continued to be consent and sexual consummation, and—unless explicitly invalidated by state law—a valid marriage could be formed with just these two ingredients. As long as a couple agreed to be husband and wife and lived together in that capacity, they were married, with or without a license or officiator. Furthermore, judicial practice suggested that the consent did not have to be explicit but that a common law marriage could be inferred by the facts of a man and woman living together as husband and wife and presenting themselves to the world as a married couple (Bowman 1996; Clark 1968; Glendon 1977; Howard 1904; Koegel 1922; Landis and Landis 1948; O'Donnell and Jones 1982; Weyrauch 1965; also see Brundage 1987 for earlier precursors of this view).

The system in the United States also allowed individual states to pass laws indicating the ways in which marriages could be contracted. For example, they could require the existence of a marriage license and a religious or governmental officiator. In fact, most, if not all, states have required some form of licensing and religious or governmental ceremony

(Clark 1968; Glendon 1976; Howard 1904; Landis and Landis 1948; Vernier 1931). However, if the states did not explicitly and definitively declare other forms of marriage to be invalid and lacking force, these common law marriages were valid (Bowman 1996; Clark 1968; Howard 1904; Landis and Landis 1948; O'Donnell and Jones 1982). The practices of American states have varied across history, and full documentation of them has been hindered by the complex and bewildering interplay of legislative action and judicial interpretation. One difficulty in interpreting laws is the nature of the language required in a statute to invalidate common law marriage. In addition, state judiciaries can accept common law marriage—or another informal marriage equivalent—even if the language of a law prohibiting it is relatively clear (Caudill, 1982; Clark, 1968; Foster, 1969; Vernier, 1931; Weyrauch, 1965b).

It thus appears that common law marriage or its equivalent has been in force in most jurisdictions in the United States throughout most of its history (Bowman 1996; O'Donnell and Jones 1982). For example, two studies in the first half of the 1900s suggested that six or fewer states explicitly and effectively repudiated or invalidated common law marriage (Howard 1904; Landis and Landis 1948). However, consistent with the confusion in the legal system, other studies in the same time period suggested that common law marriage was valid in only about half of the states even though few explicitly prohibited it (Koegel 1922; Vernier 1931).

It also appears that explicit legal support of common law marriage declined during the 1900s to about 25 percent of all jurisdictions (Atkinson 1996; Bowman 1996; Clark 1968; Ihara and Warner 1978; Weyrauch 1965, 1980). This occurred at least partially because of declining support for the historical position that common law marriage was valid unless explicitly invalidated by state law. At the same time, recent court cases have found that marriage is a basic civil right and that couples have the right to marry with minimal interference of the state (Drinan 1969; Foster 1969; Glendon 1976, 1977). Consequently, state regulation, even in those states where common law marriage is invalid, has little practical effect beyond licensing and recording of marriages (Drinan 1969; Glendon 1976, 1977; Weyrauch 1965b). And, in most states, the failure to procure a license and record a marriage is generally insufficient to invalidate a marriage, confirming the power of common law principles (Clark 1968; Foster 1969; Glendon 1977; Slovenko 1965; Weyrauch 1965, 1980). In fact, common law marriage can still be recognized even in states where it has been legally abolished (Kay and Amyx 1977; Müller-Freienfels 1987; Weyrauch, Katz, and

Olsen 1994). Thus, the ancient traditions of the supreme right of a mature couple to choose marriage over the interests of family, church, and state apparently have prevailed to the present, despite concerted efforts to the contrary (Donahue 1983; Glendon 1977). This idea is relevant for the rise of unmarried cohabitation, which we will consider later in this chapter.

Despite the continuation of the principle and practice of common law marriage or its equivalent in the United States, the movement of both religious and civil authorities toward the advocacy and practice of more formal marriage undoubtedly had important effects over the last two centuries. Marriage was probably increasingly seen as a formal institution requiring the involvement and authority of either church or state—and frequently both (Glendon 1977). Common law marriage was also often seen as an inferior and less respected form of marriage (Clark 1968; Howard 1904; Koegel 1922).

The wedding, as compared to betrothal, undoubtedly became more important and powerful across the past few centuries. The concept of betrothal was weakened by its declared lack of force, was slowly transformed into the concept of engagement, which suggested merely the plan or intention to marry, and was eventually dropped out of common language usage (Burguiére 1976; Ingram 1985; Smout 1981). Engagement in England, America, and France came to be interpreted by many as more tentative and subject to revocation than had been the promise of betrothal in earlier periods (Gottlieb 1980; Jeaffreson 1872). By the middle of the 1900s, some observers in America were describing engagement as another step in the courtship process—a time when the couple could test the wisdom of marriage (Bowman 1942; Kuhn 1955b; Landis and Landis 1948; Le Masters 1957; Modell 1989). In addition, engagement came to bestow less sexual legitimacy on the couple than had betrothal, with the wedding commonly viewed as the moment of legitimation of sexual union (Ingram 1985; Smout 1981).

It is also likely that engagement continued to carry some of the earlier meanings of betrothal for many. In the United States, couples continued to exchange rings and other tokens at engagement that designated both members as "taken" (Bowman 1942; Landis and Landis 1948; Rothman 1984). In addition, engagement continued to be a serious step that could not be easily broken.

The meanings associated with betrothal and wedding, the authority underlying them, and the power of the vows of individuals to implement them had been in existence for centuries and were not easily changed.

Many of the old meanings and approaches continued down through the centuries, and significant fractions of the population continued to marry privately and quietly as they always had (Gillis 1985; Lasch 1974; Smout 1981). And, even though engagement was less powerful than betrothal, some people continued to associate sexual legitimacy with engagement (Gillis 1985; Rothman 1984). In fact, Gillis (1985) suggests that the industrial and urban revolutions in the early 1800s in England were associated with a temporary increase in private marriages and the numbers of children recorded as illegitimate.

In Scandinavia in particular, engagement retained much of its power to legitimate sexual union and even cohabitation throughout the 1800s and 1900s (Björnsson 1971; Croog 1951; Myrdal 1941; Trost 1988). Engagement also continued to legitimize pregnancy and childbearing among many (Björnsson 1971; Croog 1951, 1952). However, at least in the 1960s, weddings in Iceland continued to be a rite of passage into full adulthood with an economically independent and self-sufficient household (Björnsson 1971). It is likely that the continued legitimation of betrothal as a license for sex and cohabitation helps to explain why unmarried cohabitation and childbearing began first and increased the most rapidly in the Scandinavian countries (Bracher and Santow 1998; Glendon 1977; Trost 1988).

Although the lack of systematic data makes it difficult to document trends in sex before engagement or marriage before the middle of the 1900s, it appears that the old norms of restricting sex to the period after betrothal continued largely intact in many places throughout the 1800s. Sexual intimacies short of intercourse continued to be allowed in courtship, but full sexual union was to be saved at least until engagement and, for most, until the wedding itself (Gillis 1985; Rothman 1984). Compliance on these norms was generally widespread in America at the beginning of the 1900s (Rothman 1984).

Despite the many changes that have occurred in the role of marriage in society, many of the past ceremonial and ritualistic features of marriage have endured to the present in many parts of the Western world. One observer has even suggested that the substantial commitment to tradition throughout English society expresses itself most forcibly in the celebration of marriages (Jeaffreson 1872). Among the rituals and ceremonies that have been inherited from the past are the hand clasp of bride and groom, the exchange of vows, the use of wedding rings, the exchange of gifts, the bridal veil, the presence of attendants, large and expensive celebrations, feasting, and dancing (Gillis 1985; Jeaffreson 1872; Sheehan 1991b). In twentieth-century England and America, marriage ceremonies became more elaborate, expensive, and ritualistic, and even included new elements[15] (Gillis 1985; Leonard 1980; Whyte 1990).

Dating and Going Steady

With the structural and cultural changes of the 1800s and 1900s came forces that influenced the ways young women and men met, interacted, courted, and eventually entered marriage and cohabitation. The expansion of school-ing into the late teens and early twenties provided a new locus for ex-tensive male-female interaction supervised by school authorities rather than by parents. School expansion also helped formulate a youth culture built around peer groups independent of parents. The growing tendency for young people to live in college dormitories or to reside in their own apartments—either alone or with others—provided new opportunities for interaction and courtship.

During the early part of the 1900s a system of dating and going steady evolved, and by the years preceding and following World War II, it had become an institution with its own expectations and norms (Bailey 1988; Fass 1977; Modell 1983, 1989; Rothman 1984). Although dating could in-clude multiple couples, it frequently involved only one two-some. Dates generally took young people away from home where they could enjoy privacy and anonymity, frequently in public settings. An automobile was not necessary for a date, but it was frequently part of the dating scene, providing both privacy—from parental supervision and surveillance—and accessibility to a wide range of activities.

As Modell (1983, 1989) has suggested, dating seems to have been closely connected with the youth culture of the high schools and their extracurricular activities, such as dancing. Dating became so extensive in high schools in the 1930s and 1940s that nearly all of the students— both male and female—had dated by the end of high school (Modell 1983, 1989). Substantial fractions had begun dating by their freshman and sophomore years. A 1960 national study of American high-school stu-dents indicated that two-thirds or more of ninth graders had commenced dating (Modell 1983; Schofield 1965 for England). During these younger years, dating was frequently a recreational activity not usually directly connected with the possibility of marriage (Bailey 1988; Fass 1977).

Frequent dating of the same person often blended into "going steady," which meant that each member of the couple was "taken," even if only temporarily, and that neither "could date anyone else or pay too much attention to anyone of the opposite sex" (Bailey 1988, 51). Going steady provided both the security and the status of having a stable partner (Bailey 1988; Modell 1989), and yet young people might have several steady boyfriends or girlfriends before becoming seriously engaged in courtship connected to the possibility of marriage. However, even with this distinction from marriage or even engagement, going steady frequently appropriated some of the symbols previously associated only with marriage—such as the exchange of tokens, including rings and articles of clothing (Bailey 1988).

As young people matured into the later years of high school and college, their dating and going-steady experiences often became more serious. Of the substantial fractions of young people who went steady in high school, many gave serious consideration to marrying their steady, and significant numbers made public or private commitments to marriage, even though these commitments may have fallen short of formal engagement (Heiss 1960; Modell 1989). Furthermore, some high-school romances blossomed into marriage, especially following World War II when many marriages occurred at young ages. In fact, approximately 30 percent of young women during the postwar years had married at age 18 or younger (Michael et al. 1994). This connection with early marriage—and the added potential for sexual intercourse—probably motivated many parents to discourage their children from going steady at a young age (Hollingshead 1949; Modell 1989).

As dating and going steady spread, they appropriated not only some of the symbols of engagement and marriage but some of the rights as well. Although firm data are scarce, it appears that kissing and fondling—previously acceptable only among older courting couples—became increasingly accepted and practiced at younger ages and at a time when marriage was only a very distant possibility (Bailey 1988; Franklin and Remmers 1961; Modell 1989; Newcomb 1937; Rothman 1984). In fact, the expression of intimacies in adolescent dating became so common and institutionalized that new terms developed—*necking, petting,* and *making out*—to describe the intimacies exchanged between dating partners. A common theme of the first half of the 1900s was increasing tolerance and frequency of necking and petting and its extension to younger and younger adolescents (Bailey 1988; Fass 1977; Franklin and Remmers 1961; Modell 1989; Newcomb 1937; Rothman 1984; Reiss 1960, 1967). By the early 1960s about one-half of adult Americans believed that petting was acceptable before marriage when accompanied by affection. Approval was even higher among young people, and greater among young men than young women (Franklin and Remmers 1961; Reiss 1967).

In more recent decades the formality of the dating and courtship system has declined substantially (Glenn and Marquardt 2001). Also, as we discuss in more detail in the following, the male-female scene has become much more sexualized.

Although dating and courtship are often viewed as a system run by youth, these activities continued to involve the advice and consent of parents throughout the mid-1900s. For example, a survey of adolescents in the state of Minnesota in the late 1940s revealed that two-thirds believed that parents should be consulted before making or accepting dates, with such parental involvement accepted more by girls than boys (Modell 1989). A national study of American high-school students in 1961 revealed that about two-thirds thought it was very desirable for their parents to approve their future spouse, again with more young women than young men holding this view (Franklin and Remmers 1961). Furthermore, it appears that some dating and courting activities continued to be located in one of the parental homes, and, with engagement, the couple increasingly became integrated into their parental families (Le Masters 1957; also see Leonard 1980 for Wales).

Changing Sexual Experience and Attitudes

Many of the views on sex and marriage in the medieval era continued to influence attitudes and laws well into the 1900s (Brundage 1987; Weyrauch 1965). For example, laws against sex outside of marriage remained in force through the late 1900s in some American states, although they were infrequently enforced (Weyrauch 1965). In fact, enforcement of these laws is now extremely difficult because the courts are increasingly ruling that the "rights of privacy" forbid the states from regulating sexual behavior among consenting adults (Ihara and Warner 1978).

At a more personal level, marriage continued to define the acceptance of sexual intercourse in the first part of the 1900s for most Americans. Although some young steadies undoubtedly experienced sexual intercourse, social norms continued to discourage full sexual union before engagement—and even before marriage (Bailey 1988; Fass 1977; Modell 1989; Reiss 1967; Rothman 1984). The extent of adherence to these standards of behavior is illustrated by findings from a national survey that only about 10 percent of women born at the turn of the century reported sexual intercourse before marriage, and about one-half of those reportedly had sex only with their future husbands (Klassen et al. 1989; also see Laumann et al. 1994). In the same survey, about five-sixths of ever-married women reaching marrying ages at mid-century reported that they had married as virgins or had premarital intercourse only with the men they married (Klassen et al. 1989; also see Michael et al. 1994; also see Kiernan 1989 for Britain). A double standard made the proscriptions against premarital sex less stringent for men than for women (Reiss, 1960). Among ever-married men born at the turn of the century, about half reported having sexual experience with someone other than their future wives, and this fraction increased significantly among subsequent birth cohorts (Klassen et al. 1989).

Proscriptions against premarital sex remained strong through the early 1960s. In a 1963 national study of adult Americans, only 7 percent reported belief in the acceptability of "full sexual relations" for a woman before marriage "if she does not feel particularly affectionate toward her partner" (Reiss 1967, 22, 29). Even with the double standard in 1963, still only 12 percent expressed approval for men under similar circumstances. In addition, although the acceptability of premarital sex increased somewhat as the hypothetical relationship increased from "not particularly affectionate," to "strong affection," to "love," to being "engaged to be married," only 17 and 20 percent respectively expressed approval of sexual relations for females and males who were engaged.

Disapproval of premarital sex declined rapidly in the late 1960s and early 1970s. By the mid-1970s only 30 percent of all American adults believed that it is always wrong for "a man and woman [to] have sex relations before marriage" (Thornton 1989, 883). Even smaller percentages of young people expressed such strong disapproval—13 percent among those under age 30 (Thornton 1989; also see Klassen, Williams, and Levitt 1989). Clearly, by 1975, the historical monopoly that marriage had in legitimating sexual intercourse had been broken for the great majority of Americans, especially the young.[16]

For most Americans who rejected the necessity of marriage for sexual union, love or affection became the legitimizing substance for sexual intercourse (Klassen, Williams, and Levitt 1989; Modell 1989; Reiss 1967; Rothman 1984). This standard for sexual intercourse was also relaxed in subsequent years as people increasingly came to view desire and consent as the only prerequisites. A national study of Americans conducted in 1992 identified three broad value systems guiding Americans today: the *traditional* of reserving sexual intercourse to marital relations; the *relational* that requires a loving relationship but not marriage for sexual union; and the *recreational* that requires neither love nor marriage for intercourse. The authors estimated the division as roughly 30, 45, and 25 percent respectively among these systems (Michael et al. 1994). In addition, the maturity of the individual remained a criteria for most Americans, as acceptance of premarital sex for unmarried teenagers was considerably less than for unmarried people in general (Thornton 1989; Thornton and Young-DeMarco 2001).

The new standards of behavior were also reflected in the behavior of young Americans. As early as 1971, premarital sexual intercourse was widespread among American teenagers. In that year, 46 percent of never-married 19-year-old women reported that they had experienced sexual intercourse. By the end of the 1980s, this figure had grown to 80 percent—and was 86 percent for 19-year-old men (Abma and Sonenstein 2001; Zelnik and Kantner 1980; also see Abma et al. 1997; Laumann et al. 1994; Morgan 1996; Santelli et al. 2000; Ventura et al. 1995; also see Schofield 1965 for England). In the early 1990s, about eight out of nine new brides reported having had sexual intercourse prior to marriage—the majority more than five years before the marriage. Although a small fraction reported having first intercourse during the engagement period, most experienced it when going steady and some in more casual relationships[17] (Abma et al. 1997). Consistent with the emerging norms, significant numbers of young people report engaging in sexual relations that are more recreational than relational (Glenn and Marquardt 2001; Whitehead and Popenoe 2001).

Marriage and Childbearing

The rather close association between marriage and childbearing has also been substantially attenuated in the past two centuries. In the north-western-European past, unmarried childbearing was both unacceptable and infrequent, while marital childbearing was "natural" in that few married couples consciously tried to restrict childbearing (Himes 1970; van de Walle and Knodel 1980). The "natural" connection between marriage and childbearing was broken in the 1800s and 1900s. Increasing numbers of couples used contraception, sterilization, and abortion to restrict their childbearing, and fertility rates fell. New and especially effective means of contraception in the 20th century made fertility regulation especially easy

(Coale and Zelnik 1963; Dawson, Merry, and Ridley 1980; Forrest and Singh 1990; Mosher and Pratt 1990; Sanderson 1979; van de Kaa 1987; van de Walle and Knodel 1980). Although fertility had declined substantially in the century before World War II, the norms for having at least one child remained strong and very few couples voluntarily remained childless. In the early 1960s, five-sixths of the mothers participating in the Intergenerational Panel Study said that all married couples who can have children ought to have them. However, the normative imperative to have children declined substantially in subsequent decades, and only about two-fifths expressed this view in the 1980s and 1990s. The adult daughters of these mothers in the 1980s and 1990s were even less insistent on universal parenthood than their mothers (Thornton 1989; Thornton and Young-DeMarco 2001; also see van de Kaa 1987 and Lesthaeghe 1995 for the Netherlands). Despite this attitude, however, little evidence indicates that personal desire for childlessness has increased (Thornton 1989; Thornton and Young-DeMarco 2001). For example, less than 10 percent of high-school seniors from the middle 1970s through the middle 1990s thought that it was unlikely that they would want to have children.

Just as the normative prescription for married couples to have children has declined, tolerance of childbearing without marriage has increased, although it is still below the acceptance of unmarried sexual union and cohabitation (Pagnini and Rindfuss 1993; Thornton 1995; Thornton and Young-DeMarco 2001). For example, among high-school seniors in the United States, the percentage saying that unmarried childbearing was destructive to society or violating a moral principle declined from about 45 percent in the mid-1970s to about 35 percent in the 1990s (Axinn and Thornton 2000; Thornton and Young-DeMarco 2001). Another study found that more than two-fifths of American adults agreed that "it should be legal for adults to have children without getting married;" similar fractions agreed that "there is no reason why single women shouldn't have children and raise them if they want to" (Pagnini and Rindfuss 1993, 334). Another study found that less than three in ten young adults agree that "single women should not have children, even if they want to" (Moore and Stief 1991, 373).

Rates of out-of-wedlock childbearing have fluctuated substantially over the past centuries. They were apparently low in many Western countries before the middle of the 1700s, then increased through the last part of the 1800s, and then declined through the initial decades of the 1900s (Laslett 1980; Shorter, Knodel, and van de Walle 1971). The decline in the late 1800s and early 1900s paralleled the decline in marital fertility and has been attributed to increasing contraception among both married and unmarried women (Laslett 1980; Shorter, Knodel, and van de Walle 1971).

Rates of nonmarital childbearing have increased dramatically again in the past half century—by more than six times between 1940 and 1993 in the United States (Ventura et al., 1995). One of the essential forces producing this dramatic increase in nonmarital childbearing was the reduction in the likelihood of marriage among pregnant, unmarried women (Abma et al. 1997; Bachu 1999; Morgan 1996; Morgan and Rindfuss 1999; Parnell, Swicegood, and Stevens 1994; Raley 2000; Ventura et al. 1995). This substantial increase in unmarried childbearing, coupled with declines in marriage and marital childbearing rates, has produced equally dramatic increases in the percentage of children born out of wedlock (Bachu 1999; Casper and Bianchi 2002; Morgan 1996; van de Kaa 1987; Ventura et al. 1995). Although the fraction of American children born to unmarried mothers remained relatively constant at around one-twentieth between 1940 and 1960, the fraction jumped to about one-third in the mid-1990s— a period when the fraction of women's *first* births that were out of wedlock reached two-fifths (Bachu 1999; Ventura et al. 1995). Substantial increases in the percentage of children born outside of marriage have also occurred throughout most of Europe (Carmichael 1995; Kiernan 1999; Lesthaeghe 1995; van de Kaa 1987, 1994). The one-third fraction of children born outside of wedlock in the United States is very similar to the fraction in the United Kingdom and France, but higher than the 13 to 15 percent in Germany and the Netherlands, and lower than the 46 to 50 percent in Denmark and Sweden (Kiernan 1999; Moore 1995; Prinz 1995). Another indication of the separation of childbearing and childrearing from marriage is the sharp decline in the percentage of children born out of wedlock in the United States who are adopted into the homes of married couples (Bachrach, Stolley, and London 1992; Ventura et al. 1995). There is also growing evidence that in many economically poor communities, childbearing is seen as a behavior that is highly valued in young adulthood while marriage should be postponed until after economic stability is achieved—often later in life (Edin and Kefalas 2005; Edin, Kafalas, and Reed 2004).

The fact that unmarried fertility has increased dramatically, and currently accounts for about one-third of all births in the United States, does not mean that "marriage is irrelevant to contemporary childbearing" (Morgan 1996, 44). Birth rates for unmarried women—both the single and the cohabiting—are still substantially lower than for married women (Carmichael 1995; Casper and Bianchi 2002; Morgan 1996; Ventura et al. 1995). Yet, it is also clear that the monopoly once held by marriage over the bearing and rearing of children has been broken (Carmichael 1995; Prinz 1995).

Birth Control

Another element of social change related to marriage in the last two centuries is the spread of the medical means of birth control. Most historical demographers agree that humans have long practiced nonmedical forms of birth control, such as rhythm methods, withdrawal, and abstinence, as a means of avoiding or delaying pregnancy. By the 1940s, more effective medical means of birth control began to be widely available (Freedman, Whelpton, and Campbell 1959). Barrier methods, such as the condom and the diaphragm, substantially increased the effectiveness of individuals' efforts to avoid or delay pregnancy even while engaging in sexual intercourse. These methods are coitally specific—that is, they must be used at the time a couple is having sex. So, although highly effective, such methods also require couples to be highly motivated *at the time of sexual intercourse* to avoid or delay pregnancy.

From the 1960s onward, a steady stream of new noncoitally-specific methods of birth control became widely available to the general public (Westoff and Ryder 1977). These methods include the oral contraceptive pill, the IUD, Depo-Provera, and implants such as Norplant. Oral contraceptive pills are generally taken daily; Depo-Provera is often taken as an injection every three months; implants or the IUD can be inserted for over a year of effectiveness. All of these methods allow the decision to avoid pregnancy to be separated, at least in time, from the decision to engage in sexual intercourse.

The availability and knowledge of these methods may have influenced cohabitation and marital behavior in the second half of the 1900s. Some argue that these birth-control methods may have encouraged women to pursue careers and delay marriage with confidence in their abilities to avoid pregnancy while engaging in sexual relations outside of marriage (Goldin and Katz 2000). Such a reaction may also have contributed to the rise in unmarried cohabitation because childbearing could be avoided among cohabitors who believed they should be married before having children. Thus, the perceived necessity of marriage as a precursor to sexuality may have declined among some because these methods of birth control reduced the link between sex and childbearing.

Unmarried Cohabitation

The necessity of a wedding for heterosexual couples setting up a joint household has also declined dramatically in recent decades. Despite the difficulties of detecting unmarried cohabitation in the historical record, especially separating it from common law marriage, evidence indicates that some fraction of couples have cohabited without marriage in many settings, including Australia in the formative years of the early 1800s, industrializing England, urban France, and Sweden (Bradley 1996; Carmichael 1995, 1996; Gillis 1985; Ratcliffe 1996). Although there were probably unmarried cohabitors in other parts of northwestern Europe and in the United States in the 1800s and early 1900s, the experience was relatively uncommon as recently as the 1950s (Bumpass and Sweet 1989; Carmichael 1995; Kiernan 2000). A national study of American adults interviewed in the late 1980s revealed that only two percent of the people born before 1928 and reaching adulthood before or shortly after World War II reported cohabitation before a first marriage (Bumpass and Sweet 1989). Experience with unmarried cohabitation increased substantially over the last half of the 1900s. About one-ninth of all persons marrying for the first time between 1965 and 1974 in the United States had cohabited previously, a fraction that was to increase by five times to 56 percent for the first-marriage cohort of 1990–94 (Bumpass and Lu 2000; Bumpass and Sweet 1989). Even higher fractions of second marriages were preceded by cohabitation. The increases in cohabitation in the United States in recent decades have been substantial enough to offset a significant fraction of the decline in marriage (Bumpass and Sweet 1989; Bumpass, Sweet, and Cherlin 1991). Trends in cohabitation have been similar in most of the countries of northwestern Europe and in countries with strong European roots, with the prevalence of cohabitation increasing sooner and reaching considerably higher levels in some countries such as Sweden than in the United States (Carmichael 1995; Cherlin 1992; Kiernan 2000, 2004; Kuijsten 1996; Prinz 1995; van de Kaa 1987, 1994). Children born to cohabiting couples account for an increasing fraction of out-of-wedlock births, about two-fifths in the early 1990s, and, in fact, explain most of the recent increase in out-of-wedlock childbearing in both the United States and most of Europe (Bumpass and Lu 2000; Carmichael 1995; Kiernan 1999).

Evidence indicates a strong generation gap in values and attitudes concerning both premarital sex and cohabitation without marriage (Bumpass 1998; Macklin 1978; Reiss 1967; Thornton 1989; Thornton and Young-DeMarco 2001). During the 1980s and 1990s, the mothers participating in our study (IPS) were opposed to unmarried cohabitation by a margin of about two to one, whereas their children accepted it by a similar or higher margin (Thornton 1989; Thornton and Young-DeMarco 2001; also see Macklin 1978; Sweet and Bumpass 1990). Today, more than three-fifths of young people in the United States agree that "it is usually a good idea for a couple to live together before getting married in order to find out whether they really get along" (Thornton and Young-DeMarco 2001, 1023—25; also see Axinn and Thornton 2000; Bumpass 1998; Moore and Stief 1991; Schulenberg et al. 1995; Thornton 1989).

It is amazing that the efforts and success of the church and state over hundreds of years to regulate marriage and intimate relations have been largely reversed in the last several decades, as individuals and couples exercised more autonomy and control of their private lives (Lesthaeghe 1995). For at least a thousand years, marriage in the Western world has been an interesting mixture of simple consent, elaborate ritual and celebration, and public recognition—with wide variation in the combination of these elements. For much of that history, social forces have moved to formalize the marriage process, which has been reflected in the involvement of the church and state, the invalidation of common law marriage in most of America, and the growing elaboration of the marriage ritual. In more recent decades this trend has reversed, and the community and state have largely withdrawn from regulating union formation, marital dissolution, and related behaviors. In addition, unmarried cohabitation has become recognized in social interaction, public opinion, legislation, and judicial action in many settings.[18] It seems that Americans and many others in the northwest-European sphere have reclaimed from the community and larger social system control over crucial elements of the union-formation process. The desire for privatization and individual control is reflected in findings from a recent survey that eight-tenths of young Americans believed "marriage is nobody's business but the two people involved," and that nearly one-half believed that "the government should not be involved in licensing marriages" (Whitehead and Popenoe 2001, 13).

Although unmarried cohabitation today has many features that make it unique from informal marriage, common law marriage, and other marital forms over the centuries, it also shares important features with some of these earlier forms. In the next chapter we shift our attention to consider cohabitation and the ways that it compares to and differs from single life and marriage in America today.

Race Differences

Recent decades have seen patterns of change over time in marriage, child-bearing, and unmarried cohabitation in the African-, Latino-, and Asian-American populations that generally follow the same trends as found among the White population (McLoyd et al. 2000; Taylor et al. 1997). Nevertheless, each of these race groups is also characterized by important differences in recent rates of change (McLoyd et al. 2000; Taylor et al. 1997). For example, declining rates of marriage and proportions remaining unmarried have been higher among African and Latino Americans than among the general population (McLoyd et al. 2000).[19] The proportion of African Americans who marry is lower than Whites, and this proportion has been dropping faster among Blacks than among Whites (Bennett, Bloom, and Craig 1989; Schoen and Owens 1992). Rates of unmarried cohabitation had been higher among African Americans than among Whites until the very recent past, when it appears these differences converged (Bumpass and Lu 2000). By contrast, rates of unmarried cohabitation have been and continue to be lower among Hispanic Americans than among Whites (Bumpass and Lu 2000). The intersection of cohabitation, marriage, and childbearing also differs by race. Rates of childbearing within cohabitations are much more similar to rates of childbearing among the married for African Americans than for Whites (Loomis and Landale 1994). Although unmarried cohabitation is less common among Hispanic groups, cohabitation accelerates childbearing more among Puerto Rican and Mexican Americans than among the general population (Manning and Landale 1996; Wildsmith and Raley 2006).

Careful historical research reveals important African-American–White differences in marital and family behaviors dating back at least a century (Landale and Tolnay 1991; Morgan et al. 1993). For example, African-American families were much more likely to be headed by women than White families, suggesting historical differences that parallel recent differences, and pointing toward explanations of race differences in family behaviors that include factors that have been persistent across a long period of time (Morgan et al. 1993). These historical results foreshadow the possibility that factors shaping the marital and cohabiting behaviors of

Whites may be different than those shaping the marital and cohabiting behaviors of other racial and ethnic groups. Although the empirical analyses we present in this book are limited to the White population, we comment on what is currently known about these potential race and ethnic differences as we summarize our results from the White population. Next we turn to conceptualization and measurement of these important relationship transitions before going on to explore empirical results in detail.

CHAPTER THREE

Comparing Marriage, Cohabitation, and Being Single

Historically, marital status in the United States and other Western societies has been defined with two master categories: single and married. Although the single status could be further divided into the subcategories of never married, widowed, and divorced, the only relevant categories for defining the status of most young people were never married and married. As we noted in the previous chapter, marriage was not a simple, unchanging, and homogeneous category, but varied in conception and practice across both time and social groups.

Conceptualizing relationship statuses has become more challenging with the widespread acceptance and practice of unmarried cohabitation in the West in recent decades. Like marriage, cohabitation is a complex category containing individuals with diverse perspectives, aims, and relationships (Carmichael 1995; Casper 1992; Casper and Bianchi 2002; Casper and Sayer 2000; Jamieson et al. 2002; Manning and Smock 2002; Smock 2000). In addition, the introduction of cohabitation has not only added a new relationship status to the mix, but introduced two new relationship contrasts: between cohabitation and being single and between cohabitation and marriage.

Our goal in this chapter is to explore the meanings of marriage, cohabitation, and being single, the contrasts among these statuses, and how cohabitation relates to marriage and being single. We also examine the heterogeneity of cohabitors by considering the motivations and expectations of people who cohabit, both at the beginning of cohabitation and later in the relationship.

Being Single

We begin with being single because it is the first relationship status experienced by young people. Although babies enter the world embedded within a complex kin and community system, their relationship status is firmly and clearly single as they are born without partner and without spouse. In Western societies this single status persists through the first decade of life and changes dramatically in the second decade with the coming of adolescence and young adulthood. Physical and social maturation dissolves many of the boundaries between the sexes, and opposites begin to attract—often in powerful ways. Male-female interactions increase and intensify, dating becomes common, steady relationships form, and sexual exploration begins. Young women and men become girlfriends and boyfriends in the romance of life—and then often ex-girlfriends and ex-boyfriends, as relationships are formed and then dissolved.

For most Americans, one of these relationships intensifies and changes in terms of intimacy, living arrangements, commitments, legal status, public presentation, and community recognition. Eventually, the young couple is no longer single but married or cohabiting.

Although Americans have historically defined being single in contrast to marriage, in this book we contrast being single with both marriage and cohabitation. Thus, we treat as single anyone who is both unmarried and not living with someone in an intimate union. This does not eliminate singles with serious and long-term stable relationships, only singles living with their partners. We use the terms *unpartnered* and *not in a union* to refer to this construct of being single, which reflects our conceptualization of the single state in contrast to the partnership or union statuses of marriage and unmarried cohabitation. In this framework, being single encompasses a variety of intimate relationships that do not involve marriage or cohabitation. Being single can also involve a variety of different living arrangements, including living with parents, in a dormitory, with housemates, or alone. Thus, being single includes a wide array of social circumstances, with the primary distinction for our purposes being that it does not include marriage or an intimate coresidential courtship.

Marriage

As we discussed in the previous chapter, the concept of marriage in the past referred to process as well as structure. The marriage process that transformed an individual from being single to being married was usually one that involved at least two steps, but could be solemnized quickly with a minimum of ceremony. In the distant past, betrothal, the first step in the process, was exceptionally powerful in transforming a person from single to married. This power apparently weakened over time, finally to be transformed into our current concept of engagement. For many people today, the second step—the wedding ceremony—is much more important than the engagement in generating marriage with all its attendant rights and responsibilities.

So, do we treat engaged couples as married or single? Here we note that the general practice today still follows the millennium-old custom of accepting the couple's presentation of their marital status. In public discourse today the concept of marriage is used without definition, and people who say they are married or who otherwise present themselves as wife and husband are accepted as married. Most researchers follow the same approach, accepting as married all couples who report this about themselves, without worrying about the rituals and processes that rendered them married (Thornton and Young-DeMarco 1996).

Our research has followed the same approach. Our marriage question was simply: "Have you ever been married?" If the respondent answered affirmatively, the interviewer probed to ascertain the number and dates of all marriages, and the dates and causes (death or discord) of any marital dissolutions. Following this approach, we treat those who say they have plans to marry, but who have not yet declared themselves as married, as single. Thus we treat engaged couples as not yet married.

Although we accept marriage as a self-defined status in our empirical research, we assume that most of our respondents understand it to be a union of husband and wife crafted out of the love, commitment, and consent of the two individuals. With these ingredients, the ritual and ceremony of wedding, usually under the authority and guidance of the government and/or church, join the couple together in matrimony. Of course, despite this common interpretation of marriage as involving ritual and external authority, marriage, as we have seen, can also be accomplished under common law or equivalent methods without ritual or external authority in most places in America.

Unmarried Cohabitation

Whereas historically marriage was the only realistic alternative to being single, in recent decades unmarried cohabitation has arisen as a common option. We agree with Davis (1985) that the key element separating unmarried cohabitation from being single is the joint occurrence of regular sexual relations and common residence. The transition from being single to cohabiting is also frequently a process rather than an event. The establishment of regular sexual relations and common residence is often spread out over weeks, months, and years. Frequently, the couple maintains two separate residences, even as they begin to experiment with sharing a household. Thus, the boundary between cohabitation and being single can also be relatively fuzzy and arbitrary.

In asking about cohabitation, most researchers provide respondents at least a partial definition of cohabitation. Sexual intimacy, common residence, and the absence of marriage are usually specified (Macklin 1978; Thornton and Young-DeMarco 1996). In our data collections we asked female study participants the question, "Have you ever lived together as a partner in an intimate relationship with a man without being married to him?" We asked a similar question of male participants about women. Like virtually all other questions about unmarried cohabitation in large-scale studies, these questions do not define marriage for respondents, but assume it to be self-evident (Thornton and Young-DeMarco 1996).[1] For respondents who had ever cohabited, information was ascertained about the number of cohabiting partners, dates of initiating cohabiting unions, and dates and reasons for terminating unions. The data-collection procedures also allowed the identification of cohabiting unions that were subsequently transformed into marital unions.[2]

Cohabitation Heterogeneity and Boundaries

The meaning of cohabitation relative to marriage and being single is complex because there are many different kinds of cohabiting couples with different goals and perspectives. Some cohabiting couples can hardly be distinguished from some single couples while others, particularly those with marriage plans, are very similar to married couples, making the boundaries between the relationship statuses fuzzy (Brown and Booth 1996). In this section of the chapter we consider these boundaries and examine the heterogeneity among cohabitors.

Is Cohabitation Really Marriage?

The boundary between cohabitation and marriage can be particularly thin
and difficult to maintain. In fact, some cohabiting unions are referred to
as marriage-like relationships, paperless marriages, or de facto marriages
because they share many similarities with marriage—including coresidence, companionship, and a sexual relationship (Brown and Booth 1996;
Bruch 1981; Caudill 1982; Müller-Freienfels 1987; Trost 1981; van de Kaa
1987).

It is also possible for unmarried cohabitation to be interpreted socially
and legally as a common-law or equivalent marriage (Caudill 1982; Estin
2001; Kiernan 2004; Regan 2001; Weyrauch, Katz, and Olsen 1994). Although cohabitation is not legally common-law marriage unless the man
and woman intend to be married and hold themselves out to the community as husband and wife, the legal and social boundary between cohabitation and common-law marriage can be fuzzy. This fuzziness has led
the authors of the *1999 Living Together Kit* to recommend that cohabiting
couples living in a state that recognizes common-law marriage should sign
a statement indicating their intent to remain unmarried so that their relationship is not mistakenly interpreted as marriage (Ihara, Warner, and
Hertz 1999; also see Kandoian 1987 on this point).

The legal distinction between cohabitation and marriage is also blurred
by the fact that many couples in the United States and elsewhere who live
together without marriage can accumulate some of the rights and responsibilities associated with marriage[3] (Bruch 1981; Caudill 1982; Estin 2001;
Fawcett 1990; Frank 1981; Glendon 1976; Kay and Amyx 1977; Kiernan
2004; Parr 1999; Regan 2001; Weyrauch 1980). In fact, in almost all circumstances today "a more or less permanent sexual union" has some legal
effect (Weyrauch 1980, 429; also see Caudill 1982; Frank 1981; Müller-
Freienfels 1987; Weyrauch, Katz, and Olsen 1994). The extension of legal rights and duties to cohabiting couples has been especially marked
in some countries where the frequency of unmarried cohabitation is un-
usually high (Blumberg 2001; Bradley 1996; Estin 2001; Müller-Freienfels
1987).

This difficulty of separating cohabitation from marriage can be illustrated by a recent decision of Washington State's Supreme Court that
distinguished marriage from a "meretricious relationship," defined by the
court as "a stable, marital-like relationship where both parties cohabit
with knowledge that a lawful marriage between them does not exist"

(Parr 1999, 1244; also see Estin 2001). Among the elements useful in identifying such "meretricious" relationships, according to the Washington court, were cohabitation, durability, continuity, functional equivalence to marriage, subjective treatment of the relationship as marriage, and pooling of resources and labor. Although many of these features suggest a common-law marriage, the court specified that in a meretricious relationship both parties "must know that they are not lawfully married" (Parr 1999, 1263). It seems that the Washington court was suggesting that a meretricious cohabiting relationship is equivalent to a common-law marriage, but making a legal distinction between the two because common-law marriage is not officially recognized in Washington. Similar equivalencies exist in other states where "parties to informal cohabitation may be considered to be in a quasi-marital state, at least for purposes of entitlements and property allocation" (Weyrauch, Katz, and Olsen 1994, 157; also see Estin 2001; Kay and Amyx 1977).

Some have suggested that substantial and stable unmarried cohabitations should be legally recognized as "modified common-law or constructive marriage" to protect the interests of the various parties (Caudill 1982, 565; Reppy 1984; also see Kandoian 1987). In fact, the American Law Institute passed a formal recommendation in 2000 for federal law to give long-term marriage-like cohabitations the same rights as marriages (Blumberg 2001; Oldham 2001; Westfall 2001). The idea behind this recommendation is that the two are the same except for the legal ceremony and certificate, which should not prevent people in a marriage-like relationship from participating in the rights and responsibilities of marriage. This approach treats long-term stable cohabitation very similarly to common-law marriage, but distinguishes its status as "marriage-like" rather than marriage.

It is not only the law that sometimes blurs the marriage-cohabitation distinction, as personal definitions of one's own relationship status can also be ambiguous and malleable. Both an in-depth qualitative study in New Zealand (Elizabeth 2000) and a large-scale British survey (Brown and Kiernan 1981) found that certain individuals will sometimes define their relationship as marriage and sometimes as cohabitation. Also, a Scottish study reported that many young adults believe the boundaries between cohabitation and marriage are so fuzzy as to be unimportant (Jamieson et al. 2002).

We recognize that the legal and social boundaries separating marriage and cohabitation are frequently indistinct, that cohabitation sometimes has almost all of the attributes of a common-law marriage, and that some cohabiting couples have probably accumulated some of the social and legal rights and duties of married couples. Yet, we also believe that for most people there are fundamental differences between cohabitation and marriage that lie at the heart of the meaning of marriage (Davis 1985; Trost 1978; Waite and Gallagher 2000). All couples who identify themselves as unmarried cohabitors are missing the key element that has defined marriage in northwestern-European societies for decades: their self-identification as married. Almost all cohabiting couples explicitly say that they are not married and do not hold themselves out to the community as wife and husband. This distinction is also generally recognized in the legal systems of most countries, where cohabitors are treated differently from married couples even though they accumulate some of the same rights and responsibilities (Bruch 1981; Müller-Freienfels 1987).

Separate categorization of cohabiting and marital unions is consistent with the fact that cohabiting unions are generally not entered into with the same commitment to the permanence of the relationship that characterizes entrance into marriage[4] (Brines and Joyner 1999; Davis 1985; Elizabeth 2000; Manting 1994; Nock 1995; Smock 2000; Thomson and Colella 1992; Trost 1978; Waite and Gallagher 2000). They are often viewed as tentative or trial relationships that will eventually be terminated or transformed into marriage—expectations that are frequently born out in practice (Axinn and Thornton 1992b; Binstock and Thornton 2003; Bumpass and Lu 2000; Bumpass and Sweet 1989; Smock 2000). Thus, the costs of terminating a coresidential union are seen as lower in cohabiting than in marital relationships (Nock 1995; Treas and Giesen 2000).

The lower commitment and durability of cohabiting as compared to marital unions are apparent in the behavior of the young adults participating in our study (Binstock and Thornton 2003). We find that cohabitors have rates of separation that are nearly five times as high as those who are married. Cohabitors also experience living apart for reasons other than relationship discord at about 60 percent higher rates than the married. Cohabitors who separate or live apart from their partner also have rates of getting back together again that are only about one-third as high as among the married who separate or live apart.

Although both cohabiting and married couples generally expect their partners to have no other sexual relationships, actual exclusivity is substantially higher in marital relationships (Forste and Tanfer 1996; Laumann et al. 1994; Treas and Giesen 2000; Waite and Gallagher 2000). In fact, the level of sexual exclusivity in cohabiting couples is much closer to that of single dating couples than to that of married couples (Forste and Tanfer 1996; Laumann et al. 1994). Concerns about flexibility and being tied down apparently underlie the concern of some cohabiting couples that marriage would constrain their freedom (Bumpass, Sweet, and Cherlin 1991). In addition, cohabitation seems to imply less economic sharing and interconnectivity (Trost 1978; Waite and Gallagher 2000).

Cohabitation also continues to be less powerful than marriage in legitimizing childbearing (Davis 1985; Manting 1994). Many young people report the view that marriage has an advantage over cohabitation for rearing children (Liefbroer and de Jong Gierveld 1993); and in fact birth rates among cohabiters are much lower than marital birth rates. In addition, pregnancy serves as a motivation to marry among substantial numbers of cohabiting couples, suggesting a desire to raise children within marriage, although there are pronounced racial and ethnic differences between those choosing to make that transition, with cohabiting white women showing significantly higher marriage rates than cohabiting black or Hispanic women, and cohabiting Hispanics showing higher marriage rates than cohabiting blacks (Carmichael 1995; Manning 1993, 2001; Manning and Landale 1996; Raley 2001). Also, there is evidence that indicates more than one-half of the pregnancies occurring in cohabiting relationships are planned, suggesting that while still less desirous than marriage, cohabitation may be becoming an increasingly acceptable context for childbearing (Manning 2001; Musick 2002; Smock and Manning 2004). Moreover, women finding themselves pregnant outside of cohabiting or marital relationships have become much less likely over the last three decades to make the transition to marriage prior to the birth of the child (Raley 2001; Smock and Manning 2004). This trend may be explained in part by what George Akerlof has described as the "technology shock" related to the legalization of abortion and easy availability of female contraception. Access to these services has afforded most women the ability to engage in sexual activities without commitment or without exacting promises of marriage from their male partners in the event of pregnancy, while at the same time placing many women who want children at a competitive disadvantage since their bargaining power for the guarantee of marriage has eroded considerably (Akerlof, Yellen, and Katz 1996).

Marriage is also an ancient institution that integrates the couple with the larger community, and cohabiting couples differ from most married couples in their relationship to the church, the state, the community, and other family members (Nock 1995; Thornton and Young-DeMarco 2001; Waite and Gallagher 2000). As we have seen, the most fundamental element of marriage is the mutual consent of the couple, but most marriages are also widely endorsed through public rituals, adherence to historical social norms, the support of parents, the attachment of legal rights, and integration with historical religious teachings. On the other hand, most cohabitations are explicitly designed independently of the larger community and polity and lack the same endorsement of family, community, church, and state given to marriage (Glendon 1976; Liefbroer and de Jong Gierveld 1993). In addition, the relationships of cohabitors with parents and others are often quite different from the family relationships of married people (Nock 1995; Rindfuss and VandenHeuvel 1990).

The separation of cohabitation from the larger family system is illustrated by data from our sample of mothers and children. In our 1993 survey we asked all of the adult children who had cohabited how their mother felt about them living with their first cohabiting partner. Nearly 10 percent of these 31-year-olds said that they did not tell their mother, and just over 40 percent said that their mother was unhappy or very unhappy about the relationship. In an effort to understand the source of maternal unhappiness with the child's cohabitation we asked the children whether the mother's unhappiness was "because she was unhappy with your choice of (NAME) or because she was unhappy that you were living together without being married?" About three-fourths of the children with an unhappy mother said it was because of living together without being married.

We also asked the mothers about the marriages and cohabitations of their children and found that, if anything, the mothers reported even higher levels of unawareness and unhappiness than were perceived by their children. Fully one-quarter of the mothers whose child had cohabited failed to report this fact. Either they never knew, forgot, or withheld the information from the interviewer. Among those mothers who did report their child's cohabitation, about 60 percent said they were unhappy about it. These mothers were asked if the unhappiness was because of whom the child was living with or because the couple was cohabiting. Nearly 80 percent said they were unhappy because the child was cohabiting (with some of them indicating unhappiness as well with the choice of partner). These data suggest that cohabitation does not enjoy the same kind of family knowledge, support, and integration historically associated with marriage.

One might expect that the mother's unhappiness with the child's co-habitation would be moderated if the child had publicly announced plans to marry before the cohabitation began. We found, however, that the level of maternal unhappiness was remarkably similar for children who had announced marriage plans and those who had no plans at all for marriage. What *did* correlate with the mother's unhappiness with her child's cohabitation was the mother's own attitudes toward cohabitation when the child was a teenager (Pearsonian correlation, $r, = .42$) and the child's views of the mother's feelings about premarital sex at the same time ($r = .31$).[5] Many of the mothers who were opposed in general to premarital sex and cohabitation when their child was a teenager were unhappy if their child later cohabited, and most of their children were aware of that unhappiness.

Cohabitation in the Marriage Process

Although cohabiting couples are not legally married and, on average, differ substantially from married couples, many connect their cohabitation to the marriage process (Casper and Bianchi 2002; Liefbroer and de Jong Gierveld 1993). Analyses using the National Survey of Families and Households (NSFH) show that one-half of all never-married Americans cohabiting in the late 1980s definitely planned to marry their partner, and another three-tenths thought they would (Brown and Booth 1996; Bumpass, Sweet, and Cherlin 1991; Sweet and Bumpass 1992; also see Carmichael 1995; also see Trost 1981 for Scandinavia and Leridon and Villeneuve-Gokalp 1989 for France). Thus, four-fifths of couples cohabiting in the 1980s were doing so within the context of the overall marriage courtship process. The fraction of cohabiting couples who expected to marry their current partner remained quite steady through the middle 1990s in the United States (Manning and Smock 2002). Although we do not know what plans these couples had when they commenced cohabitation, and 25 percent of couples disagreed about whether they planned to marry (Brown 2000), the NSFH data suggest a clear connection between cohabitation and the marriage process.

For many couples the decision to live together probably follows the explicit decision to get married. These couples are, perhaps unknowingly, following the old marriage customs in which betrothal or engagement legitimated sexual relations and living together (Björnsson 1971; Gillis 1985). This scenario suggests that once a woman and man commit to marry, they decide to live together during the engagement period when they are making wedding arrangements.

We investigated this possibility empirically with the young adults in our study who had cohabited by age 31 by asking two questions about their marriage plans with their first cohabiting partner just before they started to live together. The opening question was, "Before you started to live with (NAME), did you plan to marry (him/her)?" If the answer was yes, a follow-up question was asked: "Had you and (NAME) announced your plans to be married to other people such as friends and family *before* you started living together?"

These two questions permit us to divide cohabitors into three groups based on their marital plans before they started cohabiting: those with no marital plans; those with private marital plans; and those with announced marriage plans. Although the questions did not directly ask about engagement or betrothal, we believe that public announcements by both members of the couple are generally equivalent to the concept of engagement as currently understood in American society. We have no way to judge the seriousness of the marriage plans of the cohabitors who made no public announcement of their plans. These plans only required the endorsement of one member of the couple, and they could vary from wishful thinking to firm commitments that had not yet been shared with friends and family.[6]

Nearly three-fifths of the young people participating in our study who had cohabited reported that they had planned to marry their partner before they started to live together. Of these, somewhat more than one-half had announced their marriage plans to other people such as friends and family before beginning to live together. Four-fifths of those with public announcements, two-thirds of those with private plans, and two-fifths without marital plans did marry the person with whom they cohabited. These retrospective data concerning the marriage plans of cohabitors before they begin their first cohabitation are consistent with the NSFH data about the plans of currently cohabiting couples in suggesting that a very substantial fraction of cohabitation occurs in the context of strong plans for marriage.

Other couples undoubtedly enter cohabitation without definite commitments to marriage but with the intention of using the cohabitation period to evaluate and/or cement the relationship before becoming engaged. For these couples, cohabitation is an extension of the courtship period— an opportunity to see if they are compatible before committing to marriage (Bumpass, Sweet, and Cherlin 1991; Carmichael 1995; Casper 1992;

Casper and Bianchi 2002; Casper and Sayer 2000; Cherlin 1992; Gillis 1985; Klijzing 1992; Manting 1994; Prinz 1995; Smock 2000). Data from the National Survey of Families and Households (Bumpass, Sweet, and Cherlin 1991; Casper 1992) reveal that more than one-half of couples under age 35 who were cohabiting in the late 1980s said an important reason for cohabitation was the opportunity it gave couples to "be sure they are compatible before marriage."

We asked a similar question of cohabitors in our survey but asked them to think back to their own situation just before they started cohabiting. Among cohabitors without marriage plans nearly one-half said that wanting to try out living together before deciding about marriage was an important reason for them to cohabit,[7] and nearly one-half of these cohabitors actually went on to marry. This is nearly twice as high as the one-quarter of people without precohabitation marriage plans and without thoughts of cohabitation being a trial for marriage who went on to marry.

Adding together those with precohabitation marriage plans and those without plans but who saw cohabitation as a trial for marriage cumulates to more than three-fourths of all reported cohabitations occurring in the context of marital courtship. Thus, less than one-fourth of all our first-time cohabitors indicated that they both had no marriage plans and that they gave little or no importance to the cohabitation as a decision tool for marriage.

Interestingly, about three-fifths of those who reported either private or public marriage plans prior to cohabiting said that an important reason for cohabiting was "to try out living together before deciding about marriage." A higher fraction of those who found cohabitation unimportant as a trial for marriage went on to marry than those who started cohabitation with marriage being contingent on how the cohabitation went.[8]

The recent view and use of cohabitation as a trial period for determining marital compatibility are probably related to the high divorce rates of the past several decades and an associated fear of divorce. As we noted in the previous chapter, three-fifths of young Americans today believe that cohabitation before marriage is helpful in avoiding divorce. In fact, two-fifths of young Americans today say they would not marry someone who would not first live together (Whitehead and Popenoe 2001). Focus-group data also confirm the importance of fact-finding and testing the waters before committing to marriage as a reason for cohabitation (Whitehead and Popenoe 1999).

For many people the connection between cohabitation and marriage helps to legitimize cohabitation itself. This is illustrated by the fact that the proportion of unmarried noncohabiting young Americans (35 and younger) in the late 1980s who believed it "would be all right" for them personally "to live with someone without being married" increased from three-tenths if there was no interest in considering marriage" to about one-half if cohabitation was considered a way "to find out if [they] were compatible for marriage," and to nearly three-fifths if they "were planning to get married" (Sweet and Bumpass 1992, 153). Thus, the linkage of cohabitation with marital courtship or marriage plans substantially increases the fraction of young Americans who find cohabitation acceptable. Having said that, it should also be noted that more than two-fifths of these young adults found cohabitation personally unacceptable even in the presence of marriage plans.

Cohabitation and Single Life

Many of the people who accept cohabitation without any linkage to marriage plans probably enter cohabiting relationships as an alternative to single life—an extension of dating and sexual relationships to sharing living quarters (Casper 1992; Casper and Bianchi 2002; Casper and Sayer 2000; Cherlin 1992; Forste and Tanfer 1996; Manting 1994; Prinz 1995; Rindfuss and VandenHeuvel 1990; Smock 2000). They are in a dating or going-steady relationship that includes sexual intimacy and decide that it would be more efficient, cheaper, or convenient to live together, sometimes even continuing the maintenance of two households at least for a time. The connection between cohabitation and dating is further suggested by the fact that many couples initiate cohabitation very slowly by increasing the number of nights they spend together until cohabitation has occurred with no substantial decision concerning it (Casper and Bianchi 2002; Kline et al. 2004; Manning and Smock 2003).

Earlier we noted that people's definition of their relationship as marriage or cohabitation can vary by the circumstances and contexts one is in. The same probably holds true for people's definition of a relationship as cohabiting or living apart. In some instances, such as with peers, a person might define a relationship as cohabiting and in other contexts, for example with parents and ministers, define the relationship as dating. This probably helps explain why many parents are not aware of their children's cohabiting unions. In addition, these definitions can change over time as the relationship or one's view of it changes.

Some people who enter cohabiting relationships do so without any explicit thoughts about marrying their partners; some even plan to marry someone else later. In the National Study of Families and Households (NSFH) about one-fifth of the never-married cohabitors reported no plans to marry their current partner, and a substantial number of these expected to cohabit indefinitely with their partner (Bumpass, Sweet, and Cherlin 1991; Casper 1992). These couples may have envisioned cohabitation as a long-term relationship that served as an alternative to legal marriage (Casper 1992; Casper and Sayer 2000; Cherlin 1992; Manting 1994; Prinz 1995; Smock 2000; van de Kaa 1987).

One of the motivations for couples who choose cohabitation as an alternative to marriage appears to be the relatively greater freedom and flexibility they ascribe to cohabitation. In an in-depth qualitative study of cohabitors in New Zealand who were opposed to marriage, the social and legal constraints associated with marriage were seen as motivations to cohabit (Elizabeth 2000). Many of these couples recognized the strong institutionalized nature of marriage that formed expectations of roles and behavior and directly involved the power of the state. In contrast, cohabitation was seen as more flexible, as allowing more freedom to define relationships, as keeping the relationship more personal, and as permitting easier termination.

A national survey of young cohabitors in the United States also found that lack of independence and freedom was viewed as the primary disadvantage of marriage (Bumpass, Sweet, and Cherlin 1991). Three-tenths of the cohabiting men and one-sixth of the cohabiting women indicated the belief that their personal freedom would be curtailed if they married. In addition, about an eighth of both cohabiting women and men said that their economic independence would deteriorate if they married.

Both the National Survey of Families and Households (NSFH) and the Intergenerational Panel Study (IPS) asked cohabiting couples about reasons for cohabiting. In the NSFH, current cohabitors under age 35 were given a series of "reasons why a person might want to live with someone of the opposite sex without being married," and asked to indicate the personal importance of each. The reasons were: "it requires less personal commitment than marriage"; "it is more sexually satisfying than dating"; "it makes it possible to share living expenses"; "it requires less sexual faithfulness than marriage"; "couples can be sure they are compatible before marriage"; and "it allows each partner to be more independent than marriage" (Bumpass, Sweet, and Cherlin 1991, 920). In the IPS, 31-year-old respondents were asked to rate the importance of the following three reasons for initiating their first cohabitation: "you thought living together would cost less money than living separately"; "you wanted to try out living together before deciding about marriage"; and "you or (NAME) felt your job or his/her job was not good enough or secure enough to get married."

We have already mentioned the great importance of testing compatibility before marriage as a reason for cohabitation, and in both data sets more than one-half of cohabitors reported it as an important reason for them—a fraction substantially higher than for any of the other reasons. The second most-endorsed reason for cohabitation in each data set was saving money by capturing the economies of scale associated with sharing a household, with just over one-quarter of current cohabitors in the NSFH and about two-fifths of IPS respondents finding this an important factor (Bumpass, Sweet, and Cherlin 1991). All of the other potential reasons in both the NSFH and the IPS were endorsed by less than one-quarter of the cohabitors (Bumpass, Sweet, and Cherlin 1991).

It is also useful to know why Americans might *not* want to cohabit. The NSFH asked unmarried noncohabiting people under age 35 to characterize the importance of seven reasons for *not* wanting "to live with someone of the opposite sex without being married." The reasons were: "it is emotionally risky"; "my friends disapprove"; "my parents disapprove"; "it is morally wrong"; "it is financially risky"; "it requires more personal commitment than dating"; and "it requires more sexual faithfulness than dating."

The most frequently endorsed reason for not wanting to cohabit was emotional risk, with just over half of all currently unpartnered young people finding this a consideration. About a third indicated that financial riskiness was a reason for not wanting to cohabit. A substantial number—about two-fifths—also expressed concern that living together "requires more personal commitment than dating" and that "it requires more sexual faithfulness than dating." Clearly, the commitment and exclusivity associated with living together are factors keeping people single rather than cohabiting.

About one-third of the unpartnered young people reported that cohabitation being morally wrong and parental disapproval were important reasons not to cohabit. However, only about one-seventh considered the disapproval of friends a reason not to cohabit.

Summary

As we have discussed in this chapter, marriage, unmarried cohabitation, and being single can be usefully conceptualized as three distinct categories or states of being. This is true despite the fact that there is considerable heterogeneity of people within categories and the boundaries between categories are sometimes indeterminate in social, legal, personal, and economic terms. We use this tripartite categorization approach throughout the rest of the book.

In the next chapter we shift our focus to the transitions of people between categories, especially on the transition from being single to either being married or cohabiting. We also consider the transition of cohabiting unions into marriages. Because of the complexity of the processes moving individuals from one marital/cohabitation state to another, we consider different ways of conceptualizing those processes. We also look at the rates of transition between states.

CHAPTER FOUR

Entering Marital and Cohabiting Unions*

In this chapter we shift our focus from marital statuses to the individual transitions that transform single individuals into cohabiting and married couples. Our primary emphasis here is on union-formation rates. What are the rates of transforming single individuals into cohabitors and spouses? And, what are the rates of transforming cohabiting unions into marriages? We describe these rates and show how they differ by the age and gender of the individual.

A secondary goal of this chapter is a consideration of cumulative experience with each of the relationship statuses. What fraction of the population ever enters a union and what percentages of these new unions are entered through marriage and cohabitation? And, given the movement among the three relationship statuses, what fractions of individuals are single, married, and cohabiting at any particular point of the life course? Here our emphasis is on young adults as they mature from teenagers into their early thirties.

Conceptualizing Marriage and Cohabitation Transitions

As we have noted in previous chapters, union formation can be a complex process, in part because people vary in the ways they conceptualize mar-

*Georgina Binstock and Linda Young-DeMarco collaborated in the analysis and writing of this chapter.

riage, cohabitation, and being single. They also, undoubtedly, undergo the union-formation process in many different ways. Given this complexity and variation, researchers have used numerous conceptual and analytical strategies to study these three union statuses and the transitions that move individuals among them. In this section we identify five strategic characterizations, each of which involves an evaluation of the meanings of being single, being married, cohabitating, and the relationships among the three. Some also make assumptions about the decision-making processes underlying marital and cohabiting transitions. As we discuss these five conceptualizations, it will become clear that some are mutually exclusive and some are extensions of others.

These five conceptualizations include: (I) being single and cohabiting as equivalent contrasts to marriage; (II) marriage and cohabitation as equivalent contrasts to being single; (III) marriage and cohabitation as independent alternatives to being single; (IV) marriage and cohabitation as a choice conditional on the decision to form a union; and (V) cohabitation as part of the marriage process.

Our analysis of marital and cohabiting transitions would be simplified if we had chosen one or two of the five conceptualizations to guide us. However, because Americans maintain many different views of and approaches to union formation, and in fact may vary these in response to different partners, we found it impossible to identify a characterization that fully captures meaning and motivation for everyone. For these reasons, we have taken an eclectic approach to studying union formation and use each of the various perspectives in our analysis.

It is also important to note that these five perspectives are not independent in that they use the same information about transitions among the three union statuses, but do so in different ways. Because of these redundancies, the conceptualizations do not yield totally independent insights.

In addition, our empirical analyses do not permit a direct evaluation of which conceptualization is the most appropriate. That is, we do not approach the conceptualizations as competing hypotheses to be adjudicated by empirical evidence. Instead, we view them as different perspectives on the union-formation process that are elaborated and examined through empirical analysis. We now turn to a discussion of each of the five conceptualizations.

I. Being Single and Cohabiting as Equivalent Contrasts to Marriage

Equating being single and cohabitation as contrasts with marriage in the union-formation process treats marriage as a privileged condition—as it has been historically—and makes it the central focus of study. This conceptualization makes a crucial distinction between the social and legal categories of married and single, suggesting that cohabitation is very different from marriage and should be treated as a single status similar to dating and going steady. This perspective assumes only one central transition in the union-formation process: from either being single *or* cohabiting to being married. Thus the rate of transition from being unmarried—either single or cohabiting—to being married is the combined marriage rate of single and cohabiting people.

This perspective has several advantages. It is simple in presentation and execution. It gives primacy to marriage as a historical, legal, and highly institutionalized relationship that is expected to be permanent. And, because of its long history of use in the social sciences, this specification has been implemented in a considerable body of research (Goldscheider and Waite 1991; Koball 1998; Lehrer 2000; Lehrer 2002; Lloyd and South 1996; Marini 1985; Miller and Heaton 1991; Oppenheimer 2000; Rodgers and Thornton 1985; Sassler and Schoen 1999). Its primary disadvantage is that it ignores the similarities between unmarried cohabitation and marriage, as well as the differences between cohabiting and being single.

II. Marriage and Cohabitation as Equivalent Contrasts to Being Single

Instead of focusing on the contrast between marriage and cohabitation, the second conceptualization treats them as equivalent statuses that contrast with being single. This position suggests that sexual relations and common residence are crucial distinctions in determining relationship status, characteristics that are shared by marriage and unmarried cohabitation. It also implies that marriage provides nothing substantive or important beyond what it shares with cohabitation, which is sometimes labeled a paperless or de facto marriage that is functionally equivalent to marriage (Brown and Booth 1996; Parr 1999; van de Kaa 1987).

In this approach the emphasis is on the transition of individuals from being single to living with someone in either a marital *or* a cohabiting relationship. This analytic strategy, which has been implemented in numerous empirical studies (Clarkberg, Stolzenberg, and Waite 1995; Landale and Forste 1991; Lehrer 2000, 2002; Myers 2000), examines entrance into any intimate coresidential union without distinguishing marriage from cohabitation. Thus the rate of departure from being single is a "total union-formation rate."

This approach shares the advantage of the previous conceptualization in being simple and direct. It's also useful in focusing upon the many similarities between cohabitation and marriage. However, at the same time, it ignores the many social, legal, and personal distinctions between cohabitation and marriage. As we discussed in the previous chapter, most Americans distinguish between marriage and cohabitation, and there are often differences between cohabiting and married couples.

III. Marriage and Cohabitation as Independent Alternatives to Being Single

The third conceptualization suggests that cohabitation is sufficiently different from both marriage and being single that it should be treated as a distinct third category. It takes into account that many Americans do not view cohabitation as just another subcategory of singleness—like dating or going steady—and that there continue to be significant social and legal distinctions between marriage and unmarried cohabitation. In recognizing these distinctions, this approach broadens the classification scheme from a simple dichotomy to a trichotomy that recognizes both cohabitation and marriage as alternatives to being single (Casper 1992; Manting 1994; Prinz 1995; Rindfuss and VandenHeuvel 1990; Smock 2000).

This approach leads to a very different operationalization of the union-formation process than either of the two previous scenarios. It treats marriage and cohabitation as two comparable but different destinations or exits from the single state.[1] In this multiple destination framework, there is both a rate of transition from being single to marriage and a rate of transition from being single to cohabiting, the sum of which is equal to the total union-formation rate. This total union-formation rate is the same as the rate in the second conceptualization where the difference between cohabitation and marriage is ignored.

This third conceptualization, which has been used frequently in recent empirical studies of union formation (Clarkberg 1999; Lehrer 2000, 2002; Myers 2000), has at least two appealing features for studying union formation in America today. First, it recognizes that contemporary norms about sex and living arrangements in America provide an alternative to marriage for a single man and woman who find themselves in love and wanting to share each other's lives more fully by establishing a combined household. Second, it maintains the distinctions among the three relationship statuses—distinctions that we believe are real and substantial. This approach also has at least two drawbacks: it requires substantially more complex and difficult analyses, and it does not account for the many cohabiting couples who go on to institutionalize their relationship through marriage—a step we examine more fully in Conceptualization V, in the following.

IV. Marriage and Cohabitation as a Choice Conditional on Having a Partner

The fourth conceptualization is substantially more complex than any of the previous ones. It maintains the distinction between cohabitation and marriage, but makes the exit from being single to cohabitation or marriage a two-step process. Here we begin, as in Conceptualization II, with the desire of a single couple to transform their relationship into a coresidential union—either marriage *or* cohabitation, with no distinction between the two union statuses. The second step in the process is conditional upon this decision to share a common residence. At this point the couple decides whether they will end their single status by getting married or by living together without being married. Thus, in this conceptualization marriage and cohabitation are direct alternatives for each other for those who have decided to become a coresidential couple (Cherlin 1992; Clarkberg, Stolzenberg, and Waite 1995; Manting 1994; Prinz 1995; Smock 2000).

Here, as in Conceptualization II, the total union-formation rate is examined as the rate of entering either marriage or cohabitation, with no distinction at this point between the two forms of living arrangements. Then a second step is investigated—the choice between cohabitation and marriage for those who decide to form a coresidential union. Thus, the second step, which studies only individuals who have decided to cohabit or marry and models their dichotomous choice, does not yield a rate of transition from one status to another but a choice between two statuses for those who leave the single state. This choice is measured by the ratio of people choosing to cohabit to those choosing to marry. This approach to the study of marriage and cohabitation has also been used in previous empirical investigations (Clarkberg, Stolzenberg, and Waite 1995; Landale and Forste 1991; Myers 2000).

Conceptualization IV retains the advantages of both Conceptualizations II and III, as it begins with an examination of the total union-formation rate, but follows with a second step that maintains the distinction between marriage and cohabitation. This conceptualization also has the advantage of recognizing that all couples in America today have at least the theoretical choice between cohabitation and marriage, although some may face practical or ideological constraints on that choice, and indicate that marriage was not considered at all when they began cohabiting (Manning and Smock 2003).

Another advantage of this approach is that it makes the decision of marriage or cohabitation contingent upon having a serious relationship. This is useful because the marriage-cohabitation decision is moot without a partner with whom to make the decision. At the same time, this approach has the disadvantage of assuming a decision-making process that probably does not fit the experience of many people. That is, the theoretical ability to choose between cohabitation and marriage may not be a reality for both those who would never consider cohabitating and those who would never get married prior to trying unmarried cohabitation. In addition, qualitative research suggests many people probably make the transition from single to cohabiting so imperceptibly that the possibility of marriage is never explicitly considered. They may expand a sexual relationship into spending entire nights in one partner's home and then gradually intensify the relationship until they are living together on a regular basis (Manning and Smock 2003; Sassler 2004). As Stanley, Kline, and Markman (2005) suggest, such couples seem to slide into cohabitation rather than making explicit decisions about entering into a coresidential union.

V. Cohabitation as Part of the Marriage Process

Our last conceptualization builds upon the observation made in chapter 3 that many people view cohabitation as part of the courtship process leading to marriage (Bumpass, Sweet, and Cherlin 1991; Cherlin 1992; Gillis 1985; Klijzing 1992; Manting 1994; Prinz 1995; Smock 2000). They view the courtship process as beginning with simple dating that frequently expands to a more serious and committed relationship, including marriage. Along this trajectory many people go steady, are sexually intimate, cohabit, and get married. Many relationships, of course, do not include marriage because they are terminated at some earlier point in the courtship process. In this conceptualization, cohabitation is not an alternative to either marriage or being single, but a part of the transition process that leads from one to the other. People choose to cohabit as part of the courtship process, and if the cohabitation is successful, celebrate their new commitment in engagement and marriage.

This conceptualization of cohabitation as a potential step in the process leading to marriage suggests the operationalization of a two-step process that is different from the one posited as Conceptualization IV. Conceptualization V suggests that couples first decide whether or not to cohabit and then those who do cohabit decide subsequently whether to marry. Because many couples decide to marry without cohabitation, the first step is operationalized as a model having multiple destinations, with either marriage or cohabitation terminating the single status. This operationalization of the first step is identical to that used for the model of marriage and cohabitation as independent alternatives to being single (Conceptualization III). Rates of marriage and cohabitation are analyzed as before.

The second step, however, requires examination of the outcomes of cohabiting relationships conditional on cohabitation occurring (Smock and Manning 1997). It is operationalized by identifying all individuals who have entered cohabitation and then following these couples to see if and when they transform their cohabitations into marriages. The rate of transforming cohabitations into marriages is then analyzed. Of course, cohabitations can be terminated before marriage, which requires that dissolutions also be taken into account. This examination of marriage rates among cohabitors has been used in a number of research investigations of the union-formation process (Brown 2000; Bumpass and Sweet 1989; Bumpass, Sweet, and Cherlin 1991; Casper and Sayer 2000; Ermisch and Francesconi 2000; Manning and Smock 1995; Sanchez, Manning, and Smock 1998; Schoen and Owens 1992; Smock and Manning 1997).

The Diversity of Cohabitors

As we discussed in chapter 3, there is considerable diversity among cohabiting couples. Many people cohabit only after they are engaged, others do so with marital plans but no formal engagement, others cohabit with the idea of strengthening and evaluating the relationship before deciding about marriage, and still others cohabit without any thoughts of marriage, sometimes, as noted earlier, just sliding into cohabitation. We expect that young people are differentially selected into these types of cohabitations depending on their attitudes and expectations, and that the type of cohabitation has implications for how the cohabitation turns out (Manning and Smock 2002; Sassler 2004; Stanley, Kline, and Markman 2005).

Consistent with standard research practice, our previous discussion of conceptual approaches to marriage and cohabitation did not address this heterogeneity of cohabitors. However, because we asked respondents to tell us retrospectively about their perspectives and motivations before they started to cohabit, we know whether they were thinking about marriage when they began to cohabit, whether they were planning marriage, and how public any marriage plans might have been.

Although it is possible to consider the heterogeneity of cohabitors in several of the conceptualizations, we believe that it is most useful in Conceptualizations III and V. In Conceptualization III and Step 1 of Conceptualization V, marriage and cohabitation are treated as different destinations terminating the single state. Because we know the marital perspectives and plans of cohabitors when they began cohabiting, we can subdivide cohabitation partnerships into several categories based on those marriage perspectives and plans. We then treat each of these subdivisions of cohabitors as independent categories that, along with marriage, can be modeled as different destinations from being single in Conceptualization III and Step 1 of Conceptualization V.

These subcategories of cohabitation can also be incorporated into Step 2 of Conceptualization V. Whereas our description of Step 2 treats cohabitors as a homogeneous group, bringing marital plans into the picture permits comparison of the marriage and separation experience of the different kinds of cohabitors and provides additional insights into how cohabitation is integrated with the entire union-formation process. We conduct our analyses of Conceptualizations III and V both by treating cohabitors as multiple groups categorized by their marital plans at the time of cohabitation.

Rates of Entrance into Marital and Cohabiting Unions

As outlined in the previous section, we have identified five union-formation rates that are at the center of our empirical analysis. These monthly probabilities are calculated by dividing the number of union events in a month by the number of people at risk of the event at the beginning of the month. Union-transition probabilities and rates are not identical, but they are extremely similar when they are defined in small time units, such as a month. We use the terminology of rates and probabilities interchangeably in our discussion.

We examine these union-formation rates and choices by both gender and age of the individual in two formats. First, we graph average monthly

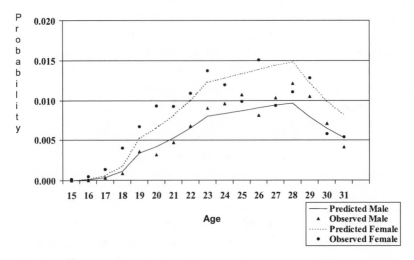

FIGURE 4.1. Monthly probability of entering marriage (ignoring cohabitation), by age and gender

probabilities (H) of making marital and cohabitation transitions separately for men and women and for each single year of age from 15 through 31. These rates are shown in figure 4.1 for marriage, ignoring whether the unmarried individuals at risk of marrying are single or cohabiting (Conceptualization I). Figures 4.2 and 4.3 respectively display first marriage and first cohabitation rates from being single with the two union forms treated as competing risks (Conceptualization III). Because the rates in these figures are estimated from relatively small samples, the sampling variation is considerable, and the curves are undoubtedly less smooth than in the population from which the sample was drawn.

Second, we summarize the effects of age and gender for all of the marriage and cohabitation rates and choices through a series of logistic equations predicting monthly marriage and cohabitation transitions. The estimation procedures for these equations are summarized in Appendix B. The trajectories implied by these estimation procedures smooth the observed ratio by age as indicated in the predicted lines graphed in figures 4.1 to 4.3.

We first consider the age pattern of union formation. The shapes of the age trajectories of marriage rates—both ignoring cohabitation (figure 4.1) and with cohabitation as a competing destination (figure 4.2)—are very consistent with first marriage schedules estimated for the entire American population (Rodgers and Thornton 1985; also see Berrington and

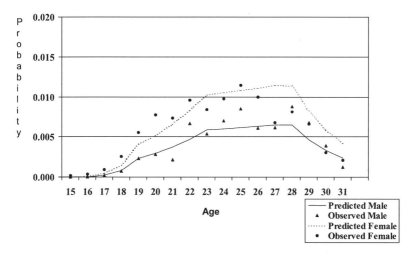

FIGURE 4.2. Monthly probability of entering marriage (with cohabitation as a competing destination), by age and gender

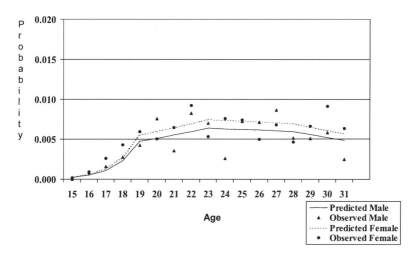

FIGURE 4.3. Monthly probability of entering cohabitation (with marriage as a competing destination), by age and gender

Diamond 2000 for Britain). For both women and men, first marriage rates are virtually zero at age fifteen, rise rapidly in the later teenage years, and increase again during the early twenties. These first marriage rates tend to peak during the middle twenties and decline during the late twenties and early thirties. The age trajectory of cohabitation rates follows the same

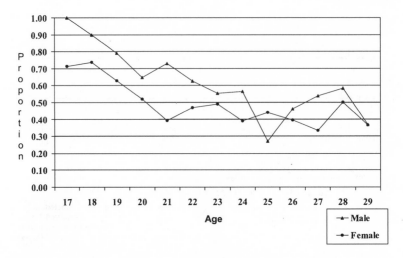

FIGURE 4.4. Proportion of first unions that are cohabitations, by age and gender

general pattern as the trajectory of marriage rates (figure 4.3), a pattern also replicated for Britain (Berrington and Diamond 2000).

Looking more carefully at the rates of transition to marriage and cohabitation from the single state, we see that for women the two rates are remarkably similar across the entire period covered, although there may be a tendency for cohabitation rates to be higher than marriage rates before about age 18 and to be lower after about age 19 (figures 4.2 and 4.3). In the late teenage years, both cohabitation and marriage probabilities (as competing destinations) are approximately .005 per month (or about .06 per year). By age 25 marriage probabilities have approximately doubled from this level to about .01 per month (or about .12 per year), with cohabitation rates being somewhat lower. This means that in the mid-twenties nearly two percent of all single women enter either marriage or cohabitation each month (or about one out of five each year).

As we noted earlier, cohabitation rates begin higher than marriage rates and do not increase as rapidly thereafter (compare figures 4.2 and 4.3). Consequently, the choice of cohabitation over marriage among those who are entering a union begins relatively high and decreases over time. This can be seen more clearly in figure 4.4, where we graph by age and gender the proportion of all first unions that are cohabitation. This proportion begins well above one-half in the younger ages and generally declines across the teenage years and early twenties to about one-half by the middle and later twenties.

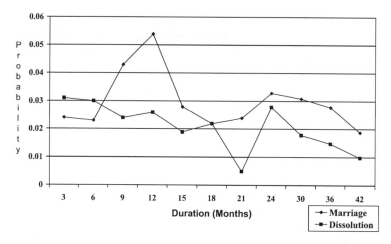

FIGURE 4.5. Monthly probabilities of terminating cohabiting relationships through marriage and through dissolution, by duration of cohabitation

In further analyses we also examined cohabitation rates distinguished by marriage plans at the time of cohabitation. We found little association between age and whether people cohabited with publicly announced marriage plans, with private marriage plans, or with no marriage plans (not shown in figures). That is, the type of cohabitation (based on marriage plans) does not appear to vary by the age of entrance into cohabitation.

Marriage rates for people who are cohabiting do not follow the same age trajectory as for people who are not cohabiting (not shown in figures). Instead, marriage rates of cohabitors are related in only very weak and statistically insignificant ways to age, which suggests that once individuals enter a cohabiting relationship, age no longer has a substantial effect on the rate of marriage.

However, further analysis (figure 4.5) demonstrates that the marriage rate is significantly related to the duration of cohabitation. The marriage rate is relatively low in the first six months of cohabitation, increases substantially in the next six months, and then declines during the subsequent six months (figure 4.5). After about 18 months of cohabitation, the rate of marriage is only about one-half of the rate at its height in the second half of the first year of cohabitation. This pattern, which suggests that many young people enter cohabitation either as a brief premarriage trial or while marriage arrangements are being made, is consistent with the notion that cohabitation is part of the marriage process for many young Americans today.

A comparison of figures 4.1 and 4.2 indicates that marriage rates based on the combined group of single and cohabiting people (marriage ignoring cohabitation) are substantially higher than marriage rates based exclusively on single people (marriage with cohabitation as a competing destination). This is because monthly rates of entering marriage for cohabitors are generally around 3 percent a month, which is approximately three times as high as the rate of marriage for single people during the peak marrying years of the middle and late twenties (data not shown in figures).

One reason this occurs is that cohabitors are in some type of relationship with a partner while many single people are not in any type of relationship with a partner. In addition, for many people cohabitation is part of the marriage process—a short interval between being single and marriage. This is not surprising given that many people enter cohabitation with marriage plans, frequently announced publicly. However, as figure 4.5 shows, the dissolution rate of cohabiting relationships is almost as high as the marriage rate, with approximately 2 percent of cohabiting couples entirely terminating their relationship each month. Thus, cohabitations are very transitory, with about 5 percent being either terminated or transformed into marriage each month. This means that less than half of all cohabitating relationships are still intact as cohabitations in just one year, and this fraction reduces to about 30 percent in two years and 15 percent in three years (Binstock and Thornton 2003; also see Bumpass and Sweet 1989; Bumpass and Lu 2000).

Only about one-tenth of people who separate from a cohabiting relationship reconcile, and many of them separate again after reconciliation. However, separated cohabitors frequently go on to establish new relationships with other people—either marriages or cohabitations—rather rapidly. About one-fifth would have cohabited or married within one year and one-third within two years of the separation. Almost nine-tenths of their second unions are cohabitations, indicating that few previously cohabiting individuals go on to marry without first cohabiting (see Binstock and Thornton 2003 for more details).

We also asked cohabitors in our study about living away from their partner for reasons other than discord—because of employment, education, family, or military matters that might cause couples to live apart (Binstock and Thornton 2003). About one in seven cohabitors experience being away from their partner within three years. These episodes are usually rather short with about three-fifths of these cohabitors being reunited within a year. Interestingly, many couples who cohabit and then spend time away from their partner get back together at the time of their wedding. This is true of about one-third of all cohabitors who live apart and then reunite with their partner. This suggests that at least some cohabitors spend part of the engagement period away from each other.

There are substantial differences in the union-formation experiences of men and women. Marriage rates are between 54 and 77 percent higher for women than for men (see Appendix B). Women also tend to cohabit at higher rates than men, but the differential (17 percent) is much lower than for marriage. Further analysis shows that women cohabit at higher rates than men only because they make the decision to marry faster and then cohabit between engagement and marriage. This conclusion is supported by the fact that women have nearly 70 percent higher rates than men of cohabiting with publicly announced marriage plans, a differential that is very similar to the gender differential for marriage itself. However, women and men have similar cohabitation rates when marriage is either not planned or has not been publicly announced. That is, compared to men of the same age, women reach the decision to marry much more rapidly than men, and some of these women marry directly while others decide to cohabit after they have publicly announced their marriages. Without this strong marriage commitment, women and men have exceptionally similar cohabitation rates. This pattern of gender differentials suggests that women are substantially less likely than men to choose cohabitation over marriage for the first union (figure 4.4). Note that the higher rates of marriage for women than for men are consistent with the well-known fact that, on average, women marry younger than men.

Of course, the age trajectories of marriage and cohabitation rates in our data are confounded with historical shifts in marriage and cohabitation. This is true because the data are drawn from a single cohort, and experiences at older ages occur at a later historical period. During the historical period when the young people in our study were making the transition to adulthood, marriage rates were declining and cohabitation rates were increasing. These historical changes may have produced more rapid increases in the observed age trajectories of cohabitation and less sharp increases in the age trajectories of marriage than would have occurred in a period of more stable rates. Despite these historical changes, however, it is likely that the shapes of the trajectories represent age effects much more than historical period effects. This is true because the shifts in marriage and cohabitation rates across the life course observed

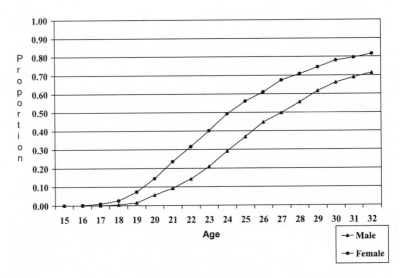

FIGURE 4.6. Cumulative proportion experiencing marriage (ignoring cohabitation), by age and gender

in figures 4.1, 4.2, and 4.3 are more dramatic than the period shifts documented elsewhere for a similar historical time. In addition, studies of life-course effects on marriage, which control for the historical period, find trajectories of marriage by age similar to those reported here (Thornton and Rodgers 1983).

Cumulative Experience with Marriage and Cohabitation

We now turn our attention from marriage and cohabitation rates to the cumulative experiences of individuals with each of the two union types. In figure 4.6 we display the percentage of individuals who had entered a first marriage by age and gender, ignoring whether the individuals had previously cohabited. Although only small numbers of people had ever married by age 20, these fractions increase rapidly during the twenties and then flatten out in the late twenties and early thirties. By age 31½, about 70 percent of men and 80 percent of women had been married.[2]

Figures 4.7 and 4.8 provide a different perspective on cumulative union-formation experience. Figure 4.7 displays the proportion of women and men by age who exited the single status for marriage, while figure 4.8 displays the proportion who exited the single status for cohabitation. Not shown

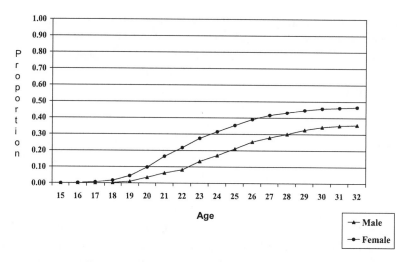

FIGURE 4.7. Cumulative proportion exiting single status through marriage (with cohabitation as a competing destination), by age and gender

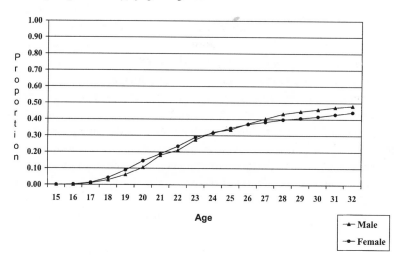

FIGURE 4.8. Cumulative proportion exiting single status through cohabitation (with marriage as a competing destination), by age and gender

in any of the figures is the percentage who exited the single status for either cohabitation or marriage, which equals the sum of the percentages exiting for cohabitation and for marriage.

Despite the fact that about 70 percent of men and 80 percent of women had married by age 31½, only about 35 percent of men and 45 percent of women exited the single status directly to marriage (figure 4.7). Another 35 percent of both men and women cohabited and then subsequently entered a first marriage by age 31½. These data, therefore, suggest that about one-half of all male first marriages and just under one-half of all female first marriages are preceded by cohabitation.[3]

Whereas 35 percent of men and 45 percent of women exited the single status for marriage by age 31½, nearly 50 percent of men and nearly 45 percent of women exited the single status for cohabitation (figure 4.8).[4] Also, of those men and women who exited the single status for cohabitation by age 31½, about 50 percent of men as compared to 60 percent of women began their unions with private or public marital plans. Adding together those who exited the single status for marriage and those who exited for cohabitations highly committed to marriage (i.e., publicly announcing their marital plans) by age 31½ cumulates to 46 percent of men and 61 percent of women (not shown in figures). Summing the percentages for marriage and all types of cohabitation together indicates that about 85 percent of men and 90 percent of women experienced an intimate coresidential relationship by age 31½, which exceeds the proportion who had married by that age by about 15 percent for men and 10 percent for women. Also, only about two-fifths of men's first unions were marriages as compared to one-half of women's first unions.

Earlier we observed that, on average, cohabitation rates for women were higher than for men (see figure 4.3). Yet, in figure 4.8 the cumulative fraction exiting the single state for cohabitation by the time people reach their late twenties is lower for women than for men. The reason for this apparent anomaly is that the marriage and cohabitation rates of figures 4.2 and 4.3 are independent, but the cumulative curves for marriage and cohabitation are not. Because women have a much higher rate of exiting the single state for marriage than men, at each age there are fewer of them at risk of cohabitation. Consequently, even though women have higher annual rates than men of exiting singlehood for cohabitation, there are fewer of them at risk of having cohabitation experience overall.

Marriage and Cohabitation Statuses by Age

Figure 4.9 shifts the focus from transition rates and cumulative experience to an analysis of marital and cohabitation statuses at particular points in the life course. The data in figure 4.9 reflect current union status, ignoring

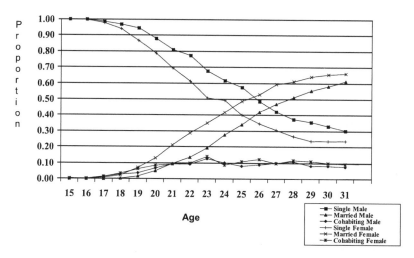

FIGURE 4.9. Current union status, by age and gender

the combination of transitions that may have brought a person into a particular status at that age. The combination of entrances into and exits from cohabiting relationships produces a slow but fairly steady increase in the fraction of people currently living in a cohabiting relationship, with that increase being fairly similar for men and women. The fraction of people currently cohabiting, however, levels off in the twenties at approximately 10 percent and remains fairly steady at this level into the early thirties.[5]

Of course, at virtually every age (except the youngest) the proportion of men and women currently in a cohabiting relationship was substantially lower than the proportion ever experiencing cohabitation. With the increasing rates of transition into cohabitation (figure 4.3) and the high rates of transition out of cohabitation either because of marriage or the dissolution of the relationship (figure 4.5), the gap between current status and lifetime experience increased across the life course. By the age of 31½, the percentage of men and women currently cohabiting was only about one-fifth as large as the percentage who had ever cohabited.[6]

The fraction of men and women currently married and living with their spouses rose substantially more rapidly than the fraction currently cohabiting. By age 25 about one-third of all men and about one-half of all women were currently married. These proportions had increased to three-fifths and two-thirds by age 31½, which are only somewhat lower than the proportions for cumulative marital experience. This indicates that relatively small fractions of the ever married were not currently married at age 31½ (about 14 percent for women and 6 percent for men).[7]

Marriage and Cohabitation in Comparative Perspective

As we explain in chapter 1, a key limitation of our most detailed analyses is the limitation to a single cohort of White Americans born in Southeastern Michigan in the early 1960s. As explained both here and in chapter 2, the cohort we analyze was preceded by cohorts with higher rates of marriage and lower rates of premarital cohabitation (Bumpass and Sweet 1989; Schoen and Owens 1992; Thornton 1988). Marriage rates have continued to decline and cohabitation rates have continued to increase across more recent cohorts (Bumpass, Sweet, and Cherlin 1991; Bumpass and Lu 2000). It is also likely that these trends have resulted in more couples today making the transition from being single to cohabiting without giving the transition the kind of serious thought—including the possibility of marriage—that seems to have characterized the behavior of most people in earlier cohorts.

Likewise, as explained in chapter 2, African- and Latino-American rates of marriage are lower than White rates of marriage (Bennett, Bloom, and Craig 1989; McLoyd et al. 2000; Schoen and Owens 1992). African-American rates of unmarried cohabitation have been higher than White rates until the mid-1990s when they converged, but Hispanic rates of unmarried cohabitation have been and continue to be lower than White rates of unmarried cohabitation (Bumpass and Lu 2000). Further, there are substantial differences among Hispanic subgroups of the population, so that Mexican-American rates of entering premarital cohabitation are actually higher than White rates of entering premarital cohabitation (Schoen and Owens 1992). Thus we have good reason to suspect important differences in the rates of marital and cohabiting transitions across racial and ethnic subgroups of the U.S. population. The analysis we present of Whites, therefore, does not reflect the behavior of other groups.

As we note in chapter 1, the State of Michigan itself appears to fall near the median of marital and cohabiting behaviors in the United States. Recent comparative research by Lesthaeghe and Neidert (2006) demonstrates that although the populations of some states exhibit relatively unique patterns of marital and cohabiting behavior, the population of Michigan is not among these outliers, but rather has behaviors quite similar to

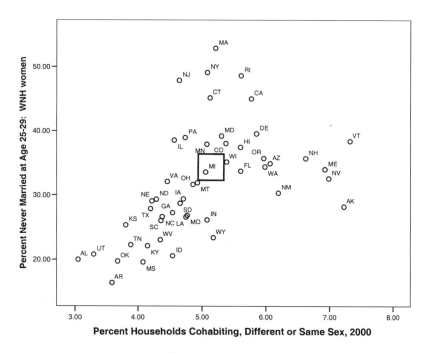

FIGURE 4.10. Location of states with respect to the postponement of marriage (y-axis) and the incidence of cohabitation (x-axis): 2000
Source: Lesthaeghe and Neidert 2006, Figure 1.

the national averages. Figure 4.10 replicates figure 1 from Lesthaeghe and Neidert's work. It presents year 2000 measures from every state in the United States, graphed by the percentage of those aged 25–29 never married on the Y-axis and the percentage of households identified as cohabiting partnerships on the X-axis. Although Lesthaeghe and Neidert identify three different groups of outlier clusters among the states, the State of Michigan is not only in the central group, it is virtually the exact center of the graph. This evidence demonstrates the strong central tendency in the population of Michigan in comparison to other states with respect to both the timing of marriage and the incidence of unmarried cohabitation.

Finally, consider U.S. marital and cohabiting behavior in an international comparative perspective. Similar to the United States, Canada, New Zealand, and many European countries are also characterized by declining rates of marriage and increasing rates of unmarried cohabitation (Heuveline and Timberlake 2004; Kuijsten 1996; Prinz 1995). In Canada the rise in cohabitation has compensated for even more of the decline in marriage than in the United States (Wu and Balkrishnan 1995). In fact, in many European countries the prevalence of unmarried cohabitation is much higher than in the United States, with the prevalence in France being perhaps the highest (Heuveline and Timberlake 2004; Toulemon 1997). However, Europe is also characterized by significant diversity in levels of unmarried cohabitation, with northern and western Europe generally characterized by substantially higher levels than eastern and southern Europe (Coleman 1992; Heuveline and Timberlake 2004; Kuijsten 1996; Lesthaeghe 2000). This diversity extends to types of cohabiting experience, not just the incidence of cohabiting experience. For example, the median durations of cohabitation vary from 4.28 years in France to 1.78 years in Switzerland, with the United States characterized by a substantially lower median of 1.17 years when calculated using a comparable method (Heuveline and Timberlake 2004). Likewise the ending of cohabitations varies greatly across countries, with some countries characterized by more than three quarters of cohabitations ending in marriage (Austria, Belgium, Finland, Slovania, and Switzerland), but others characterized by less than forty percent ending in marriage (Canada and New Zealand), compared to the United States with roughly equal numbers exiting to marriage and dissolution (Heuveline and Timberlake 2004). Thus, the international variation in unmarried cohabitation is substantial, even among countries populated primarily by Europeans and European descendants. Moreover, within this diversity the patterns of marriage and cohabitation in the United States continue to be somewhat unique (Heuveline and Timberlake 2004; Lesthaeghe and Neidert 2006). The remainder of this book is devoted to a more detailed investigation of the intergenerational influences on patterns of behavior in the United States.

This concludes Part I of the book—including a historical perspective on marriage (chapter 2), a comparison of marriage, cohabitation, and being single (chapter 3), and an overview of the process of entering marital and cohabiting unions (chapter 4). We now turn to Part II of the book and begin the process of understanding the intergenerational influences on entrance into marital and cohabiting unions.

PART II
Parental Factors during Childhood and Adolescence

CHAPTER FIVE

Influence of Parental Youth Factors before Birth of Study Child

As we discussed in chapter 1, union formation is an intergenerational process involving both young adults and their parents. In this chapter, we begin the task of evaluating the many factors in the parental generation influencing the entrance of young adults into cohabitation and marriage. Our focus concerns the parental explanatory factors from six substantive domains, each with several dimensions: (1) family organization; (2) family immigration and farm background; (3) parental socio-economic standing; (4) religion; (5) maternal marital experience; and (6) parental childbearing. We now discuss specific ways these dimensions of the parental family can influence young adult children directly as well as indirectly, through other factors in both the first and second generations.

We focus our analysis of parental influences on several dimensions of the union-formation process. First is the total union-formation rate that treats marriage and cohabitation as equivalent contrasts to being single (Conceptualization II from chapter 4). Second are the rates of entrance into marriage and cohabitation with each union status treated as an independent alternative to being single (Conceptualization III of chapter 4). The next dimension is the choice between marriage and cohabitation for those entering a union (Conceptualization IV of chapter 4). In addition, we consider the rate of transformation of cohabiting relationships into marriages (Conceptualization V of chapter 4).

Family Organization

As we noted in chapter 1, we believe that the interactions of individuals with their families, friends, and larger communities have important effects on attitudes and behavior. We hypothesize that both the amount of social interaction and its distribution between family members and friends are important.

Looking first at the amount of social interaction, we hypothesize that the overall level of parental social interaction, including interaction with both friends and family members, is likely to influence children's marital and cohabiting behavior. High levels of social interaction in the parental generation both reflect and produce a positive view of social relationships and socializing, and they may also help to bring children into contact with more potential partners. Parents with high levels of social interaction are more likely to endorse their children's entry into new social relationships, including new romantic relationships that might lead to cohabitation or marriage. It is also possible that a potential son- or daughter-in-law would integrate into a family with highly social parents more easily, or would find the family more attractive.

Parental sociability is also likely to be inherited by children through both biological and social mechanisms. Parents with greater amounts of social interaction probably have children who date more frequently, which leads to more rapid cohabitation and marriage.

Moving now from the amount of parental social interaction to the type, we hypothesize that families with low levels of family interaction and involvement and high levels of involvement with people outside the family are less likely to emphasize marriage and more likely to be open to non-marital alternatives, such as cohabitation (Coleman 1990; Thornton and Fricke 1987; Thornton and Lin 1994). The ways in which parents emphasize family and nonfamily connections may influence children's dispositions toward marriage and family life directly as the children observe their parents' behavior and priorities. It may also have indirect effects in that parental interaction patterns influence the attitudes and values of the second generation that subsequently affect family formation.

Gender-role attitudes reflect another dimension of family activities and organization—the division of labor and authority between wives and husbands. Our overall hypothesis is that parents with positive attitudes toward gender equality and the freedom for women to participate fully outside the home will have more positive orientations toward the freedom to innovate new family forms such as nonmarital cohabitation. They will also probably have less commitment to marriage because of a stronger emphasis on nonfamily roles. We, therefore, expect that gender-role egalitarianism in the parental generation will be reflected in decisions of the second generation to choose cohabitation over marriage more often.

Family Immigration and Farm Background

The research literature links immigrant and farm origins to family and demographic behavior in the United States and elsewhere (Carmichael 1995; Duncan 1965; Goldscheider and Goldscheider 1993; Hofferth and Iceland 1998; Rindfuss, Morgan, and Swicegood 1988). There are several reasons to believe that some of the roots of union-formation behavior extend back to the immigration status and rural or farm origins of parents and grandparents (see Gutmann, Pullum-Piñón, and Pullum 2002).

We begin by noting that recent immigration to the United States and family residential roots on farms or in rural areas have both been treated as indirect indicators of high levels of social organization within the family (Goldscheider and Goldscheider 1993; Rindfuss, Morgan, and Swicegood 1988). Recent immigration may be linked to high levels of social interaction within families if these levels tend to be higher in the country of origin than in the United States. However, even when the country of origin does not differ significantly from the United States, language barriers, lack of nonfamily social networks, and other obstacles to assimilation are likely to hinder new immigrants from interacting with institutions and organizations outside of the family and increase social interaction within the family, which, in turn, increases marriage.

Farm residence has historically been associated with high levels of social organization within the family for similar reasons. That is, farm work itself, which often requires input from multiple family members, may lead to high levels of social interactions within families. However, even if farm families do not differ much in this regard, their migration to urban centers may isolate them from their friends and families of orientation, causing them to be more insular than people who have always lived in cities.

To the extent that immigration and farm background lead to higher levels of family integration, we predict that both increase rates of marriage and lead to the choice of marriage over nonmarital cohabitation. However, if migration causes a separation with families of orientation, we anticipate the opposite effect. We are able to adjudicate between these effects because we have the data to determine the extent to which parents' childhood immigration status and farm background are related to later family social organization. We can also evaluate whether parental social organization when the children are born accounts for any effects of parental immigration status and farm background on children's union formation.

There are, of course, other ways in which recent immigration and farm background might influence union-formation experience. Recent international and farm migrants may have attitudes that lead to higher rates of marriage and lower rates of cohabitation among children. Although educational levels vary by both country of origin and time of migration, we anticipate that many immigrants in the first half of this century had little education. For the reasons we will hypothesize in the next section, we expect low levels of education to lead these immigrants' children to have higher rates of union formation—both marriage and cohabitation. We also know that farm background is associated with large families, a factor that we also expect to lead to higher rates of both marriage and cohabitation in the younger generation.

Parental Socioeconomic Standing

We hypothesize that higher levels of parental education and income slow down the speed of young adult entrance into marriage and cohabitation. One potential mechanism of this effect begins in the parental generation itself. We expect that high educational, occupational, and financial achievement leads to later ages at marriage, fewer premarital pregnancies, and less divorce in the parental generation, which, as we argue in the following, influence union formation in the second generation. In addition, we expect that high educational, occupational, and financial achievement leads to greater organization of social activities outside the family for both parents and children.

A second set of hypotheses builds upon the well-known positive association between parental educational, occupational, and financial attainment and children's educational and occupational achievements (Alwin and Thornton 1984; Axinn, Duncan, and Thornton 1997; Sewell et al. 1975). Compared with other parents, parents with high levels of educational, occupational, and financial achievement are likely to have and transmit higher educational aspirations for their children, to be more involved and effective in their assistance with the children's school work, and to be more willing and able to assist with college expenses. Thus, we expect that children from highly educated and financially better off families will attend school longer than others, thereby postponing the transition into both marital and cohabiting unions. However, we expect this negative effect on union formation to last only as long as the children are in school, an expectation consistent with recent research showing that parental income and education affect first-marriage timing only until age 23 (South 2001). Once the children of parents with high educational, work, or financial status finish their educations, their own higher achievements may make their transitions to marriage and cohabitation, or from cohabitation to marriage, faster than the transitions of their less-privileged peers.

Parental education can also impact young people's marriage and cohabitation through its influence on parents' and children's attitudes and values concerning family issues and courtship behavior. We know, for instance, that highly educated parents have less restrictive attitudes toward divorce and premarital sex and higher ideal ages at marriage for their children (Axinn and Thornton 1992a; Gaughan 2002; Thornton 1985a; Thornton and Camburn 1987; Waite and Spitze 1981). We also expect them to have less restrictive attitudes toward cohabitation and higher ideal ages at sexual initiation for their children. Parental education is also associated with later dating, later sexual initiation, and fewer premarital pregnancies in the younger generation (Hofferth and Hayes 1987; Longmore, Manning, and Giordano 2001; Miller et al. 1997; Plotnick 1992; Udry 1995).

A third possible mechanism linking parental educational, occupational, and financial position and family formation behavior in young adulthood is that, assuming children form their consumption aspirations in the parental home (Easterlin 1980), young people from wealthy families would have higher consumption aspirations than their less-fortunate peers (Freedman and Thornton 1990). These high-consumption aspirations are expected to lead to more investment in consumer durables and leisure, fewer resources for marriage and family life, and, ultimately, later family formation.

Religion

Marriage and family life have been powerfully and intricately interrelated with religion and religious dogma for centuries. As we have discussed in chapter 2, many religious groups have long considered marriage to be a special relationship sanctioned and governed by God. Marriage was frequently seen as so important that it was a religious sacrament or a covenant with God and the religious community.

Religious organizations have been strongly interested in marriage and its interconnections with social institutions and personal behavior for hundreds of years. Because of the preponderance of Christianity in America, it is our primary theoretical focus. For the first half of the past millennium, the doctrines and policies of the Christian church formed the law of marriage in Western countries. In subsequent centuries the state became more involved in the regulation of marriage, but even then the principles and laws governing marriage and family life reflected religious doctrine and principles.

Consequently, religious doctrines and teachings have guided the meaning of marriage, the central elements for entrance into marriage, and the form of marriage ceremonies and celebration. Ideas and norms concerning individual consent, the indissolubility of marriage, and the authority to contract a valid marriage also emanated from religious teachings. Religious teachings have also provided principles and rules about intimate relationships, childbearing, and family processes—and the ways these central human matters intersect with marriage and living arrangements.

Of course, as we noted in chapter 2, religion and its role in Western society have changed dramatically over the past few centuries, with the number of religious groups and denominations increasing and the plurality of religious beliefs expanding. In addition, the authority of religious leaders has declined, and religious beliefs and participation have been increasingly interpreted in individualistic ways and less in terms of institutional loyalty. Concomitantly, a norm of tolerance for variation in beliefs and behavior grew.

Despite these changes, most of the religious organizations in America continue to value marriage, children, and family life. Most churches also either proscribe sex outside of marriage or encourage the postponement of the initiation of sexual relations (Hadden 1983; Hargrove 1983; U.S. Catholic Conference 1977). The negative relationship between nonmarital sex and religious commitment and participation is probably even stronger when the sexual relationship includes the sharing of residential quarters (Berrington and Diamond 2000; Bracher and Santow 1998; Carmichael 1995; Liefbroer 1991; Liefbroer and de Jong Gierveld 1993; Thornton, Axinn, and Hill 1992). Because cohabitation publicly acknowledges a sexual relationship—an acknowledgment not usually made in other intimate nonmarital relationships—it can attract the attention of important reference groups to the individual's nonconformity with religious teachings and provoke a confrontation of the religious community's norms with the individual's behavior.

Given the variance in the teachings of the churches concerning sex and other family matters, religious affiliation may also influence entrance into marital and cohabiting unions (Lehrer 2000, 2002). Although most religious groups have become less restrictive about family and personal behavior in recent decades, the Catholic church and many of the more fundamentalist Protestant churches have maintained more restrictive teachings concerning sex outside of marriage than have more mainline Protestants. In addition, fundamentalist Protestants historically have held less egalitarian attitudes toward gender roles. For these reasons, we expect that Catholics and especially fundamentalist Protestants—as compared to nonfundamentalist Protestants—will enter unions more rapidly and be more likely to choose marriage rather than cohabitation (Lehrer 2000). Also, because the Catholic and fundamentalist Protestant denominations generally take stronger positions than mainline Protestants against nonmarital sex, we predict that the influence of religious participation on cohabitation and marriage is also stronger for these groups, suggesting a statistical interactive rather than additive effect.[1]

Given the important historical connections between religion and family life, it is not surprising that discussions of family and demographic behavior have devoted considerable attention to the effects of religious affiliation and participation on family formation and dissolution (Lehrer 2000, 2002; Lesthaeghe and Surkyn 1988; Lesthaeghe and Wilson 1986; Preston 1986; Sweet and Bumpass 1990; Thornton, Axinn, and Hill 1992). In a key series of articles, Lesthaeghe and his colleagues have demonstrated important associations between religious values and family behavior for several Western countries (Lesthaeghe and Surkyn 1988; Lesthaeghe and Wilson 1986). In addition, many studies document strong associations between people's religious affiliations/commitments and their family and sexual values and behavior (Chilman 1983; DeLamater and MacCorquodale 1979; Inazu and Fox 1980; Jessor and Jessor 1975; Lye and Waldron 1993; Macklin 1978; Mahoney et al. 2001; Miller et al. 1997; Sweet and Bumpass 1990; Thornton and Camburn 1989; Zelnik, Kanter, and Ford 1981).

There are several reasons to expect that the offspring of more religious parents will have higher rates of marriage, lower levels of premarital sex and cohabitation, and faster transitions out of cohabiting relationships (through marriage or relationship termination; Bracher and Santow 1998; Liefbroer and de Jong Gierveld 1993; Thornton, Axinn, and Hill 1992). One potentially significant mechanism linking parental religiosity and children's union formation is the influence of parental religiosity on the social organization of families in both the first and second generations. Research indicates that parents who attend church more frequently are more likely to be involved and spend more time with their children (Bartkowski and Xu 2000; Clydesdale 1997; Wilcox 1998, 2002). We expect that parental religiosity positively influences parents and children toward organizing activities around the family, which, as we argued earlier, is likely to lead to choosing marriage over cohabitation. A second potential mechanism is that highly religious parents tend to have highly religious children who are probably more likely to marry and less likely to cohabit than others. Third, parental religious participation and commitment may influence both children's and parents' attitudes toward a broad range of family issues, which then influence children's union formation. Fourth, because children of highly religious parents are less sexually experienced as teenagers, they probably have lower rates of premarital pregnancy, lower rates of entrance into both cohabiting and marital unions, and are more likely to enter marriage than cohabitation. Fifth, divorce is less common among highly religious people (Call and Heaton 1997; Thomas and Cornwall 1990), and, as will be discussed later, we expect parental divorce to be linked with children's union-formation behavior. Liefbroer and de Jong Gierveld (1993) suggest that much of the influence of parental religiosity on young-adult intentions for marriage and cohabitation operates through young-adult attributes such as these. However, independent of all of these intervening mechanisms, highly religious parents may actively intervene to steer their children away from cohabitation and toward marriage.

Maternal Marital Experience

The marriage experiences of parents are also likely to influence children's family formation. Among the parental marital experiences that we expect to be important for children's union formation are marital timing, pregnancy status at marriage, divorce, and remarriage experience. We expect that young people whose parents married young, were pregnant at marriage, and experienced divorce and remarriage will themselves enter unions more rapidly and tend to choose cohabitation over marriage (Kiernan and Hobcraft 1997; Musick and Bumpass 1999; Thornton 1991). Several of the many potential mechanisms linking these parental family experiences to children's behavior are outlined in the following paragraphs.

Educational, work, and financial achievement and aspirations are probably important mechanisms transmitting the influence of parental marital timing, premarital pregnancy, and divorce to children's union formation. Previous research indicates that parental divorce leads to substantial reductions in parental financial well-being, particularly for the custodial parent, and that this lowered financial well-being is passed on to the children (Alwin and Thornton 1984; Amato 2000; Amato and Keith 1991; Axinn, Duncan, and Thornton 1997; Cherlin, Chase-Lansdale, and McRae 1998; Duncan and Hoffman 1985; Furstenberg et al. 1987; Hayes 1987; McLanahan and Bumpass 1988; McLanahan and Sandefur 1994; Peterson 1996). We also know that a young age at marriage and a premarital pregnancy in the parental generation are related to lower parental educational, work, and financial achievement (Freedman and Thornton 1979). Early age at marriage among parents may also be related to lower ideal ages at marriage for children.

It has been argued that children in single-parent families grow up faster, take on adult responsibilities earlier, and operate as peers with their parents at younger ages than children in stably married families (Weiss 1979). It has also been argued that children in divorced families are exposed to lower levels of parental involvement, supervision, and monitoring (Amato 2000; Demo 1992; McLanahan and Sandefur 1994). Earlier maturation and independence among children in single-parent families would likely lower the age of first dating and heterosexual relations, and increase the risk of premarital pregnancies (Longmore, Manning, and Giordano 2001; Miller et al. 1997; Wu 1996; Wu and Martinson 1993). We expect that these factors influence the cohabitation and marital choices of young adults.

Parental divorce may affect the attitudes and values of both parents and children concerning many family matters. Consequences of divorce may include more positive attitudes toward divorce among both parents and children (Amato and Booth 1991; Thornton 1985a), and a reevaluation of marriage and childbearing that leads to postponed marriage and increased cohabitation among children (Amato and Booth 1991; Amato and de Boer 2001; Axinn and Thornton 1996; Cherlin, Kiernan, and Chase-Lansdale 1995; Li and Wojtkiewicz 1994; South 2001; Weiss 1979).

Marital dissolution and the reentry of parents into dating and courtship can modify the attitudes of both parents and children toward nonmarital sex and cohabitation (Whitbeck, Simons, and Kao 1994). Many of these divorced parents reenter the courtship system, where they must again deal personally and directly with issues of intimacy in nonmarital relationships, and many of them ultimately enter sexual and cohabiting relationships outside of marriage (Bumpass and Sweet 1989; Gwartney-Gibbs 1986). These experiences likely increase acceptance of nonmarital sex and cohabitation among both the parents themselves and their young-adult children (Axinn and Thornton 1996). Moreover, parents who have these dating/courtship experiences may be less able to restrict their children's nonmarital sex and cohabitation experience. These causal mechanisms suggest that children of divorce will be more accepting of premarital sex and cohabitation, quicker to enter into sexual relationships, more likely to have premarital fertility, more likely to experience cohabitation, and slower to enter marriage from cohabiting unions. Evidence for the influence of parental divorce and remarriage on various dimensions of marriage and cohabitation has been found in other research (Berrington and Diamond 2000; Carmichael 1995; Kiernan 2000; Kiernan and Hobcraft 1997; Musick and Bumpass 1999; Thornton 1991).

Religiosity is another mechanism linking parental marital experience with children's behavior. Parental divorce may lead to declines in religious commitment and participation among both parents and children (Thornton, Axinn, and Hill 1992), which may result in higher rates of cohabitation and lower rates of marriage among the children. It can also result in lower levels of marriage among cohabitors.

Although much of our discussion here has centered on parental divorce and remarriage, we also expect that marital satisfaction among married couples influences their children's union-formation experience. Because the affective quality of the parental home environment is an influence on departure from the parental home and the entry into marriage (DaVanzo and Goldscheider 1990; Goldscheider and DaVanzo 1985), young people with inhospitable home environments may choose to leave home, cohabit, and marry earlier than others.

Parental Childbearing Attitudes and Behavior

There is good reason to expect attitudes toward childbearing to influence the timing of marriage and cohabitation. Because marriage remains the most socially sanctioned relationship for childbearing in the United States (Bachrach 1987), and the majority of births are born to married couples (Loomis and Landale 1994; Manning 1995), we expect young people who want many children to marry more rapidly than those who want fewer children. Also, because conception requires a couple, and because child-rearing may be easier for those who have the support of a spouse or partner (Becker 1991; Preston 1986), we expect young people who want many children to enter any type of heterosexual coresidential relationship more rapidly than young people who want fewer children. However, because marriages are more stable than cohabitations, and childbearing is much more common among married couples than among cohabiting couples (Bachrach 1987; Rindfuss and VandenHeuvel 1990), we also expect that, given a choice between marrying and cohabiting, young people who want many children will be more likely to choose marriage. Thus, we expect attitudes and values regarding childbearing to influence both the timing of and the choice between cohabitation and marriage.

There are at least two good reasons to expect parental preferences for grandchildren to affect their children's marriage and cohabitation behavior. First, parental preferences for grandchildren affect children's own childbearing preferences, and these preferences, in turn, are likely to influence both cohabitation and marriage behavior. Previous research has shown that parents' preferences for their children's fertility have a strong positive effect on children's own childbearing preferences in early adulthood (Axinn, Clarkberg, and Thornton 1994). Thus parents' preferences for grandchildren may have an indirect influence on their children's cohabitation and marriage behavior, via the children's own preferences.

Second, parental desires for grandchildren may have a direct impact on their children's marriage and cohabitation behavior that is not explained by children's own preferences. Several mechanisms may produce this direct effect (Barber and Axinn 1998). For one, parents' attitudes about their children's childbearing behavior may be correlated with their attitudes about marriage and cohabitation. Those parents who want many grandchildren may hold more favorable attitudes toward early marriage (which accelerates marriage; Axinn and Thornton 1992b), or may disapprove of cohabitation (which increases the choice of marriage over cohabitation; Axinn and Thornton 1993). Or, parents who want many grandchildren may be more willing to use their money to facilitate their children's marriage than parents who want few grandchildren, which may accelerate rates of marriage (Axinn and Thornton 1992b; Waite and Spitze 1981).

Also, parents who want many grandchildren may be less likely to encourage their children to pursue education after high school or after college, which is likely to accelerate both marriage and cohabitation (Marini 1978; Thornton, Axinn, and Teachman 1995). Finally, young people with parents who want many grandchildren may accelerate their own family formation or choose marriage over cohabitation in order to please their parents, even though they themselves are not as pronatalist (Barber and Axinn 1998).

Of course, parental desires for grandchildren are closely associated with parents' own childbearing experiences and parental preferences for their own childbearing (Axinn, Clarkberg, and Thornton 1994). Because of these strong associations it is likely that parental childbearing experiences and attitudes will be associated with their children's cohabiting and marital behavior, at least indirectly through parental preferences for grandchildren. In fact, the roots of these preferences are likely to go all the way back to the size of the families in which parents were raised (Axinn, Clarkberg, and Thornton 1994). So, those parents who were raised in large families are more likely to want many children themselves, to have many children themselves, and to want many grandchildren. Thus each of these dimensions of parental childbearing experiences and attitudes may accelerate children's marriages and increase the choice of marriage over cohabitation.

Parents' unintended childbearing may also have important consequences for children's cohabiting and marital behavior. Because unintended childbearing tends to produce lower quality parent-child relationships (Barber, Axinn, and Thornton 1999), children may desire to form their own independent family living situations more quickly. This mechanism is expected to produce higher rates of both cohabitation and marriage. And, unwanted childbearing is likely to produce stronger effects than mistimed childbearing (Barber, Axinn, and Thornton 1999).

Data Analysis

We now turn to our analysis of the influence of these dimensions of the parental family on the marriage and cohabitation experience of the young adults in the Intergenerational Panel Study. We focus in this chapter on parental experiences and attributes early in the lives of the parents—from their childhoods through the birth of the child participating in the study.

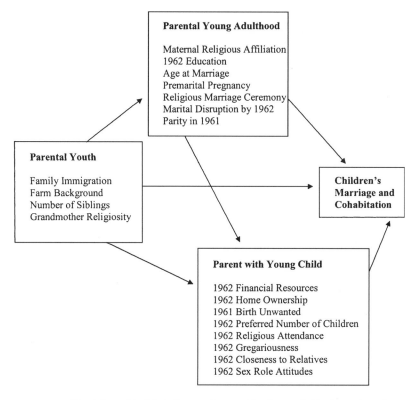

FIGURE 5.1. Heuristic model of the influence of parental family on cohabitation and marriage

In the next chapter, we examine parental family experiences occurring between the birth of the participating child and the child's adolescence.

We list in figure 5.1 the measures of parental family experience and attributes that we use in this chapter. As shown in figure 5.1, we have categorized each of the specific aspects of the parental family into one of three broad periods of the parental life course—making this categorization in order to take into account the sequencing of parental experiences. The first period of parental youth indicates the circumstances of the parents during their childhood and adolescent years. The second period of parental young adulthood indicates parental circumstances during the parents' own transition to adulthood. The third period, parent with young child, is relatively contemporaneous with the 1962 interview, just after the birth of the focal child. Although this chronological classification system has some arbitrary features, we believe that the time ordering is

TABLE 5.1 Total and direct effects of parental youth, parental young adult, and parent with young child factors on children's rate of entrance into marital and cohabiting unions (as competing destinations)[a]

	Marriage								Cohabitation							
	Total effect (min. control)[b]		Model 5.1 (equation [1b])		Model 5.2 (equation [2b])		Model 5.3 (equation [3b])		Total effect (min. control)[b]		Model 5.1 (equation [1b])		Model 5.2 (equation [2b])		Model 5.3 (equation [3b])	
	B[c]	Z[d]	B[c]	Z[d]	B[c]	Z[d]	B[c]	Z[d]	B[c]	Z[d]	B[c]	Z[d]	B[c]	Z[d]	B[c]	Z[d]
Family immigration/Farm background																
Family immigration	-0.13	2.06	-0.11	1.81	-0.11	1.57	-0.10	1.46	-0.22	3.85	-0.21	3.69	-0.20	3.24	-0.19	2.91
Farm background	0.76	3.52	0.46	2.20	0.26	1.24	0.32	1.45	0.29	1.53	0.19	0.98	0.09	0.47	0.10	0.49
Parental socioeconomic standing																
1962 education	-0.09	3.26			-0.08	2.79	-0.07	2.48	-0.08	3.16			-0.05	1.73	-0.02	0.75
1962 financial resources	-0.07	3.06					-0.06	2.83	-0.05	2.43					-0.05	2.40
1962 home ownership	-0.24	2.32					-0.21	1.95	-0.08	0.72					-.01	0.05
Maternal marital experience																
Age at marriage	-0.03	1.68			-0.02	0.91	0.00	0.24	-0.07	4.02			-0.05	2.69	-0.04	1.86
Premarital pregnancy	0.17	1.13			0.10	0.69	0.06	0.40	0.49	3.33			0.34	2.40	0.26	1.84
Religious marriage ceremony	-0.04	0.26			0.14	0.71	0.15	0.72	-0.30	2.50			-0.15	1.04	-0.04	0.30
Marital disruption by 1962	0.43	1.36			0.46	1.37	0.54	1.54	0.65	2.21			0.36	1.30	0.55	1.83
Parental childbearing																
Number of siblings	0.11	3.63	0.09	2.79	0.05	1.61	0.02	0.46	0.01	0.34	0.00	0.16	-0.02	0.70	-0.04	0.16
2nd parity in 1961	-0.09	0.79			-0.12	0.98	0.01	0.10	0.12	0.96			0.10	0.82	0.17	1.26
4th parity in 1961	-0.08	0.69			-0.11	0.92	0.08	0.52	0.10	0.80			0.06	0.45	0.06	0.38
1961 birth unwanted	-0.09	0.45					0.11	0.47	0.44	2.07					0.33	1.56
1962 preferred number of children	0.09	2.13					0.07	1.71	-0.06	1.52					-0.03	0.62

	Coef.	Z	Coef.	Z	Coef.	Z	Coef.	Z	Coef.	Z	Coef.	Z	Coef.	Z	Coef.	Z
Religion																
Grandmother religiosity	0.02	0.25	0.01	0.23	0.04	0.66	-0.02	0.30	-0.11	2.09	-0.10	2.00	-0.02	0.36	0.00	0.02
Maternal religious affiliation																
Fundamental Protestant	0.22	1.10			0.14	0.68	0.11	0.54	-0.08	0.47			-0.17	1.04	-0.14	0.82
Catholic	-0.02	0.14			-0.03	0.25	-0.25	1.96	-0.09	0.81			-0.09	0.84	0.06	0.43
Other	-0.13	0.50			-0.11	0.42	0.08	0.28	0.10	0.41			0.11	0.44	0.21	0.75
Parental religious attendance	0.12	2.70					0.13	2.69	-0.09	2.47					-0.08	2.05
Family organization																
1962 gregariousness	0.10	1.97					0.08	1.62	0.10	1.97					0.08	1.76
1962 closeness to relatives	0.00	0.01					0.04	0.25	-0.40	3.21					-0.38	3.01
1962 sex-role attitudes	-0.13	1.74					-0.09	1.16	0.15	1.93					0.12	1.59
No. of periods			103,814		103,814		103,814				103,814		103,814		103,814	
No. of events			384		384		384				432		432		432	
χ^2			360.65		376.41		406.67				209.27		242.44		274.91	
DF			9		19		27				9		19		27	

Notes: [a] All equations also control gender and age.
[b] Estimates for period 1 factors are from equation (1a), period 2 factors from equation (2a), and period 3 factors from equation (3a) in table A.1 of appendix A.
[c] Effect coefficient for logit equations transformed by equation: $[\exp(\beta) - 1]$.
[d] Z = ratio of absolute value of coefficient to its standard error.

approximately correct and provides a useful way of organizing analysis and presentation. Detailed definitions of each of our measures of these aspects of the parental family, along with summary statistics of their distribution in the sample, are provided in table C.1 of Appendix C.

Table 5.1 provides the relevant information for evaluating the total and direct effects of each of the parental factors on children's rates of entrance into marital and cohabiting unions. For this chapter we have analyzed the influence of the parental family on all of the union transitions discussed in chapter 4. However, in table 5.1 we report only the analysis of cohabitation and marriage as competing destinations (Conceptualization III of chapter 4).[2] We refer to other analyses in the text when those add to the overall picture.

As we discuss in Appendix A, we provide two estimates of the total effects of each of the parental factors on the children's marriage and cohabitation experience. One is an estimate with minimum controls for other parental factors, while another is an estimate with maximum controls of other parental factors. We provide the two estimates because the temporal and causal ordering of parental factors is sometimes ambiguous. We believe that the estimates with minimum and maximum controls are likely to bracket the true total effects. However, this bracketing of the true effects depends upon the assumption that there are no other important unmeasured factors that might be influencing both the parental factors and children's union-formation experience. If that assumption is violated, our estimates will be biased.

Our estimates of the minimally controlled total effects for all the parental factors are provided in the two columns of table 5.1 labeled "Total Effect, Min. Controls." The minimally controlled total effect for each Period 1 factor comes from an equation that includes only that one Period 1 factor and gender and age. The minimally controlled total effect for each Period 2 factor comes from an equation that includes only that one Period 2 factor, all Period 1 factors, gender, and age. Similarly, the minimally controlled total effect for each Period 3 factor comes from an equation that includes only that one Period 3 factor, all Period 1 factors, all Period 2 factors, gender, and age.

The maximally controlled total effects for Period 1 factors are estimated in Model 5.1 with all Period 1 factors in the equation. The maximally controlled total effects for Period 2 factors are estimated in Model 5.2 with all Period 1 and Period 2 factors in the equation, while Model 5.3 provides estimates of the maximally controlled total effects of Period 3 factors with all Period 1, Period 2, and Period 3 factors in the equation.

Models 5.1, 5.2, and 5.3 also provide estimates of the direct effects of each of the explanatory factors under varying conditions. Model 5.1 provides estimates of direct effects of each Period 1 factor that cannot be explained by other Period 1 factors. Model 5.2 provides estimates of the direct effects of each Period 1 and Period 2 factor that cannot be explained by other Period 1 and Period 2 factors, while Model 5.3 provides estimates of the direct effects of all the listed factors net of all the other factors.

The differences in the estimates of direct effects across Models 5.1, 5.2, and 5.3 provide estimates of indirect effects. For example, the difference between the direct effect of a Period 1 factor in Models 5.1 and 5.2 indicates the indirect effect of that Period 1 factor through Period 2 factors. Similarly, the difference between the direct effect of a Period 1 factor in models 5.2 and 5.3 indicates the indirect effect of that Period 1 factor through Period 3 factors.

Our presentation of the effect parameters for each of the parental factors follows the procedure described in Appendix B. Each coefficient (B) expresses the proportionate shift in the union-formation rate associated with each unit of the explanatory factor, and, when multiplied by 100, represents the percentage increase in the union-formation rate associated with each unit of the explanatory factor. Table 5.1 lists these effect parameters from the various equations. Also listed in table 5.1 are the Z ratios indicating the ratio of the effect parameter to its standard error.[3]

The primary analyses of this chapter are reported in table 5.1 for the entire sample of men and women, but with additive controls for age and gender. We also examined how the intergenerational forces influencing marriage and cohabitation decisions vary for men and women. We conducted these analyses by estimating Model 5.3 in table 5.1 separately for men and women. In those instances where the effects appeared to be substantially different for men and women, we estimated the Model 5.3 equations for the entire sample of men and women, but with gender interaction terms to test formally the statistical significance of the gender interactions. A modest number of the gender interaction terms was statistically significant, and we report them in the text where they arise.

Family Immigration and Farm Background

We begin our analyses looking at family immigration using a series of questions from the 1962 interview asking about the birthplace—inside or outside of the United States—for the mother and father, their parents, and their grandparents. We created a four-point scale that coded the most recent immigrants as 4 and families who had been in the United States for several generations as 1 (see Appendix table C.1).[4] Of course, these data refer to the immigration experiences of the first-generation respondents and their parents and grandparents—experiences that occurred prior to 1961. Because more recent immigration has drawn from different countries of origin, the effect of immigration status for today's young people may be different than for the families studied in this research. Furthermore, in our data set the immigrants in each generation may have arrived in the United States from predominantly a different country of origin and this, rather than their degree of assimilation into the United States, could account for the patterns observed.

Young people whose families recently immigrated to the United States have significantly lower rates of marriage than young people from families with long histories in the United States. We see in the first column of table 5.1 that the total effect coefficient (minimally controlled) for recent immigration on marriage is −.13, meaning that each unit of average immigration recency (on a 4-point scale) reduces the marriage rate by 13 percent. If we go across the entire scale and compare children of the most recent immigrants (coded 4 on our immigration scale) with children from families who had been in this country for several generations (coded 1), we find a differential of 34 percent in the marriage rate.[5]

The minimally controlled estimate of the total effect of recent immigration of the parental family on the rate of cohabitation, −.22 for each unit of immigration recency, is even larger than the effect on marriage. Across the entire scale, the cohabitation rates of children from the most recent immigrant families are 53 percent lower than those of children whose families have been in the United States the longest.

In analyses not reported in table 5.1 we examined the influence of immigration status on several additional conceptualizations of union formation from chapter 4. These analyses reveal that immigration recency has an overall negative influence on the rate of union formation. Furthermore, although recent immigration has a somewhat more negative effect on cohabitation than marriage, when we investigate the influence of immigration on the choice between cohabitation and marriage for those entering a union, we find no statistically significant effect. However, when we analyze the effect of immigration on the rate of marriage for cohabiters, we find little influence. This suggests that once a couple enters a cohabiting union, there is little effect of immigration status on the subsequent rate of marriage.

The direct effects of family immigration status are nearly identical to the total effects. Even taking into account all of the parental dimensions in Model 5.3 only reduces the estimated effects of one unit of immigration recency on marriage from −.13 to −.10, while the comparable reduction for cohabitation is from −.22 to −.19. Thus, the substantial effects of immigration status on children's union-formation decisions cannot be explained in any substantial amount by early experiences in the parental life course. Interestingly, the introduction of considerably more parental and child factors in the analyses in subsequent chapters failed to identify any particularly important intervening mechanisms explaining the observed effects of family immigration on children's union formation. Apparently, there is an effect of family immigration that is not explained by factors considered here.

Turning now from international immigration to internal migration, we note that in our preliminary analyses we considered where both the mother and father had lived longest before and after marriage—in a large city, in a small town or city, or on a farm. These analyses showed that the crucial residential distinction was growing up on a farm, with the distinction between youthful residence in large and small cities being unimportant. In addition, these preliminary analyses showed that children's union-formation decisions were influenced similarly by maternal and paternal farm background. Consequently, the family was coded as having a farm background if either the mother or father had grown up on a farm (see table C.1 in Appendix C).

Whereas recent family immigration slows down the rate of union formation, parental farming roots substantially accelerate the process. The total effect with minimum controls of having either a mother or father with a farm background is to increase the rate of marriage by .76 over the rate for children whose parents had no farm background, but this effect drops to .46 with maximum controls (marriage Model 5.1). Although not quite statistically significant, farm background also appears to speed up the rate of cohabitation from between 19 percent (maximum controls) and 29 percent (minimum controls). Because of the differences in the total effects with minimum and maximum controls, we calculated a third estimate. Here we assumed that farm background had similar causal precedence as immigration status and grandmother's religiosity, but was causally prior to number of parental siblings. This assumption is plausible because of our expectation that the fertility of the grandparents was influenced by the other grandparent factors and, therefore, endogenous to these other factors. In a supplementary equation not shown in table 5.1

that included these three parental factors, but excluded number of siblings, the estimated total effects of farm background were .70 and .20 respectively for marriage and cohabitation. If we assume that farm origins are causally prior to fertility, these are our best estimates of the total effects of farm background. In addition, the difference between the total effect estimates of farm background on marriage in the supplementary equation and in Model 5.2 (.70 versus .46) reflects a rather substantial indirect influence through number of parental siblings. This makes sense because parents with farm backgrounds have more siblings, on average, than others (mean of 4.4 versus 2.9), and, as we indicate in the following, the number of parental siblings is strongly and positively correlated with the rapidity of children's entrance into marital unions. This supplementary estimate suggests a very powerful role of fertility in accounting for the positive influence of parental farm background in increasing children's rates of entrance into cohabiting and marital unions.

The effect parameters for farm background decrease substantially with the introduction of parental factors from the parents' young adulthood and early childrearing years in Models 5.2 and 5.3. With the parental factors of Periods 2 and 3 taken into account, the effect on marriage rates shrinks from .46 in Model 5.1 to .32 in Model 5.3 and the effect on cohabitation rates shrinks from .19 to .10 (table 5.1), indicating important indirect effects.

A more detailed examination of the data reveal several important parental intervening factors transmitting the effects of parental farm background on children's union-formation experience. In fact, three specific parental factors—parental religious affiliation, education, and being close to relatives—can each explain substantial portions of the influence of parental farm background on children's union-formation decisions.

The indirect effect of farm background on children's marriage behavior through parental religious affiliation is between .04 and .06.[6] Because we believe that religious affiliation is probably causally prior to the other parental factors included as intervening factors, we also believe that the higher estimate of .06 is the most plausible. Parents with farm backgrounds are more likely than others to be fundamentalist Protestants (31.8 percent compared to 9.9 percent), and children with fundamentalist origins have higher rates of marriage than people of other religious affiliations. We interpret these results as suggesting that one of the reasons children of parents with farm backgrounds have higher rates of marriage than others is that their parents are also likely to be fundamentalist Protestants and children of fundamentalists marry more rapidly. However, religious affiliation explains very little of the farm background effect on children's cohabitation experience.

Parental education is another major intervening mechanism transmitting the influence of farm background. By itself, parental education can account for between .06 and .09 of the effect of parental farm background on marriage rates and from between .03 and .08 of the effect on cohabitation.[7] If we assume that parental education is causally prior to the other intervening parental factors (except religious affiliation), then the estimates of the indirect effects of farm background on marriage and cohabitation through education are both equal to .08. The causal interpretation of these results is relatively straightforward: parental farm origins are associated with lower levels of parental education, which in turn lead to higher rates of entrance into marital and cohabiting unions.[8] That is, farm-origin parents receive less education than others, and this factor alone increases children's rates of marriage and cohabitation by about 8 percent.[9]

Maternal closeness to relatives can also explain part of the parental farm-background effect on children's cohabitation rates. The indirect effect of parental farm background on children's cohabitation rates through maternal closeness to relatives is .08.[10] Apparently, parents in this sample who grew up on farms are less likely than others to have relatives who are also their closest friends and companions (means of .30 and .37 respectively). Because children whose parents are friends with their relatives have the lowest cohabitation rates, this lower rate of maternal family closeness among farm migrants results in children experiencing higher rates of cohabitation. This intervening factor alone increases the cohabitation rates of the children of farm parents by about 8 percent.

However, even with these indirect pathways of influence controlled, farm background still has a direct (although not statistically significant) effect on marriage. Furthermore, analyses in subsequent chapters indicate that the positive effect of farm background on marriage remains strong even with controls for a range of additional intervening factors. In addition, these subsequent analyses reveal no additional indirect causal pathways explaining the positive effect of parental farm background on children's union-formation experience.

The positive influence of farm background on cohabitation is surprising because we expected individuals from rural areas to have less positive attitudes toward premarital sex and cohabitation than others. However, when we break down cohabitors into subgroups based on their commitment to marriage at the time of cohabitation, we find that farm background has a positive influence on cohabitation only for young people who are already engaged. This suggests that farm background accelerates the speed of deciding to marry, with some of these couples marrying directly and others deciding to cohabit while engaged. Other than this engaged-cohabitation phenomenon, we found no further effect for farm background on cohabitation.

Also, in supplementary analyses we found that once a couple is cohabiting, farm background has no further effect on the rate of marriage (Conceptualization V).

Our investigation of gender interactions revealed that the positive influence of parental farm background on the rapidity of children's entrance into both marriage and cohabitation is substantial and positive only for males. This gender interaction is statistically significant only for cohabitation (results not shown in tables).

Parental Socioeconomic Standing

We incorporate into our analyses several indicators of parental socioeconomic status (SES): the average years of education of the mother and father; parental financial resources (the average of 1961 income and 1962 assets—in thousands of dollars);[11] and home ownership—a simple dichotomous indicator of whether the family owned its own home in 1962, with or without a mortgage.[12] The total effects of parental SES on children's subsequent marriage and cohabitation decisions are remarkably similar across these three SES measures, and consistent with most of the hypotheses we discussed earlier: education, financial resources, and home ownership are each related to lower rates of entrance into unions (table 5.1). Furthermore, except for the effect of home ownership on the rate of entrance into cohabitation, each of these effects is statistically significant. Also, with the exception of home ownership, the magnitudes of the effects of these socioeconomic indicators on marriage are very similar to their effects on cohabitation. This suggests that these factors operate to slow down the rate of entrance into both marital and cohabiting unions, but have virtually no effect on the choice between the two types of unions. Also note that because parental SES is related to lower rates of both marriage and cohabitation as competing destinations, it is not surprising that a supplementary analysis shows that it slows down the overall rate of marriage ignoring whether or not cohabitation had already occurred. Parental financial resources, but not education and home ownership, also slow down marriage among cohabiters.

The data show a strong negative total effect of parental education on children's rates of entrance into marital and cohabiting unions. The minimally controlled and maximally controlled estimates of the total effect of parental education on marriage are remarkably uniform in suggesting that each year of average parental education decreases children's marriage rates by 8 to 9 percent. The minimally constrained effect on cohabitation is also in this same range, but the maximally constrained effect on cohabitation is a negative 5 percent (Model 5.2 of table 5.1).

Further investigation reveals that the difference between the two estimates of the total effect of education on cohabitation can be explained entirely by the association between parental education and the circumstances surrounding the marriage of the parents. Highly educated parents are substantially more likely than less educated parents to marry at an older age, be married by a religious official, and not be pregnant at the time of marriage.[13] And, as we show in the following sections, each of these dimensions of parental marriage is very strongly related to low rates of cohabitation in the next generation.

It is plausible to argue that parental educational attainments are, for the most part, causally prior to parental marriage. A substantial body of research demonstrates that education influences subsequent marriage experience, especially age at marriage (Blossfeld and Huinink 1991; Goldscheider and Waite 1986; Marini 1978; Thornton, Axinn, and Teachman 1995). In addition, previous work with this same data set reveals that most of the parents in the study who were premaritally pregnant married after they were out of school (Freedman and Thornton 1979). For these reasons, it is plausible that parental education influences parental marriage circumstances, which in turn influence children's union-formation experience.

We implemented this idea by estimating the total effect of education in a model that contains only family immigration, farm background, number of siblings, grandmother religiosity, religious affiliation, and education (results not shown). In that model the estimated effect of education on cohabitation is −.09—an effect that equals the effect of parental education on children's rate of marriage. If we add the parental marriage factors to this equation, the effect of education is reduced to −.05. The causal model with parental education preceding parental marriage, thus, suggests that the difference between the new estimated total effect of –.09 and the maximally controlled estimate of –.05 can be interpreted as the indirect effect of education on cohabitation through the circumstances surrounding parental marriage. If we accept this interpretation, it means that higher levels of educational attainment negatively influence children's cohabitation by increasing parental age at marriage, increasing the likelihood the parents had a religious marriage ceremony, and decreasing the likelihood the mother was pregnant at marriage.

Further specification of this indirect effect, however, is difficult because all of the empirically relevant parental marriage factors are correlated and simultaneously determined, making it difficult to construct a causal model that specifies differential causal ordering. Nevertheless, more detailed analyses with alternative specifications reveal the relative strengths of these three parental marriage factors in explaining this difference in the educational total effect on cohabitation, with the largest effect being age at marriage and the smallest being a religious marriage ceremony (results not shown).

In addition, even if one believed that the causal ordering were reversed—with parental marital decisions preceding educational decisions—the total effect of education on cohabitation would still be –.05 (rather than –.08 to –.09). Although we recognize that marital decisions sometimes influence education, we believe the preponderance of the influence between these two factors is from education to marriage. This reasoning suggests that the total education effect may be smaller than –.08, but closer to –.08 than to –.05. But in either event, the effect is substantial and important.

Extrapolating the educational effect of –.09 for marriage across four years of education, from both parents having graduated from high school to both parents having graduated from college, reveals a 31 percent drop in the marriage rate.[14] The decrease is only slightly smaller for children's cohabitation rates across four years of parental education.

We have already suggested that the circumstances of the parents' marriage can explain part of the education effect on cohabitation. Here we note that the addition of parental attributes when the study child was an infant reduces the parental education effect close to zero, suggesting additional intervening factors (compare Models 5.2 and 5.3).

Further investigation shows that 1962 parental financial resources help transmit the effects of parental education on children's cohabitation. The indirect effects of parental education on cohabitation through financial resources equal between −.02 and −.03. That is, each unit of education is associated with a 2 to 3 percent lower rate of cohabitation because higher educational attainment leads to greater financial resources ($r =$ .38), which, in turn, decrease the entrance of children into cohabitation. A small part of the total effect of parental education on children's entrance into cohabitation can be explained by parental attendance at religious services in 1962. Educated parents in this sample attend religious services more frequently ($r = .19$), which, as we will see later in this chapter, significantly reduces the cohabitation experience of young people.

Detailed analysis also shows a similar indirect negative effect of education on children's marriage rates through financial resources.[15] Nevertheless, the negative effect of parental education on children's marriage remains very large even with all the parental factors included in Model 5.3. This suggests that parental education has a direct negative effect on children's marriage that cannot be explained by the other parental factors considered here. Understanding the reasons education affects children's marital timing will require inclusion of additional factors beyond those examined in this chapter.

The total effects of parental financial resources and home ownership also appear to be very substantial with both maximum and minimum controls. Each thousand dollars of average economic resources reduces the marriage rate by 6 to 7 percent and the cohabitation rate by 5 percent, so that a difference of $10,000 in average financial resources in 1962 would mean a substantial difference in second-generation union-formation rates. And, home ownership reduces the marriage rate between 21 and 24 percent.

We checked the possibility of an age interaction between parental socioeconomic status and children's union formation by investigating rates separately at ages 22 and younger and ages 23 and older. We investigated this age interaction because of the hypothesis that parental socioeconomic status would delay children's union formation primarily by increasing children's school attendance, and we broke the age range at 23 because ages 22 and younger are the main school-attendance years.

We found the effects on marriage are larger at the younger ages for all three socioeconomic factors—education, financial resources, and home ownership. For example, the maximally controlled coefficient for education on marriage rates at ages 22 and under is −.15, compared to −.03 at ages 23 and older. We also found age differences in the same direction for financial resources and home ownership (not shown in tables). Thus, the coefficients for the socioeconomic factors listed in table 5.1, which are for the entire age range up to 31, fall between the coefficients for the two separate age groups.

This age interaction is not apparent in cohabitation rates. If the interaction of parental SES with children's age is due to an indirect effect of SES factors on union formation through the children's school attendance, as we hypothesize, the lack of an interaction effect with cohabitation may mean that children's school attendance has less effect on cohabitation than on marriage. This is consistent with earlier analyses by Thornton, Axinn, and Teachman (1995). We will return to this hypothesis in chapter 10.

Maternal Marital Experience

Four dimensions of marriage and marital dissolution are examined in this section. We begin with the mother's age at marriage, measured in number of years. The other three dimensions are dichotomous measures of whether (a) the mother was pregnant at the time of marriage, (b) she experienced a prior marital dissolution through death or marital discord, and (c) the marriage of the mother and father was performed by a religious official. Because all of these dimensions of marriage are interrelated, we discuss them as a group here.

The empirical data provide strong support of our hypotheses about the relationship of maternal marriage experience and children's union formation. For cohabitation, all of the minimally controlled total effects are substantial and statistically significant, with premarital pregnancy, prior marriage, and religious marriage ceremony being associated, respectively, with +49, +65, and −30 percent differentials in the children's rate of cohabitation. Each year of maternal age at marriage is associated with a 7 percent decline in children's cohabitation rates. All of these factors have estimated total effects on second-generation marriage rates that are in the same direction but these are both statistically insignificant and much smaller than for cohabitation.

Although the estimates of the effects on cohabitation in Model 5.2 are smaller than the minimally controlled total effects, each remains substantial. Premarital pregnancy, prior marriage, and religious marriage ceremony continue to have differentials of +34, +36, and −15 percent on children's cohabitation rates. Further, each year of maternal age at marriage is associated with a 5 percent decline in cohabitation. The effect of maternal age at marriage and premarital pregnancy remain statistically significant, but the effects of the other two factors do not.

It is plausible that these estimates with maximum controls are closer to the "true" total effects on cohabitation than those with minimum controls. The reason is that both parental religion and education are probably primarily exogenous to maternal marriage, indicating that they should be controlled in analyses of the effects of maternal marriage factors. In addition, only parental parity in 1961 is endogenous to maternal marriage, and its exclusion from the equation for cohabitation changes only slightly the estimated coefficients for the maternal marriage factors. The new estimates (with maximum controls minus maternal parity in 1961) for the four maternal marital factors on children's cohabitation are: −.05 for each year of maternal age at marriage, +.35 for premarital pregnancy, +.37 for prior marriage, and −.14 for religious marriage ceremony. These coefficients are very close to those estimated as the effects with maximum controls, and, we believe, a close approximation to the total effects of these marriage factors on cohabitation rates.

We emphasize, however, that the effects estimated in the new equation and in Model 5.2 are net of each other. This means that if we were to take them as a package and compare young people whose mothers married young, were premaritally pregnant, were previously married, and did not have a religious marriage ceremony, their cohabitation rates would be tremendously higher than those whose mothers had the opposite marital circumstances. This attests to the strong influence of union-formation experiences across generations.

The introduction of additional dimensions of the parental family in Model 5.3 further decreases the estimated effects of age at marriage, premarital pregnancy, and religious marriage ceremony on children's cohabitation rates. In fact, religious marriage ceremony has *no* direct effect on cohabitation once influences from the time of the study child's birth are taken into account.

One important factor explaining the effects of maternal age at marriage and premarital pregnancy is parental socioeconomic standing. Mothers who marry young and who are pregnant at marriage tend to have fewer financial resources, which in turn is associated with higher marriage and cohabitation rates among children. This indirect effect through financial resources is sufficiently large that for each additional year of maternal age at marriage it produces a one percent decline in both marriage and cohabitation rates. In addition, a premarital pregnancy has an indirect effect through financial resources of increasing both marriage and cohabitation by about 2 percent, and has an indirect effect through parental home ownership of increasing cohabitation by about 4 percent (with no effect on marriage).

Note that parental educational attainment is controlled in estimating the indirect influence of parental age at marriage and premarital pregnancy through 1962 financial resources and home ownership. With education controlled, we suggest the following interpretation of these findings: young maternal ages at marriage and premarital pregnancy lead to lower levels of parental financial resources and home ownership in subsequent years that, in turn, speed up the rate of union formation among children.

Maternal gregariousness in 1962 can also explain part of the total influences of parental marriage age and premarital pregnancy on children's union-formation rates (figures 9.3 and 9.4). Maternal age at marriage has a –.01 per year indirect effect through 1962 maternal gregariousness on both marriage and cohabitation, which aggregates to a considerable amount across several years. In addition, parental premarital pregnancy has a positive indirect effect (.02 to .04) on children's marriage and cohabitation through 1962 maternal gregariousness. Maternal gregariousness is an intervening mechanism because mothers who married rapidly and were premaritally pregnant are more gregarious than others.[16]

The interpretation of maternal gregariousness intervening between parental marriage and children's marriage is consistent with the fact that maternal gregariousness was measured in 1962, after the parents had been married, often for many years. An alternative explanation of these results, however, is that gregariousness is a relatively stable personality trait, our 1962 measure of which would reflect the mothers' gregariousness during their years of adolescence and young adulthood (not shown in figures). If this is true, gregariousness might decrease maternal age at marriage and increase premarital pregnancy, which would increase children's union-formation rates. This scenario would also imply that at least portions of the total effects of maternal age at marriage and premarital pregnancy on children' union-formation rates are spurious because of maternal gregariousness influencing union formation in each generation.

Parental religiosity also helps explain the positive influence of parental premarital pregnancy on the rate of entering cohabiting unions. Premaritally pregnant mothers attend religious services less frequently (mean = 3.2 in 1962) than their counterparts (mean = 3.7 in 1962). And, as we will see later in this chapter, low levels of parental religiosity are associated with more rapid entrance by children into cohabiting unions. That is, a maternal premarital pregnancy is likely to lower maternal religiosity, and the lower levels of religiosity increase the rate of children's entrance into cohabitation.

The indirect effect of a premarital pregnancy on children's marriage through parental religiosity is of similar magnitude but opposite in direction to the indirect effect on cohabitation. The reason is that the lower levels of parental religiosity among the premaritally pregnant—including infrequent attendance at religious services—are associated with lower marriage and higher cohabitation rates in the next generation. The indirect effect on marriage through 1962 religiosity is a negative 3 percent, and the indirect effect on cohabitation is a positive 2 percent. Clearly, parental religiosity is an important element in explaining the effects of a parental premarital pregnancy on children's union-formation experience.[17]

We believe that the interpretation of a causal structure whereby premarital pregnancy reduces religiosity, which in turn influences children's union formation, is plausible for many people. But for others, it is likely that low levels of religiosity lead to a premarital pregnancy, which then speeds up cohabitation and slows down marriage in the second generation. In this case, at least part of the premarital pregnancy total effect on union formation is spurious in that both parental premarital pregnancy and children's union formation are the joint outcomes of parental religiosity.

We noted earlier that a religious marriage ceremony in the parental generation was negatively related to the entrance of children into cohabitation unions, but that most of this effect was due to intervening effects through subsequent parental factors. Here we suggest that the primary indirect effects of a religious marriage on cohabitation operate through these couples' higher levels of religiosity later in life and their greater closeness to their relatives—both of which we report later to decrease children's rates of cohabitation.[18] The indirect effect through parental religiosity in 1962 is either –.04 or –.05 (depending on the controls used) and the indirect effect through closeness to relatives is –.06.

Despite the many indirect effects we have identified, the direct effects of maternal age at marriage and premarital pregnancy on second-generation cohabitation remain substantial and statistically significant, even with the full controls of Model 5.3. There is an estimated decline of 4 percent in cohabitation for each year of maternal age at marriage and an increase of 26 percent for a premarital pregnancy.

It is interesting to note that parental premarital pregnancy does not influence all types of cohabitation in the second generation the same (results not shown). In fact, the only cohabitation group it influences substantially is cohabitation with no plans of marriage. Furthermore, this effect is very substantial, with children of mothers who were premaritally pregnant entering cohabitation without marriage plans at rates that were about two-thirds higher than those of other young people. The effects of maternal premarital pregnancy on rates of cohabitation with either private or public plans to marry are similar to those on marriage rates. Thus, premarital pregnancy in the parental generation is related to the most nonnormative or unaccepted form of cohabitation—that without any plans for marriage. This suggests a tendency toward nonnormative union behavior that is transmitted across generations.

Before leaving the parental marital factors of premarital pregnancy and age at marriage, we note that each of them interacts with age of the children in affecting the children's union formation. As with parental socioeconomic factors, the effects of premarital pregnancy and age at marriage affect children's marriage rates primarily at the young ages (−.06 versus .02 in Model 5.2 for maternal age at marriage and .22 versus −.08 for premarital pregnancy). However, unlike parental socioeconomic factors, effects of maternal age at marriage and premarital pregnancy on cohabitation also depend on children's age, with the effects of these two maternal factors being strong primarily at the young ages (−.07 versus −.02 for maternal age at marriage in Model 5.2 and .43 versus .13 for premarital pregnancy).

Unlike maternal age at marriage, premarital pregnancy, and religious marriage ceremony, the estimated effects of a prior maternal marriage on both marriage and cohabitation are larger in Model 5.3 than Model 5.2. These results suggest that marital dissolution and remarriage even before a child's birth are important influences on that child's union-formation decisions many years later, and that those effects are independent of the other parental dimensions we have considered in this analysis.

This finding has important substantive implications. Many studies have shown that marital disruption during childhood is related to children's premarital sex and cohabitation behavior. As we noted earlier, several causal mechanisms could explain that effect. However, these potential explanations, which are linked to the children's direct experience with marital disruption, do not apply to the current findings, which are related to marital dissolutions *before* the birth of the child.

This suggests mechanisms that operate independent of the children's direct experience with marital dissolution. One possibility is that mothers who have experienced marital dissolution may have different attitudes toward premarital sex and cohabitation that, in turn, influence their children's union-formation behavior (Axinn and Thornton 1996). Another possibility is a biogenetic connection, with both mothers and children in families experiencing marital disruption having predispositions that lead to different approaches to marriage, cohabitation, and divorce. One might also expect a socioeconomic connection, as maternal marital dissolution is associated with educational attainment, financial well-being, and home ownership. Yet, the data are inconsistent with this hypothesis as the marital disruption effect persists in Model 5.3 with these socioeconomic factors controlled.

Parental Childbearing Attitudes and Behavior

We consider several dimensions of family size and fertility experience, each with a different focus and temporal ordering. Our first family size dimension is the average number of siblings in the families of orientation of the mothers and fathers.[19] Our second family size dimension is the total number of children ever born to the mothers in our study, counting the children born in 1961. Because the sample was drawn to represent only families with one, two, or four births, we have coded each parity group as a dummy variable with first parity families being the reference category.

Two additional measures of fertility are included in our analysis. The first is a dichotomous variable that indicates whether the mother said at the 1962 interview that she did not want to have another child when she became pregnant with her 1961 child (our focal child). The second is a continuous variable and measures the mother's preferred number of children at the time of the 1962 interview.

The data summarized in table 5.1 indicate that both the mean number of siblings in the parental families and the mother's preferred number of children have positive total effects on the children's rate of entrance into marriage. An increase of one sibling in the parental families of orientation increases the marriage rate in the following generation by between 9 and 11 percent. An increase of one child in the mother's preferred number of children increases the second-generation marriage rate by between 7 and 9 percent. For the total marriage rate ignoring cohabitation

(Conceptualization I), the respective increases in marriage associated with the two fertility indicators range between 5 and 8 percent for each additional sibling or preferred child (data not shown in tables). Both fertility indicators also influence the rate of marriage among cohabitors by about 8 percent, although this is not statistically significant for preferred number of children.

Neither fertility indicator has a statistically significant effect on the children's rate of cohabitation, although the negative influence of preferred family size is substantial and nearly statistically significant with minimum controls. Further analysis shows that both number of siblings and preferred number of children have statistically significant and positive influence on the second generation's choice of marriage over cohabitation (not shown in tables).

The actual number of children born to the mothers as of 1961 is not related significantly to the children's rate of entrance into either cohabitation or marriage. The positive influence of grandparent fertility and mother's preferred number of children clearly does not extend to the mother's actual fertility as of 1961. One possible explanation for this difference is that actual fertility in 1961 does not include children born in subsequent years, and is, therefore, only a partial indicator of family size. We will return to this issue in the next chapter as we introduce measures of completed family size.

The effect of the number of siblings in the parental generation on children's marriage rates is substantially explained by the other factors in the model. With the full controls of Model 5.3, the positive effect of number of siblings on marriage is reduced to 2 percent, a rather substantial decrease, suggesting important indirect effects through other parental factors.

Part of the indirect effect of number of siblings operates through parental education (.02 to .03) and a smaller amount through home ownership (.01). This suggests that each sibling is associated with a 2 to 3 percent increase in the children's marriage rates entirely because of the indirect influence through parental education and a 1 percent increase through home ownership. We believe that these results can best be interpreted as a causal chain with a larger number of parental siblings decreasing parental education ($r = -.35$) and home ownership, and thereby leading to increased rates of their children entering marriage.[20]

We know that family size preferences and behavior are transmitted intergenerationally, yielding a positive correlation in fertility across generations (Axinn, Clarkberg, and Thornton 1994). In our study the mothers who came from larger families preferred more children themselves ($r =$ .16). Given this positive association and the positive effect of parental fertility preferences on children's entrance into marriage, parental family size has an indirect effect of .01 through parental fertility preferences.

Interestingly, being an unwanted child increases the rate of cohabitation but has little effect on the marriage rate. Furthermore, the total effect of being an unwanted child on cohabitation is substantial—44 percent in the estimation with minimum controls and 33 percent in Model 5.3 with maximum controls.[21] Our examination of gender interactions suggests that the positive effect of being an unwanted child on cohabitation may exist only for daughters and not for sons (not shown in tables).

Religion

Several dimensions of religion and religiosity are examined in this analysis. The first refers to the religiosity of the maternal grandmother when the mother was growing up. It is measured on a scale ranging from zero to three, with three being the most religiously observant. The second measure, already discussed in the context of marriage, is a dichotomous variable for whether or not the parental marriage was performed by a church official. The third dimension is the religious affiliation of the mother in 1962, coded into three dummy variables: fundamentalist Protestants; Catholics; and others (including no affiliation). The reference religious group is mainline or nonfundamentalist Protestants. More detailed specification of religious denomination was not possible because of sample size limitations. The fourth dimension is the average attendance of the mother and father at religious services in 1962, which is coded from 1 (both parents never attending) to 6 (both parents attending several times a week).[22]

As we explained earlier, numerous theories predict that parental religiosity will have a strong positive relationship with children's marriage rates and a strong negative relationship with cohabitation. The data in table 5.1 provide ample support for these expectations. The effect of religion operates across generations, as even the religiosity of the maternal grandmother has a strong negative total effect on the child's subsequent experience with cohabitation. Each unit of the grandmother's religiosity (measured on a 4-point scale) is associated with about a 10 percent lower cohabitation rate. However, grandmother's religiosity has no substantial effect on entrance into marriage.

Consistent with our expectations, we also find that the average attendance of the parents at religious services in 1962, shortly after the focal child was born, increases marriage while decreasing cohabitation. Furthermore, the total effects of parental service attendance are substantial, with each unit of average religiosity increasing marriage by 12 or 13 percent and decreasing cohabitation by 8 or 9 percent. Over the full range of a six-point scale, the effects of parental religiosity at the time of the child's infancy are remarkable—increasing the marriage rate by at least 76 percent and decreasing the cohabitation rate by at least 34 percent. If we focus our attention on the choice between cohabitation and marriage for those who enter a coresidential union, we find that each unit of religiosity decreases cohabitation by 20 percent. Going across the entire six points of the religiosity scale produces a difference in the odds of cohabitation versus marriage of nearly two-thirds.

Although parent and grandparent religiosity influences the rate of entrance into marital and cohabiting unions from being single, supplemental analyses show that they have little influence on the rate of transforming cohabitations into marriages.

It is important to note that Model 5.3 of table 5.1 is sufficient to explain virtually all of the total effects of both grandmother's religiosity and parental religious marriage. As one would expect, the stability of religiosity between generations is one important mechanism accounting for the influence of early parental religiosity on children's cohabitation experience. Parents who themselves have more religious parents are more likely than others to be married by a religious official and to attend religious services more frequently.[23] Consequently, grandmother religiosity influences the grandchildren's cohabitation experience by affecting the religiosity of parents. The indirect effect through parental religious marriage ceremony is between –.01 and –.03, and the indirect effect through parental religious attendance in 1962 is –.02. As we noted earlier in this chapter, parental religious marriage ceremony, in turn, has an indirect effect through parental attendance at religious services and being close to relatives.

Several other parental dimensions—education and maternal age at marriage—operate to explain the total effect of grandmother religiosity on children's cohabitation experience. The indirect effect of grandmother religiosity through parental education is between –.01 and –.03, and the indirect effect through parental age at marriage is between –.02 and –.04. We interpret these results as indicating that grandmother religiosity operates to increase parental educational attainment ($r = .13$) and age at marriage ($r = .18$), which, in turn, decrease the children's rate of entrance into cohabitation.

Although religiosity substantially influences children's union-formation experience, religious affiliation does not appear to have any significant total effects on marriage or cohabitation. Fundamentalist Protestants experience somewhat higher marriage rates and somewhat lower cohabitation rates than nonfundamentalist Protestants, but these differences are not statistically significant. If we contrast the choice between cohabitation and marriage for those entering a union, fundamentalists have a 30 percent lower rate of choosing cohabitation rather than marriage—another difference that is not quite statistically significant (results not shown).

The effect of being Catholic as compared to being a mainline Protestant is intriguing. If we focus only on the total effect, we see that Catholics are similar to mainline Protestants in their entrance into both cohabitation and marriage. However, when we shift our attention to Model 5.3 with its wide range of controls, we find that children of Catholics marry at a statistically significant 25 percent lower rate than do children of mainline Protestants. This implies that the strong direct negative effect of Catholicism is offset by an equally strong positive indirect effect through one or more intervening dimensions of the parental family.

Detailed analyses show that a substantial portion of the positive indirect Catholic effect operates through two key parental dimensions: attendance at religious services and fertility preferences. The indirect positive effect of being Catholic on marriage rates through parental religious attendance is between .17 and .18. This indirect effect flows directly from two facts: Catholic parents attended religious services much more frequently in 1962 than did others (a mean of 4.3 compared to 2.7); and parental religiosity significantly increases the rate of marriage in the younger generation. This result suggests that, if all else were equal, children of Catholic parents would have 17 to 18 percent higher marriage rates than others because of the higher service attendance of their parents.

Similarly, being Catholic has an indirect effect on marriage rates through fertility preferences of between .05 and .08. This occurs because Catholic parents had substantially higher fertility preferences (a mean of 4.3 compared to 3.3), and, as we have seen, parental desires for high fertility are reflected in higher rates of marriage in the next generation.

There may also be interesting indirect effects of parental Catholic religious affiliation on cohabitation that operate through church attendance and fertility preferences. As we saw earlier, the estimated total effect of parental Catholic affiliation on children's cohabitation is not statistically significant, but children of Catholics are estimated to have 9 percent lower cohabitation rates than mainline Protestants. However, this effect totally disappears with the full controls in Model 5.3 (table 5.1). More detailed examination shows a .10 to .12 indirect negative effect of Catholicism on children's cohabitation experience that operates through the religious attendance of the parents, and a .02 to .05 indirect negative effect that operates through fertility preferences. These results suggest that Catholic parents attend services more frequently and have higher family size preferences, which, in turn, decrease their children's entrance into cohabitation. Once these factors are taken into account, children of Catholic families enter cohabitation at about the same speed as mainline Protestants.

Family Organization

Our last group of 1962 parental factors predicting children's union-formation behavior centers on family organization and interaction. These analyses focus on two dimensions of maternal interactions with friends and relatives. The first is the sum of the mother's contacts with friends and relatives.[24] It is labeled gregariousness and is coded from zero for never seeing friends or relatives to eight for seeing both friends and relatives almost every day (Appendix table C.1). The second family organization dimension, constructed by averaging two separate indicators, measures whether the mother feels closer to relatives than friends.[25] The measure ranges from zero for being closest to friends to one for being closest to relatives (see Appendix table C.1).

These two dimensions of maternal interactions with friends and relatives relate very differently with the children's union-formation experience. Consistent with our expectations, maternal gregariousness substantially increases the rate of both cohabitation and marriage in the younger generation. Furthermore, the total effects on marriage and cohabitation are nearly identical, with each unit of maternal gregariousness being associated with an 8 to 10 percent increase in children's union formation. Given the nine-point gregariousness scale, this produces substantial differences between children of mothers who are low and high on contact with friends and relatives. For example, the increase in union formation between children of mothers scoring two and six on the scale would be approximately 40 percent $(1.09^4 - 1)$.

We posit two indirect mechanisms transmitting the influence of parental gregariousness on children's union formation. The first is that high levels of parental sociability are transmitted across generations either socially or biologically, and high sociability in the second generation enhances union formation. Second, highly sociable parents may give their children a more positive view toward social interactions and help them in meeting and attracting prospective partners, thereby accelerating the rate of marriage and cohabitation.

The mother's closeness to relatives is not associated with children's rate of entrance into marriage, but is substantially negatively correlated with the children's cohabitation experience. In fact, going across the range of the scale from having all friends who are not relatives to having all friends as relatives is associated with about a 40 percent reduction in the rate of children's cohabitation. It is possible that parental integration into more familial networks than nonfamilial networks creates in the children a greater commitment to marital and familial relationships that reduces the likelihood of entering a cohabiting union.[26]

We also examined mothers' views concerning appropriate gender roles within the family as a dimension of family organization. Our maternal sex-role attitudes measure ranges from 1 to 5 where a score of 5 signifies the most egalitarian response and a score of 1 signifies the least egalitarian response (see Appendix table C.1).[27] Our gender-role attitude index, of course, captures only one aspect of gender roles—attitudes about the segregation of family roles. It provides little information about such issues as gender identity and beliefs about masculinity and femininity. Consequently, our data set provides no resources for addressing these important aspects of gender roles. In addition, our questions were designed to measure attitudes about important gender issues in the early 1960s and cannot take into account the evolving nature of these issues.

The data in table 5.1 demonstrate that maternal sex-role attitudes significantly influence the union-formation decisions of children. We can conclude that egalitarian sex-role attitudes speed up cohabitation and slow down marriage—with the total effect being in the range of 9 to 15 percent per unit on the sex-role attitudes index for both types of union. We can also conclude that maternal sex-role attitudes have little to do with the overall rapidity of the union-formation process, but that they do substantially affect the choice between cohabitation and marriage. In fact, among those who do enter a union, each unit on the sex-role index increases the choice of cohabitation over marriage by 32 percent (data not shown in tables). Going across the full four-point range produces more than a *doubling* of the choice of cohabitation over marriage.

This dramatic linkage of maternal sex-role attitudes and children's union-formation experience is consistent with the idea that family values are transmitted in some way across generations, and that these values have strong behavioral implications. In this case, egalitarian attitudes in the parental generation are clearly associated with choosing cohabitation over marriage in the second generation.

Summary and Conclusions

The roots of children's union-formation behavior lie far into the past. In fact, as we have shown in this chapter, even knowledge of the parents when they were very young provides predictive power concerning the children's marriage and cohabitation. In addition, many parental factors from the time leading up to and including the child's birth have implications for the children's marriage and cohabitation behavior.

The data show that recent immigration status to the United States is related to low rates of entrance into both cohabitation and marriage while farm background is related to high rates of marriage and cohabitation. Parental socioeconomic standing is consistently related to low rates of both cohabitation and marriage, although the effects seem slightly stronger for marriage than cohabitation. The effects of parental socioeconomic status seem to be particularly strong at young ages.

Our results suggest a strong intergenerational transmission of union-formation behavior. Parents who marry at older ages have children who also marry later. A parental premarital pregnancy is related to more rapid union formation in the second generation. Parents who had a religious marriage ceremony have children with slower union-formation rates. These effects of parental experiences are all more substantial for the children's cohabitation than for their marriage. Maternal marital disruption even before the child is born is positively related to the child's subsequent cohabitation behavior.

Considerable evidence indicates that parental childbearing patterns are related to children's union-formation experience. Both the number of siblings and the preferred number of children in the parental family are related to more rapid entrance of children into marriage. However, the actual fertility of the parents by the time the children were born has no significant relationship to the children's rate of entrance into marriage. This apparent anomaly is cleared up in the next chapter where we find that total parental fertility when the children are age 15 is related to the children's rate of marriage.

Religion is also a central factor in explaining children's union-formation behavior, with religious commitment seeming to have a stronger effect than religious affiliation. The effects of religion are also intergenerational: the religiosity of both grandparents and parents is negatively related to the rate of children's cohabitation, while parental religiosity has a positive influence on marriage.

Finally, family organization has important relationships to children's union-formation behavior. The gregariousness of the mother is positively related to both early cohabitation and marriage. Maternal closeness to family rather than friends is related to a low incidence of cohabitation. In addition, the attitudes of mothers about sex roles are strongly related to the children's choice between cohabitation and marriage, with more egalitarian mothers having children who are much more likely to choose cohabitation over marriage. This finding suggests an important attitudinal component in the intergenerational influences on cohabitation and marriage.

Race Differences

Of course these results from the Intergenerational Panel Study come from White respondents, and have no immediate inference to other groups in the United States, such as African Americans or Hispanic Americans. Nevertheless, the results provide some information useful for understanding marriage and cohabitation in those groups as well. First, the strong effects of immigration status we find among this non-Hispanic sample suggest immigration status per se may be a factor shaping the marital and cohabiting behaviors of various racial and ethnic subgroups of the population, including subgroups within both the Hispanic- and the Asian-American populations. Second, it is quite reasonable to expect the extremely strong intergenerational associations we find among Whites are also present among other racial and ethnic groups. To the extent strong intergenerational influences are present in other groups, particularly in the intergenerational transmission of union-formation behavior, these intergenerational mechanisms may help to explain the persistence of racial differences in marriage and family behavior across long periods of time—

periods characterized by many different economic conditions (Morgan et al. 1993). Third, we find important intergenerational influences on marital and cohabiting behavior span many different substantive dimensions among the White population. This is likely to be true among other racial groups as well, though the specific influences with the most effect on behavior are likely to vary across groups (Bennett, Bloom, and Craig 1989; Landale and Tolnay 1991; Teachman, Polonko, and Leigh 1987).

Conclusion

Intergenerational factors have strong and lasting consequences for marital and cohabiting behavior. These consequences span a broad range of substantive domains including parents' socioeconomic characteristics, parents' marital and childbearing experiences, parents' religion and religiosity, and the social organization of parental families. Moreover, the effects of each of these dimensions are largely independent of one another, so that each different dimension of the parental family exerts its own influence. Of course it is not possible to randomly assign children to parents, so that all studies of intergenerational influences are forced to rely upon observational research designs. As a result, the strong empirical associations we observe may or may not reflect independent causal forces. Nevertheless, the associations documented in this chapter are consistent with our theoretical framework predicting strong, multidimensional intergenerational influences on the timing of union formation, the choice between marriage and cohabitation, and the rates of both marriage and cohabitation.

In chapter 6 we switch our attention from the first three periods of the parental life course to the fourth period—when the children in the study were maturing from birth to age 15. We consider many of the same kinds of parental factors, but now at a later point in the lives of the parents and children. A particular interest of this next chapter is the relative influence of early and late life factors. We also focus our attention on the ways by which parental factors during the children's adolescence operate to transmit the influence of parental factors from earlier periods.

CHAPTER SIX

Influence of Parental Factors during Childhood and Adolescence of the Children*

The key message of the previous chapter is that the influences on children's union-formation experiences can be traced backward for at least two generations, to the immigration status, farm background, religious affiliation and commitment, and childbearing experience and preferences of parents and grandparents. The union-formation behaviors of young people are also influenced by their parents' marital experiences, family organization, and patterns of interactions. Most remarkable is the fact that many dimensions of the parental family observed before or soon after a child is born can have strong implications for the union-formation behavior of the child many years later.

This chapter is motivated by the observation that parental families are not static entities, but dynamic and evolving organizations. Although children may experience many continuities in family life from infancy through childhood and into adolescence, most also experience numerous changes in their family environments. Many of these changes can be dramatic—even shocking—as in the case of parental divorce, death, or remarriage. Other parental family changes may also seem significant for the child, such as parental unemployment, entering the labor force for the first time, religious conversion, having a new baby, or going back to school. Other parental family changes may happen more slowly—sometimes even imperceptibly—yet

---

*Li-Shou Yang collaborated in the analysis and writing of this chapter.

profoundly modify children's environments between infancy and adolescence. Dimensions that may evolve over the years include parental familial and friendship networks, attitudes about appropriate roles for women and men, participation in religious communities, and financial well-being.

All these familial changes of childhood and adolescence have the potential for great influence in the lives of children. Changes in the composition of families and their economic well-being can modify the resources available to children as they transition to adulthood and make decisions about schooling, employment, and the formation of residential unions. Shifts in parental involvement in religious, familial, and friendship networks can change who children associate with and the values that permeate their environments. Parental experiences with divorce and remarriage may modify the views of both parents and children concerning union formation and dissolution, which, in turn, may affect the decisions of children as they make the transition to adulthood.

In this chapter we follow our study families as the children mature from infants in 1962 to teenagers in 1977. We examine how the children's marital and cohabitation decisions are related to their familial experiences during these years of childhood and early adolescence. Two types of family factors are considered. First, we examine how the educational, employment, childbearing, divorce, and remarriage experience of parents from birth to age fifteen relate to children's subsequent marital and cohabitation decisions. We also examine how parental financial resources, family size preferences, attendance at religious services, sex-role attitudes, and relationships with family and friends when the children are age 15 relate to the children's subsequent decisions about marriage and cohabitation. Inherent in these examinations is a comparison of the effects of parental factors and familial circumstances when the child is age 15 (1977) to the effects when the child was an infant (1962). That is, do parental factors observed relatively late in the lifetimes of children have similar influence as those relatively early in the lives of the children? We also ask to what extent parental experiences during these fifteen years operate as intervening factors transmitting the effect of parental factors earlier in the lives of the parents.

Data and Analytical Approach

In this chapter we examine information from the parental family between 1962 and 1977 when the child was maturing from infancy to adolescence.

We do so within five of the substantive domains of the parental family identified earlier: (1) socioeconomic standing, (2) marital experience, (3) childbearing, (4) religion, and (5) family organization. The three main parental socioeconomic dimensions we consider are the mother's educational attendance during these fifteen years, the mother's total years of education in 1977, and the family income in 1977 when the child was age 15. In the marriage arena we examine whether the parents experienced a marital dissolution during these fifteen years, and, if so, whether the mother remarried. Two dimensions of parental fertility are considered: the number of children born to the mother between 1962 and 1977 and the mother's preferred number of children when the child was 15. The only new religious dimension we introduce is maternal attendance at religious services in 1977. We consider four dimensions of family organization and interactions, each measured in 1977 when the child was 15: the mother's gregariousness, the mother's closeness to relatives, the mother's sex-role attitudes, and the mother's total years of employment from 1962 to 1977. Appendix table C.2 provides detailed definitions of each of these parental dimensions and summary statistics of their distribution in the sample. We do not introduce any new measures of migration or farm experience.

Our examination of the influence of parental experiences between the child's infancy and adolescence on children's decisions about marriage and cohabitation builds directly upon the work of the last chapter analyzing the features of the parental family at the child's infancy or earlier. We first reestimate Model 5.3 from table 5.1, predicting the children's rates of cohabitation and marriage using *only* the dimensions of the parental family observed by infancy in 1962 and examined in chapter 5. Results from these reestimated equations are listed in table 6.1 as Model 6.1. Model 6.1 is different from Model 5.3 in that it excludes two parental factors of Model 5.3—grandmother religiosity and religious marriage ceremony—because their total effects were entirely explained by the other parental dimensions in Model 5.3. The second difference between Models 5.3 and 6.1 is that families in which the mother died between 1962 and 1977 are excluded from Model 6.1 because they yield no 1977 information to use as predictors of children's union-formation experience.

We begin our examination by estimating the minimally controlled and maximally controlled total effects of each dimension of the parental family observed after the child's infancy in 1962 until the child was age 15. We do this by estimating the series of equations noted as Equations 4a and 4b in table A.1 of Appendix A. We estimate total effects with minimal

TABLE 6.1 **Adding the effects of parental circumstances during children's ages 1–15 to the effects of parental youth, young adulthood, and with young child experiences and circumstances on children's rates of entrance into marital and cohabiting unions (as competing destinations)**

	Marriage						Cohabitation					
	Model 6.1		Total effect (minimum control)		Model 6.2		Model 6.1		Total effect (minimum control)		Model 6.2	
	B[a]	Z[b]	B[a]	Z[b]	B[a]	Z[b]	B[a]	Z[b]	B[a]	Z[b]	B[a]	Z[b]
Family immigration/Farm background												
Immigration	−0.10	1.41			−0.14	1.95	−0.19	2.82			−0.16	2.29
Farm background	0.37	1.65			0.42	1.80	0.10	0.52			0.14	0.65
Parental socioeconomic standing												
1962 education	−0.07	2.28			−0.03	0.10	−0.03	0.91			−0.05	1.46
Additional maternal education 1962–77			−0.24	2.44	−0.15	1.36			−0.01	0.13	−0.17	1.65
1962 financial resources	−0.06	2.85			−0.06	2.31	−0.05	2.29			−0.04	1.83
1976 family income			−0.01	1.57	−0.01	2.06			−0.01	1.63	−0.01	1.16
1962 home ownership	−0.20	1.84			−0.28	2.53	−0.02	0.18			0.04	0.33
Maternal marital experience												
Age at marriage	0.00	0.24			0.00	0.03	−0.04	1.96			−0.01	0.58
Premarital pregnancy	0.04	0.31			0.07	0.45	0.28	1.92			0.14	1.04
Marital disruption by 1962	0.52	1.56			0.62	1.76	0.56	1.85			0.56	1.78
1962–1977 dissolution/remarriage												
Divorce not remarried 1962–1977			−0.20	0.95	−0.14	0.63			0.56	2.72	0.30	1.52
Divorce remarried 1962–1977			0.12	0.51	0.41	1.47			1.08	4.55	0.94	3.85
Widowed 1962–1977			−0.49	1.99	−0.48	1.87			0.74	2.34	0.88	2.59
Parental childbearing												
Number of siblings	0.01	0.22			0.00	0.06	−0.01	0.24			−0.01	0.29
2nd parity in 1961	0.01	0.09			0.13	0.87	0.17	1.25			0.24	1.63

	Model 1		Model 2		Model 3		Model 4	
	b[a]	Z[b]	b[a]	Z[b]	b[a]	Z[b]	b[a]	Z[b]
4th parity in 1961	0.10	0.60	0.32	1.54	0.06	0.36	0.28	1.45
1962–1977 children born	0.13	2.68	0.08	1.58	0.25	1.20	0.10	2.02
1961 birth unwanted	0.07	1.61	0.10	0.41	−0.03	0.60	0.16	0.79
1962 preferred number of children			0.02	0.48	−0.13	0.75	0.00	0.10
1977 preferred number of children	0.07	1.62	0.02	0.56	0.08	0.57	−0.03	0.93
Religion								
Maternal religious affiliation								
Fundamental Protestant	0.09	0.44	−0.02	0.10	0.22	0.78	0.02	0.13
Catholic	−0.22	1.76	−0.18	1.33	−0.08	2.08	0.04	0.33
Other	0.11	0.35	0.43	1.23	0.09	1.79	0.15	0.55
1962 religious attendance	0.13	2.88	0.09	1.87	−0.39	3.05	−0.03	0.75
1977 maternal religious attendance	0.11	2.70	0.10	2.26	0.12	1.54	−0.09	2.63
Family organization								
1962 gregariousness	0.09	1.84	0.09	1.67	0.07	1.50	0.04	0.77
1977 gregariousness	0.09	2.17	0.07	1.67	−0.03	0.89	0.06	1.48
1962 closeness to relatives	0.04	0.25	−0.06	0.39	−0.13	4.00	−0.32	2.43
1977 visiting relatives/friends	−0.03	0.56	−0.03	0.62	0.03	0.76	−0.08	1.96
1962 sex-role attitudes	−0.08	1.10	−0.03	0.39	−0.08	2.08	0.08	1.04
1977 sex-role attitudes	−0.22	2.91	−0.18	2.14	0.48	4.23	0.42	3.84
1962–1977 maternal employment	−0.03	1.77	0.00	0.08	0.03	1.90	0.00	0.16
No. of periods	102,726		102,726		102,726		102,726	
No. of events	380		380		426		426	
χ^2	399.38		435.43		269.72		332.68	
DF	25		37		25		37	

Notes: [a] Effect coefficient for logit equations transformed by equation: $[\exp(\beta) - 1]$.
[b] Z = ratio of absolute value of coefficient to its standard error.

controls through a series of equations that adds to Model 6.1 one (and only one) parental factor observed *after* the child's infancy. These estimates are listed in table 6.1 as "Total Effect Minimum Control." We estimate maximally controlled total effects of these new parental factors by including all of them simultaneously in Model 6.2, presented in table 6.1.

Model 6.2 also lists the coefficients for the parental factors observed by the child's infancy in 1962 and examined in chapter 5. These coefficients indicate the direct effects of these parental factors that do not operate through any of the parental factors considered in this chapter.

Although Model 6.2 contains parental dimensions from both early and late in the lives of the children, we do not use these data for direct comparisons of early and late effects. The reason is that in some cases we used somewhat different measures (in content and metric) of early and late parental dimensions, making direct comparisons of the early and late effect parameters in Model 6.2 difficult.[1]

These differences compelled us to estimate a different version of Model 6.2 where we maintain exact comparability between early and late measurement. We label these equations as Model 6.3 and report the results in table 6.2. Model 6.3, thus, provides comparisons of the effects of early and late parental characteristics on children's union-formation behavior in an equation containing all of the parental factors from the child's infancy and adolescence.

By estimating the effects of early and late parental characteristics simultaneously, we estimate the effect of each while controlling for the other. Thus, Model 6.3 controls for any indirect effects of early parental factors through later ones, as well as for any association between a late parental characteristic and children's union-formation experience that results from both being correlated with the early parental factor.

It is also useful to estimate the effects of late parental characteristics in one equation that does not include the comparable early parental dimension and contrast these effects with estimates of the effects of early parental factors in a second equation that does not include the comparable late parental dimensions. This approach provides comparisons of early and late parental factors without controlling the effects of each other. We estimated these two equations and report their results in table 6.3. In both equations we include six parental factors that we treat as fixed in this analysis: immigration, farm background, age at marriage, premarital pregnancy, 1962 religious affiliation, and 1961 birth unwanted. In our first equation, reported as Model 6.4 of table 6.3, we add to these fixed parental dimensions the 1962 versions of the other parental factors. In

TABLE 6.2 **Single equation comparisons of the effects of early and late dimensions of parents on children's rates of entrance into marital and cohabiting unions (as competing risks)**

	Marriages Model 6.3		Cohabitations Model 6.3	
	B^a	Z^b	B^a	Z^b
Family immigration/Farm background				
Immigration	−0.14	2.09	−0.16	2.35
Farm background	0.47	2.00	0.21	0.99
Parental socioeconomic standing				
Mother's 1962 education	−0.05	1.44	−0.02	0.55
Additional maternal education 1962–77	−0.16	1.45	−0.13	1.26
1961 family income[c]	−0.03	1.36	−0.02	1.19
1976 family income	−0.01	2.08	−0.01	1.46
1962 home ownership	−0.29	2.56	0.04	0.34
Maternal marital experience				
Age at marriage	0.00	0.16	−0.02	0.80
Premarital pregnancy	0.06	0.43	0.18	1.28
Marital disruption by 1962	0.50	1.49	0.55	1.75
1962–1977 dissolution/remarriage				
Divorce not remarried 1962–1977	−0.14	0.60	0.31	1.56
Divorce remarried 1962–1977	0.43	1.53	0.95	3.88
Widowed 1962–1977	−0.48	1.88	0.79	2.38
Parental childbearing				
Number of siblings	0.00	0.04	−0.01	0.29
2nd parity in 1961	0.15	1.01	0.26	1.78
4th parity in 1961	0.39	1.82	0.29	1.48
1962–1977 children born	0.09	1.76	0.09	1.79
1961 birth unwanted	0.03	0.12	0.19	0.91
1962 preferred number of children	0.03	0.69	−0.01	0.24
1977 preferred number of children	0.02	0.36	−0.04	0.92
Religion				
Maternal religious affiliation				
Fundamental Protestant	0.01	0.06	−0.01	0.07
Catholic	−0.17	1.28	0.07	0.48
Other	0.32	0.96	0.04	0.15
1962 maternal religious attendance[d]	0.07	1.54	−0.02	0.59
1977 maternal religious attendance	0.10	2.28	−0.10	2.96
Family organization				
1962 gregariousness	0.10	1.90	0.06	1.20
1977 gregariousness	0.07	1.65	0.06	1.48
1962 visiting relatives/friends[e]	0.02	0.50	0.01	0.24
1977 visiting relatives/friends	−0.04	0.72	−0.10	2.32
1962 sex-role attitudes	−0.03	0.35	0.07	0.90
1977 sex-role attitudes[f]	−0.14	1.77	0.24	2.65
1962–1977 maternal employment	0.00	0.16	0.01	0.95
No. of periods	102,726		102,726	
No. of events	380		426	
χ^2	430.91		315.05	
DF	37		37	

Notes: [a] Effect coefficient for logit equations transformed by equation: $[\exp(\beta) - 1]$.
[b] Z = ratio of absolute value of coefficient to its standard error.
[c] 1961 family income is measured the same as 1976 family income.
[d] 1962 maternal religious service attendance is measured the same as in 1977.
[e] 1962 close to relatives is measured the same as in 1977.
[f] 1977 sex-role attitudes are measured the same as 1966 sex-role attitudes.

TABLE 6.3 Two equation comparisons of the effects of early and late dimensions of parents on children's rates of entrance into marital and cohabiting unions (as competing destinations)

	Marriage				Cohabitation			
	Model 6.4		Model 6.5		Model 6.4		Model 6.5	
	Bᵃ	Zᵇ	Bᵃ	Zᵇ	Bᵃ	Zᵇ	Bᵃ	Zᵇ
Family immigration/Farm background								
Immigration	-0.12	1.75	-0.13	1.84	-0.19	2.90	-0.13	1.92
Farm background	0.40	1.78	0.32	1.48	0.16	0.79	0.28	1.31
Parental socioeconomic standing								
1962 maternal education[c]	-0.07	2.36			-0.01	0.36		
1977 maternal education[c]			-0.06	1.92			-0.05	1.64
1961 family income[d]	-0.05	2.82			-0.02	1.49		
1976 family income			-0.01	2.23			-0.01	1.79
Maternal marital experience								
Age at marriage	0.01	0.30	-0.02	0.79	-0.04	2.21	-0.03	1.47
Premarital pregnancy	0.09	0.63	0.20	1.27	0.31	2.18	0.22	1.57
Marital disruption by 1962	0.36	1.12			0.57	1.86		
1962–1977 dissolution /remarriage								
Divorced/not remarried 1962–1977			-0.17	0.77			0.34	1.70
Divorced/remarried 1962–1977			0.44	1.64			0.95	4.15
Widowed 1962–1977			-0.37	1.37			0.88	2.63
Parental childbearing								
Number of siblings	0.02	0.65	0.04	1.10	-0.01	0.20	-0.01	0.23
2nd parity in 1961	-0.02	0.13			0.18	1.39		
4th parity in 1961	0.03	0.18			0.09	0.59		
1962–77 children born			0.12	2.65			0.04	0.97
1961 birth unwanted	0.11	0.47	0.01	0.06	0.29	1.34	0.25	1.32
1962 preferred number of children	0.08	1.77			-0.04	0.89		
1977 preferred number of children			0.02	0.62			-0.02	0.73

Religion

	b	Z	b	Z	b	Z	b	Z
Maternal religious affiliation								
Fundamental Protestant	0.70	0.36	0.03	0.15	-0.13	0.78	0.03	0.18
Catholic	-0.20	1.57	-0.05	0.41	0.10	0.70	0.05	0.39
Other	0.10	0.32	0.27	0.83	0.04	0.15	0.03	0.11
1962 maternal religious attendance[e]	0.11	2.48	0.10	2.56				
1977 maternal religious attendance					-0.08	2.19	-0.12	3.79
Family organization								
1962 gregariousness	0.11	2.18	0.08	1.91				
1977 gregariousness					0.10	2.15	0.06	1.44
1962 visiting relatives/friends[f]	0.06	1.10	0.00	0.10				
1977 visiting relatives/friends					-0.02	0.46	-0.08	1.94
1962 sex-role attitudes	-0.09	1.21	-0.14	2.05				
1977 sex-role attitudes[g]					0.11	1.40	0.26	2.96
No. of periods	102,726		102,726		102,726		102,726	
No. of events	380		380		426		426	
χ^2	394.67		408.09		254.14		303.72	
DF	24		25		24		25	

Notes: [a] Effect coefficient for logit equations transformed by equation: $[\exp(\beta) - 1]$.
[b] Z = ratio of absolute value of coefficient to its standard error.
[c] Mother's years of education in 1962 and 1977 respectively.
[d] 1961 family income is measured the same as 1976 family income.
[e] 1962 religious service attendance is measured the same as in 1977.
[f] 1962 close to relatives is measured the same as in 1977.
[g] 1977 sex-role attitudes are measured the same as 1962 sex-role attitudes.

our second equation, Model 6.5 of table 6.3, we add to the fixed parental factors the 1977 versions of the other parental dimensions. The content and scale metrics used in table 6.2 are also used in table 6.3 to facilitate comparisons across the different estimates.

Parental Socioeconomic Standing

We include two aspects of parental socioeconomic status between the child's infancy and adolescence in our analyses. One is the mother's direct report in 1977 of her attendance at educational programs during the 15 years between the child's infancy and adolescence. This additional maternal educational factor is measured dichotomously and includes participation in both formal educational courses and training programs associated with employment.[2] Our second new socioeconomic dimension is family income when the child was age 15 in 1977, measured in thousands of 1962 dollars. Although we had a measure of 1977 parental assets, we did not use this dimension in our final analysis because it did not have substantial or significant effects on children's decisions about cohabitation and marriage.[3]

In chapter 5, we observed the strong negative influence of parental socioeconomic status measured shortly after the birth of the children on the rates of children's entrance into marital and cohabiting unions. From the data of table 6.1, we learn that parental socioeconomic achievements during the childhood and adolescent years of the children are also substantially negatively related to the rapidity of the children's entrance into marital and cohabiting unions. The minimally controlled total effects indicate that each thousand dollars of family income is associated with about a one percent lower rate of both cohabitation and marriage in the second generation. The mother receiving additional education between 1962 and 1977 was associated with between 15 and 17 percent lower rates of marriage and cohabitation among the children (maximally controlled). As with 1962 parental socioeconomic factors, the 1977 parental socioeconomic factors tend to have stronger effects on children's union-formation at ages 22 and younger than at ages 23 and older (not shown in tables).

The introduction of the post-1962 parental factors modifies the estimated influence of parental average education in 1962, when the child was an infant. This indicates that factors from the parental family during the children's adolescence are probably intervening mechanisms for the influence of parental education, with the effect of each unit of parental education on children's marriage rates more than halved—from −.07 to −.03—with the introduction of these factors (compare Model 6.2 with Model 6.1). More detailed analysis shows that 1976 family income and 1977 maternal sex-role attitudes are the most significant intervening factors. Parental education is positively associated with family economic resources, which tend to slow children's entrance into marriage and cohabitation. Parental education has a strong positive influence on the egalitarianism of maternal sex-role attitudes (Thornton and Freedman 1979). And, as we will discuss further later, children of egalitarian mothers enter marriage more slowly than others. Here, maternal egalitarianism alone accounts for between 1 and 2 percent lower rates of marriage for each unit of parental education.

Interestingly, the introduction of parental factors during the children's adolescence increases the magnitude of the effect of parental education on children's cohabitation from −.03 to −.05 (table 6.1). This means that there is an indirect positive effect of parental education through at least one of the parental factors during the children's adolescence that is suppressing the direct negative influence of education. The primary factor of importance here is 1977 maternal sex-role attitudes. High parental education is strongly related to 1977 egalitarian attitudes, which are positively associated with high rates of cohabitation in the second generation. The result is that each unit of parental education increases children's cohabitation rates by 3 to 4 percent.

The data in table 6.1 provide little information for evaluating the relative effects of early and late parental education. To address this issue we estimated the effects of mother's years of educational attainment in 1962 and 1977 in separate equations.[4] The results are shown in table 6.3 where we present estimates of the effects of 1962 maternal education in Model 6.4 and the effects of 1977 maternal education in Model 6.5. These data do not provide any compelling evidence that either early or late education had a stronger influence.

Family income in 1976 when the child was age 14 is also negatively related to the rapidity of the child's entrance into both cohabitation and marriage. Although the effect depends somewhat on the specification, each thousand dollars of income is associated with about a one percent lower rate of entrance into cohabitation and marriage (table 6.1). If we extrapolate this one percent difference across several thousand dollars of family income, the difference in union-formation rates can be rather substantial—being more than a 10 percentage point difference for a ten-thousand-dollar spread.[5]

The introduction of the post-1962 parental factors in Model 6.2 reduces only slightly the observed effects of 1962 parental financial resources on cohabitation and marriage. This means that parental resources during infancy have their own independent effect on the children's union-formation decisions, net of parental financial levels when the child is a teenager (i.e., not just because early financial resources are correlated with later financial resources).

In fact, the data provide evidence that parental resources in infancy may have a greater influence on children's union-formation decisions than parental resources when the children are age 15. This is suggested by our earlier observation that parental assets in 1977 are not significantly related to the children's subsequent union-formation decisions while 1962 parental assets are. Also, the results in table 6.2 suggest that parental family income in 1962 has a stronger influence on children's union-formation experience than parental family income in 1977. With the definitions and metrics of the two family income measures held constant, the estimated effect of 1962 income is substantially larger than the estimated effect of 1977 income in the same equation (Model 6.3 of table 6.2). The comparative coefficients for 1962 and 1976 family incomes on marriage are $-.03$ and $-.01$ respectively; for cohabitation the comparisons are $-.02$ and $-.01$. Similar differences between the 1962 and 1976 effects are observed for the two effects in separate equations (table 6.3).

These results suggest that parental financial resources have an influence that extends far beyond the simple availability of money for assistance and guidance during the years when children are making decisions about marriage and cohabitation. In fact, the influences of parental resources on children's union-formation decisions through early childhood socialization may be even more important than the influences of parental resources during young adulthood. To foreshadow a conclusion in chapter 11, we note here that we were unable to identify the intervening factors explaining this socioeconomic effect. The direct effects of parental socioeconomic standing remained strong despite the introduction of numerous additional factors.

Maternal Marital Experience

In the previous chapter we observed that maternal young age at marriage, premarital pregnancy, and marital dissolution before the birth of the child are all associated with more rapid entrance into residential unions in the second generation. Moreover, the effects are stronger for cohabitation than for marriage, suggesting that these dimensions of maternal marital experience not only influence the rapidity of union formation, but also the choice between marriage or cohabitation.

In this chapter we extend our investigation of the influence of maternal marital experiences by considering events between the birth of the child and the time the child turned age 15. We consider whether or not the parental marriage dissolved after the 1962 interview and, if so, whether the dissolution was caused by divorce or widowhood.[6] We further divide the group of dissolutions produced by divorce according to whether or not the mother remarried by 1977.[7]

One of the consistent effects of parental marital dissolution through both divorce and widowhood during the child's lifetime is its association with a substantially higher rate of cohabitation in the second generation (table 6.1). In the estimates with minimal controls, the total positive effects of parental marital dissolution on children's cohabitation rate range from 56 to 108 percent. Most of these effects are reduced with maximum controls but still range from 30 to 94 percent with the full controls of Model 6.2. There are no statistically significant positive effects of marital dissolution on children's marriage, and the effect of coming from a widowed family on marriage is negative.[8]

This differential effect of parental marital dissolution on children's marriage and cohabitation rates suggests it is closely tied to the choice between cohabitation and marriage. Our formal statistical tests confirm this expectation in that we find that the total effect for each of the three maternal marital experience categories—divorced/not remarried, divorced/remarried, and widowed—is to increase substantially children's likelihood of choosing cohabitation over marriage. Note that a strong influence of a parental marital dissolution on children's union-formation experience has been observed in numerous countries (Carmichael 1995; Kiernan 2000).

The apparent opposite effects of maternal marital history on marriage and cohabitation suggests that parental marital history may have little influence on the overall rate of entrance into unions. Estimation of total effects for this total union-formation rate are generally consistent with this expectation. The exception is the category of divorced/remarried, which is associated with a total union-formation rate that is 64 to 73 percent higher than the rate among children of the continuously married (results not shown).

A marital dissolution followed by maternal remarriage has a similar effect on children's union-formation rates regardless of whether it occurred before the birth of the child or during the child's infancy and adolescence. A dissolution/remarriage that occurs either before or after the birth of the child is associated with a higher total union-formation rate, increasing it by at least 50 percent (not shown in tables), and with higher rates of both cohabitation and marriage (although statistical significance is marginal). The most important difference is that dissolution/remarriage after the birth of the child is strongly associated with the child's choice of cohabitation over marriage whereas these events before the birth of the child are not. Interestingly, just as the marital factors observed at the time of the child's birth are more strongly related to the child's union formation at ages 22 and younger than at ages 23 and older, parental marital experience between the child's birth and age 15 is also more closely related to the child's union formation at the younger ages.

The similarity of the effects of marital dissolution/remarriage before and after the birth of the child suggests that it may not be the child's direct experience with parental marital dissolution that matters. The parental marital dissolution effect may have more to do with the transmission of attitudes or biogenetic characteristics from parents to children.

As we discussed in chapter 5, many parents experience cohabitation following a marital dissolution. We also know that this experience is especially common among those who remarry. There are reasons to believe that the children of mothers who cohabit following a marital dissolution have especially high rates of cohabitation themselves, and data from the 1995 National Survey of Family Growth are consistent with this expectation (Teachman 2003). We were able to evaluate this hypothesis in our own data set because we asked the mothers in 1993 about their histories of marital dissolution, remarriage, and cohabitation. These measures permit us to ascertain whether the mothers had experienced a nonmarital cohabitation between 1962 and 1977. Although the samples of widowed women or divorced/not remarried women reporting cohabitation between 1962 and 1977 were too small for separate analyses, the distribution of divorced/remarried women between those who had cohabited and those who had not was sufficient for tentative comparisons between these two groups.

Our comparisons showed that the cohabitation rates of the children of these two groups are nearly identical—both being about twice as high as the rates of the children of continuously married women. The children of cohabiting remarried women had slightly higher marriage rates, but this difference is far from statistically significant. Thus, our results are inconsistent with our hypothesis that maternal cohabitation is related to higher rates of cohabitation among the children. Our samples of cohabiting and noncohabiting remarried women, however, are relatively small, suggesting that our test of this hypothesis is weak.

In chapter 5 we observed that premarital pregnancy in the parental generation is associated with a higher rate of cohabitation. Here, we note that the marital dissolution experience of the mothers between 1962 and 1977 is an important intervening factor transmitting that effect. Couples in the parental generation who were pregnant at marriage had higher dissolution rates between 1962 and 1977, and, as we have just reported, a marital dissolution was associated with much higher cohabitation rates in the second generation.[9] The magnitude of this indirect effect is approximately 3 percent.

In addition, part of the effects of a parental premarital pregnancy operate through maternal sex-role attitudes in 1977. Mothers who were premaritally pregnant hold substantially more egalitarian sex roles than others, which in turn are related to higher rates of children's entrance into cohabiting unions. This indirect effect alone can account for children of premaritally pregnant mothers having about 3 percent higher cohabitation rates.

Parental Childbearing Attitudes and Behavior

We examined two dimensions of parental childbearing in the children's postinfancy period between 1962 and 1977. The first is the number of children born to the mother in this 15-year interval, and the second is the mother's preferred number of children as reported in 1977 (a replication of the measure for preferred number of children in 1962).

Both 1962–1977 childbearing and fertility preferences in 1977 have significant total effects on children's union-formation decisions. Each child born during this 15-year interval is associated with between 8 and 13 percent higher marriage rates and between 7 and 10 percent higher cohabitation rates in the second generation. With minimal controls, family size preferences in 1977 when the child was an adolescent have a positive total effect on the children's marriage rate but not on the children's cohabitation rate. However, with the introduction of maximum controls in Model 6.2, the effect of maternal fertility preferences on children's marriage virtually disappears. In addition, the effect of 1962 fertility preferences is virtually eliminated by the controls of Model 6.2, suggesting that fertility preferences when the child was an infant have an influence on children's union formation by virtue of their influence on subsequent maternal childbearing (pearsonian correlation, $r = .29$). Similarly, 1977 fertility preferences are probably not important influences on children's union-formation experience, but are positively associated with them because they are correlated with the actual fertility of the mother ($r = .32$).[10]

With the introduction of Model 6.2 controls, the estimated effects of 1961 parity also change in very interesting ways. The effects of having both two and four children in 1961, as compared to having only one child, increase dramatically with Model 6.2 controls. This occurs because of the strong negative correlation between number of children in the family in 1961 and the number born between 1962 and 1977.[11] Model 6.2 eliminates the suppressor effect of this negative correlation on the positive effect of 1961 parity by controlling for additional childbearing, which increases the estimated positive effect of 1961 parity substantially.[12]

A more detailed examination of Model 6.2 shows that the effects of the various indicators of actual family size are remarkably consistent across the entire period from the birth of the sample child to age 15. Looking first at the effect of the mother having two children in 1961 versus having only one, we see that in Model 6.2 it increases the marriage rate by 13 percent and the cohabitation rate by 24 percent. The effect of the mother having four children rather than one is to increase the marriage rate by 32 percent and the cohabitation rate by 28 percent. These fourth-parity coefficients suggest that each additional child is associated with an approximately 10 percent increase in children's marriage and cohabitation rates. Although this interpolated rate per child is lower than implied by the difference between children of first- and second-parity mothers in 1961, it is almost identical with the 8 to 10 percent increase associated with each child born after 1962. These findings suggest that each additional sibling— irrespective of whether the siblings are older or younger than the study child—is associated with an approximately 10 percent higher rate of entrance into marital and cohabiting unions.

In a separate equation we estimated the effects of the total number of children ever born to the mother—a measure that is the sum of 1961 parity and children born between 1962 and 1977. We substituted this summary indicator of fertility for its two components and for preferred fertility in 1962 and 1977. With this specification we estimated the positive effect of each additional child ever born to be 11 percent for the children's marriage rate and 6 percent for the children's cohabitation rate.

Religion

We introduce one postinfancy indicator of religiosity in this chapter: the attendance of the mother at religious services when the child was age 15 in 1977. This information was collected and coded identically to the information about the mother's attendance at religious services when the child was an infant in 1962. Data were also collected from the mothers about their husbands' attendance in 1977. However, we are not using the husband's data in this chapter because many of the mothers were divorced or widowed and had either remarried someone other than the study child's father or had not remarried and so had no husband about whom to report. In chapter 8 where we focus more exclusively on religion, we include the religious service attendance of fathers who remained continuously married to mothers between 1962 and 1977.

The data in table 6.2 indicate that the direction of the effects of maternal 1977 religious service attendance when the child was 15 are extremely similar to the effects we reported in chapter 5 for 1962 parental service attendance when the child was an infant. Children of mothers who attended religious services frequently in 1977 have substantially higher marriage rates and substantially lower cohabitation rates than other children. In fact, each additional unit on our six-point attendance scale is associated with a 10 or 11 percent increase in the marriage rate and a decrease of 9 to 13 percent in the cohabitation rate. If we shift the dependent variable from entrance into cohabitation and marriage to the choice between the two residential forms, we find that each unit on the attendance scale is associated with a reduction of between 20 and 24 percent in the odds of choosing cohabitation over marriage (not shown in tables). Extrapolating this difference across three units of the attendance scale (for example, from attending less than once a month to attending once a week), lowers the odds of choosing cohabitation over marriage about one-half.[13]

A supplemental analysis of the total union-formation rate (ignoring the cohabitation-marriage distinction) indicates that maternal religious attendance has no effect (not shown in tables). The high rates of marriage and low rates of cohabitation among the children of more religious mothers cancel each other, leaving no effect of religiosity on the total union-formation rate. Additional analyses not shown in tables indicate that enough of the children who initially cohabit go on to marry that each unit of maternal service attendance is associated with only a 4 percent increase in the total marriage rate that ignores whether cohabitation occurred earlier.[14]

Turning our attention from 1977 maternal attendance to the attendance of both parents in 1962, we find that the introduction of multivariate controls in Model 6.2 reduces the influence of 1962 parental attendance on both marriage and cohabitation. The reductions between Models 6.1 and 6.2 in the effects of a one-point unit change in average parental attendance on the three central factors of interest are: from .13 to .09 on marriage; from −.08 to −.03 on cohabitation; and from −.20 to −.14 on the choice of cohabitation over marriage. Note that although the effect of 1962 religious attendance on cohabitation is reduced to nonsignificance in Model 6.2, the effects on the rate of marriage and on the choice between cohabitation and marriage remain strongly significant. These results clearly show an effect of early religiosity in the parental home that is not mediated by subsequent parental religiosity. Although early parental religiosity may influence children's union-formation behavior through the subsequent religiosity of the parents and other later dimensions of the parental family, this is clearly not the entire story. Even when all of the parental factors from the child's adolescence are controlled (Model 6.2), there remains a direct influence of early parental religious attendance on children's subsequent behavior.

Having emphasized the enduring direct effects of 1962 parental religious attendance, we do note that its influence is significantly reduced by the additional parental controls of Model 6.2—primarily by 1977 religious attendance. That is, our findings indicate that, in addition to the direct effects of 1962 parental religiosity, it also affects children's decisions indirectly, through its influence on 1977 parental religiosity. This interpretation is substantiated further by an equation that adds only 1977 service attendance to Model 6.1. This yields coefficients for the effects of 1962 attendance on both marriage and cohabitation that are very similar to those estimated in Model 6.2 (results not shown).

These results indicate that the persistence of parental religiosity across the life courses of parents and children is an important explanation of the influence of early parental religiosity on children's union-formation behavior (not shown in figures). Parental religiosity tends to be stable from the children's births to their adolescence, and parental religiosity during adolescence influences children's cohabitation and marriage. This indirect effect through parental religiosity when the child is an adolescent produces a 4 to 5 percent increase in marriage rates and a 4 to 6 percent decrease in cohabitation rates for each unit of 1962 parental religiosity. Given that our measure of parental religiosity contains several gradations, these

are substantial indirect effects. Thus, the consistency of parental religiosity across the life course is an important element of the union-formation
process among young adults.

Family Organization

We examine four dimensions of family organization and interaction during the years between the child's infancy and adolescence, two of which
flow directly out of the measures analyzed in chapter 5 for the child's infancy. Maternal gregariousness in 1977 is measured the same as it was in
1962—the sum of the frequency of getting together with friends and relatives. Sex-role attitudes in 1977, conceptually identical to the 1962 measure, is gauged as the average response (on a five-point scale) to eight sex-
role attitude items—a repeat of the four used in 1962 plus four additional
items (Thornton, Alwin, and Camburn 1983). A third indicator, new in
1977, measures the difference between the frequency of seeing relatives
and seeing friends. The fourth family organization dimension examined
here, also new in 1977, is the 1962–1977 employment of the mother, measured in number of years of full-time equivalent work hours.

A perusal of the total effects of table 6.1 indicates that, as expected,
the 1977 indicators of these dimensions of family organization have similar effects to those observed in 1962. As in 1962, maternal gregariousness
in 1977 is associated with a more rapid rate of entrance into residential
unions, being statistically significant for marriage but not for cohabitation.
In a supplemental analysis, we ignored the difference between cohabitation and marriage and found that a unit of gregariousness is associated
with a statistically significant 6 or 7 percent increase in the overall rate of
union formation (not shown in tables). Also, the observed effect on the
choice between cohabitation and marriage is neither large nor statistically
significant (results not shown). Thus, 1977 maternal gregariousness is related to a higher overall rate of union formation but has little relationship
to the choice between cohabitation and marriage—a conclusion that is
identical to our chapter 5 results for the effects of 1962 maternal gregariousness.

Looking at the effects of maternal gregariousness when the child was
an infant, we find that the introduction of Model 6.2 controls reduces its
effect on the total union-formation rate from 10 to 7 percent (not shown
in tables). That is, approximately three percentage points of the effect of

1962 gregariousness that did not operate through 1962 parental factors is now found to operate through post-1962 parental factors.

However, even with these Model 6.2 controls, the direct influence of 1962 maternal gregariousness remains substantial (7 percent) and statistically significant. This means that early childhood socialization with a gregarious mother has an effect on the child that carries over to adulthood quite independently of later maternal gregariousness. Furthermore, the direct effects of maternal gregariousness in 1962 and 1977 on the total union-formation rate are nearly identical when estimated in the equation of Model 6.2. For example, in Model 6.2 the estimated effects of 1962 and 1977 maternal gregariousness are both 7 percent (not shown in tables). Even the effects of 1962 and 1977 gregariousness on the individual components of marriage and cohabitation are similar, as can be seen in table 6.1.[15] Because both the 1962 and 1977 gregariousness measures range from zero to eight, this implies a very dramatic difference in the union-formation rates of children whose mothers were high on the scale in both years as compared to children of mothers who were low in both years.[16]

Maternal visiting with relatives compared to friends in 1977 uses the same two measures used for the 1977 gregariousness indicator—frequency of visiting relatives and frequency of visiting friends. However, instead of summing the indicators, we subtract them to indicate whether visiting is more frequent with relatives than with friends. The 1977 maternal visiting dimension, thus, varies from minus four (never seeing relatives and seeing friends almost every day) to plus four (seeing relatives almost every day and never seeing friends).

Maternal visiting with relatives versus friends has no statistically significant influence on the marriage rate, but each unit on the scale reduces the rate of cohabitation by 8 percent. Given that this indicator ranges across 9 points, this represents a substantial difference between the cohabitation experience of children of mothers who only see relatives and visit with them frequently and children of mothers who only see friends and visit with them frequently.

Table 6.1 does not contain a comparable indicator of Visiting Relatives/Friends in 1962, but in tables 6.2 and 6.3 we construct one that is identical to the 1977 measure. These analyses clearly indicate that late maternal visiting patterns affect children's cohabitation decisions much more than early visiting patterns. In fact, whereas the 1977 indicator has a substantial influence, the effect of 1962 visiting is small and statistically insignificant in these models.

Although maternal visiting patterns early in a child's life do not seem to be related to the child's union-formation decisions, we saw in chapter 5 that early parental closeness to relatives is negatively related to children's cohabitation. The data in table 6.1 show that while the controls in Model 6.2 reduce the observed effect of 1962 maternal closeness to relatives on cohabitation, it remains substantial even with full controls. Children are apparently strongly influenced by whether or not their mothers feel close to relatives during childhood, and this influence carries over into the cohabitation decisions of the children many years later.[17]

In chapter 5 we noted that the effect of maternal closeness to relatives on children's cohabitation experience operates primarily by decreasing the rate of entrance into cohabitations where there is no commitment to marriage. Here we note that the same is true for maternal visiting with relatives more than friends when the child is an adolescent. That is, maternal connections with relatives does not limit children's cohabitation when there are marital plans, but they do when there are no marriage plans.

The effects of maternal sex-role attitudes in 1977 directly parallel the effects of 1962 maternal sex-role attitudes, but with greater force. Children of mothers with more egalitarian sex-role attitudes marry substantially slower and cohabit substantially faster than other children. As documented in table 6.1, an increase of one unit on the sex-role attitude scale is associated with an 18 to 22 percent decline in children's rate of marriage and a 42 to 48 percent increase in the rate of cohabitation. Because the 1977 sex-role attitude scale is the average of eight individual sex-role attitude items, an increase in one unit on the scale is equivalent to an increase of one unit on each of the eight items. Mothers who agreed with all of the individual egalitarian items (an average score of 4 on the scale) would have children with marriage rates about 40 percent lower and cohabitation rates at least twice as high as the children of mothers who disagreed with all of the individual egalitarian items (an average score of 2 on the scale). If we compare the choice between cohabitation and marriage for those children who experience either, we find that each unit on the 1977 sex-role attitudes scale is associated with a doubling of the odds of cohabitation (not shown in tables).

As one would expect, the effect of 1977 sex-role attitudes on marriage ignoring cohabitation is not as great as the effect of these attitudes on marriage with cohabitation as a distinct destination (results not shown). The reason is that many of the young people who cohabit subsequently enter marriage very rapidly. Nevertheless, each unit on the 1977 sex-role

attitude scale reduces marriage ignoring cohabitation by a statistically significant 13 to 16 percent, as compared to a reduction of about 20 percent
on marriage with cohabitation as a competing destination.

The observed effects of 1962 sex-role attitudes are almost completely
eliminated by the introduction of the Model 6.2 controls—primarily by
the factor of 1977 maternal sex-role attitudes.[18] This suggests that 1962
maternal sex-role attitudes influence children's union-formation decisions
primarily because of their association with 1977 attitudes. Very little of
the 1962 maternal attitudes effects operate independently of the 1977 attitudes.

Although the coefficients for 1962 sex-role attitudes in table 6.1 are
much smaller than those for 1977 sex-role attitudes, one must be cautious
about comparing them because the content and metric of the 1962 and the
1977 sex-role attitude scales are different. To compare the magnitudes of
the effects of the two scales we turn to table 6.2, where we define the 1977
scale exactly as we did in 1962, dropping the four new items and averaging only the four items that were used in 1962. From table 6.2 we see
that the direct effects of 1962 maternal attitudes on children's marriage
is −.03 compared to the effect of −.14 for 1977 maternal attitudes. Similarly, each unit of 1962 maternal attitudes on children's cohabitation is .07
compared to the same unit effect of .24 for 1977 attitudes. The effects of
1977 attitudes are even stronger than the effects of 1962 attitudes when
the two are evaluated in separate equations (see table 6.3). These results
suggest that the direct effects of early maternal attitudes are smaller than
the effects of later maternal attitudes.

Turning now to maternal employment, we find that the children of
mothers who worked extensively have significantly lower rates of marriage and significantly higher rates of cohabitation than other children.
Each full-time-equivalent year of maternal employment between the child's
birth and age 15 is associated with a 5 percent higher likelihood of choosing cohabitation over marriage (not shown in tables). This effect of maternal employment is, thus, in exactly the same direction as 1962 and 1977
sex-role attitudes. However, the introduction of additional multivariate
controls in Model 6.2 totally eliminates these effects. This indicates that
maternal employment between 1962 and 1977 is associated with the marriage and cohabitation decisions of children only because it is related to
other post-1962 parental factors that are highly related to children's decisions.

We have one more comment to make about the direct effects of the
family organization factors. In subsequent chapters, we introduce many

additional factors associated with children's union-formation experience. However, the effects of maternal gregariousness, closeness to relatives, and visiting relatives/friends are not substantially modified and remain strong throughout. This indicates that additional research will be required to identify the intervening mechanisms transmitting these effects to children's union-formation experience. However, as we will report in chapter 9, we are successful in identifying factors transmitting the effects of maternal sex-role attitudes.

Summary and Conclusions

The analyses in this chapter provide strong support for the idea that the circumstances of the parental family during childhood and adolescence are strongly related to the children's later union-formation experience. Every dimension of the parental family that we examined—socioeconomic standing, marital experience, childbearing, religion, and family organization—is related to children's union-formation experience. Furthermore, the effects of the parental factors from the children's childhoods and adolescence are remarkably similar to those of the parents' own childhood and early adulthood. This provides strong support for the idea that the effects of parental factors are very similar throughout the life courses of children.

The results of this chapter also indicate that, for the most part, both early and late parental factors are important. Although some of the effects of early parental characteristics operate primarily through later characteristics, most early parental characteristics have direct effects as well. Furthermore, many of the effects of parental factors occurring at or before the child's birth are as large as parental effects during childhood and adolescence. In fact, for the socioeconomic factors, there is a tendency for the effects of the early parental factors to be stronger than the effects of later parental factors. This is an important observation because it suggests that the experiences of very young children in the parental home have important and lasting influences that cannot be explained by later parental circumstances.

The primary exceptions to this strong conclusion about the importance of early parental factors are in the areas of parental religion and family organization. Although these early parental factors have strong total effects, their influence is reduced substantially—although not eliminated—when the later parental factors are introduced into the analysis. This suggests that the effects of these early factors are primarily indirect through later parental factors.

Finally, we summarize the results of this chapter through the creation of a new base model that will serve as the package of 1962–1977 controls for analyses of the effects of parental and child factors from later in the life course. This new base model trims and consolidates the factors included in Model 6.2 by dropping factors that do not have direct effects on either marriage or cohabitation in that model. Also, in those instances where the direct effects of comparable factors from 1962 and 1977 are of similar magnitude, we combine them into a single scale. This more parsimonious model is presented as Model 6.6 of table 6.4.

More specifically, our new base model of 1962–1977 effects (Model 6.6) deviates from Model 6.2 by dropping mother's number of siblings, 1962 parity, 1962–1977 children born, and 1962 and 1977 preferred number of children, and by adding number of children ever born by 1977. As documented earlier in the chapter, 1977 children ever born provides a parsimonious summary of the effects of parental and preferred family size on children's union-formation experience. We also drop 1962 sex-role attitudes and 1962–1977 employment experience because any direct effects of these factors work through the other factors included in our analysis, especially 1977 sex-role attitudes. Finally, because of the very similar direct effects of 1962 and 1977 maternal gregariousness, we combine these two factors into a scale by taking their average.

Race Differences

Again these results from the Intergenerational Panel Study come from White respondents, and have no immediate inference to other groups in the United States, such as African Americans or Hispanic Americans. Nevertheless, the results provide some information useful for understanding marriage and cohabitation in those groups. We document strong, long-lasting consequences on union formation of many dimensions of the parental family in the White population. Though the data used here cannot demonstrate this directly, it seems likely there may be long-lasting effects of these factors among other racial and ethnic groups as well. For example, such intergenerational influences are consistent with known race differences such as consistently lower rates of marriage among African Americans across long time periods (Morgan et al. 1993) and lower desires to get married among African Americans (South 1993).

TABLE 6.4 **New summary base model of the effects of 1962 and 1977 dimensions of parents on children's rates of entrance into marital and cohabiting unions (as competing destinations)**[a]

| | Model 6.6 | | | |
| | Marriage | | Cohabitation | |
	B	Z	B	Z
Family immigration/Farm background				
Immigration	−0.14	2.03	−0.15	2.14
Farm background	0.43	1.96	0.13	0.67
Parental socioeconomic standing				
1962 education	−0.04	1.04	−0.05	1.46
Additional maternal education 1962−1977	−0.15	1.38	−0.18	1.79
1962 financial resources	−0.05	2.31	−0.04	1.96
1976 family income	−0.01	1.97	−0.01	1.21
1962 home ownership	−0.27	2.72	0.06	0.55
Maternal marital experience				
Age at marriage	0.00	0.05	−0.01	0.67
Premarital pregnancy	0.07	0.47	0.16	1.14
Marital disruption by 1962	0.62	1.82	0.51	1.71
1962−1977 dissolution/remarriage				
Divorce not remarried 1962−1977	−0.17	0.75	0.35	1.75
Divorce remarried 1962−1977	0.40	1.46	0.89	3.90
Widowed 1962−1977	−0.46	1.82	0.81	2.49
Parental childbearing				
1962−1977 children born	0.11	2.84	0.06	1.59
1961 birth unwanted	0.07	0.30	0.18	0.98
Religion				
Maternal religious affiliation				
Fundamental Protestant	−0.03	0.15	0.04	0.19
Catholic	−0.17	1.24	0.04	0.32
Other	0.42	1.21	0.16	0.60
1962 religious attendance	0.10	1.96	−0.03	0.86
1977 maternal religious attendance	0.10	2.27	−0.09	2.76
Family organization				
Average gregariousness 1962−1977	0.16	2.62	0.10	1.70
1962 closeness to relatives	−0.07	0.43	−0.32	2.41
1977 visiting relatives/friends	−0.03	0.67	−0.08	2.00
1977 sex-role attitudes	−0.19	2.44	0.46	4.35
No. of periods	102,726		102,726	
No. of events	380		426	
χ^2	434.37		328.59	
DF	29		29	

Notes: [a]Model 6.6 utilizes data for the entire sample by imputing values for the few cases with missing data.
[b]Effect coefficient for logit equations transformed by equation: $[\exp(\beta) - 1]$.
[c]Z = ratio of absolute value of coefficient to its standard error.

Conclusion

Both early childhood and adolescent intergenerational factors have strong, long-lasting consequences for marital and cohabiting behavior. Early childhood parental socioeconomic characteristics and marital and childbearing experiences have strong consequences for marriage and cohabitation that cannot be explained by later childhood parental characteristics and experiences. By contrast, later childhood parental religion and religiosity and the social organization of parental families in later childhood both explain much of the early childhood effects in these same domains. Equally important, the effects of these different parental dimensions remain largely independent of one another. Multiple dimensions of the parental family simultaneously shape young adults' marital and cohabiting choices. Of course, as we have stated before, the strong empirical associations we observe may or may not reflect independent causal forces. Nevertheless, the associations documented in this chapter are consistent with our theoretical framework predicting strong, multidimensional intergenerational influences on the timing of union formation, the choice between marriage and cohabitation, and the rates of both marriage and cohabitation.

PART III

**Parent and Child Factors during the
Children's Young Adulthood**

CHAPTER SEVEN

The Courtship Process and Union Formation*

In this part of the book, Part III, we shift from an exclusive focus on parental influences during the years of childhood and adolescence to examination of the influence of both parents and children during the years when the children are making decisions about union formation. In these chapters we add parental aspirations and values, as well as the behavior, experiences, and values of the young adults themselves, as predictors of union formation. Our goal here is to examine the many ways in which the attitudes, plans, experiences, and behaviors of young adults influence subsequent decisions about marriage and cohabitation.

The chapters in Part III focus on the courtship process; religious affiliation and commitment; family attitudes and values; educational aspirations and experience; and occupational achievements. We considered several of these domains in terms of first-generation influence in chapters 5 and 6 of Part II. In Part III we examine each of these domains of influence on behavior more intensively by devoting a chapter to each of them.

Many of the predictors of union formation that we examine in this part of the book are, themselves, interconnected in a complex nexus of causal relationships. That is, parental aspirations and values; children's religiosity and courtship; and the educational and occupational aspirations and achievements of the children are all causally interrelated. This makes it

*Linda Young-DeMarco collaborated in the analysis and writing of this chapter.

difficult to construct a model specifying the nature of their total, direct, and indirect influences on union-formation experience. Consequently, the primary goal of this part of the book is to establish the total effects of these factors on union formation with minimal controls. We do this by considering the influence of the individual factors in equations that control for parental factors measured through age 15, but that do not control for later explanatory factors. This examination of total effects is supplemented with some effort to examine which aspects of a particular domain may be the most relevant or important. In the later chapters of Part III, we provide a detailed examination of some of the direct and indirect pathways accounting for the influences of the explanatory factors considered here.

In the present chapter we focus on how the heterosexual experiences of the children during their adolescent years—specifically dating, going steady, and sexual initiation—are related to the timing of union formation and the choice between cohabitation and marriage. We consider the effects of both the timing of the initiation of these courtship experiences and the intensity and extensiveness of heterosexual relationships during late adolescence. We also investigate how pregnancies occurring before the initiation of residential unions influence entrance into marriage and cohabitation.

Theoretical Framework

Marriage and cohabitation in young adulthood are in many ways the culmination of years of heterosexual interaction and experimentation. Adolescence finds young women and men experiencing intense physiological changes. Social constraints change and the forms of heterosexual experience expand in an experimental and cumulative process played out across the years of adolescence and young adulthood (Ehrmann 1959; Miller, McCoy, and Olson 1986; Miller et al. 1997; Thornton 1990). As children mature into adolescence, they usually begin to date, form steady relationships, and make decisions about sexual intimacy. For most young people this process eventually leads to cohabitation and/or marriage.

Of course, the timing of the initiation of dating and going steady varies substantially across the adolescent years, as does sexual experience (Cooksey, Mott, and Neubauer 2002; Hofferth and Hayes 1987; Miller, McCoy, and Olson 1986; Miller et al. 1997; Moore et al. 1995; Thornton 1990). The experience of intimacy and commitment within relationships can be slow or rapid, with possible reversals as well as expansions of commitment

(Furman, Brown, and Feiring 1999; Surra 1990). Many dating relationships—even ones that become quite steady—end because of conflict, lack of interest, or better alternatives. Nevertheless, most young people increase their involvement in dating across time, spend more time together as couples, and become more intensely involved in the courtship process (Surra 1990).

Previous research demonstrates that the tempo of dating and going steady is important for the initiation of sexual relationships (Cooksey, Mott, and Neubauer 2002; Ehrmann 1959; Miller, McCoy, and Olson 1986; Miller et al. 1997; Peplau, Rubin, and Hill 1977; Reiss 1960, 1964, 1967; Reiss and Miller 1979; Schofield 1965; Thornton 1990; Whyte 1990; Zelnik, Kanter, and Ford 1981). Those who begin to date at an early age also tend to develop steady relationships early and continue to date more frequently, which all have implications for the initiation of sexual relations (Cooksey, Mott, and Neubauer 2002; Ehrmann 1959; Reiss and Miller 1979; Schofield 1965; Thornton 1990; Whyte 1990). Young people who begin dating early and who develop steady relations early are more likely to be sexually experienced, to have had more sexual partners, and to have more permissive attitudes concerning premarital sex (Miller et al. 1997; Thornton 1990; Whyte 1990).

These findings suggest that as young women and men gain experience with one level of involvement, they become prepared for more intensive courtship and sexual involvement, and momentum builds toward more intensive commitment. Thus we hypothesize that early and intensive dating, going steady, and entrance into a sexual relationship lead to early formation of coresidential unions. This hypothesis is consistent with past research showing that active dating and early sexual involvement is associated with early marriage (Bartz and Nye 1970; Gaughan 2002; Klassen et al. 1989; Marini 1985; Miller and Heaton 1991; Otto 1979; Whyte 1990), and we expect a similar relationship for entrance into cohabiting unions (Laumann et al. 1994; Kiernan and Hobcraft 1997).

In fact, we expect the effect of early dating and sexual initiation to be stronger for cohabitation than for marriage because those with early and frequent nonmarital sexual experiences may find it easier than their counterparts to transition into a cohabiting union, and may be more likely to choose cohabitation over marriage. In addition, among people who choose to cohabit, those with early sexual experience may feel less compelled than others to transform the cohabitation into marriage. The influence of these courtship processes on entrance into cohabitation and marriage can be particularly important when they result in a nonmarital pregnancy. Although the forces requiring marriage to legitimate nonmarital pregnancies are less powerful today than in the past, pregnancy and childbearing can still provide an important impetus to marriage (Manning 1993, 1995; Manning and Landale 1996).

Attitudes toward sex outside of marriage may be a particularly important factor linking early sexual experience with later union-formation experience. Consensual, nonmarital sexual relations in adolescence are an indication of acceptance of sex outside of marriage. It is likely that such attitudes in adolescence continue into young adulthood, where they are associated with greater willingness to enter cohabiting unions. The likely result is that young people with adolescent sexual experience enter coresidential unions more rapidly than others—and more often choose cohabitation rather than marriage.

We also posit two main paths through which early dating, going steady, and sexual initiation can *indirectly* influence union formation. One is through their influence on religious commitment and attitudes, values, and aspirations toward marriage and family. People who initiate romantic and sexual experiences early may decrease their religious commitment and become more approving of premarital sex, cohabitation, and divorce, which in turn influence entrance into marriage and cohabitation (Billy et al. 1988; Salts et al. 1994; Thornton and Camburn 1989; Zelnik, Kanter, and Ford 1981). Second, early dating and sex may also affect union formation indirectly through their effects on educational experiences. Romantic relationships require a person to devote time and energy that can jeopardize school performance and aspirations (Billy et al. 1988; Jessor et al. 1983; Zelnik, Kanter, and Ford 1981). These indirect mechanisms suggest that early dating, going steady, and sex lead to higher rates of union formation, with preference for cohabitation over marriage, and lower rates of marriage among cohabitors.

We also expect that additional causal factors contribute to a positive correlation between the timing of union formation and the tempo of courtship experience in adolescence. Foremost among these is the possibility that early dating and sexual experience is selective of people with characteristics that also lead to early cohabitation and marriage. That is, there may be some enduring factors of individuals early in life—for example, physical appearance, social skills, or hormonal levels—that lead to higher or lower levels of emotional, dating, and sexual involvement at many points in the life course. Especially attractive young people with strong social skills and interests in the opposite sex may be more interested and more successful in pursuing (or being pursued for) dating, courtship, and union formation (Miller and Heaton 1991; Thornton 1990).

Data and Analytical Approach

The data for this chapter were obtained primarily from the 1980 interview with the young adults when they were eighteen years old. During this interview all of the young adults were asked about the timing of the initiation of first dating, first going steady, and first sexual intercourse (see Appendix C, table C.3).[1] The ages of first dating, first going steady, and first sexual intercourse are provided in table 7.1. As we note there, only about 3 percent of these eighteen-year-olds indicated that they had never had a date, 24 percent said that they had never gone steady, and 39 percent reported no sexual experience. The initiation of dating begins early in the teenage years, with about one-third of our sample reporting dating before age 15; one-fourth while age 15; and three-tenths while age 16. Going steady generally begins at an older age, but still about one-third reported going steady before age 16, and about one-fifth at each of ages 16 and 17. Sexual debut generally occurs at yet older ages. Although a few teenagers reported first sexual intercourse at ages 13 and 14 (about one in twelve), more than four-fifths reported they were 16 or older. Interestingly, males generally report younger initiation of dating and sexual intercourse, but are similar to females in their reports of age of first steady relationship.

It is important to note that reports of sexual experience are subject to recall error (Lewontin 1995). There is not only the issue of random misreporting, but the possibility of conscious underreporting or exaggeration. Furthermore, given the sexual double standard, it is possible that the nature and direction of misreporting varies by the gender of the respondent, with men exaggerating and women minimizing sexual experience. Such errors can bias the estimates of actual effects.

In our analyses predicting entrance into marital and cohabiting unions we turned the data about the ages at first dating, going steady, and sexual intercourse into a series of categorical zero-one variables. As documented in Appendix table C.3, we categorized age at first date into four zero-one variables: age 13 or younger, age 14, age 15, and age 16. People who had never dated or who first dated at age 17 or older comprise the omitted category. We categorized age at first going steady into the same four age

TABLE 7.1 **Percentage distribution of timing of first date, going steady, and sexual intercourse**

	Males	Females	Total
Age at first date			
13 or younger	21	9	15
14	18	17	18
15	22	32	27
16	29	30	29
17–18	7	10	8
No dates by age 18	3	2	3
Total	100	100	100
No. of cases[a]	477	469	946
Age at first steady			
13 or younger	10	8	9
14	9	11	10
15	12	15	13
16	20	21	20
17–18	22	24	23
No steady by age 18	27	21	24
Total	100	100	100
No. of cases[a]	477	469	946
Age at first intercourse			
13 or younger	6	2	4
14	6	3	4
15	10	6	8
16	15	10	13
17–18	27	36	32
No intercourse by age 18	36	43	39
Total	100	100	100
No. of cases[a]	475	468	943

Note: [a]The number of cases consists primarily of children interviewed in 1980 at age 18. For those who had missing data or were not interviewed in 1980, the information was obtained from the 1985 interview, with the 1985 data coded into the same categories as the 1980 data. Respondents providing no data in either 1980 or 1985 are excluded from this table.

divisions just listed, and then added a fifth one for age 17 (with those who never went steady or did so at age 18 comprising the omitted category). We categorized age at first sex into three zero-one categorical variables: age 15 or younger, age 16, and age 17 (with those who were sexually inexperienced or had first sex at age 18 comprising the omitted category).

In an attempt to summarize the dating, going steady, and sexual experience of the young people we created two additional summary zero-one categorical variables based on heterosexual experience before age 18. The first such variable indicated young adults who reported going steady before age 18 but reported no sexual intercourse by that time. The second such variable indicated those young adults with sexual experience before age 18. The omitted category for these zero-one variables consists of all people who had never gone steady and had never had sexual intercourse before their 18th birthdays.

In addition to the information about the timing of first date, first going steady, and first sexual intercourse, young adults who had never been married were asked an additional battery of questions in the 1980 interview. These included the number of dates the young people had had in the past four weeks, whether the respondents were dating the same person or different people, and if they were dating someone they planned to marry. Sexually experienced respondents were also asked how many different sexual partners they had ever had and how many times they had intercourse in the previous four weeks. As documented in table C.3 of Appendix C, we converted the answers to most of these questions into dummy variables. The exception was the number of dates in the past four weeks, which we treated as a continuous variable.

Finally, we asked the young adults with children for the birth date of their first child. From this information, we coded the timing of the first pregnancy, if any, occurring before the first marital or cohabiting union.[2] We used this information to code whether or not a female respondent or the partner of a male respondent was pregnant with a first birth during each month at risk of entering a first union. Thus, a preunion pregnancy is a time-varying covariate used to predict subsequent union-formation experience.

Our analysis of the influence of adolescent courtship experience is conducted using Model 6.6 of chapter 6. This model includes all of the factors from the parental family from 1962 through 1977 that were found to have direct effects on the children's union-formation experiences.[3] We conduct all of our analyses by estimating a series of equations that contain all of these parental factors from 1962 through 1977 as control variables, plus one adolescent courtship factor. We do not enter multiple courtship factors into the same equation because of the strong correlations among the courtship factors. This approach provides minimally controlled estimates of the effects of these factors on union formation. It is also important to observe that these minimally controlled estimates do not control for other factors in the life of the child or in the life of the parent after the child was age 15 in 1977. It is likely that control of these other factors would modify the magnitude of the estimated effects. We turn to this issue later in the book, but note here that even with many additional controls, the dramatic effects reported in this chapter remain substantial.

Age at First Dating, Going Steady, and Sexual Relations

The primary results of our analyses of the influence of age at first dating, going steady, and sexual relations are summarized in table 7.2, where
we indicate the percentage effect of each of these factors on various dimensions of union formation, including the total union-formation rate,
the marriage rate with cohabitation as a competing destination, and cohabitation with marriage as a competing destination. The data in table 7.2
demonstrate substantial relationships between virtually every dimension
of the timing of adolescent courtship—dating, going steady, and sexual
relationships—and entrance into cohabitation and marriage. Early initiation of dating, going steady, and sexual relations is associated with dramatically higher rates of union formation. Furthermore, early adolescent
courtship is also associated with the choice of cohabitation over marriage
for those entering coresidential unions.

Looking first at the total union-formation rate (last two columns of
table 7.2), we observe a strong monotonic total effect of the early initiation of dating on the rate of initiation of coresidential unions. Children
who began dating at age 13 or younger have union-formation rates that
are 146 percent higher than those who began dating at age 17 or older.
Even the one-year difference between those who begin dating at age 16
and those who wait until 17 or later is 41 percent.

Age at first going steady also has a strong total effect on the union-
formation rate, with people experiencing a first steady relationship before
age 18 having 86 to 154 percent higher union-formation rates than those
who had their first steady relationship at age 18 or later. This effect is not
entirely monotonic, however. Those first going steady at age 13 or younger have particularly high union-formation rates and those having their
first steady at age 17 have particularly low rates, but there is very little systematic difference across ages 14 to 16.

The association between age at first sexual experience and the total
union-formation rate is also strong. People with first sexual experience at
ages 16 and 17 have union-formation rates nearly twice as high as those
whose first sexual experience occurs at age 18 or older. The difference in
total union-formation rates rises to over 200 percent for those who have a
first sexual experience at age 15 or younger. Similarly, those who have had
sexual relations by age 17 have union-formation rates nearly 200 percent
higher than those who have neither gone steady nor had sexual relations
before age 18.

TABLE 7.2 **Total effects with minimum controls of timing of adolescent courtship experience on children's rates of entrance into marital and cohabiting unions (as competing destinations)[a] and the total rate of union formation**

	Marriage		Cohabitation		Total	
	B[b]	Z[c]	B[b]	Z[c]	B[b]	Z[c]
Age at first date[d]						
13 or younger	0.87	2.64	1.84	5.22	1.46	5.97
14	1.11	3.49	1.27	4.17	1.18	5.40
15	0.86	3.18	0.58	2.44	0.69	3.88
16	0.79	3.02	0.17	0.80	0.41	2.54
Age at first steady[e]						
13 or younger	0.71	2.26	2.11	6.54	1.54	6.74
14	0.78	2.74	1.42	4.98	1.12	5.57
15	1.20	4.44	1.14	4.46	1.18	6.35
16	1.62	6.29	0.88	4.18	1.16	7.20
17	0.92	4.15	0.82	3.84	0.86	5.60
Age at first sex[f]						
15 or younger	0.46	1.97	4.40	11.94	2.12	10.59
16	0.02	0.11	2.30	8.07	0.96	5.94
17	0.34	2.04	1.80	7.52	0.91	6.62
Sex and steady experience before age 18[g]						
Sex before age 18	0.98	4.60	2.92	9.72	1.95	10.74
Steady before age 18 but no sex	1.14	5.34	0.22	1.23	0.70	5.00
No. of periods	103,814		103,814		103,814	
No. of events	384		432		816	

Notes: [a] A separate equation is estimated for each of the adolescent courtship factors listed. Each of these equations also control for the parental factors listed in table 6.4, age, whether the mother was interviewed in 1980, and whether the child was interviewed in 1980.
[b] Effect coefficient for logit equations transformed by equation: $[\exp(\beta) - 1]$.
[c] Z = ratio of absolute value of coefficient to its standard error.
[d] Omitted category is never went on a date or first date at age 17 or older.
[e] Omitted category is never went steady or first steady at age 18 or older.
[f] Omitted category is never had sex or first sex at age 18 or older.
[g] Omitted category is never went steady or had sex before age 18.

These data, thus, provide strong support for the ideas motivating this chapter. Adolescent courtship experiences have a substantial relationship to entrance into marital and cohabiting unions, with early entrance into dating, steady, and sexual relationships being strongly linked to early union formation. These findings are consistent with all of the causal mechanisms discussed earlier, including enduring personal attributes influencing both adolescent courtship and union formation and the idea that rapid entrance into adolescent relationships leads to younger entrance into coresidential unions.

Decomposing the union-formation rate into its two components—marriage and cohabitation—however, demonstrates that adolescent courtship experiences are not related uniformly to rates of cohabitation and marriage. Rather, in every comparison the relationship of the timing of adolescent courtship experience and union formation is stronger and more monotonic for cohabitation than for marriage. For example, the gap between the cohabitation rates of the youngest and oldest first daters is 184 percent, compared to a gap of only 87 percent for marriage. Similarly, the gap between the youngest and oldest in initiating steady relationships is 211 percent for cohabitation and 71 percent for marriage. The difference by age at first sex is even more dramatic—440 percent for cohabitation and only 46 percent for marriage. Furthermore, the effect of courtship timing is monotonic for cohabitation, while it is not at all monotonic for marriage.

Note, however, that the relationships between the rate of marriage and the timing of first date, first going steady, and first sex are stronger if we consider the marriage rate ignoring cohabitation rather than the marriage rate with cohabitation as a competing destination. For example, the gap between those who had their first sexual experience at age 18 or older and those who did at age 15 or younger increases from 46 percent when the outcome of interest is marriage with cohabitation as a competing destination to 64 percent when the outcome is marriage ignoring cohabitation (data not shown in tables). This is because many people who have sex at a young age cohabit early and rapidly go on to marriage. Thus, early sexual experience also leads to a substantially higher overall rate of marriage than suggested using the competing destination analysis summarized in table 7.2.[4]

The data we have presented so far suggest that the timing of adolescent courtship is related both to the overall rate of union formation and the choice between cohabitation and marriage. We confirmed this insight by examining directly the choice between cohabitation and marriage for those who had entered a union. This investigation revealed that among those entering a union (at any age) there was no significant association between age at first date and the choice between marriage and cohabitation. However, there was a strong association between age at first going steady and this choice, with the odds of cohabiting being 72 percent higher for those who first went steady at age 13 or younger than for those who waited until age 18 or older (data not shown in tables). The gap between those having first sex at age 15 or younger and those who waited until age 18 or later was even more remarkable at 218 percent. Interestingly, those who had sex by age 17 had odds of choosing cohabitation that were 78 percent higher than those who had neither gone steady nor had sex. However, those who went steady without having sex were 39 percent less likely to choose cohabitation. This strongly suggests that it is sex rather than going steady that leads to the choice of cohabitation over marriage.

Thus the data we have presented reveal that the association between the rapidity of adolescent courtship and union formation is not just a simple maturational process. Young people do not merely move from one level of courtship and union type to another without any thought about the kinds of unions they are entering. Although such maturation processes are probably operating—as suggested by the linkage between adolescent courtship timing and the overall rate of union formation—the processes are clearly more intricate and fine-tuned than this. Similarly, these results suggest that the influence of any enduring personal attributes such as hormones, physical attractiveness, and sociability that influence both adolescent courtship and union formation are not operating in a simple uniform way. Instead, whatever selectivities are operating work differently for entrance into cohabitation and marriage.

These findings highlight the potential importance of cognitive processes in the relationships between adolescent courtship processes and union formation. For example, adolescents who initiate sexual relationships at young ages are indicating some approval of nonmarital sex—an attitude that is likely to persist into young adulthood where it may help legitimize unmarried cohabitation. Attitudes toward premarital sex may thus be an important element in shaping both courtship processes and the subsequent choice between cohabitation and marriage. This view is buttressed by the fact that the choice of cohabitation over marriage is more strongly associated with the timing of first sex than with the timing of first date or first going steady. It is also supported by the fact that sex before age 18 is associated with much higher odds of choosing cohabitation over marriage, but going steady without sex before age 18 is associated with lower odds of choosing cohabitation.

A graphical summary view of the relationship between the timing of first sex and the total union-formation rate is provided in figures 7.1 and 7.2. In figure 7.1, the cumulative proportion of young singles who enter either cohabitation or marriage (total union formation) is graphed against age. Figure 7.2 graphs the same information by the number of years since sexual debut. Figure 7.1 demonstrates the strong and generally monotonic association between age at first sex and the cumulative fraction entering either cohabitation or marriage. However, figure 7.2 shows virtually no

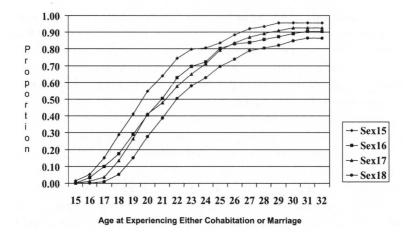

FIGURE 7.1. Cumulative proportion experiencing either cohabitation or marriage by age and age at first sex

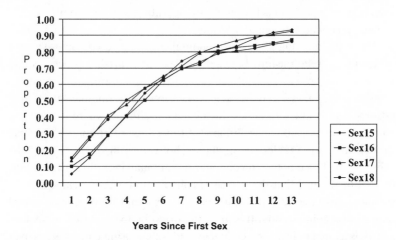

FIGURE 7.2. Cumulative proportion experiencing either cohabitation or marriage by age at first sex and years since first sex

association between age at first sex and the rapidity of entering a union thereafter. That is, the cumulative proportion entering a union at various time intervals after sexual debut is virtually identical across categories of age at sexual debut. This suggests that the relationship between the rapidity of adolescent courtship and entrance into coresidential unions is entirely explained by maturational momentum, with little effect of age at first sexual debut on the waiting time to entrance into a coresidential union once that sexual debut occurs.

Figures 7.3 and 7.4 decompose the relationship between the age at first sex and the cumulative proportion entering unions thereafter into its two components of marriage and cohabitation. In contrast to the total union-formation rate (figure 7.2), the individual rates of entering cohabiting unions and marital unions after sexual debut are both strongly and

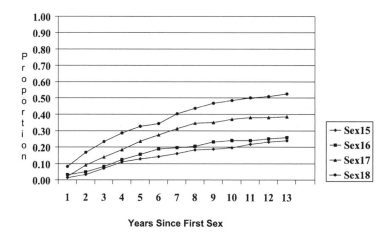

FIGURE 7.3. Cumulative proportion experiencing marriage as a first union by age at first sex and years since first sex

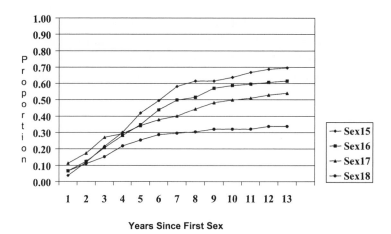

FIGURE 7.4. Cumulative proportion experiencing cohabitation as a first union by age at first sex and years since first sex

oppositely related to the age of first sexual experience. That is, when looking at the tempo of entering first unions following sexual debut, individuals with a younger sexual debut enter marriage less rapidly than others
(figure 7.3) and enter cohabitation more rapidly (figure 7.4). Furthermore,
both of these relationships are strong and monotonic. These results further illustrate that the association between sexual debut and coresidential
union formation is not just the result of simple maturational momentum,
but involves a close connection between adolescent courtship experiences
and the process of choosing cohabitation or marriage.

Intensity of Courtship Experience at Age 18

We now shift our attention from the timing of the initiation of various heterosexual experiences to the intensity of courtship at age 18 (at the time of
the 1980 interview). We do so by relating the five adolescent courtship factors at age 18—number of dates at age 18, dating same or different people
at age 18, dating someone planning to marry, number of sexual partners,
and sexual experience by age 18—to subsequent rates of entrance into
marriage and cohabitation (as competing risks). Like the analyses in the
previous section, we control for all of the relevant parental variables from
1962 through 1977 (from children's infancy to age 15) examined in chapter
6. However, unlike the previous analyses we limit the examination to the
period after the 1980 interview at age 18 to maintain the proper temporal
ordering of the measures. The courtship-intensity measures indicate behavior and experiences at age 18 and should be used only to predict subsequent cohabitation and marriage experience. The results of this analysis
are summarized in table 7.3. The coefficients for the adolescent courtship
factors listed there are estimated in separate equations—one equation for
each adolescent courtship factor.

As seen in the last two columns of table 7.3, the intensity of courtship
experience at age 18 is strongly and positively associated with the subsequent tempo of coresidential union formation. In every comparison,
the more intense the courtship involvement at age 18, the more rapid the
subsequent pace of forming coresidential unions. For example, each additional date reported by these 18-year-olds in 1980 is associated with an
8 percent increase in the rate of subsequent union formation. Having recent sexual experience (in comparison to having none) increases the rate
of union formation by 112 percent. Having 1, 2 or 3, and 4 or more sexual

TABLE 7.3 **Total effects with minimum controls of early courtship intensity on children's rates of entrance into marital and cohabiting unions (as competing destinations)[a] and the total rate of union formation**

	Marriage		Cohabitation		Total	
	B[b]	Z[c]	B[b]	Z[c]	B[b]	Z[c]
Number of dates during last 4 weeks	0.09	6.15	0.08	5.56	0.08	8.02
Dating patterns during last 4 weeks[d]						
Dating the same person	1.51	6.03	0.69	3.54	1.05	6.75
Dating different people	0.20	0.99	0.82	3.70	0.54	3.54
If dating someone plan to marry	1.61	8.17	0.38	2.54	0.88	7.43
Number of sex partners[e]						
If 1 sex partner	0.70	3.75	0.77	3.49	0.70	4.96
If 2–3 sex partners	0.48	2.49	1.59	6.17	0.94	6.08
If 4 or more sex partners	−0.17	0.89	3.41	9.83	1.23	6.98
If sex during the last 4 weeks[f]						
Has had sex, but not during last 4 weeks	0.18	1.04	1.24	5.52	0.63	4.69
Has had sex during last 4 weeks	0.56	3.43	2.01	8.30	1.12	8.24

Notes: [a] A separate equation is estimated for each of the adolescent courtship factors listed. Each of these equations also control for the parental factors listed in table 6.4, age, and whether the mother was interviewed in 1980. Because the predictor variables in this analysis refer to the time immediately prior to and at the 1980 interview, this analysis was limited to months subsequent to the 1980 interview. The number of person-periods in the respective analyses ranges from 59,708 to 60,023, the number of marriages from 341 to 348, the number of cohabitations from 350 to 352, and the total number of unions from 691 to 700. The differences in number of periods and events result from differences in missing data on the independent variables.
[b] Effect coefficient for logit equations transformed by equation: $[\exp(\beta) - 1]$.
[c] Z = ratio of absolute value of coefficient to its standard error.
[d] Omitted category is never went on a date by the 1980 interview.
[e] Omitted category is no sex partners by the 1980 interview.
[f] Omitted category is never had sex by the 1980 interview.

partners (compared to having none) increases the rate of union formation by 70, 94, and 123 percent respectively.[5]

In the previous section we noted that the timing of first date, going steady, and sexual intercourse was more closely related to cohabitation than to marriage. Here we observe a similar relationship for the two sexual-experience variables measuring the intensity of courtship experience through age 18. Both the number of sexual partners and recent sexual experience have a much stronger relationship to cohabitation than to marriage. Furthermore, the effects of both of these factors on cohabitation are strong and monotonic. For example, moving up each category for number of sexual partners (from none to 1 to 2–3 to 4 or more) is associated with an increase in the cohabitation rate of 77 percent, 159 percent, and 341 percent. Similarly, going from no sexual experience, to some sexual experience but none in the past four weeks, to sexual experience in the past four weeks is associated with increases of 124 and 201 percent.

However, only one of these two sexual-experience factors—recent sexual experience—is monotonically related to the timing of entrance into marriage. Those who had sex, but not recently, had marriage rates that were 18 percent higher than those with no sexual experience, while those with recent sexual experience had rates that were 56 percent higher. On the other hand, for the number of sexual partners, as we move from low levels of sexual involvement to high levels of sexual involvement, the rapidity of marriage declines rather than increases. For example, as compared to having no sexual partners, those with 1 partner have 70 percent higher marriage rates; however, those with 2 or 3 sex partners only have 48 percent higher marriage rates, and those with 4 or more partners actually have 17 percent lower marriage rates.

As noted in the previous section, this pattern of results suggests that the intensity of sexual involvement is not only related to the timing of union formation but to the choice between cohabitation and marriage. In supplementary analysis we investigated the influence of these sexual experience factors on the choice between cohabitation and marriage for those who entered a union. As compared to having no sexual experience, having had sex (either in the past four weeks or at some time prior) is associated with a 72–101 percent higher odds of choosing cohabitation over marriage (not shown in tables). Furthermore, increases in the number of sex partners (from none to 1 to 2 or 3 to 4 or more) increases the odds of the choice of cohabitation over marriage from 11 to 75 to 354 percent.[6]

Unlike the extent of sexual experience at age 18, the intensity of recent dating at age 18 is not more strongly related to cohabitation than to marriage. Instead, as documented in table 7.3, the recent frequency of dating is about equally related to the rapidity of entrance into marriage and cohabitation—with no impact on the choice between the two. Furthermore, although dating the same person and dating different people—as compared to not dating—seem to have similar effects on the cohabitation rate, dating the same person increases the marriage rate substantially over dating different people. This suggests that exclusively dating one person is more associated with marriage than with cohabitation. Young adults dating someone they plan to marry have higher rates of both cohabitation and marriage, but the effect is much greater for marriage. This observation holds up in an analysis focusing on the choice young adults make between cohabitation and marriage, with dating someone they plan to marry being associated with a 51 percent lower odds of cohabitation over marriage, as compared to not dating someone they plan to marry.

Therefore, these results about the intensity of courtship experiences at age 18 provide further support for some of the conclusions of the previous section about the tempo of adolescent courtship experiences. Both the timing and the intensity of heterosexual relations are related to the rapidity of entrance into cohabiting and marital unions in young adulthood, with younger ages and greater intensity increasing the tempo of cohabitation and marriage—as one would expect with a model of maturational momentum.

Equally interesting, however, is that both the timing and intensity of heterosexual relationships are related to the subsequent choice between cohabitation and marriage. Generally, young and intensive courtship involvement is related to the choice of cohabitation over marriage. However, this choice is much more pronounced when the measures of courtship involvement—both timing and intensity—are related to sexual experience rather than dating or going steady. In fact, for some measures of dating intensity, we found no correlation to the choice of cohabitation over marriage.

This provides further evidence that the union-formation experience is not simply one of implementing one's physical and social maturation in relationships. That the choice of cohabitation over marriage is more strongly related to premarital sexual experience than to dating and going steady suggests the strong role played by attitudes about premarital sex in both adolescent courtship and union formation. It is likely that sexual attitudes and values permeate a broad range of decisions about courtship, cohabitation, and marriage (also see Laumann et al. 1994).

Before leaving the effects of early sexual experience on cohabitation and marriage, we note that very little of the total effects of early sexual experience on union-formation experience can be explained by the other factors that we consider later in the book. That is, these estimated effects are not reduced substantially by the other parent and child factors brought into the analyses. Thus, we posit an independent direct effect of early sexual experience on the rate of entrance into unions, with that effect being larger for cohabitation than for marriage. This large positive direct effect is one of the major stories of our book. Note that we discuss potential age and gender interactions with the sexual and dating experience factors in the following paragraphs, after our discussion of pregnancies before unions.

Pregnancy before Union

We now switch our attention from the timing and intensity of adolescent courtship to pregnancies occurring when a young adult is still single (not married or cohabiting). As we discussed in chapter 2, marriage in the Western world has long been the social institution legitimizing sexual relations, pregnancy, and childbearing. Although sex, pregnancy, and childbirth have always been biologically possible without marriage, marriage has been the social institution that legitimized these central human experiences. And the social forces requiring marriage for all of these experiences have been historically strongest for childbearing. This can be seen in the fact that although some single couples were sexually involved before marriage and became pregnant, they felt enormous social pressures to marry to legitimize the birth. Many of these couples followed the social conventions and married before the child was born.

The social forces limiting sex, pregnancy, and childbearing to marriage have, as we discussed in chapter 2, become much weaker in recent decades. The result has been dramatic increases in sex, pregnancy, and childbearing outside of marriage. In fact, a common theme in the family literature is the declining incidence among singles of marriage following pregnancy.

The purpose of this section of the chapter is to investigate the residual power of pregnancies among single individuals to lead to the formation of a coresidential union. We examine how much the rate of union formation—either cohabitation or marriage—increases during periods of pregnancy, compared to nonpregnancy. We also consider the extent to which this pregnancy effect is the same or different for cohabitation and marriage. That is, does a pregnancy outside of a coresidential union more strongly motivate a marriage or a cohabiting union?

Because we lack information about pregnancies that did not result in childbirth, we focus entirely on pregnancies ending in a live birth. This limitation prevents investigation of the entire decision-making process—including whether or not to have an abortion—for people dealing with a pregnancy outside of a union. Instead, we can only address the decision to enter a cohabiting or marital union among those who decide to give birth to the child.

It should also be noted that the causation between having a baby and union formation may be in the opposite direction to that posited previously. That is, the proximity of marriage or cohabitation—or even the actual decision to enter a union in the future—could increase the likelihood of pregnancy or the likelihood of a pregnant woman deciding to have the baby. This possible endogeneity of effects needs to be kept in mind as we discuss our estimates.

We ascertained the dates of birth of all children of female respondents or the partners of male respondents through our life-history calendar. Dating of the timing of the pregnancy is more difficult as the length of the gestation period varies across individuals. In addition, for this analysis we are most interested in the date when the pregnant woman and her partner learned of the pregnancy, because only then could the fact of the pregnancy enter into decisions about forming a coresidential union. This adds a period past the date of pregnancy—a period that also varies across individuals.

Because we have no independent information about the timing of the pregnancy or when the couple became aware of it, we had to make assumptions about this timing from the reported date of birth of the child. We used three different markers of the timing of pregnancy awareness: eight months before birth; seven months before birth; and six months before birth. Because preliminary analysis revealed only very modest differences in results across the three definitions, we discuss only the results for the middle alternative—assuming knowledge of pregnancy by the seventh month before a birth. As indicated in Appendix table C.3, we coded all months between the time of the birth and seven months prior to the birth as months with a pregnancy before the union.

We estimated the total effect of a pregnancy outside of a union in an identical fashion as the other effects considered in this chapter—by adding this variable to the base model created from the analyses of chapter 6 (Model 6.6). The results of this analysis reveal that a nonunion pregnancy has an enormous total effect (with minimum controls) on the rate of entrance into unions (not shown in tables). The odds of entering a coresidential union—either marriage or cohabitation—are approximately 17 times higher during months of pregnancy than during other months. This suggests that Americans still make a powerful connection between childbearing and living in a coresidential union—despite the dramatic increase in nonmarital childbearing.

The effect of a nonunion pregnancy on union formation is not, however, uniform across cohabitation and marriage. A nonunion pregnancy increases the likelihood of marriage by about 27 times, as compared to $5\frac{1}{2}$ times for cohabitation. We also found that among all couples entering a union, the likelihood of choosing marriage over cohabitation was about 5 times larger for those facing the birth of a child than those who were not.

TABLE 7.4   **Percentage distribution of union status of respondents at the timing of first pregnancy and first birth[a]**

Union status	At pregnancy	At birth
Single	20	6
Cohabiting	11	6
Married	68	86
Separated/Divorced/Widowed	1	2
Total (%)	100	100
No. of cases	295	295

Note: [a] First pregnancy and first birth refer to the same pregnancy—the one resulting in the respondent's first live birth. Partnership status at birth is figured at the exact month of birth. Partnership status at pregnancy is figured at nine months prior to the birth.

TABLE 7.5   **Percentage distribution of union status at birth within categories of union status at beginning of pregnancy**

Union status at pregnancy	Union status at birth					Total[a] (%)	N
	Single	Cohabiting	Cohabited, then married	Married	Seperated/ Divorced/ Widow		
Single	28	8	13	50	0	100	60
Cohabiting	0	38	0	59	3	100	32
Married	0	0	0	99	1	100	201
Total	6	6	3	85	1	100	293

Note: [a] Rounding error may prevent the individual percentages from summing to 100. Rounding error, different categories, and a slightly different number of cases in tables 7.5 and 7.4 make the total percentage distribution of union statuses at birth slightly different in table 7.5 and table 7.4.

This provides evidence that many single people continue to prefer marriage over cohabitation as a living arrangement in which to give birth to a child.

Further insights into the relationships between pregnancy (resulting in a live birth) and union status can be seen in table 7.4, where we report the union status of all first births reported to females in our sample at both the beginning and end of the pregnancies. Table 7.4 reports the percentage distribution of births at both conception and birth. Table 7.5 is a transition table reporting the union status at the end of the pregnancies by union status at the beginning of the pregnancies. That is, the percentages in table 7.5 represent the percentage in each union status at birth within each category of union status at conception.

The first panel of table 7.4 indicates that approximately two-thirds of the pregnancies occurred to individuals who were married at the beginning of the pregnancy. Thus, despite the dramatic increase in sex and pregnancy outside of marriage, two-thirds of all first births in this sample were conceived within marriage. About one-fifth occurred when the couple was single and one-tenth when the couple was cohabiting.

Interestingly, the distribution of union status at the time of birth was more weighted toward marriage than the union status at the time of conception. That is, 86 percent of all first births in this sample occurred to married women, 6 percent to single people, 6 percent to cohabiting couples, and 2 percent to previously married people. This suggests a substantial shift from unmarried statuses at the time of pregnancy into marriage during the course of the pregnancy. This distribution also indicates that births to cohabiting couples comprise a large fraction of the births to all unmarried people, a finding consistent with national U. S. data (see Bumpass and Lu 2000). Bumpass and Lu (2000) report that the high fraction of out-of-wedlock births to cohabiting mothers, along with the recent increase in cohabitation, can account for a significant part of the substantial increase in out-of-wedlock childbearing between the early 1980s and the early 1990s.

Further insight into the transitions between union statuses during pregnancy can be seen in table 7.5, where we indicate the percentage in each union status at birth within each union status at time of conception. Looking at the first row for individuals who were single at the time of conception, we see that only 28 percent remained single at the time of the birth. Twenty-one percent of pregnant singles chose to cohabit before the birth of the child (the sum of columns 2 and 3), but the majority subsequently transformed their cohabiting relationships into marriages. In all, only 8 percent of the women who conceived their first birth while single were cohabiting at the time of the birth (column 2), in comparison to the 63% who were married at the time of the birth (sum of columns 3 and 4).

Further evidence of the power of marriage in defining childbearing is provided by data for the people who were cohabiting at the time of the pregnancy leading to a first birth (row 2 of table 7.5). The fraction of these cohabiting individuals who decided to marry between the time of pregnancy and the time of the birth (59%) is remarkably similar to the fraction of single individuals who decided to marry between pregnancy and birth (63%). Thus, even couples who had a coresidential union before pregnancy were very likely to move toward marriage once a pregnancy occurred (also see Manning 1993; Manning and Landale 1996). This strong tendency is undoubtedly related to the presumption that the bearing and rearing of children are accomplished better within marriage than in cohabiting or single relationships.

Although our sample of parents is relatively small, consists entirely of Whites, and originates from the Detroit Metropolitan Area, the pattern of relationships in these data are very similar to estimates using national data (Bumpass and Lu 2000; Manning 1993; Manning and Landale 1996). We estimate that 20 percent of first births are conceived to single women and 11 percent to cohabiting women, as compared to 21 and 7 percent, respectively, for White women nationally (Manning and Landale 1996). We estimate that 6 percent of first births are born to single women and 6 percent to cohabiting women, which compares to 9 and 4 percent, respectively, for women in a national survey (Manning and Landale 1996).[7] Our estimate of the fraction of pregnant single and cohabiting women who marry by the birth of the child (approximately 60%) is close to Manning's (1993) national estimate for White women[8] (52% and 63% respectively for single and cohabiting women). However, other research shows that for Hispanic and African-American women the fraction conceiving children outside of marriage is substantially higher and the fraction marrying following a nonmarital conception is substantially lower than for non-Hispanic whites (Manning 1993; Manning and Landale 1996; Morgan and Rindfuss 1999).

The number of people experiencing a birth prior to cohabitation or marriage in our sample is too small to examine the influence of a nonunion birth on subsequent union formation. However, Bennett, Bloom, and Miller (1995), who analyzed data from women participating in four large national American studies, found that having a birth while single is substantially related to lower rates of marriage. This depressing effect of an out-of-wedlock birth on subsequent marital prospects is particularly dramatic if the woman does not marry within six months of the birth of the child. In fact, Bennett and colleagues estimate that the monthly likelihood of a first marriage is about 20 to 50 percent lower for women who have a first birth and do not marry within six months of the birth than for women who do not have a premarital birth (also see Graefe and Lichter 2002; Lichter, McLaughlin, and Ribar 2002). The lower rates of marriage for people who have a baby may be related to having traits, such as being opposed to marriage, that decrease their desire for or attractiveness to marriage partners. Another possibility is that the presence of the child itself is an impediment to marriage. The second explanation is consistent with research showing that the presence and number of children results in lower rates of remarriage among the previously married (Bumpass, Sweet, and Martin 1990; Lampard and Peggs 1999; Peters 1986; Teachman and Heckert 1985; Thornton 1977).

Interestingly, Bennett and colleagues (1995) found in the National Survey of Family Growth that women with a first birth before a union not only had significantly lower rates of entering a formal union but also had higher rates of entering an informal union. These results indicate that women with a birth who enter unions are much more likely than others to choose cohabitation over marriage.[9] Thus, not only is early sex associated with the choice of cohabitation over marriage, but so is having a birth outside of a coresidential union—which suggests a strong ideational linkage between cohabitation, sex, and nonmarital childbearing. The Bennett, Bloom, and Miller study also indicated that the overall rate of union formation (combining formal and informal unions) was negatively related to having a child.

Contrasting our own findings of the positive influence of a premarital pregnancy on marriage with others' findings of a negative influence of a premarital birth on marriage suggests the importance of the decision making during pregnancy for future marital prospects. These results suggest that a pregnancy to single couples frequently leads to the decision to transform that relationship into a marital union. The result is an especially heightened rate of marriage immediately following pregnancy and preceding the birth of the child. However, pregnant young women who decide to have the child but do not marry at that time—either because of their own or their partner's desires or circumstances—face a long period of lower chances of marriage. In fact, these single mothers face substantially elevated chances of never marrying, being from "two to three times as likely not to marry by age 35 as those who do not bear a child out of wedlock" (Bennett, Bloom, and Miller 1995, 50; also Graefe and Lichter 2002). Furthermore, Bennett and colleagues estimate that the increase in nonmarital childbearing in the United States between 1970 and 1988 can account for about one-quarter of the increase during the same period in the fraction of women in their early forties who had never married.

Substantive Interactions

As part of this research, we investigated the extent to which the influence of various dimensions of dating, going steady, sexual relations, and pregnancy on the initiation of marriage and cohabitation varied by gender and age. Our analysis of gender interactions was motivated by the expectation that courtship experiences were more meaningful and powerful in the lives of young women than young men. That is, dating, going steady, and sexual intercourse are all deeply gendered activities that probably affect women more powerfully than men. There is also a double standard whereby proscriptions against nonmarital sex have historically been applied more vigorously to women than to men (Modell 1989; Reiss 1960, 1964, 1967). These considerations led to the expectation that the effects of dating, going steady, sexual experiences, and pregnancy would have stronger effects for women than for men.

Our investigation of this gender-interaction hypothesis revealed little support for the hypothesis of stronger effects among women. For example, we found that the effects of sexual experience by age 17 on marriage and cohabitation rates were remarkably similar for females and males (and any gender interaction did not even approach statistical significance). Similarly, we found no statistically significant gender interactions with the effect of going steady but not having sexual intercourse on both cohabitation and marriage. The effect of a nonunion pregnancy was also found to be similar for young women and men. All of these results, therefore, cast doubt on the hypothesis of stronger effects for young women.

We investigated age interactions by dividing the period of exposure to union formation into two periods: before age 23, and age 23 and older. As expected, the effects of courtship timing on subsequent union formation is substantially greater at the younger ages. For example, at ages 22 and under, those having sex at 15 or younger have marriage, cohabitation, and total union-formation rates that are 88, 572, and 308 percent higher than those who experienced first sex at ages 18 or older. These effects are substantially larger than the comparable effects of 3, 193, and 66 percent at ages 23 and above (data not shown in tables). An important implication of this finding is that the effects at ages 22 and younger are even greater than those reported in table 7.2 for all ages combined.

Summary and Conclusions

The data presented in this chapter provide strong support for the idea that the tempo of adolescent courtship is strongly related to the rapidity of entering marital and cohabiting unions. Young people who begin dating, going steady, or having sexual intercourse at a young age enter coresidential unions much faster than others. This effect is stronger in young adulthood than it is in older adulthood. This is likely true because proximate causes are usually more powerful than distal ones. Nevertheless, this effect remains important at ages 23 and older. Similarly, young people who date frequently, who have had many sex partners, and who are sexually active at age 18 enter coresidential unions much faster than others. In addition, union formation is substantially hastened by a pregnancy.

These data are consistent with the idea that there is a momentum in the formation of heterosexual unions. This means that young people who date, go steady, and have sex early are prepared and motivated to have more intensive courtship and earlier formation of coresidential unions. These data are also consistent with the idea that there are enduring physical, psychological, or social factors that influence heterosexual relations across the entire life course. That is, the individual attributes leading to early dating, sex, and pregnancy also lead to early coresidential unions. Unfortunately, separating these two effects is extremely difficult.

Interestingly, neither of these causal mechanisms can entirely explain the results presented in this chapter. The reason is that the timing and intensity of dating, sex, and pregnancy are not only related to the timing of union formation but to the choice between cohabitation and marriage. Early and intense experience with going steady and sexual relations are strongly related to the choice of cohabitation over marriage. However, the differential effect of a pregnancy on cohabitation and marriage is in the opposite direction, with the effect of a pregnancy being much higher on marriage than on cohabitation.

This pattern of results suggests that cognitive processes, attitudes, and beliefs have an important role in explaining the tempo and choice between cohabiting and marital unions. Young adults with early and frequent sexual experience have clearly indicated an approval of nonmarital sexual relationships, or, alternatively, their early and intense sexual relationships lead to more accepting attitudes. These tolerant attitudes toward sex outside of marriage probably persist into young adulthood where they help to legitimize coresidential unions. It is, thus, likely that attitudes toward sex outside of marriage are an important influence on both adolescent courtship and subsequent experience with cohabitation and marriage. Research by Laumann et al. (1994) is consistent with this hypothesis in that they find that sexual attitudes help to account for the relationship between early sexual experience and subsequent choices between cohabitation and marriage.

It is also likely that cognitive processes and social values help to explain the strong choice of marriage over cohabitation for couples who experience a first pregnancy leading to a live birth. Despite the long-term increase in the acceptance and frequency of childbearing outside of marriage, it appears that many young adults still believe that marriage is the most appropriate social relationship for bearing and rearing children. Thus, many noncoresiding couples who are expecting a child not only speed up their joint living arrangements, but also frequently enter marriage itself. That is, they decide not only to raise the child jointly, but also to have the child and relationship sanctioned by marriage itself. In addition, many couples who experience a pregnancy while cohabitating decide to marry before the child is born.

Race Differences

The links among dating, sexual, and pregnancy experience on the one hand and cohabitation and marriage on the other have received more research attention among the White population than among other racial and ethnic subpopulations. These factors have received greater attention among African Americans than among Hispanic- or Asian-American subpopulations, and among African Americans the consequences of premarital pregnancy have probably received the greatest attention. Pregnancy increases rates of marriage, and rates of converting cohabitations into marriage, among African Americans just as it does among Whites (Manning 1993; Manning and Smock 1995). On the other hand, a premarital childbirth at young ages reduces rates of marriage (Bennett, Bloom, and Craig 1989). This is also true among Hispanics (Graefe and Lichter 2002). Those who experience premarital births are also more likely to choose cohabitation over marriage (Qian, Lichter, and Mellott 2005). There are important race differences early in courtship and in dating behavior. White women are more likely than African-American women to date and more likely to participate in serious dating relationships that increase expectations of marriage (Crissey 2005).

Conclusion

Dating, steady dating, sex, multiple sexual partners, and premarital pregnancy all accelerate the rates of entering marital and cohabiting unions. On the other hand, early steady dating, early sex, and multiple sexual partners increase the chance of choosing cohabitation over marriage, but pregnancy greatly increases the chance of choosing marriage over cohabitation. The links between the pace of entering dating and sexual relationship with entry into cohabitation and marriage suggest a positive momentum in relationships as well as enduring physical, psychological, or social factors that influence heterosexual relationships. By contrast, the links from dating, sex, and pregnancy to the choice between cohabitation and marriage suggest cognitive and attitudinal processes that unfold across the life course. Of course, random assignment of individuals to specific dating, sexual, or pregnancy experiences is not likely to be part of the social sciences any time soon, forcing us to rely on observational study designs to investigate these links, leaving open the possibility that our results may be biased by the misspecification bias. Yet, even though the strong empirical associations we observe may not reflect independent causal forces, the associations documented in this chapter are consistent with hypotheses predicting extremely strong links among courtship, relationship, and marital and cohabiting behaviors.

CHAPTER EIGHT

Religious Affiliation and Commitment

W e included in chapters 5 and 6 a brief analysis of the influence of the religious experience of parents and grandparents on young people's entrance into cohabiting and marital unions. Those analyses showed that four different dimensions of the parental family—grandmother's religiosity, parental religious affiliation, a religious marriage ceremony for the parents, and parental religious service attendance—are related in some way to the union-formation process. The primary conclusion of these analyses is that religious participation and commitment in the parent and grandparent generation are connected to lower rates of cohabitation and higher rates of marriage among young adults. Both grandmother religiosity and parents being married by a church official seem to be related to the children's union-formation experience by way of their relationship to parental religious service attendance. Interestingly, religious commitment and participation seem to be stronger predictors of marriage and cohabitation experience than religious affiliation, although Catholic affiliation is associated with lower rates of marriage once factors correlated with affiliation are controlled.

In this chapter we broaden our examination of religious influences on entrance into unions by raising several additional questions and issues. First, we compare the effects of paternal and maternal religious activity on children's union-formation experience, asking explicitly whether mothers or fathers influence their children the most. Second, we compare the effects of parental religiosity early in a child's life with the effects of parental religiosity when the child is a teenager and making decisions about dating, intimacy, and living arrangements. Third, we introduce indicators of the children's religious commitment, examining the extent to which the children's participation in religious services, their evaluation of the importance of religion in their lives, and their belief in the validity and reliability of religious texts affect their marriage and cohabiting experience (see Appendix table C.4 for wording of questions). We also compare the effects of children's religiosity to the effects of similar maternal religiosity factors. A related question is whether parental religious influences on children's union formation operate entirely through the children's religious commitment or have an independent effect. Fourth, we examine whether the effects of religiosity on young people's marriage and cohabitation vary across religious groups. Finally, we examine the extent to which the influence of religiosity varies by the gender of the child.

The inclusion of young-adult religious participation, commitment, and belief in the analysis is particularly important because it is the young people who are making the actual decisions about cohabitation and marriage. We expect that the personal religious commitment and frequent attendance at religious services by young adults would increase contact and agreement with the messages of the churches about intimate and family behavior (Petersen and Donnenwerth 1997). Active involvement in religious institutions also enhances interaction with both adults and peers holding similar values. These factors lead us to expect that young people with high levels of religious participation and commitment will have positive attitudes toward marriage and marital childbearing and negative attitudes toward divorce, premarital sex, cohabitation, and childbearing outside of marriage. These factors are likely to increase marriage because they increase the desire to marry and provide community support for it. They also probably decrease cohabitation because they restrict both readiness and willingness to cohabit.

We also posit that highly religious young people have lower rates of cohabitation than others even if they have not internalized restrictive values concerning premarital sex and cohabitation. This is because cohabitation involves public acknowledgment of a nonmarital sexual relationship, which young people with high levels of religious participation and commitment are likely to want to avoid even if they are personally accepting of cohabitation. Furthermore, religious young people are more likely to date and interact with other religious young people who may tend to have positive feelings about marriage and opposition to cohabitation. As with the indirect effects of religiosity through attitudes and values, these direct mechanisms also suggest that religious participation leads to higher rates of marriage and lower rates of cohabitation.

It is likely that religious people who choose to cohabit do so when they are more committed toward marriage. Although still disapproved, the prospect of a brief period of cohabitation during engagement might result in fewer negative sanctions by parents, peers, and religious tutors than unions without formal marriage plans (Binstock 2001).

Religious commitment and participation are also expected to play a role in the transformation of cohabiting unions into marriages. We expect that religious people who choose to cohabit will feel more desire and social pressure to either terminate the relationship or transform it into marriage (Binstock 2001).

Comparing Maternal and Paternal Effects

We now turn our attention to the relative influence of paternal and maternal religiosity on the union-formation experiences of children. This analysis is possible because we asked the mothers in both 1962 (just after the child was born) and 1977 (when the child was 15) how frequently she and her husband (if married at the time) attended religious services. We limited the analysis to families in which the child's mother and father were still married and living together in 1977.[1]

It is important to note that the religious participation of the mother and the father is highly correlated: the Pearson correlation coefficient was .74 for 1962 and .73 for 1977. This is undoubtedly a reflection of the fact that many husbands and wives attend religious services together. These correlations may also be inflated somewhat by the fact that attendance is reported for both parents by the same individual.

The results of our analysis of the relative importance of maternal and paternal religious service attendance on children's union-formation experience are reported in table 8.1. The top panel of table 8.1 reports the comparative analysis for 1962 parental religiosity, while the bottom panel reports the comparative analysis for 1977 parental religiosity. The total effects listed in table 8.1 represent the effects of each of the parental religiosity factors estimated in a series of equations, with each equation containing only the control variables and one of the listed religiosity factors.

TABLE 8.1 **Effects of maternal and paternal religious service attendance on children's rates of entrance into marital and cohabiting unions (as competing destinations)**[a]

	Marriage				Cohabitation			
	Total effect		Direct effect		Total effect		Direct effect	
	B^b	Z^c	B^b	Z^c	B^b	Z^c	B^b	Z^c
1962 analysis[d]								
Maternal religious attendance	0.11	2.54	0.08	1.46	−0.07	1.93	−0.05	1.22
Paternal religious attendance	0.09	2.29	0.05	0.96	−0.06	1.74	−0.03	0.74
Average religious attendance	0.13	2.69			−0.08	2.05		
No. of periods	103,814		103,814		103,814		103,814	
No. of events			384				432	
χ^2			406.80				274.98	
DF			28				28	
1977 analysis[e]								
Maternal religious attendance	0.08	1.87	0.04	0.66	−0.15	4.17	−0.08	1.52
Paternal religious attendance	0.08	2.19	0.06	1.30	−0.16	4.57	−0.12	2.55
Average religious attendance	0.10	2.26			−0.18	4.82		
No. of periods	83,737		83,737		83,737		83,737	
No. of events			325				299	
χ^2			351.83				230.01	
DF			23				23	

Notes: [a]The total effects are estimated in equations that contain all of the base model variables plus only *one* of the religiosity factors listed. The direct effects are estimated in equations that contain all base model variables plus the religiosity factors listed—separately for 1962 and 1977.
[b]Effect coefficient for logit equations transformed by equation: $[\exp(\beta) - 1]$.
[c]Z = ratio of absolute value of coefficient to its standard error.
[d]For the 1962 analysis, the base model is Model 5.3 of chapter 5, minus the original 1962 religious service attendance factor in Model 5.3.
[e]The 1977 analysis includes only those families where the mother was continuously married through 1977. For the 1977 analysis, the base model is Model 6.5 of chapter 6, minus 1977 religious service attendance and the 1962–1977 marital history variables.

The equations estimating the direct effects include the multiple parental religiosity factors listed plus the base model controls. In addition to the individual maternal and paternal religious service attendance factors, we list the average of the two, as in the analysis of chapter 5.

Looking first at the top panel of table 8.1, we see that paternal and maternal attendance at religious services in 1962, just after the child was born, have remarkably similar effects on children's union-formation rates. In separate equations, each additional unit of maternal religious service attendance has a −.07 effect on cohabitation, as compared to the −.06 effect of paternal attendance. Each unit of maternal attendance also has a .11 effect on marriage, as compared to a .09 effect for paternal attendance. With maternal and paternal attendance in the same equations, the estimated effects of maternal and paternal attendance on cohabitation are, respectively, −.05 and −.03. The comparative effects on marriage are .08 and .05. These results suggest that the effects of maternal and paternal attendance are very similar, although maternal attendance at the time of a child's birth may have a somewhat greater influence.

This general similarity of maternal and paternal effects is observed again in 1977, when the child was age 15 (bottom panel of table 8.1). In separate equations, the effect of each unit of maternal attendance on cohabitation is −.15, compared to −.16 for paternal attendance. For marriage, maternal and paternal attendance have the same per-unit effect of .08. With the two variables in the same equation, the effects on cohabitation diverge to −.08 for each unit of maternal attendance compared to −.12 for paternal attendance. Similarly, in the same equation the effect of maternal attendance on marriage is .04 compared to .06 for paternal attendance. Whereas the maternal effects were somewhat larger than the paternal effects in 1962, they were somewhat smaller in 1977. Thus, these findings provide little evidence of a greater effect of either maternal or paternal service attendance on children's union-formation experience.[2]

Comparing Effects of Parental Religiosity in Early Childhood and Adolescence

The data in table 8.1 also provide insights into the relative influence of parental religious involvement when the children were born and when they were adolescents. Those data show remarkably similar effects of parental religiosity at birth and during adolescence on the rate of entrance into marriage. At the same time, the data show stronger correlations between cohabitation rates and parental religiosity in 1977 than in 1962. In fact, the 1977 coefficients are about twice as high as the 1962 coefficients. This suggests that parental religiosity during the children's adolescence may be more important for predicting cohabitation than parental religiosity during early childhood.[3]

The data in table 8.1 are not appropriate for assessing whether early or late parental religiosity has the stronger *direct* effect on children's behavior. This is because the estimates for early and late childhood in table 8.1 do not come from the same sample with the same explanatory factors in the equations. To address the question of direct effects of early and late parental religiosity, we refer back to table 6.2 where we included both early and late maternal religiosity in the same equation.

The results of table 6.2 indicate that maternal religious service attendance has stronger direct effects during the teenage years than during infancy. The direct effect of 1977 maternal religiosity on marriage is .10 compared to .07 for 1962. For entrance into cohabitation, the 1977 direct effect is −.10 as compared to −.02 for 1962. If we shift our attention to the choice between cohabitation and marriage, the effect of 1977 maternal religiosity is −.20 on the choice of cohabitation over marriage compared to −.07 for 1962 (not shown in tables).

The reduction of the 1962 maternal religiosity effect with the introduction of 1977 maternal religiosity suggests that one important component of the 1962 direct effect is the indirect effect that it has through 1977 maternal religiosity. This conclusion is consistent with the results of chapter 6. This indirect effect is made possible, in part, because of the strong correlation between the mother's attendance in 1962 and 1977—which is .46 (the comparable correlation for fathers who remained married to the child's mother is .55).

Religious Participation, Importance, and Beliefs in Young Adulthood

We now turn our attention from the religiosity of mothers and fathers during the early childhood and adolescence of the children to the religiosity of the children and mothers during the children's young adulthood. More specifically, we consider in 1980, when the children were age 18, measures of the children's and mother's participation in religious services and the importance of religion in their lives. We also use a measure of children's beliefs about the authority of religious teachings that was ascertained in 1993 when the children were age 31.

As documented in Appendix C (table C.4), the participation of children and mothers in religious services in 1980 was measured as it was in 1962 and 1977. The importance of religion to the children and mothers was ascertained in 1980 by the question: "Quite apart from attending religious services, how important would you say religion is to you—very important, somewhat important, or not important?" These response categories were coded from 1 (not important) to 3 (very important). Finally, religious beliefs were measured in 1993 by asking the children and mothers the extent to which they agreed or disagreed with the following two statements: "The Bible is God's word and everything happened or will happen pretty much as it says"; and "The Bible is the answer to all important human problems." The answers were coded from 1 (strongly disagree) to 5 (strongly agree), with 3 reserved for those who responded that it depends, that they did not know, or that they were undecided. The responses to the two belief questions were very highly correlated, suggesting that they were measuring the same underlying concept and could be combined into one scale for analysis.[4] Of course, the belief questions were measured in 1993—after the union-formation experience being studied— which violates the temporal assumptions associated with causal analysis. We were forced to use 1993 measures of religious beliefs because the earlier data collections did not ask explicitly about such beliefs.[5] All of this information from the mothers and children was obtained in separate interviews.

Table 8.2 provides a summary of the estimated effects of the attendance, importance, and belief indicators of maternal and child religiosity on the children's union-formation experience. All of the indicators of children's religiosity have substantial and statistically significant total effects on both marriage and cohabitation rates. For example, each unit of children's religious attendance is associated with a .24 increase in the marriage rate and a .23 decline in the cohabitation rate. Each unit of the importance of religion to the children is associated with a .41 increase in the rate of marriage and a .30 decrease in the rate of cohabitation. Note that although the per-unit difference is greater for importance than attendance, the number of units in the religious attendance scale is greater (5) than the number of units in the religious importance scale (2), so that across the full range of response alternatives these two measures of religiosity actually have quite similar effects on cohabitation and marriage. In addition, each unit on the children's belief scale is associated with a .33 higher rate of marriage and .18 lower rate of cohabitation. These are all substantial differences, attesting to the large influence of religiosity on the union-formation experience of young adults.

As expected, the coefficients for all of the children's religious factors are reduced substantially in the multivariate equations, and especially the estimates for importance of religion, which were reduced below statistical significance for both marriage and cohabitation. At the same time, the coefficients for both children's religious attendance and belief remained substantial and statistically significant for both cohabitation and marriage, suggesting that these dimensions are more important influences on the

TABLE 8.2 **Effects of mother and child religiosity on children's rates of entrance into marital and cohabiting unions (as competing destinations)[a]**

	Marriage				Cohabitation			
	Total effect		Direct effect		Total effect		Direct effect	
	B^b	Z^c	B^b	Z^c	B^b	Z^c	B^b	Z^c
1980 maternal religious attendance	0.10	2.45	0.06	1.35	−0.14	3.84	−0.11	2.65
1980 maternal religious importance	0.37	2.65	0.26	1.75	−0.21	2.61	−0.06	0.60
1993 maternal religious belief	0.08	1.32	0.03	0.45	−0.16	3.04	−0.12	2.02
No. of periods	56,597		56,597		56,597		56,597	
No. of events	337		337		331		331	
			122.53				94.01	
DF	24		26		24		26	
1980 child's religious attendance	0.24	5.11	0.16	3.18	−0.23	6.10	−0.20	4.57
1980 child's religious importance	0.41	3.76	0.13	1.20	−0.30	4.33	−0.12	1.36
1993 child's religious belief	0.33	5.71	0.26	4.44	−0.18	4.13	−0.12	2.41
No. of periods	57,219		57,219		57,219		57,219	
No. of events	340		340		336		336	
χ^2			170.18				124.70	
DF	24		26		24		26	

Notes: [a]The total effects are estimated in a series of equations that contain all of the base model variables from Model 6.5 of chapter 6, minus the mother's 1977 religious service attendance. To this base model is added one of the religiosity factors listed. The direct effects are estimated in equations that contain all of the base model factors plus all the religiosity factors listed. Mother effects are estimated from women interviewed in both 1980 and 1993. Child effects are estimated from children interviewed in both 1980 and 1993. Equations were estimated using only person periods after the 1980 interview.
[b]Effect coefficient for logit equations transformed by equation: $[\exp(\beta) - 1]$.
[c]Z = ratio of absolute value of coefficient to its standard error.

rapidity of union formation than is self-assessment of the importance of religion.

Of course, all of these dimensions of children's religiosity are substantially intercorrelated. Importance and attendance correlate at .47, importance and belief at .35, and attendance and belief at .26.[6] Because of these correlations, the estimated effects of the items are substantially reduced in the multivariate analyses.

As is children's religiosity, maternal religiosity tends to be positively associated with the children's marriage rate and negatively associated with the children's cohabitation rate. However, the results are not quite as consistent for maternal religiosity and all of the total effects for maternal religiosity are smaller than the comparable total effects for children's religiosity. As with the children, the multivariate analysis substantially reduced the estimated effects of the various maternal religious factors. These findings suggest that maternal religiosity, although important, is less influential on children's union formation than the children's own religiosity.

More insights are provided in table 8.3 where direct effects are estimated in a series of equations, each of which includes the same religiosity indicator for both the parent and child and all of the base model variables as controls. The results in table 8.3 consistently suggest that the direct effects of children's religiosity are more substantial than the direct effects of maternal religiosity. In every comparison, the estimated coefficients of child's religiosity are larger than the estimated coefficients for the comparable maternal religiosity factor. In many instances the differences are substantial. For example, each unit of child's religious service attendance has a .22 effect on the rate of marriage and a −.24 effect on the rate of cohabitation, while the comparable effects of maternal attendance are .01 and −.04. Similarly, each unit of the belief of the child in the Bible has an effect of .32 on the marriage rate and a −.16 effect on the cohabitation rate, whereas the comparable effects of maternal religious belief are .01 and −.12. The contrasts between mothers and children in the effects of the importance of religion are in the same direction. These results reveal that children are more directly influenced by their own religiosity than their mother's when making union-formation decisions.

Furthermore, the data in table 8.3 suggest that taking the child's religiosity into account dramatically decreases the estimated effect of maternal religiosity. This can be seen by comparing the direct effects for the maternal religiosity factors in table 8.3 with the total effects for the same factor estimated in table 8.2. In fact, the direct effects of maternal religiosity in table 8.3 are relatively modest in size and with two exceptions—the effect of maternal religious importance on the children's marriage rate and the effect of maternal belief on the children's cohabitation rate—are not even marginally statistically significant.

All of this suggests that maternal religiosity is highly relevant for children's union-formation experience, but that this effect largely works through the children's own religiosity. The direct effect of maternal religiosity net of the children's religiosity, for the most part, is of less importance than this indirect effect through the children's religiosity.

This indirect effect is associated with a strong intergenerational connection of religiosity between mothers and children. The correlations between mother's and children's religiosity are .55 for service attendance in

TABLE 8.3 **Comparing the direct effects of mother and child religiosity on children's rates of entrance into marital and cohabiting unions (as competing destinations)[a]**

	Marriage						Cohabitation					
	B[b]	Z[c]	B[b]	Z[c]	B[b]	Z[c]	B[b]	Z[c]	B[b]	Z[c]	B[b]	Z[c]
1980 maternal religious attendance	0.01	0.22					−0.04	0.95				
1980 maternal religious importance			0.26	1.85					−0.09	0.93		
1993 maternal religious belief					0.01	0.09					−0.12	2.13
1980 child's religious attendance	0.22	4.09					−0.24	5.27				
1980 child's religious importance			0.35	3.09					−0.32	4.26		
1993 child's religious belief					0.32	5.22					−0.16	3.37
No. of periods	52,963		52,963		52,963		52,963		52,963		52,963	
No. of events	322		322		322		311		311		311	
X^2	132.63		126.92		139.20		110.45		90.12		81.14	
DF	25		25		25		25		25		25	

Notes: [a]The direct effects are estimated in a series of equations that contain all of the base model variables from Model 6.5 of chapter 6, minus the 1977 religious service attendance of the mother plus the religiosity factors listed. Effects are estimated for mother and child pairs interviewed in both 1980 and 1993. Equations were estimated using only person periods after the 1980 interview.

[b]Effect coefficient for logit equations transformed by equation: $[\exp(\beta) - 1]$.

[c]Z = ratio of absolute value of coefficient to its standard error.

1980, .30 for the importance of religion, and .36 for religious beliefs. These correlations suggest that mothers have considerable success in passing on their religious commitments and beliefs to their children, which then have a strong influence on children's union-formation experience.

Because in most instances the positive influence of parent and child religiosity on children's marriage rates is countered by a similar negative effect on cohabitation rates, religiosity should have little effect on the overall rate of union formation. We confirmed this by direct empirical testing of the religiosity factors on the total union-formation rate (not shown in tables). This difference in the direction of effects also means that religiosity has a dramatic influence on the choice between cohabitation or marriage. Children with highly religious parents and high personal religiosity are much less likely than their counterparts to choose cohabitation over marriage.

In a separate analysis we replicated the marriage estimates of table 8.2, but substituted the outcome of marriage ignoring cohabitation for the outcome of marriage versus cohabitation. The effects of each of the religiosity variables are substantially reduced in this analysis because many of those who initially cohabit go on to marry quickly, and because many of those who marry after cohabitation are probably less religious than those who went directly to marriage. Adding those who previously cohabited to the married population increases the overall marriage rate for those with low religiosity more than it increases the marriage rate of the highly religious. Nevertheless, the more religious still have higher rates of marriage. The total effects for the children's religiosity factors are both substantial and statistically significant. These results thus suggest that less religious individuals are not only more likely to cohabit before marriage, but that this substitution of cohabitation for marriage leads to lower rates of marriage overall.

Although the data that we have discussed so far demonstrate a powerful and pervasive effect of religiosity on young people's entrance into marriage, they do not show the full strength of this relationship. This is because cohabitation is a heterogeneous category containing many types of individuals and relationships, including some who have public plans to marry, some with private plans to marry, and some who have no expectations of marriage whatsoever. When we disaggregate cohabiters into these three groups, we find that the size of the effect of children's religiosity is directly correlated with the distance the couple was from marriage when they began cohabiting. That is, in models estimating the total effects

of children's religious attendance, religious importance, and religious beliefs, each unit of the children's religiosity is associated, respectively, with
35, 42, and 23 percent lower rates of entering cohabitation without any
marriage plans, and 10, 21, and 14 percent lower rates of entering cohabitation with public marriage plans (not shown in table).[7] Clearly, when
cohabitation is not associated with marriage, religiosity has an especially
strong inhibiting influence. Having marital plans weakens but does not
eliminate the negative influence of religiosity on entrance into cohabitation. These results also suggest that engagement and the commitment to
marry reduces the force of religious proscriptions against sexual expression outside of marriage.

Religious Affiliation Interactions

Earlier, we hypothesized that the effects of religious participation and involvement on union-formation experience would vary by religious groups—
with the effects being weaker for nonfundamentalist Protestants than for
either Catholics or fundamentalist Protestants. We evaluated this hypothesis by estimating the total effects of religiosity indicators in tables 8.1 and
8.2 separately for the three religious groups.

These analyses provide no support for the hypothesis that the effects of
religious involvement and commitment on children's rates of entrance into
marital and cohabiting unions are lower for nonfundamentalist Protestants than for others. All of the indicators of parent and child religiosity
have positive effects on the rate of marriage and negative effects on cohabitation for nonfundamentalist Protestants. In fact, many of the coefficients for nonfundamentalist Protestants are larger than the coefficients
for the total sample and very few are even marginally smaller. Thus, we
found no evidence to support the original hypothesis motivating this particular investigation of differential effects across religious groups. Apparently, the effects of participation and involvement in nonfundamentalist
Protestant groups are similar to the effects in Catholic and fundamentalist Protestant groups. These findings, therefore, suggest the general conclusion that religious participation and commitment are important and
similar for all major denominational groups, with high levels of religiosity
in both the parental and child generation associated with higher rates of
marriage, lower rates of cohabitation, and the tendency to choose marriage over cohabitation as a first union.

Gender Interactions

Earlier we found that paternal and maternal religiosity had similar over-all effects on children's rates of union formation. Here, we take up two additional questions concerning gender. The first concerns whether the influence of the religiosity of parents and children on children's union formation depends on the gender of the child. The second question focuses on whether mothers influence daughters more than sons, while fathers affect sons more than daughters.

We begin with the first and simpler issue by estimating separately for males and females the direct effects of the parent and child religiosity factors listed in tables 8.1 and 8.2. As one would expect, coefficient estimates are not precisely the same for males and females, but these analyses do not support any conclusions of substantial and consistent differences in the effects of either parent or child religiosity on males and females. The conclusion is that religiosity affects males and females similarly and sub-stantially. Our analyses also do not provide any consistent and substan-tial support to the second hypothesis that intergenerational influences are greater for same-sex parent-child pairs than for opposite-sex pairs. The entrance of sons or daughters into marital and cohabiting unions is gen-erally affected similarly by maternal and paternal religiosity.

Summary and Conclusions

Religion—and its association with family, marriage, and intimacy—con-tinues to be an important element in the formation of marital and cohab-iting unions. Young people with strong connections and commitments to religious institutions enter marriage and cohabitation differently than those with weak connections and commitments.

Our data suggest that highly religious young people generally enter first coresidential unions at about the same rate as others, but they are more likely to choose marriage over cohabitation and consequently have higher rates of marriage and lower rates of cohabitation. This difference gener-ally applies to both young women and young men and across major reli-gious denominations.

Our data also indicate that all the religious dimensions examined—at-tendance at religious services, the importance given to religion in one's life, and belief in religious text—are strongly related to the rate at which young people enter marital and cohabiting unions. The inhibiting force of religiosity on cohabitation, however, appears to be strongest when the couple has no plans for marriage and is weakest when the couple is engaged to marry. It also appears that religious attendance, importance, and belief may have more important influences on marriage and cohabitation than does religious affiliation, at least as measured here.

Interestingly, the religiosity that affects the formation of marital and cohabiting unions has deep roots within families. The union-formation experience of young adults can be predicted by the religiosity of their grandparents, mothers, and fathers.

The pathways of the influence of family religiosity on children's union formation are generally indirect rather than direct. Family religiosity is important mostly because parents are socialized by their own parents and then the parents pass on their religiosity to their own children. It is this transmission of religiosity across generations and its persistence across time within generations that makes grandparent and parent religiosity such important influences on children's union-formation experiences. Although the intergenerational transmission and intragenerational persistence of religiosity are far from perfect—that is, many highly religious grandparents have less religious grandchildren and vice versa—they are sufficient to make both grandparent and parent religiosity important influences on the union-formation experiences of children.

Finally, our research may provide insight concerning national trends in marriage and cohabitation in recent decades. Religion became less important and central to Americans during the 1960s and 1970s, and confidence in religious authorities and teachings declined (Alwin 1988; Glenn 1987; Roof and McKinney 1987; Thornton 1989). At the same time, cohabitation emerged as a new coresidential choice and the marriage rate fell substantially (Bumpass and Sweet 1989; Rodgers and Thornton 1985; Thornton 1988). Other research has suggested that aggregate trends in religion may have important effects on familial trends (Lesthaeghe and Surkyn 1988; Lesthaeghe and Wilson 1986; Thornton 1985b, 1989).

Our analysis is consistent with the idea that aggregate religious trends may have been important influences on changes in marriage and cohabitation nationally. The decline in the centrality and importance of religious commitments during this period may have led to a weakening of the religious proscriptions against sexual relations and living together outside of marriage, or a weakening of church-member compliance with these norms. These changes may have influenced large fractions of young

Americans to substitute cohabitation for marriage, at least temporarily, with the resulting increase in cohabitation and the decline in marriage.

Highly religious young people generally enter first coresidential unions at about the same rate as others, but they are more likely to choose marriage over cohabitation. As a result, highly religious young people have higher rates of marriage and lower rates of cohabitation than others. These powerful effects of religiosity are much greater than observed effects of religious affiliation, at least given the measures available in these panel data. Transmission of religiosity across generations and its persistence across time within generations makes grandparent and parent religiosity important influences on children's marital and cohabiting decisions—most of the influence of the family dimensions of religiosity are explained by young peoples' own religiosity. As with other results, the observational design means the strong empirical associations we observe may not reflect independent causal forces. Nevertheless, the results presented in this chapter suggest that low levels of religiosity will produce low rates of marriage and high rates of premarital cohabitation.

The Influence of Attitudes, Values, and Beliefs*

Introduction

Attitudes, values, and beliefs are central factors in theoretical models of family formation behavior and key elements in understanding changing patterns of family formation. Our central goal in this chapter is to examine the influence of a broad range of attitudes on young people's experiences with premarital cohabitation and marriage. We examine attitudes toward dimensions of family formation, such as cohabitation, premarital sex, marriage, and childbearing, as well as attitudes toward nonfamily activities that may compete with family formation, such as education, careers, and consumer spending. We examine the impact of young people's attitudes on their cohabiting and marital behavior, controlling for the effects of the family factors documented in chapters 5 and 6.

A related goal is to examine the role of parental attitudes in shaping children's attitudes and behavior. Although both the previous chapters and the research literature in general examine a wide range of parental family characteristics, up until now we have concentrated mainly on structural characteristics of parental families. The importance of social-psychological aspects of the family of origin, such as preferences or aspirations, has long been acknowledged in the status-attainment literature (e.g., Sewell

*Georgina Binstock collaborated in the analysis and writing of this chapter.

et al. 1975). Here too, we argue that values, beliefs, and attitudes expressed
in the family of origin are important aspects of the families themselves
and have significant effects on adult children's family formation behavior.
Thus, we add an examination of the role of mothers' attitudes in shaping
children's attitudes and behavior to our analysis.

Theoretical Framework

As discussed in chapter 1, the framework of reasoned action and planned
behavior predicts that positive attitudes toward a behavior increase the
likelihood of that behavior (Barber, Axinn, and Thornton 2002; Fishbein
and Ajzen 1975; Liefbroer and de Jong Gierveld 1993). This can occur
both by making a person more ready for a transition and by cutting down
the psychological and social barriers to a decision. In the case of cohabitation or marriage, positive attitudes toward cohabitation or marriage,
coupled with social pressure or social support, increase the likelihood
of cohabiting or marrying (Barber, Axinn, and Thornton 2002; Clarkberg, Stolzenberg, and Waite 1995; Liefbroer and Gerritsen 1994; Musick
and Bumpass 1999). Therefore, we predict that young people who believe
that marriage is an important and positive institution and who would be
very disappointed if they never married will form intimate coresidential
unions faster than those with less commitment to marriage. We expect
that desires for an early marriage will also lead to more rapid union formation (Bayer 1969; Gaughan 2002). It is also likely that positive attitudes
about marriage and preferences for early marriage will (a) cause couples
forming unions to more likely choose marriage than cohabitation, and (b)
enhance the rate of cohabiting relationships being transformed into marriage (Binstock 2001). Furthermore, although we expect these effects to
operate across all the young-adult years, we believe that they will increase
in importance as the children mature. This expectation is based on the
belief that the differential motivation to marry will be expressed most
strongly in behavior as young people draw close to and exceed their desired age of marriage.

Similar lines of argument suggest that couples forming unions who
hold positive attitudes toward cohabitation would be more likely to enter
a cohabiting union, at least for a period of time, but those with negative
attitudes toward cohabitation would be more likely to marry. Also, to
the extent that positive attitudes toward cohabitation lead to long periods
of cohabitation, they may ultimately delay entrance into marriage itself,

especially if the cohabiting couple would have chosen to marry in the absence of cohabitation as a viable alternative (Bumpass and Sweet 1989; Ermisch and Francesconi 2000). Entrance into marriage can be delayed even more if the cohabiting relationship breaks up, an eventuality that can lead to another extensive period of courtship and cohabitation before marriage occurs (Ermisch and Francesconi 2000).

Positive attitudes toward cohabitation may also speed up the overall rate of entry into coresidential unions if it leads couples not yet ready for marriage to decide to cohabit. This could happen for couples who decide to cohabit in the interval between engagement and marriage or for those who are not yet ready to commit to marriage but who want to take advantage of the perceived economic or social benefits of living with their partner. All of these causal mechanisms would result in a higher overall rate of union formation among those with positive cohabitation attitudes. It would also result in those with positive attitudes toward cohabitation being more likely to choose cohabitation over marriage, and a lower rate of marriage among cohabitors.

Of course, attitudes toward a variety of behaviors may affect decisions to cohabit or marry. Those who feel positive toward behaviors that are easily combined with coresidential unions, such as childbearing in the case of marriage or premarital sex in the case of cohabitation, are likely to enter unions more quickly. Thus, we expect that young people who desire to have several children, who view childbearing as a key part of adulthood, and who would be disappointed if they did not have children will be more likely to enter coresidential unions. However, because marriage is still the preferred union type for the bearing and rearing of children (Liefbroer and de Jong Gierveld 1993; Loomis and Landale 1994; Manning 1995), we also expect that positive attitudes toward children will more likely lead to the choice of marriage over cohabitation (Barber and Axinn 1998), and to more rapid transformations of cohabiting relationships into marriage. All of these childbearing attitude effects could operate directly on young adults' union formation or indirectly through aspirations and plans for marriage.

Similar considerations suggest that those with positive attitudes toward premarital sex will be more likely to cohabit than their counterparts, and will be slower to transform a cohabiting relationship into marriage. In contrast, young adults with less positive attitudes toward premarital sex might cohabit only with a strong commitment to marriage (such as being engaged), which would hasten transformation of the relationship into marriage.

Attitudes toward family formation may affect union-formation behavior via their impact on early adult experiences. For instance, preferences for large families speed the entry into marriage and decrease the likelihood of cohabitation (Barber and Axinn 1998), which in turn increase the rate at which young people enter parenthood (Loomis and Landale 1994; Manning 1995; Manning and Landale 1996). Similarly, because of perceived role conflict, preferences for large families may reduce educational attainment or slow rates of entry into the labor force. In both cases, young people's subsequent experiences may be a key mechanism linking family formation attitudes to cohabitation and marriage behavior (Barber, Axinn, and Thornton 2002).

We also expect that preferences for family versus nonfamily social activities influence entrance into marital and cohabiting unions. We believe that three dimensions of these preferences are particularly relevant for present purposes: (1) preferences for spending time in family social activities; (2) preferences for spending time in nonfamily activities; and (3) preferences for the choice between family and nonfamily activities. By preferences for family social activities, we mean enjoyment of caring for children, playing with children, working within the family, and interacting with adult family members. By preferences for nonfamily social activities, we mean enjoyment of working outside the family, engagement in nonfamilial recreational activities, and investment in careers outside the family.

We expect that preferences for spending time in family social activities will increase both the rate of union formation and the choice of marriage over nonmarital cohabitation. Young people who prefer to spend their time in social activities with children and adult family members are likely to desire early family formation, especially marriage, so that they have access to their own marriage and family life more quickly. These expectations are consistent with the findings of Clarkberg, Stolzenberg, and Waite (1995) that valuing residential closeness to parents is related to a choice of marriage over cohabitation.

Preferences for spending time in nonfamily social activities are expected to reduce both the rate of union formation and the choice of marriage over nonmarital cohabitation (see Clarkberg, Stolzenberg, and Waite 1995). Young people who prefer to spend their time in social activities outside the family probably desire to postpone family formation because they find rewards outside of family life. Also, the pursuit of these nonfamily activities may compete with the pursuit of family formation (Rindfuss 1991; Rindfuss, Swicegood, and Rosenfeld 1987; Thornton, Axinn, and Teachman 1995).

Another dimension of family organization is the division of labor between husbands and wives. Particularly important for young people who have never married or cohabited are their beliefs and attitudes concerning appropriate roles for men and women who are in partnerships. There are several reasons to expect an influence of gender-role attitudes on cohabiting and marriage behavior. Some researchers argue that positive attitudes toward egalitarian roles for men and women reflect an underlying disposition toward innovative family forms (Clarkberg, Stolzenberg, and Waite 1995). In this view, attitudes favoring the gendered division of labor that characterized the United States in the 1950s are expected to be associated with preferences for marital behavior that was typical of the 1950s, and thus lead to high rates of marriage and low rates of cohabitation (Clarkberg, Stolzenberg, and Waite 1995).

Another perspective suggests that a gendered division of labor within the family may increase efficiency through returns to specialization and trade (Becker 1991). To the extent that couples wish to take advantage of specialization and trade, they will be motivated to marry early. Marriage provides an institutional context for gender-based specialization in housework and nonfamily work by providing legal and social interdependence among men and women. This view of the relationship between the gendered division of labor and marriage predicts high marriage rates among those who are positive toward highly specialized roles for men and women, and a preference for marriage over cohabitation because cohabitation provides fewer legal and social supports for long-term interdependency.

Positive attitudes toward education and work roles—roles with demands that can conflict with those of union-formation roles—may also affect cohabitation and marriage (Barber 2001). First, holding favorable attitudes toward a competing behavior may reduce favorable attitudes toward the focal behavior. For example, researchers have found attitudes toward childbearing and work careers to be negatively correlated (Crimmins, Easterlin, and Saito 1991; Stolzenberg and Waite 1977; Waite and Stolzenberg 1976). One component of any behavior's outcome is its opportunity cost, which in turn influences attitudes toward that behavior. Thus, a young person who holds strong positive attitudes toward education and careers may have negative attitudes toward early marriage because it limits time available for school and work.

Second, forming intentions for two or more competing behaviors may compromise an individual's ability to implement those intentions (Barber 2001). If fulfilling one role makes the fulfillment of another role difficult in terms of time, money, effort, psychological well-being, or other resources, an individual experiences role conflict. For instance, a young person who intends to get married while attaining a graduate degree may find him or herself too busy working toward graduation to focus time or energy on his/her desire to get married.

Overall, individuals who hold positive attitudes toward education and careers are less likely to hold positive attitudes toward marriage and bearing children. Those who decide to marry and have children, attain high levels of education, and achieve demanding careers are likely to experience difficulty implementing all of those intentions simultaneously. As a result, we follow Barber, Axinn, and Thornton (2002) in predicting that individuals with positive attitudes toward education and careers will be more likely to delay union formation than will their peers with less positive attitudes toward these alternatives.

In addition to their independent effects, attitudes toward alternatives to family formation may also affect family formation behavior via their influence on early adult experiences. For example, expectations for high levels of education are associated with college attendance. Overall then, we predict that early adult experiences will explain a portion of the impact of attitudes toward family formation alternatives, but that these attitudes will have important independent effects as well.

In thinking about educational and financial aspirations, we note Easterlin's arguments for the importance of consumption aspirations for family formation (Easterlin 1980; also see Clarkberg, Stolzenberg, and Waite 1995). Easterlin suggests that feelings about the economic resources needed to marry vary across individuals—with higher consumption aspirations being positively related to standard of living in the parental family. Because substantial financial resources are needed to fulfill aspirations for high levels of consumer spending, higher consumption aspirations are likely to motivate greater commitments to education, work, and careers. Given the potential role conflict between education, work, and careers on the one hand and entrances into family formation on the other hand, these commitments are likely to delay entrances into cohabiting and marital relationships. And given the differences between cohabitation and marriage discussed earlier, we expect that consumer spending aspirations will be less important for cohabitation than for marriage. Consequently, we expect that with all else equal, young people with expectations for a high standard of living will enter marriage more slowly than others. As argued previously, these consequences may be produced by a direct effect of consumption aspirations on cohabiting and marital behavior, or they may be produced by indirect effects via education and work behavior.

Parental attitudes, values, and beliefs about a range of issues can in-fluence children in multiple ways (Axinn and Thornton 1996; Bengtson 1975). Through socialization, parents' preferences for their children shape the children's own attitudes, preferences, and intentions. Because chil-dren are socialized to evaluate behaviors similarly to their parents, they may be conforming to their parents' wishes by behaving in accordance with their own attitudes and preferences (Barber 2000).

Parents also influence their children's behavior *independent* of chil-dren's attitudes via social control techniques (Barber 2000; Liefbroer and de Jong Gierveld 1993). Social control refers to parents' attempts to have their children behave in ways that parents find appropriate, or to chil-dren's alteration of their behavior simply to please their parents. These influences operate independently of how children themselves might pre-fer to behave through mechanisms such as punishment or reward (Axinn and Thornton 1993; Barber 2000; Gecas and Seff 1990; Liefbroer and de Jong Gierveld 1993; Smith 1988). Thus, we expect children's behavior to be directly related to their parents' attitudes, because children consider their parents' attitudes when deciding how to behave (Liefbroer and de Jong Gierveld 1993). In addition, because children also respond to their own attitudes when deciding how to behave, we expect children's atti-tudes to be related to their own behavior, regardless of their parents' at-titudes.

Children may also respond to parental attitudes independently of their own attitudes because they prefer to please their parents (Barber 2000; Liefbroer and de Jong Gierveld 1993). Love, admiration, and respect for parents may lead children to behave in accordance with their parents' at-titudes and preferences, even when parents do not invoke social control techniques. So, children may refrain from cohabitation or terminate co-habiting relationships in order to please their parents, to avoid embarrass-ing their parents, or to maintain positive relationships with their parents.

Of course, socialization, social control, and the desire to please parents are not completely independent processes. For instance, some aspects of social control require socialization—a mother who shows her child that an action has hurt or disappointed her is employing a social control tech-nique that assumes the existence of socialization (Coleman 1990). And, some socialization techniques could be considered social control mecha-nisms. For instance, parents who try to convince their child to reform his or her attitudes are attempting to control the child's behavior indepen-dent of what the child might prefer. In addition, the desire to please and respect parents is related to the kind of socialization experienced during the childhood years in the parental home.

Although the relevance of parental preferences for children's behaviors may decline over time, the considerable influence that parents have over their children's behavior during the transition to adulthood is likely to be a significant factor in the set of opportunities and constraints that children face in later adulthood. Parents may set processes in motion— such as residential location, college attendance, and work behaviors—that will have long-term influences on their children's lives (Axinn and Thornton 1992a; Sewell et al. 1975). For example, children whose parents discourage college attendance may face limited career options in later adulthood, and children whose parents encouraged marriage postponement in favor of career goals may face limited prospects for marriage. Thus, even though parental preferences may become less directly relevant as children grow into adulthood, they are likely to exert considerable influence on cohabiting and marital behavior via their earlier influence on education, work, and other behaviors. Overall then, we predict that mothers' positive attitudes toward family formation will speed their children's family formation and that mothers' positive attitudes toward behaviors that compete with family formation will delay their children's family formation (Barber 2000; Barber, Axinn, and Thornton 2002).

Data and Analytic Approach

To test the complex and multidimensional reasoning presented, we draw on a wide range of attitudinal measures available from our intergenerational panel study. Our main focus is on measures of attitudes collected in 1980 from separate interviews with the 18-year-olds and their mothers. In both generations we examine attitudes toward family formation in general, as well as preferences and expectations regarding specific family outcomes.

Appendix table C.5 provides a comprehensive summary of the attitude measures we report in subsequent analyses. We also explored the influence of a few other attitude measures, but we do not include them in table C.5 because they do not have important observed effects on cohabiting and marrying experiences.

Our analytic approach begins with an examination of the total effects of the mothers' attitudes. As argued in our theoretical framework, we believe that mothers' attitudes play an important role in shaping children's attitudes, so that part of the total effect of mothers' attitudes is an indirect effect via children's attitudes.[1] Note that, as in chapters 7 and 8, we begin our exploration of total effects in 1980 controlling for the intergenerational effects established in chapters 5 and 6, which represent a wide range of parental experiences before 1980.

Our second step is to examine the total effects of the young adults' own attitudes on subsequent cohabiting and marital behavior. As an extension of this analysis, we also explore children's beliefs about maternal attitudes. In these analyses we also treat the intergenerational effects established in chapters 5 and 6 as controls in our models of these total effects of children's attitudes. We do not, however, include measures of the mothers' attitudes in these initial models of the effects of the children's attitudes.

The third step in our analytic approach is to examine the effects of mothers' attitudes net of the children's attitudes. Here our work is facilitated by the fact that several specific survey items, across a range of domains, were asked of mothers and children in exactly the same way. This helps to ensure that differences between children's and mothers' attitudes are not produced by differences in the ways the items were measured. This analysis also reveals the remaining direct effects of mothers' attitudes on children's behavior that are not mediated by the children's own attitudes in the same specific domain.

The fourth and final step in our analytic approach is to examine the extent to which the influence of maternal attitudes depends on the quality of mother-child relationships. This analysis uses measures of mother-child and father-child relationship quality to ascertain the extent to which the effects of parental attitudes is strongest when parent-child relationship quality is the most positive. Together, these analyses give us a comprehensive view of how the interplay between mothers' attitudes and children's attitudes affect the children's subsequent cohabiting and marital behavior.

The intergenerational forces described previously lead us to expect that both mothers' and fathers' attitudes will have importance influences on children's behavior. Although our analysis is limited to items about mothers' attitudes, we assume responses to these items reflect a family environment that often includes paternal attitudes as well. As a result, we interpret our findings as informative of both the mothers' and the collective parental influence.

TABLE 9.1 **Total effects with minimum controls of mother's attitudes on children's rates of entrance into marital and cohabiting unions (as competing destinations)[a]**

	Marriage		Cohabitation	
	B[b]	Z[c]	B[b]	Z[c]
Mother's attitude toward premarital sex/cohabitation	−0.16	2.32	0.22	3.02
Mother's preferred age at marriage for child	−0.11	3.79	0.00	0.17
Mother's preferred family size for child	0.19	2.59	−0.11	1.54
Mother's educational expectation for child	−0.08	2.59	−0.07	2.23

Notes: [a] All equations also include the factors from Model 6.6 of chapter 6 (table 6.4). Estimates are from four separate equations (with no controls for the other factors listed).
[b] Effect coefficient for logit equations transformed by equation: $[\exp(\beta) - 1]$.
[c] Z = ratio of absolute value of coefficient to its standard error.

Intergenerational Effects of Attitudes

Table 9.1 summarizes our findings for the total effects of mothers' attitudes on children's cohabiting and marital behavior. Each row of coefficients represents the effects of that specific attitude on the rate of marriage and cohabitation, controlling for the intergenerational effects reported in chapter 6. Note that these are estimates of total effects with minimum controls in that each coefficient is estimated in a separate equation without controls for the other maternal attitudes.

Mothers' attitudes toward premarital sex and cohabitation are coded so that higher values reflect more positive attitudes.[2] Consistent with our theoretical perspective, positive maternal attitudes toward premarital sex and cohabitation increase the rate of cohabitation and reduce the rate of marriage among children (first row of table 9.1). Thus, among young people entering coresidential relationships, those who have mothers with more tolerant attitudes toward premarital sex and cohabitation are much more likely to enter cohabitation rather than marriage (not shown in tables).

Turning now to the mother's preferred age for her child to marry, we note that it is coded so that higher values represent a desire for later ages at marriage. So, the negative effect on marriage displayed in table 9.1 (row 2) means that mothers who prefer later ages at marriage have children who marry at significantly lower rates than mothers who prefer earlier ages at marriage. Moreover, mothers' preferences regarding their children's ages at marriage have a large range, so that the effect on children's rate of marriage is quite strong. For example, mothers who prefer their children marry at age 20 have children who marry at more than three times the rate of children with mothers who prefer they marry at age 30.

Note that mothers' preferences regarding their children's age at marriage has virtually no effect on children's rate of entering cohabitation. Interestingly, this zero effect is a result of counteracting positive and negative effects of maternal preferences on the different kinds of cohabitation. There is a positive effect of maternal preferred age at marriage on the rate of cohabitation without marital plans but a negative effect when there are marital plans. Thus, the mothers who prefer older marriage ages for their children not only have children who marry later, but also have children with lower rates of cohabitation with plans for marriage (results not shown).

The negative influence of parental age at marriage preferences on the rate of marriage extends to cohabitors as well as single people. Mothers with high marriage-age preferences have children who marry slower after cohabitation than mothers with low marriage-age preferences (results not shown).

The influence of other maternal attitudes regarding marriage, remaining single, and divorce is quite varied. First considering maternal attitudes toward remaining single, we used a composite of the extent to which mothers would be bothered if their child did not marry and mothers' attitudes toward remaining single. That measure has no significant impact on either cohabitation or marriage rates (results not shown). Second, we investigated mothers' general attitudes toward marriage, including views that married people are usually happier than single people, that there are few good or happy marriages these days, and that it is better to go through life married than single. We found no significant associations between these maternal attitudes about marriage and children's cohabiting and marital behavior (results not shown). Third, maternal attitudes toward tolerance of divorce significantly increase children's rates of cohabitation (results not shown). Mothers who strongly agree that "divorce is usually the best solution when a couple can't seem to work out their marriage problems" have children who cohabit at rates more than fifty percent higher than children with mothers who strongly disagree with the same statement.

Mothers' preferences for children's family size has a total negative effect on the rate of cohabitation and a positive effect on the rate of marriage (row 3 of table 9.1). Thus, among young people who begin coresidential unions, those with mothers who want many grandchildren are substantially more likely to choose marriage over cohabitation (not shown in tables). This finding is consistent with both the expectations described earlier and previous research linking mothers' desires for grandchildren to their children's marital behavior (Barber and Axinn 1998). The large range of mothers' preferences for children's family size means that this effect is substantial. For example, the estimates suggest that mothers who prefer that their children have six children have children who marry at twice the rate of children with mothers who prefer their children have one child.

Mothers' preferences regarding their children's educational attainment also appear to be a powerful force in the lives of young-adult children (row 4 of table 9.1), with preferences for higher educational attainments reducing the rates of both cohabitation and marriage. These effects are large and consistent with our prediction that mothers' preferences for achievements that compete with marriage will delay marriage. The results are also consistent with research on the timing of childbearing that shows mothers' preferences for higher educational attainments among children substantially delay children's own childbearing (Barber 2000; Barber, Axinn, and Thornton 2002). Clearly, mothers' expectations for children's education slow children's family transitions, including cohabitation, marriage, and childbearing.

Mothers' preferences that the child work for a year or two before marrying has a substantial negative effect on children's rates of marrying (not shown in tables). As with the effects of education discussed previously, these findings are consistent with our hypothesis that preferences for nonfamily activities, which may compete for time and attention with family formation, will in general delay the entrance into marriage.[3]

Taken as a whole, these results constitute evidence of powerful influences of maternal attitudes and preferences on children's union-formation behavior. Mothers' tolerance of premarital sex and cohabitation increase cohabitation rates and decrease marriage rates, mothers' preferences that their children marry early and produce many grandchildren increase rates of marriage, and maternal preferences for high minimum levels of schooling delay entrance into marriage. These results join a growing body of evidence pointing toward powerful effects of parental attitudes and preferences on their children's behavior (Axinn and Thornton 1992a, 1993; Barber 2000, 2001; Goldscheider and Goldscheider 1993; Marini 1978).

Independent Effects of Specific Maternal Attitudes

The estimated effects of maternal attitudes in table 9.1 are total effects with minimum controls in that they are estimated in separate equations. Because some of these total effects may be the product of intercorrelations among measures and would be reduced if they were estimated in

TABLE 9.2 **Total effects with maximum controls of mother's attitudes on children's rates of entrance into marital and cohabiting unions (as competing destinations)**[a]

	Marriage		Cohabitation	
	B[b]	Z[c]	B[b]	Z[c]
Mother's attitude toward premarital sex/cohabitation	−0.09	1.16	0.20	2.62
Mother's preferred age at marriage for child	−0.08	2.67	−0.02	0.64
Mother's preferred family size for child	0.17	2.17	−0.08	1.11
Mother's educational expectation for child	−0.07	2.19	−0.06	1.85
No. of periods	58,703		58,703	
No. of events	342		350	
χ^2	180.72		120.92	
DF	32		32	

Notes: [a] All equations also include the factors from Model 6.6 of chapter 6 (table 6.4). Estimates are estimated in an equation including all of the factors listed.
[b] Effect coefficient for logit equations transformed by equation: $[\exp(\beta) - 1]$.
[c] Z = ratio of absolute value of coefficient to its standard error.

the same equation, we estimate effects of all the maternal attitudes simultaneously. These estimates, displayed in table 9.2, are total effects with maximum controls in that all maternal measures are included.

The results indicate that nearly all of the maternal attitudes that were statistically significant in table 9.1 also have independent effects on the children's behavior, even with maximum controls. As one would expect, the effects estimated in this summary model are generally smaller than when estimated individually. This is particularly true in the case of maternal attitudes toward premarital sex and cohabitation, where the effect on marriage rates is reduced by nearly 50 percent by controlling for the other maternal attitudes (comparing column 1, row 1 of table 9.2 to column 1, row 1 of table 9.1). However, the effects of the other factors significant in table 9.1 remain statistically significant in the full model. This attests to the significant independent effects on children's behavior of a broad range of parental attitudes. In a later section we examine the extent to which these parental factors influence children's behavior directly or indirectly (through children's own attitudes), but before doing so we turn to an analysis of the influence of the young adults' attitudes.

Young People's Attitudes and Preferences

Table 9.3 shows our estimates of the total effects with minimum controls of young people's attitudes on their subsequent rates of cohabitation and

TABLE 9.3 **Total effects with minimum controls of children's attitudes on children's rates of entrance into marital and cohabiting unions (as competing destinations)[a]**

	Marriage		Cohabitation	
	B[b]	Z[c]	B[b]	Z[c]
Attitude toward premarital sex/cohabitation	−0.13	2.46	0.44	5.58
Preferred age at marriage	−0.16	6.67	−0.02	1.04
Attitude toward remaining single	−0.25	4.08	0.03	0.51
Preferred family size	0.03	0.79	−0.05	1.36
Attitude toward abortion	−0.05	0.47	0.45	3.42
Educational expectations	−0.04	1.55	−0.03	1.07
Attitude toward careers	−0.32	4.52	0.06	0.76
Attitude toward child-oriented spending	0.48	2.47	0.38	2.08
Sex-role attitudes	−0.20	2.43	−0.01	0.15
Attitude toward men prioritizing family more highly than career	0.28	3.30	0.02	0.30

Notes: [a] All equations also include the factors from Model 6.6 of chapter 6 (table 6.4). Estimates are from ten separate equations (with no controls for the other factors listed).
[b] Effect coefficient for logit equations transformed by equation: $[\exp(\beta) - 1]$.
[c] Z = ratio of absolute value of coefficient to its standard error.

marriage. Each coefficient in table 9.3 represents a separate model, which includes the same control variables used in the previous analyses.

Attitudes toward Premarital Sex and Cohabitation

Our results show, as expected, that positive attitudes toward premarital sex and cohabitation significantly reduce rates of marriage and increase rates of cohabitation. Individuals who feel strongly positive toward premarital sex and cohabitation have cohabitation rates that are more than twice as high and marriage rates that are a third lower than individuals who feel strongly negative toward premarital sex and cohabitation. And among those young people who enter either marriage or cohabitation, those with strong positive attitudes toward premarital sex and cohabitation are nearly five times more likely to cohabit for their first union than those with strong negative attitudes toward premarital sex and cohabitation (not shown in tables).

We also investigated young people's reports of their friends' and their mothers' attitudes toward premarital sex. It is important to note that these reports are probably influenced by the young people's own viewpoints. Nonetheless, both mothers and friends are important socializing forces in the lives of adolescents and young adults, and we expect that views on their attitudes toward premarital sex will influence the young adults' subsequent union-formation experiences. The results are consistent with this expectation (not shown in tables).

Young people who believe their mother or friends hold positive attitudes toward premarital sex enter cohabiting relations at significantly higher rates than young people who believe their mother or friends hold negative attitudes toward premarital sex. The public nature of cohabitation makes it difficult to hide the fact that premarital sex is occurring. The belief that these significant others are tolerant of premarital sex probably increases cohabitation rates because young people can then anticipate more support of cohabiting relationships. On the other hand, the belief that their mother or friends are not tolerant of premarital sex raises the psychological costs of cohabiting. The result is a strong positive relationship between beliefs regarding mothers' and friends' attitudes toward premarital sex and subsequent decisions about entrances into cohabiting relationships (not shown in tables).

Attitudes toward Marriage and Divorce

Rows 2 and 3 of table 9.3 show that our two measures of attitudes toward marriage both have strong effects on young people's subsequent marital behavior. However, neither of them has a significant influence on cohabitation behavior. More specifically, individuals who prefer later marriage or who have more positive attitudes toward remaining single enter marriage later than their peers.

Each additional year added to preferred age of marriage results in a 16 percent decrease in the rate of marriage, which translates to a marriage rate that is only one-sixth as high for those who prefer to marry at age 30 compared to those who prefer to marry at age 20. This depressing effect on the marriage rate holds for cohabitors as well as single people. That is, cohabitors with high age at marriage preferences marry at a slower rate than those with low age at marriage preferences (results not shown).

Similarly, those who feel positive toward remaining single[4] marry at significantly lower rates than those who feel negative toward remaining single (row 3 of table 9.3). Although this attitude does not affect cohabitation rates over the full period from age 18 to age 31, we found that those with positive attitudes toward remaining single have a significantly elevated rate of entering cohabiting relationships between ages 18 and 23 (results not shown). Thus, positive attitudes toward remaining single lead to an important substitution of cohabitation for marriage at younger ages.

The Intergenerational Panel Study also includes a number of different measures of generalized attitudes toward marriage. These include the beliefs that married people are happier than single people, that it is better to go through life married, and that there are few happy marriages these days. Previous research has demonstrated that these generalized attitudes toward marriage predict marital and cohabiting behavior between ages 18 and 23, with positive attitudes toward marriage increasing marriage rates and decreasing cohabitation rates (Axinn and Thornton 1992b). However, when we examine the effects of these same generalized attitudes over the entire age range from 18 through 31, we find that—although the effects remain in the same direction—they are smaller and no longer statistically significant (not shown in tables). This is because the influence of generalized attitudes toward marriage and divorce at age 18 weakens as young people mature from age 18 through age 31.

Our results for attitudes toward divorce follow a similar pattern. Tolerance of divorce, as measured by agreeing with the idea that divorce may be the best solution for couples experiencing problems in their marriage, increases rates of premarital cohabitation and reduces rates of marriage (not shown in tables). Although both effects are statistically significant between the ages of 18 and 23, neither is statistically significant for cohabitation and marriage rates through the whole period from age 18 to 31. Thus, at younger ages positive attitudes toward divorce produce an important substitution of premarital cohabitation for marriage, but these effects become weaker at older ages.

The panel study also includes another measure of attitudes toward marriage and divorce: the belief that married people should stay together if there are children in the family. Those who strongly disagree with this idea cohabit at rates 33 percent higher than those who strongly agree with this idea, and this effect is statistically significant throughout the ages from 18 to 31 (not shown in tables). Disagreement with this item also reduces rates of marriage, though this effect is not statistically significant (not shown in tables). Overall then, the associations we find are consistent with the conclusion that positive attitudes toward divorce reduce rates of marriage and increase rates of cohabitation, particularly at younger ages.

Attitudes toward Childbearing

Next we consider the influence of childbearing attitudes on cohabiting and marital behavior. Preferences for large families have a mild but not statistically significant negative effect on cohabitation rates, and no significant effect on marriage rates (row 4 of table 9.3). Enjoyment of activities with children, on the other hand, has no effect on cohabitation rates but significantly increases marriage rates (not shown in tables). The belief that children cause worry and strain to parents has no significant effect on either cohabitation or marriage rates (not shown in tables). Overall we expected positive attitudes toward childbearing to lead those forming coresidential unions to choose marriage over cohabitation. Our results provide some support for this prediction.

Attitudes toward Abortion

We also explore the influence of the 18-year-olds' attitudes toward abortion on their rates of cohabitation and marriage. Our measure of this factor comes from the responses representing views on whether or not "it would be all right" to have an abortion under six different circumstances (see table C.5 of Appendix C). Positive attitudes toward abortion—indicating higher acceptance of abortion for the six described reasons—are associated with significantly higher rates of premarital cohabitation, but have no significant effects on marriage rates (row 5 of table 9.3). The dramatic effects of abortion attitudes on cohabitation behavior add a complex dimension to our overall thinking about the relationship between childbearing attitudes and cohabitation. It may be that acceptance of abortion reduces young people's perceived risk of having the ongoing premarital sexual relationship associated with cohabitation. Put another way, strong negative attitudes toward abortion may reduce cohabitation rates because of the associated risk of premarital pregnancy combined with an unwillingness to consider medical means of pregnancy termination. It is also possible that both abortion and unmarried cohabitation are strongly counter to historical norms and that positive attitudes toward each of them are reflective of an overall positive orientation to individual rights and autonomy.

Educational Expectations

Next we test the effects of educational expectations on cohabiting and marital behavior. Positive attitudes toward education, as indicated in the theoretical framework presented previously, are expected to promote activities, such as schooling, that may compete with cohabitation and marriage. The empirical results indicate that young people's expectations for the highest amount of schooling they will attain may have modest negative effects (not statistically significant) on both cohabitation and marriage rates (row 6 of table 9.3). Likewise, young peoples' willingness to choose completing college over marriage is associated with significantly lower marriage rates. Those who say at age 18 that they would not drop out of college to get married, go on to marry at rates that are 35 percent lower than those who say they would (not shown in tables). Thus these alternative measures of commitment to education produce the expected delays in entrances into marriage.

Attitudes toward Careers

We also expect positive attitudes toward careers will promote educational and work activities that compete with cohabitation and marriage, at least in early adulthood. As shown in table 9.3 (row 7), positive attitudes toward careers significantly reduce rates of marriage. Those with strong career orientations enter marriage at about half the rate of their peers with weak career orientations.[5] Thus, positive attitudes toward careers substantially delay marriage.

Attitudes toward Spending

We consider the theory that higher consumption aspirations reduce rates of entry into marriage and childbearing by investigating two different forms of consumption aspirations: attitudes toward spending on luxury goods, an activity that would compete with marriage and childbearing, and attitudes toward spending on child-oriented goods, an activity compatible with marriage and childbearing.

Our results are consistent with the expectation that positive attitudes toward luxury spending (buying items such as televisions, recreational vehicles, stereos, and fashion clothing) have a modest negative effect on marriage rates. Although this reductive effect is not statistically significant across the entire age span from ages 18 to 31, it is statistically significant ($p < .10$) at ages 18 to 23 (not shown in tables).[6] So, at least at younger ages, positive attitudes toward luxury goods delay marriage (see also Barber, Axinn, and Thornton 2002).

Positive attitudes toward child-oriented spending (e.g., lessons, camps, education for children), on the other hand, have strong, statistically significant effects increasing rates of both cohabitation and marriage (row 8 of table 9.3). Young people who feel positively about spending on goods for children enter both cohabitation and marriage at significantly higher rates than those who do not. Thus, our results are consistent with the conclusion that attitudes toward spending are an important element in the overall package of attitudes and values that influence choices about family formation.

Note that our findings regarding attitudes toward spending on children are particularly interesting because they do not fully support the relative deprivation hypothesis that high consumer-spending preferences delay family formation (Clarkberg, Stolzenber, and Waite 1995; Easterlin 1980; Easterlin and Crimmins 1985). They also run contrary to key microeconomic theories of fertility (Becker 1991; Willis 1973) related to the "quantity-quality trade-off" hypothesis. That is, parents will limit the quantity of their children in order to increase the quality of each child. This hypothesis predicts that parents with high aspirations for their children will delay family formation until they have accumulated the resources necessary to invest heavily in each child (Barber, Axinn, and Thornton 2002; Becker 1991). Our results, however, indicate that only those spending preferences *not* oriented toward children delay family formation. Preferences for spending on children actually hasten family formation. This may be because those preferences are associated with an underlying orientation toward children and family formation (Barber, Axinn, and Thornton 2002). Further research will be required to better understand these findings. However, these results are consistent with our theoretical framework, which predicts positive attitudes toward family and family-related behaviors increase rates of family formation behavior.

Sex-Role Attitudes

Chapters 5 and 6 provide a detailed investigation of the influence of mothers' sex-role attitudes on children's cohabitation and marriage behavior. Our findings for the effect of young adults' sex-role attitudes are quite consistent with those we found for the mothers. Young people with more egalitarian sex-role attitudes enter marriage at significantly lower rates than other young people (row 9 of table 9.3). This is not surprising, as marital relationships tend to facilitate the specialization of spouses into separate roles.

For the young adults, we also investigate attitudes regarding men's roles in families. Some scholars have argued that a key consequence of the gender-role revolution of the 1960s and 1970s in the United States is that only those with positive attitudes toward men's involvement in family matters will form new families through marriage and childbearing (Goldscheider and Waite 1991). If this is true, we expect that those who have positive attitudes toward men prioritizing family roles more highly than career achievement will marry at higher rates than those who do not. And as shown in the final row of table 9.3, we find that young adults who believe that men should prioritize family over career marry more quickly than others, with each unit of the attitudinal factor being associated with a 28 percent higher rate of marriage. This finding provides strong support for the idea that attitudes toward men's family roles have an important effect on entrance into marriage.

Differences by Gender

The tensions between work and family roles are generally greater for women than for men because most men continue to specialize in market work while many women combine and integrate work and family roles. For this reason, we expect the effects of sex-role attitudes, attitudes about careers, and the role of men within their families will be greater for women than for men.

We investigate this hypothesis directly in our analysis of marriage by introducing interaction terms between gender and the three family/career factors in question: sex-role attitudes; attitude toward careers; and attitude toward men prioritizing family more highly than career. For each of the family/career factors, the estimated effects for women were stronger than the effects for men. Furthermore, although the differences were modest and not statistically significant for sex-role attitudes and attitudes toward careers, the difference was statistically significant for attitudes toward men prioritizing family over career. Whereas each additional unit of positive orientation of men toward family life increased men's rate of marriage by 12 percent, it increased women's marriage rate by 43 percent. Clearly, the beliefs of women about the role of men in the family have a strong influence on the speed at which they enter marriage.

Direct and Indirect Effects of Maternal Attitudes

Mothers' family experiences and attitudes are known to influence children's family formation attitudes (Axinn and Thornton 1996), which in turn exert a strong influence on family formation behavior. Thus it is reasonable to expect the close association between mothers' attitudes and children's attitudes may explain some of the total effects of mothers' attitudes on children's behavior.

A particular parental attitude might influence children's behavior through many causal pathways. Most obvious is through a replication of a parental attitude in the second generation—for example maternal attitudes about school influencing children's union formation through the children's attitudes about school (Marini 1978). However, it is also possible for a particular parental attitude to affect children's behavior via a wide array of children's attitudes. For example, maternal attitudes about schooling might influence children's attitudes about marriage, premarital sex, and childbearing—all of which influence children's union-formation experiences. For this reason, we consider all of the children's attitudes together in a combined model of maternal and child attitude effects, the results for which are shown in table 9.4.

A comparison of the results in the top panel of table 9.4 with those in table 9.2 reveals that the addition of the children's factors substantially reduces the estimates of all the maternal attitude effects except for maternal educational expectations for the child. Whereas all of the maternal attitudes had statistically significant effects on marriage and/or cohabitation behavior without controls for children's attitudes, most do not after the children's attitudes are added to the model. The sharp reduction of the effect of mothers' attitudes on children's behavior reflects the substantial indirect effects of mothers' attitudes via the full array of children's attitudes included in the models presented in table 9.4. This substantial reduction is also consistent with a broad version of the socialization hypotheses, in which mothers' attitudes and values in any one domain influence children's attitudes and values across a broad set of domains. This broad socialization model thus also accounts for much of the influence of parental attitudes on children's behavior.

Further analysis revealed which of the children's attitudes were most important in transmitting the effects of first-generation attitudes on second-generation experience with marriage and cohabitation. For maternal attitudes toward premarital sex and cohabitation the central intervening mechanisms are children's attitudes toward premarital sex and cohabitation and preferred age at marriage. Given the transmission of attitudes and behavior across generations, it should not be surprising that mothers with permissive attitudes toward premarital sex and cohabitation have

TABLE 9.4 **Direct effects of adult children's attitudes and mother's attitudes on children's rates of entrance into marital and cohabiting unions (as competing destinations)**[a]

	Marriage		Cohabitation	
	B[b]	Z[c]	B[b]	Z[c]
Mother's attitudes				
Attitude toward premarital sex/cohabitation	−0.08	0.98	0.10	1.31
Preferred age at marriage for child	−0.06	1.71	0.00	0.15
Preferred family size for child	0.07	0.91	−0.09	1.19
Educational expectations for child	−0.07	1.75	−0.06	1.42
Children's attitudes				
Attitude toward premarital sex/cohabitation	−0.06	0.98	0.32	3.69
Preferred age at marriage	−0.12	4.18	−0.05	1.79
Attitude toward remaining single	−0.13	1.70	−0.07	1.01
Preferred family size	−0.05	1.15	−0.03	0.72
Attitude toward abortion	0.20	1.44	0.28	2.06
Educational expectations	0.03	0.70	−0.01	0.24
Attitude toward careers	−0.18	2.03	0.01	0.09
Attitude toward child-oriented spending	0.58	2.68	0.36	1.85
Sex–role attitudes	0.02	0.19	0.00	0.04
Attitude toward men prioritizing family more highly than career	0.25	2.74	0.04	0.49
No. of periods	56,788		56,788	
No. of events	325		334	
χ^2	229.79		151.54	
DF	42		42	

Notes: [a] All equations also include the factors from Model 6.6 of chapter 6 (table 6.4). Estimates are estimated in an equation including all of the factors listed.
[b] Effect coefficient for logit equations transformed by equation: $[\exp(\beta) - 1]$.
[c] Z = ratio of absolute value of coefficient to its standard error.

children with permissive attitudes ($r = .36$) that, in turn, enhance the rate of forming a cohabiting union. In addition, mothers who have permissive attitudes have children who prefer to marry at older ages ($r = .10$)—and this is, in turn, related to higher rates of cohabitation.

There are two additional potential pathways of influence through which maternal attitudes toward premarital sex and cohabitation may operate: going steady and sexual experience; and the religiosity of the young adult. Just as mothers with permissive attitudes have children with more permissive attitudes, their children also have more early dating and sexual experience. In addition, mothers who are more permissive have children who are less religious ($r = -.35$). And, we know from earlier chapters that low levels of religiosity and early dating and sexual experience are related to high rates of cohabitation.

Turning now to the mother's preferred age at marriage for the child, we find a relatively straightforward and simple story. The introduction of the attitudes and experiences of the young adults reduces substantially the estimated effect of maternal preferred age at marriage on the young-adult marriage rate. Virtually all of the indirect effect is transmitted through one young-adult factor, the preferred age at marriage of the child. There is a strong correlation ($r = .38$) between maternal and child preferred ages at marriage, and young adults with later preferred marital ages marry more slowly than others. The estimated influence of maternal preferred age at marriage through children's preferred age at marriage is $-.04$ to $-.05$. Thus, for each year of maternal preferred age at marriage there is a 4 to 5 percent decline in the marriage rate that operates entirely through the young adult's own preferred age at marriage. Given a range of several years for preferred marital ages, this indirect effect can be substantial.

Moving now to the indirect effects of maternal fertility preferences on children's marriage behavior, we note several indirect effects through young-adult attitudes: attitudes about sex and cohabitation before marriage; preferred age at marriage; attitudes toward remaining single; and attitudes toward careers.[7] It turns out that mothers with high fertility desires for their children tend to have young-adult children with the following attributes: less positive attitudes toward premarital sex and cohabitation ($r = -.11$), preferences for a lower age at marriage ($r = -.05$), negative attitudes toward remaining single ($r = -.11$), and less positive attitudes toward careers ($r = -.17$). Because each of these dimensions of young adulthood is associated with higher rates of marriage, they act as indirect pathways for the positive influence of parental family-size preferences on the rate of entrance into marriage.

At the same time, and paradoxically, maternal preferences for many grandchildren are related to both greater religiosity ($r = .18$) and greater premarital sexual involvement in the second generation—again factors that increase the rate of marriage. Thus, many indirect pathways transmit the influence of maternal fertility preferences on young-adult entrance into marriage, and these indirect pathways account for nearly all of the influence of maternal fertility preferences.

Nevertheless, even in the model including all these measures of children's attitudes, we find that mothers' preferred ages for children to marry and mothers' educational expectations for children each have a statistically significant, independent effect on the timing of children's marriage. Mothers who prefer their children to marry later and mothers who expect their children to attain higher levels of education have children who do in fact marry later. Although these maternal effects are reduced by the inclusion of children's own attitudes, they represent an important intergenerational influence of maternal attitudes on children that cannot be explained by the children's own attitudes. Thus, our results join a growing body of evidence that parental attitudes constitute an important influence on children's behavior net of their influence on children's attitudes (Barber 2000). This effect can occur through various forms of parental control and through the desire of children to please their parents even when the attitudes of parents and children do not coincide.

The attitudes and values of the children operate not only as mechanisms transmitting the influence of maternal attitudes but as mechanisms transmitting other parental experiences, such as maternal marital and childbearing experiences. We now turn to a discussion of these indirect effects of maternal experience through children's attitudes.

Explaining Effects of Maternal Divorce and Remarriage

An important finding of chapter 6 was the substantial influence of a parental marital dissolution on the rate of children entering cohabitation and marriage. We reported there that children who have grown up in families in which the mother has experienced a marital dissolution and then remarried have higher rates of marriage than children who have not. We found no positive effect for maternal marital disruption on marriage rates when mothers do not remarry. However, all kinds of maternal marital dissolutions—whether or not they are followed by remarriage—are associated with substantially higher cohabitation rates.

Interestingly, when children's factors at age 18 are introduced, the direct effect of maternal divorce and remarriage on young-adult cohabitation is reduced, suggesting an indirect effect of maternal experience through the children's attitudes and aspirations. Further exploration suggests no single dominant pathway of indirect influence from experience with maternal divorce and remarriage to second-generation cohabitation experience, but several relatively modest pathways through the child's family attitudes. Most important here are attitudes toward premarital sex and cohabitation; sex-role attitudes; and attitudes toward abortion. Young people who grow up in families with a divorced and remarried mother have more permissive attitudes toward premarital sex and cohabitation, more egalitarian gender-role attitudes, and more positive attitudes toward abortion—factors all positively related to the decision to cohabit.[8] We also note the relevance of high school grades, a factor to be studied

in the next chapter. Children of mothers experiencing divorce and remarriage have lower grades, a factor related to higher rates of cohabitation.[9]

Explaining Effects of Parental Childbearing

One of the important findings of chapter 6 was the substantial positive influence of parental family size on the rate of union formation. Young people from large families both marry and cohabit substantially more rapidly
than others.

Our examination of indirect effects reveals that parental family size influences children's entrance into marriage indirectly through the mother's
preferred family size for her child. Mothers with large families prefer large
families for their children (Pearson correlation, $r = .20$), a factor that leads
to higher rates of marriage. Note that the introduction of the 1980 maternal attitudes in the equation predicting cohabitation does not result in a
reduction of the direct effect of parental fertility. The reason is that although parental fertility and family size preferences are positively correlated, high fertility preferences lead to lower, not higher, rates of entrance
into cohabitation.

Interestingly, the attitudes of the young people themselves serve as
a pathway through which parental fertility has the indirect effect of decreasing rather than increasing marriage rates in the second generation.
This is in the opposite direction of the direct effects reported in chapter 6.
Two main second-generation attitudes transmit this negative indirect effect of parental fertility on marriage rates: attitude toward child-oriented
spending; and attitude toward men prioritizing family more highly than
career. Young people from large families have weaker aspirations for
child-oriented spending ($r = -.08$) and emphasize less strongly men's
family responsibilities relative to their careers ($r = -.08$)—all of which are
associated with slower rates of entering marriage. Consequently, parental
fertility has an indirect negative effect on second-generation marriage
rates through each of these second-generation factors.[10] One nonattitu-
dinal second-generation factor also produces a negative indirect effect
from parental fertility to children's marriage. It is the children's experience with going steady and sex. Young people from large families have
less going-steady and sexual experience, which is associated with a slower
rate of entering marriage.

With the negative indirect effects of parental fertility through the children's factors controlled, the net or direct effect of parental family size on the rate of entrance into marriage is particularly substantial and important. Each additional sibling is associated with a 15 percent increase in the young adults' rate of marriage, net of other factors.[11] Explanations of this intergenerational effect will require examination of factors beyond those considered in this book.

Explaining Effects of Parental Religion

In the previous chapter we observed that the intergenerational transmission of religiosity was an important mechanism transmitting the influence of maternal religiosity on children's union-formation experiences. Here we note that the family attitudes of both mothers and children are also intervening factors transmitting the influence of maternal religiosity. In addition, the child's sex and dating experiences transmit some of the maternal religiosity effect. In fact, the family attitudes of mothers and children, the religiosity of the children, and the dating and sexual experience of the children can account for much of the 1977 religiosity effect.

Within the parental generation, the main story is through attitudes toward premarital sex and cohabitation. Religious mothers have less permissive attitudes toward premarital sex and cohabitation ($r = -.40$), which lead to lower rates of cohabitation and higher rates of marriage. Thus, there is a positive indirect influence of parental religiosity through maternal premarital sex attitudes on marriage that ranges from .02 to .03, depending on whether the estimate has maximum or minimum controls. This means that for each unit of maternal religiosity, there is a two or three percentage point increase in the rate of marriage through maternal attitudes toward premarital sex and cohabitation. Similarly, there is between a two and three percent decline in the rate of cohabitation with each unit of religiosity because religiosity decreases parental permissiveness, which in turn leads to lower rates of cohabitation. Clearly, maternal attitudes about premarital sex and cohabitation are important elements in the influence of maternal religiosity on the union-formation experiences of young adults.

Similar indirect pathways are operating across generations. The religious attendance of the mother in 1977 has negative indirect influences on second-generation cohabitation through the young adults' dating and sexual experience and attitudes about premarital sex and cohabitation.

We estimate these indirect effects to range from −.01 to −.02 for dating and sex, and to range from 0 to −.01 for attitudes about premarital sex and cohabitation. These negative indirect effects occur because the children of more religious mothers postpone dating and sexual experience as teenagers and have less positive attitudes toward premarital sex and cohabitation ($r = -.27$), both of which lower the likelihood of entering cohabitation.

Explaining Effects of Maternal Sex-Role Attitudes

In chapter 6 we observed that the attitudes of the mother toward appropriate roles for women and men were strongly related to both marriage and cohabitation in the second generation. More specifically, egalitarian gender-role attitudes are positively related to cohabitation and negatively related to marriage. Here we note three factors that can help to explain these effects: mother's attitude toward premarital sex and cohabitation; mother's preferred age at marriage for the child; and mother's preferred family size for the child. Mothers with egalitarian sex-role attitudes have substantially more permissive attitudes toward premarital sex and cohabitation ($r = .37$), prefer higher ages at marriage ($r = .24$), and prefer smaller family sizes ($r = -.15$). Permissive attitudes toward premarital sex and cohabitation, preferences for delayed marriage, and preferences for small families are also all related to low rates of marriage in the second generation, thereby forming indirect pathways of influence from maternal sex-role attitudes to the marriage experience of young adults. Similarly, permissive attitudes toward premarital sex and cohabitation and preferences for small families are both related to high rates of cohabitation, completing the indirect pathways from maternal sex-role attitudes to cohabitation rates in the second generation.

Thus, these results suggest that maternal sex-role attitudes are interrelated with other maternal attitudes that have important connections with second-generation marriage and cohabitation behavior. Note that we have structured this analysis with the assumption that 1977 maternal sex-role attitudes are causally prior to maternal attitudes toward other dimensions of life measured in 1980. Although this assumption is consistent with the temporal ordering of measurement, we also know that maternal attitudes toward family issues are quite stable over time (Thornton and Binstock 2001). This suggests that the maternal attitudes and preferences about premarital sex, cohabitation, age at marriage, and family size measured in 1980 are highly correlated with the same attitudes held in 1977 or earlier. Consequently, it is possible that instead of these other family attitudes forming indirect pathways of causal influence, they are part of a package of interrelated family attitudes. Of course, even if this latter interpretation is correct, sex-role attitudes may still form the central core of that interrelated package of family attitudes.

Interestingly, although egalitarian maternal sex-role attitudes are generally related to high rates of cohabitation in the second generation, our examination of indirect effects has revealed one substantial negative indirect effect of maternal sex-role attitudes on cohabitation. This negative indirect pathway (of between −.07 and −.10) operates through the going steady and sexual experience of the young adults. That is, mothers with more egalitarian sex-role attitudes have children who wait longer to go steady and have sex, factors that slow down the rapidity of entrance into cohabiting unions. Note that the indirect effect through young adults' steady and sexual experience is negative, in contrast to the positive indirect effect through the mother's attitudes toward premarital sex and cohabitation. This is possible because maternal egalitarian sex-role attitudes are positively correlated with permissive attitudes toward premarital sex and cohabitation, yet negatively correlated with the rapidity of entrance into dating and sexual relationships. Thus, despite having more permissive attitudes toward premarital sex, mothers with egalitarian sex-role attitudes have children who enter intimate premarital relationships more slowly than others.

Direct Effects of Children's Attitudes

We now turn to the direct, or net, effects of each dimension of the children's attitudes and preferences on behavior. We do so by controlling for each of the maternal attitudes and the full range of attitudes and preferences of the second generation. We use the same measures as in previous analyses, and the results are displayed in the second panel of table 9.4.

It is impressive to note the number of effects of children's attitudes that remain quite strong despite the large number of controls. As shown in table 9.4, positive attitudes toward both abortion and premarital sex/cohabitation[12] significantly increase cohabitation experience without significantly influencing marriage. Those with positive attitudes toward remaining single and those with positive attitudes toward careers have significantly lower rates of marriage, but do not vary significantly in the rate of cohabitation. Those who value men's roles in the home marry more quickly, but have no significant difference in cohabitation rates. Interestingly, those with later preferred ages at marriage both marry and cohabit at lower rates than others. Furthermore, those with positive attitudes toward spending for children both marry and cohabit significantly faster than others, even controlling for many other factors. Only preferred family size, expected educational attainment, and sex-role attitudes no longer have a significant influence on cohabiting and marital behavior. These specific domains of young people's attitudes do not influence cohabiting and marital behavior independently of the mothers' attitudes in these same domains and the other attitude domains in the children's generation.

These results suggest that researchers investigating the influence of attitudes on behavior must recognize that attitudes across multiple domains of meaning are likely to affect behavior in any single domain (Barber 2001). Moreover, as predicted, positive attitudes toward family, or toward specific dimensions of family formation processes, are associated with higher rates of union formation. By contrast, positive attitudes toward nonfamily alternatives, such as careers or remaining single, are associated with lower rates of union formation.

Intertwining of Effects of Children's Attitudes

Despite the many strong direct effects of the individual attitudinal factors on children's cohabitation and marriage, many of the direct effects of these attitudes in table 9.4 are smaller than the total effects in table 9.3. This suggests that several of these attitudinal factors are closely correlated, with their total and indirect effects intertwined. We now turn to an explication of which factors reduce the observed effects of other factors.

As we explain in Appendix A, our approach to estimating indirect effects requires a causal and temporal ordering of the factors in the lives of the young adults being studied. This is difficult in the present case because all of the child's attitudinal factors were measured simultaneously at age 18, and there is no clear causal ordering among them. Without this clear causal ordering of the attitudinal factors, it is difficult to be definitive about which set of attitudes explains the effects of other attitudes on union formation. Nevertheless, this analysis will show how the effects of the various attitudes on marriage and cohabitation are intertwined.

Attitudes toward Premarital Sex and Cohabitation

We first note that the estimated effect of attitudes toward premarital sex and cohabitation on the rate of cohabitation is reduced slightly with the introduction of abortion attitudes into the analysis. This occurs because of the strong positive correlation between attitudes toward abortion and attitudes toward premarital sex and cohabitation ($r = .41$) and the fact that both are positively related to the rate of entrance into cohabitation. This finding illustrates that attitudes about a range of family and intimate matters—including abortion, sex, and cohabitation—are intertwined in their influence on entrance into cohabitation.

Another attitude with a substantial correlation with attitudes toward premarital sex and cohabitation is the acceptance of remaining single ($r = .21$). This positive correlation between two historically proscribed behaviors is important because both slow down the rate of entrance into marriage. Thus, when the acceptance of remaining single is controlled, the observed effect of attitudes toward premarital sex and cohabitation is reduced.

Attitudes toward Abortion

Just as we observed earlier that abortion attitudes were relevant to understanding the effects of premarital sex and cohabitation attitudes on cohabitation behavior, here we note that premarital sexual attitudes are important in understanding the effect of abortion attitudes. More specifically, attitudes toward premarital sex and cohabitation can explain part of the total effect of abortion attitudes on the rate of cohabitation.

Attitudes toward Being Single

Turning now to the acceptance of remaining single, we note that some of its negative effect on rates of entrance into marriage can be accounted for by preferred age at marriage. In fact, preferred age at marriage can account for between $-.07$ and $-.09$ of the effect of attitudes toward remaining single on the rate of marriage. That is, acceptance of singleness and preferences for older ages at marriage are positively correlated ($r = .30$), which helps explain the low rates of marriage among people accepting of being single. Causation may run in either direction—that is, acceptance of remaining single could lead to preferences for higher ages of marriage (and thus lower rates of marriage), or preferences for higher ages at marriage could lead to acceptance of remaining single.

In addition, acceptance of staying single is positively related to career aspirations $(r = .19)$ and acceptance of premarital sex and cohabitation $(r = .21)$. Because both of these factors are associated with low rates of marriage, they transmit some of the negative influence of positive attitudes toward staying single on the rate of marriage. This suggests an important interrelationship among attitudes toward being single, sex, cohabitation, and careers that is reflected in a pattern of joint influence on the rate of entrance into marriage.

Career Aspirations and Gender-Role Attitudes

As we just noted, career aspirations are strongly and negatively related to the rate of entrance into marriage. Here we add the observation that some of the effect of career aspirations on the rate of marriage is due to the other attitudinal factors considered. Further examination reveals a web of factors that are associated with career aspirations in influencing marriage, including attitudes toward marriage, being single, and the commitment of men to family life.

The major correlated factor transmitting the effect of career aspirations on marriage are marital age preferences and attitudes toward being single. Those with strong career aspirations have later preferred ages at marriage $(r = .28)$ and greater acceptance of remaining single $(r = .19)$, two factors that lead to lower rates of marriage. Also, people with strong career aspirations place less emphasis on men's involvement in the family $(r = -.14)$, another factor related to low rates of marriage. Although these other factors explain some of the effect of career aspirations on marriage, a strong direct effect remains that is not mediated by any other factors considered here, indicating the direct relevance of career aspirations for marriage.

Another substantial predictor of marriage rates is sex-role attitudes, with those holding more egalitarian attitudes having substantially lower rates of marriage than others. Furthermore, we are able to account for that entire effect with the factors considered here, indicating many potential indirect pathways of influence and suggesting the centrality of sex-role attitudes in the network of influences on marriage rates.

Egalitarian sex-role attitudes are positively associated with three other important predictors of the rate of entrance into marriage: attitudes toward premarital sex and cohabitation ($r = .26$), preferred age at marriage ($r = .15$), and career aspirations ($r = .31$). Each of these factors is, in turn, related to lower rates of marriage. Clearly, these associations are important explanations of the negative influence of sex-role attitudes on the rate of marriage.

Young-Adult Attitudes, Religiosity, and Sexual Behavior

Just as the young-adult attitudes are intertwined and jointly influence marriage and cohabitation, they are interrelated with young-adult religiosity and sexual experience. These interconnections play an important role in influencing young-adult union formation. We now turn to these interconnections, noting that their simultaneous occurrence and measurement makes the causal model interconnecting them ambiguous.

Religiosity

We begin our discussion with young-adult religiosity and remind the reader of the strong conclusion of chapter 8 that high levels of religiosity are related to high rates of entrance into marriage and low rates of entrance into cohabitation, with highly religious youths choosing marriage over cohabitation more frequently than the less religious. These effects of religiosity on both cohabitation and marriage remain large and statistically significant, even with the full controls utilized in later chapters. This indicates that young-adult religiosity has an important effect on the union-formation process that cannot be explained through the young-adult factors observed in our study.

However, the direct effects of religiosity are reduced with the introduction of young-adult attitudes and sexual experience in the analyses, indicating that the influence of young-adult religiosity on union formation is part of a more general relationship between religiosity and personal behavior and attitudes. Our results indicate that religiosity is correlated with a wide range of family attitudes and behaviors—including attitudes toward premarital sex and cohabitation, adolescent sexual behavior, preferred ages at marriage, and preferences for the involvement of men in family life—each of which is related to the union-formation experiences of young adults.

Particularly important here is the fact that, compared with those who are less religious, those young adults who are highly religious are much less sexually experienced as teenagers and have much less positive attitudes toward premarital sex, cohabitation, and abortion.[13] This is important because, as we have seen earlier, low levels of sexual involvement in the teenage years and restrictive attitudes toward premarital sex, cohabitation, and abortion are related to low levels of cohabitation. If we make the assumption that young-adult religiosity is causally prior to sexual behavior and attitudes toward sex, cohabitation, and abortion, then the latter young-adult factors form important intervening pathways through which young-adult religiosity influences the rate of entrance into cohabiting unions. Of course, if the causation is entirely in the opposite direction, then part of the estimated total effect of religiosity would be spurious. Specifying the nature of this causal network is beyond our capability in this book.

Interestingly, premarital sex, attitudes toward premarital sex and cohabitation, and attitudes toward abortion provide much less leverage in explaining the high marriage rates of the highly religious. The reason for this relates to an observation of an earlier chapter: these factors have less influence on marriage than on cohabitation, thereby lowering their power as intervening mechanisms for marriage compared to cohabitation.

The important indirect influences of religiosity on marriage operate through age at marriage preferences and attitudes about the roles of men in the home. Highly religious young adults have lower preferred ages at marriage ($r = -.17$) that lead to higher rates of marriage. This factor alone can account for about half of the total influence of religiosity on the rate of marriage. Highly religious young adults also have stronger positive attitudes about men's active involvement in the home ($r = .16$), a factor that substantially increases the rate of marriage. These interpretations are, of course, dependent upon the assumption that religiosity is causally prior to attitudes toward men's home roles and age at marriage.

It is important to note that just as family attitudes and adolescent sexual experience can explain a substantial part of the religiosity effect on union formation, religiosity can explain part of the observed effects of family attitudes. That is, the introduction of religiosity into equations with family attitudes reduces the estimated effects of some of those attitudes. One example of this is attitudes toward premarital sex and cohabitation, where the introduction of religiosity into the analysis reduces the effect of these attitudes on cohabitation between .04 and .07, (with maximum or minimum controls). This happens because positive attitudes toward premarital sex and cohabitation are associated with low religiosity that, in turn, increases the cohabitation rate. Of course, as in earlier analyses, the interpretation of this reduction of the attitude effect with the introduction of religiosity depends upon the assumptions made about the causal connections between religiosity and attitudes toward premarital sex and cohabitation.

Interestingly, just as religiosity plays a substantial role in explaining the positive effect of premarital sex and cohabitation attitudes on cohabitation behavior, it also helps to explain the negative effect of such attitudes on the rate of marriage. Positive attitudes toward premarital sex and cohabitation are associated with low rates of religiosity that, in turn, slow down the rate of entrance into marriage.

Adolescent Sexual Behavior

Just as religiosity can explain part of the influence of premarital sex and cohabitation attitudes on cohabitation behavior, adolescent sexual experience can explain another part of that attitudinal effect. More specifically, premarital sexual experience can explain between .14 and .17 of the total effect of attitudes toward premarital sex and cohabitation (depending on whether the estimate is made with maximum or minimum controls). This is, of course, due to the strong correlation between sexual attitudes and behavior.[14] If we assume that attitudes toward premarital sex and cohabitation are causally prior to sexual behavior, this means that a substantial part of the attitude effect on cohabitation operates through adolescent sexual behavior. However, if we assume that adolescent sexual behavior is causally prior to sexual attitudes, then much of the effect of attitudes on cohabitation is spurious in that it is the result of sexual behavior influencing both sexual attitudes and cohabitation behavior. It is difficult to distinguish between these two possible explanations, even though our behavioral indicators refer to the period up through age 18 and the attitudes were measured at age 18. This is because attitudes are relatively stable, making it possible for earlier attitudes toward premarital sex to influence sexual experience during the teenage years.

Sexual experience as a teenager can also help explain the effect of abortion attitudes. Young adults with positive attitudes toward abortion have, on average, earlier experience with sex as teenagers, a factor strongly associated with high rates of cohabitation.

The Impact of Parent-Child Relationship Quality

Some scholars have argued that the magnitude and direction of the effect of parental attitudes on children's behavior is likely to depend on the quality of the relationship between parent and young adult. This argument proposes that parents' attitudes probably have the strongest influence on children's behavior when parent and child have a high-quality relationship, and that the influence of parents' attitudes is probably weakest, or even reverses, when parent and child have a low-quality relationship. Such arguments hypothesize a statistical interaction effect rather than an additive effect in that the influence of parental values on children's values and behavior depends on how well parents and children communicate and get along. This interactive model has been demonstrated in the arena of premarital sexual attitudes and behavior (Moore, Peterson, and Furstenberg 1986; Weinstein and Thornton 1989). Thus, it is prudent to examine our models of cohabitation and marital behavior for similar interactions between the effects of maternal attitudes and the quality of parent-child relationships.

This task is facilitated by the fact that the Intergenerational Panel Study includes multiple measures of the quality of the mother-child and father-child relationship from the children's points of view (see Appendix table C.5). Although we focus on the effect of mothers' attitudes on the children's behavior, we explore the effects of both father-child and mother-child relationship quality. Previous research on the measurement properties of these measures of parent-child relationship quality demonstrates that the multiple measures for each parent can be combined into a single scale (Thornton, Orbuch, and Axinn 1995). Therefore, we combined the items measuring the mother-child relationship into one scale and the items measuring the father-child relationships into another scale, and we also combined these two scales into a parent-child scale (Thornton, Orbuch, and Axinn 1995).

We estimated separate models for each of the maternal attitudes as in table 9.2, but added the main effect of the mother-child relationship quality and the interaction between the attitude and the mother-child relationship quality. We repeated this procedure using father-child relationship

quality and for our summary measure of parent-child relationship quality. None of these interactions were statistically significant or substan-
tively large (not shown in tables). We find that the influence on children's
behavior of each item of the mothers' attitudes does not depend on the
child's relationship to the mother or to the father—a result that is not consistent with the body of ideas motivating this specific inquiry. Our inability
to find strong results may be a consequence of our focus on cohabiting and
marital behavior, or of the specific maternal attitudes we examine.

However, in the process of this inquiry we found that the quality of
mother-child and father-child relationships has strong, important, and statistically significant effects on young people's rates of marriage. We estimated three separate models, each including all the same controls used
elsewhere in this chapter, but now including mother-child relationship
quality, father-child relationship quality, and the summary parent-child
relationship quality. Although no measure of relationship quality has any
significant effect on young people's cohabitation behavior, each has a significant positive effect on rates of marriage (not shown in tables). In fact,
those young people who feel they always have a positive relationship with
their mothers go on to marry at nearly two and a half times the rate of
those young people who feel they never have a positive relationship. The
effects of father-child and parent-child relationships are of similar magnitude. These results provide strong evidence that those young people
who believe they have extremely positive relationships with their parents
go on to form families of their own, via marriage, at substantially higher
rates than others.

In additional analyses, we added our summary measure of parent-child
relationship quality to the models of table 9.4, which include mothers' and
children's attitudes across multiple domains. Although the introduction
of these additional controls somewhat reduced our estimate of the effect
of parent-child relationship quality, we found that high parent-child relationship quality still results in significantly higher rates of marriage. In
addition, the estimates of the parent and child attitude effects from models that include this measure of parent-child relationship quality look extremely similar to those displayed in table 9.4 (not shown in tables).

The theoretical framework we outlined previously does not provide
direct prediction of this effect. Nonetheless, several of the key ideas presented there help to explain it. First, that framework predicts that those
who feel positively about families and spending time in family life will
marry more quickly than those who do not. Second, that framework predicts

that situations and experiences early in life will shape young people's later behavioral decisions. Together, these two ideas provide a possible explanation of the observed effects of the quality of relationships with parents on the rates of entering marriage during early adulthood. Young people who perceive strong positive relationships with their parents probably have more positive dispositions toward family life in general, and may have a more rapid entry into marriage as a way of building their own adult family life. These data also provide no support for a counter explanation that children marry early to escape a negative relationship with their parents.

Summary and Conclusion

We find strong relationships between family formation behavior and attitudes in a variety of domains. Furthermore, these relationships are not limited to parallel attitudes and behavior. For instance, positive attitudes toward premarital sex and cohabitation increase cohabitation rates, but decrease rates of marriage. Positive attitudes toward both marriage and childbearing increase rates of marriage, and positive attitudes toward careers decrease marriage rates and increase cohabitation rates. Finally, positive attitudes toward luxury spending decrease marriage rates, but positive attitudes toward child-oriented spending increase rates of both marriage and cohabitation.

Overall, we find that parents' and children's attitudes both have a substantial influence on family formation behavior. It appears that children's attitudes toward a broad range of family formation behaviors and nonfamily activities largely explain the effects of mothers' attitudes on children's behavior, implicating socialization mechanisms as the link between maternal attitudes and children's behavior. We hesitate to draw firm conclusions about this pattern of results because of the relatively limited number of attitude measures in each domain. Some maternal attitudes, in fact, maintain important direct effects on children's behavior that are not explained in our analyses by children's own attitudes. The data we use are unique in terms of the breadth of attitudes measured directly from each generation over a relatively long period. Nevertheless, other children's attitudes, not measured here, may explain the remaining direct effects of maternal attitudes. Thus, although we recognize that further research is necessary to draw firm conclusions, the results documented here suggest the search for mechanisms linking parental attitudes to children's behavior should take into consideration an extremely broad array of children's attitudes.

Clearly, comprehensive explanations of family formation behavior benefit from consideration of social-psychological explanations of behavior—explanations that draw attention to the important role of attitudes, values, and beliefs in shaping behavioral choices. Some research has suggested that society-level values are becoming more varied as a broader range of behaviors is considered acceptable, paving the way for individuals to act on their own attitudes and preferences in making behavioral decisions (Bellah et al. 1985; Bumpass 1990; Lesthaeghe and Surkyn 1988; Preston 1987; Thornton 1989; Veroff, Douvan, and Kulka 1981). If this is the case, then we might expect to see a rising importance of individuals' own attitudes in relation to the attitudes of important others (Barber, Axinn, and Thornton 2002). Or, it may be that the diminishing strength of norms in the larger society about personal and family behavior will lead to a stronger reliance on close family members like parents for behavioral guidance (Barber, Axinn, and Thornton 2002). Both of these scenarios are likely to increase the importance of attitudes, values, and beliefs as influences on family formation behavior in the future.

Race Differences

Again, results from this White cohort provide some useful information for understanding potential race differences in marital and cohabiting behaviors in spite of the fact they cannot be used for direct inference to other groups. We conclude that variation in attitudes and beliefs about the family and competing nonfamily alternatives are an important influence on young people's decisions about marriage and cohabitation. Research based on other studies featuring more race variation find similar results—with a broad range of attitudes affecting both the rate of transitions into a coresidential union and the choice between cohabitation and marriage—among the general population including both African Americans and Whites (Clarkberg, Stolzenberg, and Waite 1995). Second, a substantial body of research demonstrates race and ethnic differences in attitudes and beliefs about the family—differences that are likely to affect marital and cohabiting behaviors. For example, studies indicate Hispanic Americans prefer more rapid transitions to marital and childbearing roles, South-Asian Americans prefer less rapid transitions to marital

and childbearing roles, and African Americans' prefer long intervals between sex and the first birth, but short intervals between marriage and
the first birth, and they perceive a high likelihood of premarital childbearing (East 1998). Some of the African-American–White difference may be
because African Americans are less likely than whites to participate in
serious romantic relationships at young ages that raise marital expectations (Crissey 2005). Research on specific Hispanic-American subgroups
also suggests that there are potentially important differences in attitudes
and beliefs among these groups (Oropesa 1996), so that generalizations
about Hispanic or Asian Americans may not reflect the full ethnic diversity within these groups. More research on racial and ethnic differences in
a broad range of attitudes and beliefs is needed, but these studies, combined with our results in this chapter, suggest racial and ethnic differences
in attitudes and beliefs may help to produce differences in marital and cohabiting behavior. Other research on race differences in marital behavior
also suggests that there may be race and ethnic differences in the relationship between attitudes and marital behavior (Clarkwest Forthcoming).
This means that in addition to attitude differences across groups, there
may also be differences in the ways that attitudes shape actions across
groups.

Conclusion

Attitudes, values, and beliefs do have important independent effects on
marital and cohabiting behaviors, even after all the other powerful influences are controlled in our models. These influences span a broad range of
attitudes, values, and beliefs. Mothers' attitudes, values, and beliefs also
have important consequences for their children's behavior, though much
of this influence is mediated by the children's own attitudes, values, and
beliefs. As with other results, the observational design means the strong
empirical associations we observe may not reflect independent causal
forces.

   Nevertheless, social scientists are not likely to be able to randomly assign beliefs to individuals, and the results presented in this chapter suggest
that these ideational influences do in fact reflect important independent
effects on marital and cohabiting behavior (see also Jayakody, Thornton,
and Axinn Forthcoming).

   Of course, attitudes, values, and beliefs operate indirectly on family formation behavior via their influence on other related behavioral

choices. We examine this issue in detail in the following chapters. Chapter 10 explores the educational experiences that link educational expectations to cohabitation and marriage, and chapter 11 explores the work experiences that link attitudes toward careers to cohabitation and marriage.

CHAPTER TEN

Educational Influences

In this chapter we shift our emphasis from religion and family attitudes to consider the influence of educational aspirations and achievement on marriage and cohabitation in young adulthood. We do so because as we emphasized in our historical review in chapter 2, marriage has long been intricately interrelated with economic standing and prospects. Because marriage in Western societies historically meant the establishment of independent households and economic units, couples who wanted to marry required the earning capacity to maintain considerable residential and economic independence from their parents. This earning capacity was historically obtained through a joint economic enterprise centered on the family and household. With industrialization and geographical separation of much productive work from the home, the husband provided the family's primary economic support though wages from employment outside the home while the wife took care of the home and children. More recently, both husband and wife have contributed to the economic well-being of the family through nonfamily employment, although men continue to specialize more in market work and women in the care of home and family.

The significance of economic considerations in Western marriage suggests an important effect of earning capacity on the ability to marry (Lichter et al. 1992; Oppenheimer 1994, 1988, 2003; Oppenheimer and Lew 1995). This leads to the expectation that young people with high skill levels, extensive training in educational programs, high-quality jobs, and good long-term job prospects will be able to marry and establish independent households earlier than those with fewer of these resources. These same people are also likely to be more attractive partners in the marriage market.

The linkages between educational, occupational, and financial attainments and entrance into marriage are further complicated by the fact that the same school attendance that builds human capital inhibits financial independence and the ability to marry. Because school attendance limits the amount of time available for other activities, including marriage and employment at steady and remunerative jobs, we expect school enrollment to inhibit entrance into marital unions (Blossfeld and Huinink 1991; Carmichael 1984; Goldscheider and Waite 1986; Kravdal 1999; Oppenheimer 2003; Oppenheimer and Lew 1995; Oppenheimer, Blossfeld, and Wackerow 1995; Teachman, Polonko, and Leigh 1987; Thornton, Axinn, and Teachman 1995; Waite and Spitze 1981).

We expect that the roots of the connections between socioeconomic and marriage experiences extend back to the high-school years. We know that success in high school—as measured by mental ability, grades, and program of study—as well as high educational and occupational aspirations are strong predictors of postsecondary school attendance and occupational success (Sewell et al. 1975). We also expect that the perceived importance of education relative to marriage and the enjoyment of school have similar effects. The importance of all these early school factors for subsequent school and employment experience leads to several hypotheses about the role they play in marriage. We expect that these early educational factors have strong negative influences on the pace of entrance into marriage indirectly through their positive influence on school attendance.

We also expect direct effects of some of these early school factors on subsequent entrance into marriage. We hypothesize that having greater mental ability, better school grades, and a higher quality education will increase attractiveness in both the labor and marriage markets and thus have a positive influence on marriage net of both school attendance and the amount of schooling accumulated—especially once schooling has been completed.

We anticipate that dating and courtship provide another connection between educational success and entrance into marriage. Previous research has shown that school success and aspirations are related to delayed entrance into dating and heterosexual relations, and this likely postpones marriage (Gaughan 2002; Miller et al. 1997; Zelnik, Kanter, Ford 1981).

So far our discussion of the socioeconomic influences on union formation has focused entirely on marriage without considering the implications
for cohabitation. Many of the socioeconomic influences on marriage discussed previously are expected to have similar effects on cohabitation,
while others are expected to affect cohabitation and marriage differently.

Looking at the similarities between cohabitation and marriage, we
note that both involve intimate relationships, the sharing of living quarters, a time-intensive relationship with a partner, intermingling of personal finances, and at least some economic independence (Davis 1985). These
similarities suggest that school aspirations and achievements, work experience, and financial success influence the cohabitation rate in similar ways
as marriage.

However, there are differences between cohabitation and marriage that
suggest the influence of educational, occupational, and economic factors to
be less important for cohabitation than for marriage. Centrally important
here is the fact that for many people cohabitation does not imply the long-
term commitment generally associated with marriage (Whitehead and
Popenoe 1999). This view of cohabitation as a short-term or transitional
arrangement, in contrast to the ideal of marriage as a lifetime arrangement, suggests that long-term concerns about financial accomplishments
and stability are probably less influential in cohabitation than in marriage.

Another important difference between cohabitation and marriage is
the transaction costs of the event itself. In general, cohabitation requires
few out-of-pocket expenses and time other than those associated with ac-
quiring a common residence and the relocation of one or more of the
partners. Although, in principle, the transition costs of marriage could be
nearly as low, in many instances a formal wedding entails a large ceremony and celebration that require considerable time, money, energy, and
patience. Such expenses could inhibit the marriage desires of young couples, especially those with limited personal and family resources. A recent
Norwegian study has found that a substantial fraction of cohabitors suggest this as a disadvantage to marriage (Kravdal 1999).

Cohabitation and marriage also have different implications for the
bearing and rearing of children (Bachrach 1987; Carmichael 1995; Davis
1985; Manning 1993; Manning and Landale 1996; Rindfuss and Vanden-
Heuvel 1990) and for long-term financial independence from parents—
with cohabiting couples receiving more assistance from parents than married couples (Rindfuss and VandenHeuvel 1990). These differences suggest that school attendance, high skills, educational attainment, steady

employment, and earning power may affect cohabitation less than marriage.

It is likely that some couples who would like to marry conclude that they are unable to assume the commitments of marriage because of limited skills, educational attainment, financial resources, and employment prospects, yet believe that they have the financial resources to cohabit (Oppenheimer 2003). In fact, because the desire to share living expenses is cited by some as a motivation to cohabit, people with fewer economic resources may be *more* motivated than others to cohabit, whether or not they plan to marry the partner eventually (Bumpass, Sweet, and Cherlin 1991; Ross 1995). Any substitution of cohabitation for marriage by less educated and financially established couples would mean that lower educational achievements, income, occupations, and employment prospects would be associated with less rapid entrance into marriage and higher prevalence of cohabitation. We expect that other socioeconomic influences on union formation such as mental ability and grades, curriculum, educational aspirations, and actual and prospective earnings also have differential effects on cohabitation and marriage.

We expect that the completion of schooling and entrance into employment provide a strong impetus toward marriage among cohabiting couples because it removes one of the institutional constraints restricting marriage opportunities. We also expect that as cohabiting couples procure better and steadier jobs with high wages that they will feel more motivated to transform their relationships into marriage. Given the gender division of labor in many families and cultural expectations that the husband should be a stable provider (Cherlin 2000; Wilkie 1993), we expect that the transition from cohabitation to marriage depends more on the earning capacity of the man than the woman. This expectation is consistent with earlier research showing that this transition is positively related to men's economic resources but generally unrelated to women's economic resources (Manning and Smock 1995; Smock and Manning 1997).

In this chapter, we begin our empirical evaluation of these ideas by documenting the independent effects of school enrollment and educational attainment on the rate of entering marriage and premarital cohabitation. We also examine the differences between the effects of full-time and part-time enrollment, and the potential dissipation of these effects as young people age. Then we go on to estimate the effect of early variations in individual's aspirations, ability, and enjoyment of school experiences.[1] Finally, we examine the extent to which experiences with school enrollment and attainment explain the effects of early variations in aspirations, ability, and enjoyment of school. Together the results provide an extensive documentation of the influence of education on marriage and cohabiting behavior. In the next chapter we extend this line of inquiry by examining the influence of earning capacity on union formation.

Data and Analytic Approach

To test the multidimensional reasoning previously presented regarding the influence of education on cohabiting and marital behavior, we draw on a broad range of education measures available from our intergenerational panel study. We use time-varying measures of educational experience ascertained using a life-history calendar, which provided a month-by-month history of school attendance. We recorded whether or not the person was enrolled each month, and if so, whether the enrollment was part or full time.

Our coding of school enrollment was complicated by summer vacations and other temporary periods away from school. If the operationalization of school enrollment focused exclusively on a single month, short periods of time between episodes of education would be counted as time away from school. If the people involved still considered themselves as continuing students during such periods, this coding scheme would underestimate their actual educational involvement. This problem can be solved by counting people as continuing students if they experienced enrollment in any month across a longer period of time. However, this approach has the opposite problem in that many people who discontinue school with no intention of returning in the near future would be coded inappropriately as students for a period of time.

To handle this measurement difficulty we used two definitions of school enrollment. The first takes a restrictive interpretation of school enrollment and focuses exclusively on the previous month. Two dummy variables were created to summarize that experience—one coding part-time enrollment and the second coding full-time enrollment, with no enrollment being the reference category. The second approach focuses on school enrollment during the previous six months. People enrolled full-time during *any* of those months were coded as full-time students. All of those who had solely part-time enrollment were counted as part-time students. All others were coded as being out of school.

Neither of these solutions is appropriate for the years prior to age 18, when most young people are enrolled continuously in school except for regularly scheduled vacations. Most nonenrollment during these years is simply a result of school breaks, which makes it very difficult to estimate union-formation experience for those who are actually out of school. Furthermore, education influences marriage and cohabitation differently before age 18 than in subsequent years (Thornton, Axinn, and Teachman 1995). As a result, we limited our analysis in this chapter to ages eighteen and older.

Our measure of educational accumulation was constructed by calculating the number of months of enrollment between age 16 and the beginning of the month in question. In calculating this variable we assigned each month of full-time school a value of one, each month of part-time school a value of one-half, and each month of no school a zero. All months, including summer ones, were included in these calculations.

Note that, as in chapters 7 through 9, we begin our analysis of educational effects controlling for a variety of parental experiences before 1980, when the children turned 18. Thus, the effects of young people's own educational enrollment and attainment we document are net of those important intergenerational effects.

Once we have established the consequences of school enrollment and educational attainment we go on to explore the influence of young peoples' educational expectations, ability, and enjoyment of school. These key dimensions of early relationship to the educational attainment process were measured in 1980, when the young people were age 18, and are described in Appendix C, table C.6.

School Enrollment

Table 10.1 summarizes the total effects of school enrollment and accumulation on marriage and cohabitation treated as competing risks. Looking first at the effects of school enrollment, we find strong and consistent support for many of the hypotheses discussed earlier. School enrollment consistently reduces the rate of entrance into both marital and cohabiting unions, and many of the observed effects are strikingly large. For example, being enrolled in school full time in the previous month reduces the rate of marriage by nearly three-quarters and reduces the rate of cohabitation by more than one-half (total effects of table 10.1). Put the other way, those who were not enrolled in any schooling in the previous month cohabited at twice the rate and married at nearly four times the rate of those who were enrolled full time in the previous month.

Enrollment in the previous six months has somewhat weaker total effects than enrollment in the previous month (table 10.1), but still exerts significant delaying effects on both cohabitation and marriage.[2] The introduction of school accumulation into the equations (Models 10.1 and 10.2) modifies somewhat, but does not change, the strong negative effects of school enrollment. These results support the hypothesis that the role of student conflicts in some way with the role of coresidential partner and thereby delays entrance into marriage and cohabitation.

The data support our expectation that full-time school enrollment reduces union formation more than part-time attendance. For example, full-time enrollment in the past month reduces the rate of marriage by 74 percent, while part-time enrollment reduces the rate by 44 percent (total effects of table 10.1). The differences between part- and full-time enrollment observed using the six-month definition of school enrollment are even larger. The greater effects of full-time enrollment are consistent with the idea of role incompatibilities between educational attendance and union formation. Also, part-time students may have lower educational aspirations than full-time students, making their opportunity costs smaller for discontinuing school.

The hypothesis that school enrollment reduces marriage more than cohabitation also receives strong support. For full-time enrollment, the estimated effects are always greater for marriage than for cohabitation, and in some instances the differential effects are striking. For example, in models without controls for educational accumulation, full-time enrollment in the past month reduces the cohabitation rate by 54 percent as compared to a 74 percent reduction in marriage (total effect). This differential is even larger when school accumulation is entered into the equations. These results provide support for our hypothesis of more incompatibility of full-time school enrollment for marriage than for cohabitation. The differences in effects of part-time enrollment are smaller and the direction of the difference varies.

Additional analysis shows that the effects of full-time school enrollment on marriage are similar regardless of whether cohabitation is treated as a competing destination or ignored (not shown in tables). The combination of strong negative effects of enrollment on both cohabitation and marriage also produces a strong negative effect on the total union-formation

TABLE 10.1 Total and direct effects of school enrollment and accumulation on the rates of entrance into marital and cohabiting unions (as competing destinations)[a]

	Marriage						Cohabitation					
	Total effect (min. control)[b]		Model 10.1		Model 10.2		Total effect (min. control)[b]		Model 10.1		Model 10.2	
	B[c]	Z[d]	B[c]	Z[d]	B[c]	Z[d]	B[c]	Z[d]	B[c]	Z[d]	B[c]	Z[d]
School enrollment in previous month[e]												
Full time	-0.74	6.31	-0.77	6.82			-0.54	4.60	-0.49	3.82		
Part time	-0.44	2.80	-0.47	3.06			-0.45	2.77	-0.42	2.51		
School enrollment in previous six months[e]												
Full time	-0.59	5.53			-0.66	6.34	-0.52	4.99			-0.47	3.95
Part time	-0.18	1.23			-0.24	1.64	-0.38	2.60			-0.35	2.32
School accumulation (in years)	0.04	0.90	0.15	3.14	0.16	3.30	-0.16	3.96	-0.11	2.54	-0.10	2.11
No. of periods			60,386		60,386				60,386		60,386	
No. of events			357		357				360		360	
χ^2			228.59		205.44				150.89		149.31	
DF			31		31				31		31	

Notes: [a]Each of these equations also includes gender, age, and the parental factors listed in Model 6.6 of table 6.4. [b]The total effects with minimum controls were estimated in equations that included only one of the school factors. That is, each was estimated in a separate equation. [c]Effect coefficient for logit equations transformed by equation: $[\exp(\beta) - 1]$. [d]Z = ratio of absolute value of coefficient to its standard error. [e]No enrollment is the omitted category for the school-enrollment dummy variables.

rate. Full-time enrollment reduces the rate of formation of any type of union by 65 percent, and part-time enrollment reduces the same rate by 44 percent (not shown in tables).

In investigating possible gender differences, we found the influence of school enrollment on both cohabitation and marriage was remarkably similar for men and women (not shown in tables). Although there were small gender differences in the estimated magnitude of these negative effects depending on whether enrollment was measured in the previous month or previous six months, we found none of these differences to be statistically significant.

Finally, we investigated the possibility that the delaying effects of school enrollment dissipate with age. As individuals age, the incompatibility between the role of student and the role of marital or cohabiting partner may be reduced, and the negative effect of school enrollment may decline. If this is true, then an interaction between school enrollment and age should have a statistically significant, positive effect on rates of cohabitation and marriage—reducing the magnitude of the negative effects of enrollment as individuals age.

In fact, this is exactly what we find in models of marriage, where the interactions between enrollment and age are each positive and statistically significant. As young people age the delaying effect of school enrollment on marriage dissipates until it no longer has any significant influence. This dissipating effect is significant for both full-time enrollment and part-time enrollment, and the effects are quite similar among both men and women (not shown in tables). We find a similar change in the effect of school enrollment on cohabitation with age, although these effects are not statistically significant (not shown in tables). Overall, these results mean that enrollment in education delays entry into marital and cohabiting relationships, but this delaying effect mainly occurs in early adulthood. Early adulthood, of course, is a period when enrollment status varies greatly in the United States, and those differences go on to produce important variance in the timing of starting marital and cohabiting relationships.

Educational Attainment

Our theoretical reasoning suggests a positive effect of educational attainment on rates of marriage. However, if the delaying effect of enrollment in school is not controlled, we may not observe these effects because the positive effects of attainment are confounded by the negative effects of enrollment. Likewise, although our theoretical framework predicts a negative effect of attainment on rates of cohabitation, estimates that do not account for the negative effects of school enrollment will probably over-represent the effects of educational attainment.

The results presented in table 10.1 demonstrate this issue. Our estimated total effect of school accumulation, which does not control for enrollment in school, is strongly negative on rates of cohabitation, but is positive, although statistically insignificant, for rates of marriage. In Model 10.1, however, which controls for school enrollment in the previous month, we observe a somewhat weaker, but statistically significant negative effect of educational attainment on rates of cohabitation and a strong, statistically significant positive effect on rates of marriage (table 10.1). Each additional year of educational attainment in Model 10.1 reduces the rate of premarital cohabitation by 11 percent, which means that six additional years of education—for example completing a master's degree rather than completing high school alone—would cut the rate of entering cohabiting relationships in half.

The effect of educational attainment on rates of marriage is even stronger and in the opposite direction. Each additional year of education increases the rate of marriage by 15 percent (Model 10.1 of table 10.1). This means that six additional years of education would more than double the rate of marriage. The directions of these effects remain the same when we control for enrollment in the past six months (comparing Models 10.1 and 10.2).

The main effect of educational attainment is thus a strong influence on the choice of union type, with young adults who have higher levels of educational attainment being much more likely to choose marriage over cohabitation, and vice versa. Because educational attainment has a strong positive influence on the rate of marriage and a strong negative influence on the rate of premarital cohabitation, it has no significant influence on the total rate of entering any union (not shown in tables).

These results are quite consistent with the theoretical ideas described earlier. Greater educational attainment enhances individuals' human capital, conferring skills, and certification that serve to increase future employment opportunities and earning power. These advantages lead to greater resources to establish an independent household and family. As a result, once they are out of school, young people with higher educational attainment cohabit at significantly lower rates and marry at significantly higher rates than their counterparts. We investigate the specific employment and earnings mechanisms that may be responsible for these strong effects of educational attainment in chapter 11.

In investigating potential differences by gender, we found that the negative effect of educational attainment on cohabitation rates was somewhat stronger among women than among men, and the positive effect of educational attainment on marriage rates was somewhat stronger among men than among women. This gender difference in the effect of educational attainment was not statistically significant in models of marriage but it was in models of cohabitation. Specifically, each additional year of schooling reduces rates of cohabitation by nearly 20 percent for women but only about 9 percent for men (not shown in tables). These gender differences in the effect of educational attainment on marriage and cohabitation foreshadow important gender differences in the influence of employment and earnings on marital and cohabiting behavior, which are a key theme of chapter 11.

Educational Expectations, Ability, and Enjoyment

We now expand our analysis to include three additional dimensions of education: educational expectations, ability, and enjoyment. Using the heuristic causal model of figure 10.1, we examine educational expectations, ability, and enjoyment as temporally and causally prior to enrollment and attainment; enrollment as prior to attainment; and both enrollment and attainment intervening between educational expectations, ability, and enjoyment and union formation. This model posits that ability, expectations, and enjoyment will have direct effects on marriage and cohabitation as well as indirect effects through both enrollment and accumulation.

Estimates of the effects of expectations, ability, and enjoyment across the age range from 18 through 31 are provided in table 10.2. Each of the equations in Model 10.3 was estimated by including all three of the educational variables as measured at age 18. We do not estimate total effects with minimum controls because expectations, ability, and enjoyment are all positively correlated, and overlap temporally, making it very difficult to adjudicate the causal relationships among them. A consequence of this decision is that the total effects presented in Model 10.3 (with maximum controls) are of somewhat smaller magnitude than the total effects of each individual dimension of education would be when evaluated

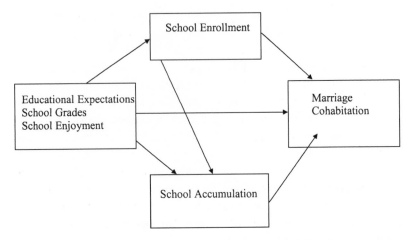

FIGURE 10.1. Heuristic model of the influence of educational factors on cohabitation and marriage

in a separate equation with minimum controls (not shown in tables). We added the one-month measure of school enrollment to Model 10.4 and both enrollment and attainment to Model 10.5.[3]

Expectations for Educational Attainment

First we examine the influence of educational expectations on young people's rates of marriage and cohabitation. Young people who aspire to achieve high levels of education marry at lower rates than other young people (row 1, table 10.2). This negative effect is strong and statistically significant, with expectations for each additional year of education reducing marriage rates by 6 percent. The effect of these expectations on rates of cohabitation is neither large nor statistically significant.

Our estimates of the effects of educational expectations change as we add measures of school enrollment, and then attainment, to the models. With the negative effects of enrollment on marriage controlled in Model 10.4, the negative effect of expectations is reduced by one half. This means that part of the negative influence of aspirations operates through school enrollment. Educational expectations increase enrollment, which, in turn, reduces the rate of marriage. When we add attainment to the model of marital behavior in Model 10.5, the effect of expectations, however, becomes more negative. This means that expectations increase overall school

TABLE 10.2 **Direct effects of educational ability, expectations, and enjoyment on the rates of entrance into marital and cohabiting unions (as competing destinations)**[a]

	Marriage						Cohabitation					
	Model 10.3		Model 10.4		Model 10.5		Model 10.3		Model 10.4		Model 10.5	
	B[b]	Z[c]	B[b]	Z[c]	B[b]	Z[c]	B[b]	Z[c]	B[b]	Z[c]	B[b]	Z[c]
Educational expectations	-0.06	2.04	-0.03	0.82	-0.07	2.07	-0.01	0.42	0.03	0.80	0.07	1.90
School grades	0.18	1.62	0.21	1.86	0.15	1.39	-0.19	2.29	-0.16	1.89	-0.12	1.34
School enjoyment	0.02	0.80	0.03	0.97	0.02	0.71	0.01	0.40	0.01	0.31	0.02	0.56
School enrollment in previous month[d]												
Full time			-0.75	6.13	-0.77	6.51			-0.54	4.47	-0.50	3.90
Part time			-0.45	2.80	-0.47	2.98			-0.45	2.77	-0.42	2.50
School accumulation (in years)					0.18	3.23					-0.15	3.05
No. of periods	60,168		58,569		58,569		60,168		58,569		58,569	
No. of events	341		338		338		356		347		347	
χ²	162.40		215.70		226.07		118.99		145.64		155.04	
DF	31		33		34		31		33		34	

Notes: [a] Each of these equations also control for gender, age, and the parental factors listed in table 6.4.
[b] Effect coefficient for logit equations transformed by equation: $[\exp(\beta) - 1]$.
[c] Z = ratio of absolute value of coefficient to its standard error.
[d] No enrollment is the omitted category for the school-enrollment dummy variables.

achievement, which, in turn, increases marriage, making for a positive indirect effect of aspirations through achievement. With both enrollment
and attainment controlled in Model 10.5, high expectations for educational accomplishment have a negative, statistically significant direct effect on marriage. This means that educational expectations have an independent effect of slowing down the rate of entrance to marriage net of
their operation through school enrollment and attainment.

Models of cohabitation tell a somewhat different story. Adding enrollment to the model of cohabitation rates in Model 10.4 produces a slight,
statistically insignificant, positive effect of educational expectations on cohabitation. When enrollment and attainment are both added, in Model
10.5, the slight positive effect of expectations increases and becomes statistically significant. Thus, school expectations increase both school attendance and attainment, which decrease the rate of cohabitation. Once
these negative indirect effects through attendance and attainment are
controlled, the direct effect of expectations on cohabitation is positive.
Thus, the direct effects of high educational expectations are to slow the
rate of marriage and speed the rate of cohabitation.

This juxtaposition is quite interesting. For those entering a union, high
educational expectations, net of their indirect effects via enrollment and
attainment, lead to a choice of cohabitation over marriage, thereby postponing marriage. This result is consistent with the idea that, at any given
level of educational enrollment and attainment, those entering unions who
have high expectations for educational attainment tend to choose cohabitation and postpone marriage. Earlier, our findings from the analysis of
school enrollment suggested that role incompatibility is greater between
enrollment and marriage than between enrollment and cohabitation. The
extent to which those with high educational aspirations believe this is true
likely fuels the decision to enter cohabiting unions rather than marital
unions.

School Ability

Our measure of educational ability is the young people's reports of their
grades in the most recent semester of school they had experienced at age
18 (see Appendix C, table C.6). Without controls for educational attainment and enrollment, grades have a positive effect on rates of marriage
and a negative effect on rates of cohabitation (row 2 of Model 10.3, table
10.2).

In Model 10.4, where we add enrollment to these equations, we see a slight increase in the positive effect of grades on marriage and a slight decline in the negative effect of grades on cohabitation. This occurs because people with high grades in secondary school go on to attend postsecondary school more often, which leads to lower rates of both cohabitation and marriage. That is, when the negative indirect effect of grades through school enrollment is controlled, the direct effect of grades is more positive on marriage and less negative on cohabitation.

In Model 10.5 we add educational attainment to the model with grades and school attendance, and see that its introduction reduces the direct effect of grades on both marriage and cohabitation. This happens because school grades positively influence the amount of education attained, which increases the rate of marriage. Controlling for this positive indirect effect of grades through educational attainment reduces the positive direct effect of grades on marriage. The indirect effect of grades through educational attainment on cohabitation, however, is negative because grades increase attainment, which, in turn, leads to lower rates of cohabitation. Once this negative indirect effect is taken into account, the direct negative effect of grades on cohabitation is reduced to statistical insignificance.

Looking more closely at the direct effects of grades on marriage and cohabitation (with enrollment and attainment controlled), we see that these direct effects are very similar in direction to the effects of school attainment. That is, like high educational attainment, good grades increase the rate of marriage and decrease the rate of cohabitation. This means that people with high grades who enter a coresidential relationship are more likely than others to choose marriage over cohabitation. In further analysis we found that each additional unit of grades predicted a 27 percent increase in choosing marriage over cohabitation, an effect that is just below statistical significance ($Z = 1.61$). The similarity of the grades and attainment effects suggests that both may increase people's ability to marry, thereby leading those who enter a union to choose marriage over cohabitation.

More detailed analysis of the ways in which school grades affect marriage rates identifies the acceptability of remaining single as a primary indirect mechanism for this influence on marriage. Young people with high grades have less positive attitudes toward remaining single ($r = -.61$), a characteristic associated with higher rates of marriage. However, even with full controls for all factors considered in this book, high school grades retain a negative direct effect on cohabitation rates.

Enjoyment of School

The 1980 interview with the young adults also asked how much they enjoyed a number of different activities—rating each item on a scale from zero to ten, with zero being "dislike a great deal," ten being "enjoy a great deal," and five being "don't care." Included on the list were "doing school work" and "going to school," which we combined into the measure of school enjoyment (table C.6 of Appendix C).[4] We found that this measure had no statistically significant effect on rates of either marriage or cohabitation from age 18 through age 31 (row 3 of Model 10.3 of table 10.2). The small effect of school enjoyment remains statistically insignificant once the indirect effects via enrollment and attainment are controlled in Models 10.4 and 10.5.

More detailed analyses, not displayed here, reveal that school enjoyment influences marriage timing in a complex interaction with age. Among 18- to 22-year-olds, those who reported enjoying school at 18 marry at significantly lower rates than others. However, among young adults 23 and older, those who reported enjoying school as 18-year-olds marry at significantly higher rates than others. So, in early adulthood (before age 23), when differentials in educational enrollment are greatest, enjoyment of school, like school enrollment, delays marriage. However, later in adulthood (age 23 and older), when most adults are no longer enrolled in school, the effect of enjoyment of school is similar to the effect of educational attainment, increasing rates of marriage. Moreover, these total effects of enjoyment of school are not changed by controlling for the indirect effects via enrollment or attainment, as the direct effect of enjoyment on marriage between ages 23 and 31 is the same magnitude as the total effect (not shown in tables).

Direct Effects of School Enrollment and Educational Attainment

Of course, the expectations, ability, and enjoyment of school at age 18 are both temporally and causally prior to the educational enrollment and attainment observed between ages 18 and 31 (figure 10.1). Therefore, the models estimating the effect of enrollment and attainment displayed in table 10.1 are, in some sense, misspecified because they do not include controls for prior educational aspirations, ability, and enjoyment. In the last three rows of table 10.2, we reestimate the effects of educational enrollment and attainment, this time controlling for expectations, ability, and enjoyment. We display only the past-month version of enrollment because the pattern of results is identical for the six-month version of enrollment (not shown in tables).

Two results deserve mention. First, the effects of school enrollment are virtually unchanged from table 10.1, even now that previous educational expectations, ability, and enjoyment are included in the models (table 10.2). Clearly, enrollment in schooling has a strong delaying effect on both marriage and cohabitation that is not explained by other dimensions of education. Second, compared to the effects estimated in table 10.1 (Model 10.1), neither the positive effects of educational attainment on marriage nor the negative effect of educational attainment on cohabitation is decreased by controlling for expectations, ability, and enjoyment of school (last row of table 10.2). This again confirms the importance of educational attainment in the marriage and cohabitation process.

Direct Effects of Maternal Aspirations for the Child's Education

As we discussed in chapter 9, mothers' aspirations for children's educational attainments have a significant negative influence on rates of entry into both marriage and cohabitation that is independent of the young people's own expectations for educational attainment. Here we note that this effect of maternal aspirations on marriage is also independent of educational enrollment, educational attainment, grades, and school enjoyment (not shown in tables). Thus, maternal expectations for educational attainment have a significant, independent delaying influence on marriage that is not explained by other relevant dimensions of educational experience. The introduction of additional parent and child factors in the analysis also failed to explain a substantial part of the effect of maternal aspirations on children's marriage.

However, the story is very different for cohabitation. The introduction of factors from the lives of the young adults explains virtually all of the negative maternal educational expectations effect on cohabitation (not shown in tables). The specific mechanisms of indirect influence of parental educational expectations on cohabitation include adolescent steady and sexual experience, school grades, and school attendance, with each transmitting a negative influence of maternal expectations on cohabitation. Mothers with high educational aspirations for their children have children who dated less, were less sexually precocious, had higher grades ($r = .31$), and had higher levels of attendance in school. Because each of these young-adult attributes leads to lower rates of entrance into cohabitation, they act as indirect mechanisms through which maternal aspirations influence children's cohabitation behavior. Clearly, there is a package of educational accomplishment and delayed sexual experience that is associated with high maternal aspirations and low experience with cohabitation.

Summary and Conclusions

The empirical results presented in this chapter lead to several useful insights concerning the influence of education on marriage and cohabitation. One important empirical finding is the lower rate of both cohabitation and marriage among those enrolled in school, which counters the common belief that cohabitation is an experience concentrated among college students. Low rates of union formation among students are predicted by our theoretical framework, which posits that those who cohabit or marry assume adult roles that conflict with school attendance. Cohabitation and marriage also involve substantial time and energy—commitments that can disrupt the ability of students to handle the demands of school. Although people could, of course, discontinue their educations to cohabit or marry, this decision could truncate the accumulation of knowledge, skills, and credentials necessary for success later in life.

Our results also indicate that school enrollment has less of a negative impact on cohabitation than on marriage. This finding is consistent with the observation that the role demands of cohabitation are less than those of marriage, making cohabitation relatively easier to handle with the demands of school attendance. This finding also supports the idea that, whereas many people view marriage as a permanent role, they view cohabitation as more temporary—making it less incompatible with the transitional student role. Because school enrollment affects cohabitation less than it does marriage, students who enter a union are more likely than nonstudents to choose cohabitation. This relative preponderance of cohabitation over marriage among students may explain why earlier observers emphasized the importance of cohabitation among students.

Our empirical findings replicate earlier research in showing that the effects of school enrollment on marriage decline across the life course. We interpret this finding as suggesting that the opportunity costs associated with the discontinuation of education decline sharply as larger fractions of educational aspirations are attained. Also, as more education is completed, the time that married students are involved in role overload diminishes. Our research provides the additional insight that the effects of school attendance on cohabitation also decline with age.

Our empirical findings are consistent with the theoretical expectation that the effects of part-time enrollment on marriage are less negative than the effects of full-time enrollment. This apparently reflects the lower time demands of part-time enrollment, which produces fewer incompatibilities with marriage. In addition, the opportunity costs of discontinuing part-time school are probably less than those of quitting full-time enrollment.

Our research also provides insights concerning the influence of school attainment on the union-formation process. Although the accumulation of schooling has little influence on the total union-formation rate, it affects both cohabitation and marriage, but in opposite directions. That is, young people with little educational attainment have higher rates of cohabitation and lower rates of marriage than those with greater school attainments. We interpret these findings as suggesting that people with modest accumulations of education substitute cohabitation for marriage, at least for a period of time, while those with greater school attainments have a greater tendency to enter coresidential unions directly through marriage rather than through cohabitation. This substitution of cohabitation for marriage among the less educated suggests that they may lack the financial resources to make the extensive commitments of marriage, but may be able to assume the smaller commitments associated with cohabitation. Another possibility is that the less educated are less successful in finding marriage partners that have the financial resources considered necessary for marriage.

It is also useful to note that the inability to afford marriage but not cohabitation may be more perceptual than actual when children are not involved. The costs of housing, food, and clothing can be the same for a cohabiting partner as for a married couple. This suggests that many couples have higher perceptual or aspirational prerequisites for marriage than for cohabitation.[5] One such perceptual necessity associated with marriage in the minds of many is an elaborate wedding and celebration that is often expensive. This additional anticipated economic requirement may add to the perception that marriage is the higher-cost variety of living together.

It is also possible that the continuing linkage of marriage and childbearing is relevant here (see chapter 7). Couples who may be able to afford cohabitation and marriage may not perceive themselves as being able to afford children. Such couples may cohabit until they believe they are able to afford children and then enter marriage.

Our empirical results confirm the usefulness of expanding the conceptualization of education used in union-formation studies to include educational expectations, ability, and enjoyment. These three dimensions of education influence the union-formation process both directly and indirectly through school enrollment and attainment. Interestingly, grades in high school have direct effects on marriage and cohabitation net of their indirect effects through educational enrollment and attainment. They do so by influencing couples entering a union to choose marriage over cohabitation, thereby increasing the marriage rate and decreasing the cohabitation rate. The direct effects of educational expectations are in the opposite direction, being associated with lower rates of marriage, higher rates of cohabitation, and the choice of cohabitation over marriage. Enjoyment of school, however, decreases marriage during the younger ages and speeds it up in the later years. These influences depend both on the type of union and the age of the person.

Race Differences

Our results from Whites provide some useful information for understanding potential race differences in marital and cohabiting behaviors. A substantial body of social-science literature documents strong racial and ethnic differences in college attendance, postgraduate educational enrollment, and educational attainment (Bennett and Xie 2003; Hauser 1993; Hurtado et al. 1997; Jasinski 2000; Light and Strayer 2002; Morgan 2005; Perna 2000; Portes and Wilson 1976; Rivkin 1995; Wolfle 1985). Based on our findings in this chapter, racial or ethnic groups with lower rates of college and postgraduate educational attendance are likely to both marry and cohabit at higher rates than other groups. This difference is likely to be larger for marriage than for cohabitation and larger at young ages than at older ages. On the other hand, racial and ethnic groups with lower educational attainments are more likely to cohabit and less likely to marry than other racial and ethnic groups. As we discuss in the next chapter, less-positive employment prospects are often cited as a key reason for lower rates of marriage among the African-American population compared to the White population (Bennett, Bloom, and Craig 1989; Lichter et al. 1992; Oppenheimer, Kalmijn, and Lim 1997; Raley 1996). To the extent that lower educational attainments reduce employment prospects, race differences in educational attainment may also contribute to race differences in marital and cohabiting behavior indirectly via employment. We return to this topic in the following chapter.

Conclusion

Enrollment in school reduces rates of both cohabitation and marriage, with somewhat stronger effects on marriage than on cohabitation and somewhat stronger effects at younger ages than at older ages. Role incompatibility between educational enrollment and intensive coresidential unions appears to be the most likely explanation. On the other hand, once these consequences of enrollment are taken into account, educational attainment has opposite consequences for marriage and for premarital cohabitation. Those with high educational attainment are more likely to marry and less likely to cohabit than those with low educational attainment. Enjoyment of school, performance in school, and expectations for more schooling also influence marital and cohabiting behavior, and some of these effects are independent of enrollment and attainment experiences. As with other results, the observational design means the strong empirical associations we observe may not reflect independent causal forces. Nevertheless, the strong effects of education on marriage and cohabitation we observe are consistent with theories of the consequences of role incompatibility and human capital accumulation for marital and cohabiting behavior.

In the next chapter we turn to the influence of work experience and earnings on marital and cohabiting behavior. The lessons learned in this chapter about the influence of education on cohabitation and marriage will be brought forward into that chapter, as educational attainment processes are closely linked to work and earnings.

Work, Earnings Potential, and Career Aspiration*

As stated in chapter 1, our approach to the subject of marriage and co-habitation is guided by the life-course perspective, a principal tenet of which is that different domains of the human life influence each other throughout the life course. That is, significant events and transitions in an individual's life are interrelated to and contingent upon (but not determined by) other personal experiences and societal forces. In the previous chapter, we examined the influence of various educational experiences on the entry into marriage and cohabitation. We now turn to the influence of work in the labor force on marriage and cohabitation.

Theoretical Background

Like education, work can have both negative and positive effects on union formation. On the one hand, because successful careers often require substantial investments of time and energy early in the life course, they can compete with union-formation behavior. Thus, role conflict may preclude early union formation among individuals pursuing career ambitions. On the other hand, because financial independence has long been viewed in the Western world as a prerequisite for marriage, success in the labor market may facilitate union formation. In this sense, union formation can be

*Chapter 11 draws heavily from a published paper authored by Yu Xie, James Raymo, Kimberly Goyette, and Arland Thorton (2003).

seen as a form of consumption that may be hastened by, or even signal, one's financial capability.

In linking economic resources and marriage, researchers have paid close attention to differences in the roles played by men and women in society and within the family (e.g., Becker 1991; Easterlin 1980). In "breadwinner-homemaker" families, the husband is expected to specialize in generating economic resources outside the household, while the wife is assumed to specialize in household production (such as childcare). Indeed, historical evidence suggests that men's ability to accumulate resources adequate to support a family has been a principal determinant of marriage timing in many societies (e.g., Dixon 1971, 1978; Hajnal 1965; Landale and Tolnay 1991). For women, however, greater economic resources have typically been viewed as a marriage deterrent. This conventional reasoning reflects the domestic focus of women's family responsibilities and the presumed conflict between economic and domestic roles for women (Goldin 1990; Waldfogel 1997).

Empirical evidence indicates that the historical division of labor between women and men has influenced the preferences of women and men for partners, with women more than men emphasizing social status and economic prowess as an important trait in a spouse. Since women's economic roles have historically been less important, men were less concerned about such dimensions in a partner and emphasized instead such elements as physical attractiveness (Buss 1994; Buunk et al. 2002; Kenrick et al. 1990).

One of the most cited formulations of the relationship between economic resources and marriage is provided by Gary Becker's (1973, 1974, 1991) neoclassical economic theory of marriage. Emphasizing comparative advantage in market and domestic production, economies of scale, and a rational desire to maximize joint household production, Becker argues that the gains to marriage are maximized when gender differences in comparative advantage and specialization are the greatest. Because gender-role specialization within marriage requires the reduction or cessation of (presumably) the wife's market-labor supply, it follows that higher female wages raise the opportunity cost (i.e., foregone wages) of marriage for women, and thus may act to suppress it. On the other hand, greater economic resources for men (i.e., a larger comparative advantage in market production) should increase their attractiveness as marriage partners and thus facilitate marriage.

This theoretical argument suggests that both greater economic opportunities and higher earnings potential for women reduce the attractiveness of marriage for women, while poor economic circumstances reduce the feasibility of marriage for young men. To the extent that women's labor-market resources resemble those of men, the gains to gender-role specialization within marriage are expected to decline, thus making marriage less attractive for both women and men (e.g., Espenshade 1985; Goldscheider and Waite 1986; Preston and Richards 1975).

Much of the support for the argument of reduced gains to gender-role specialization is derived from analyses of aggregate-level data and cross-sectional survey data that find a negative relationship between indicators of women's economic status (i.e., educational attainment, employment, earnings) and the prevalence or incidence of marriage (Espenshade 1985; Fossett and Kiecolt 1993; Lichter, LeClere, and McLaughlin 1991; McLanahan and Casper 1995; Preston and Richards 1975). However, studies using more appropriate longitudinal, micro-level data tend to find an insignificant or even a positive relationship between measures of women's economic status and the likelihood of marriage (Bennett, Bloom, and Craig 1989; Blossfeld and Huinink 1991; Cherlin 1980; Goldscheider and Waite 1986; Lichter et al. 1992; Mare and Winship 1991; Oppenheimer, Blossfeld, and Wackerow 1995; Oppenheimer and Lew 1995; Oppenheimer 1997; Teachman, Polonko, and Leigh 1987; Thornton, Axinn, and Teachman 1995; Sassler and Schoen 1999; Sweeney 2002; Waite and Spitze 1981).[1] Results from investigations of men's marriage behavior are less dependent on the nature of the data analyzed. Consistent with theoretical expectations, analyses of both cross-sectional and longitudinal data have consistently shown that greater economic resources significantly increase the rate of marriage for men (e.g., Cooney and Hogan 1991; Goldscheider and Waite 1986; Lloyd and South 1996; MacDonald and Rindfuss 1981; Mare and Winship 1991; Oppenhiemer 2003; Oppenheimer, Kalmijn, and Lim 1997; Sweeney 2002; Sassler and Schoen 1999; Teachman, Polonko, and Leigh 1987).

The lack of empirical support for the reduced gains argument as an explanation of women's marriage timing has prompted several scholars to seek alternative explanations. One common criticism of the traditional exchange framework described previously is that, given the large increases in women's market-labor supply across the life course, the underlying assumption of gender-role specialization between spouses is no longer tenable in the United States. Indirect support for this critique can be found in a growing body of evidence suggesting that women's economic resources are of increasing importance as a spouse-selection criterion (Mare 1991; Qian and Preston 1993; South 1991).

The reduced gains argument has also been called into question on theoretical grounds. Valerie Oppenheimer, in particular, has argued that its emphasis on the economic returns to gender-role specialization within marriage effectively renders it an explanation of why economically independent women should choose not to marry rather than why they should marry later than other women (Oppenheimer 1988, 1994, 1997; Oppenheimer, Blossfeld, and Wackerow 1995; Oppenheimer and Lew 1995). With attitudinal data providing little support for a rejection of marriage among economically independent women, she proposes an alternative model of marriage timing in which the spouse-search process is prolonged for women with greater economic resources. In this "extended spouse search" hypothesis, greater economic resources promote later marriage by increasing women's incentive as well as their financial ability to conduct longer and more exacting searches in the marriage market. This search-theoretic model of women's marriage timing has been increasingly adopted as a framework guiding empirical studies (Lewis and Oppenheimer 2000; Lichter, Anderson, and Hayward 1995; Lichter, LeClere, and McLaughlin 1991; Lichter et al. 1992; Oppenheimer, Blossfeld, and Wackerow 1995; Oppenheimer and Lew 1995; Sweeney 2002). Empirical results have been generally consistent with expectations derived from this theory. For example, Oppenheimer and Lew (1995) report positive effects of higher earnings on the probability of marriage after age 23 for a sample of white women in the United States, suggesting that greater economic resources are being used to delay marriage rather than to buy out of it altogether (also see Qian and Preston 1993 for related findings).

Because cohabiting unions are less formal, less stable, and less likely to involve children, role specialization is likely to play a smaller role in cohabitation than in marriage. Thus, even among men, we expect the positive influence of financial capacity to be weaker on cohabitation than that on marriage.

In this chapter we consider how different dimensions of work and career influence the union-formation process. We begin with what has been a common expectation in the Western world—the husband needs to have a paid job to support a family—and examine the extent to which this expectation holds true for cohabitation. We then consider the effect of earning capacity on entrance into marriage; the effect of earning power on entrance into cohabitation; and the effect of career aspirations on entrance into cohabitation and marriage.

Work Status

As we discussed in chapter 2, families in the Western world have long been centered on the married couple and their dependent children. In this family system it was necessary for a couple to obtain the economic resources—usually a farm—to marry and set up an independent household. As society has changed in recent generations, the source of economic independence to marry and establish a household moved from the family farm to wage employment. It became necessary for someone in the family—usually the husband—to have a steady job and income to support a new family and household.

We examine the linkage between employment and entrance into marriage and cohabitation by focusing on the work status of individuals during the period that they are most likely to enter a union. In the life-history calendar used in the study, young adults reported their work status for each month between ages 15 and 31 in four categories: no work, working 1–9 hours per week, working 9–29 hours per week, and full-time employment. Following the approach of the previous chapters, we limit the analysis to the period after the 1980 interview, when the young adults were age 18.

After experimenting with different methods to use the work-status information, we chose a summary indicator that measures the proportion of time a person has been employed in the previous six months. This factor thus varies between 0 and 1, with 0 indicating that a person has never worked full time in the previous 6 months and 1 meaning that a person has been employed full time for the entire previous six months.[2] This variable provides a simple measure of work experience, yet retains the original information.

In table 11.1, we present the results from event-history models predicting entries to marriage and cohabitation using this measure of work experience. As in the preceding chapters, we add this measure to the baseline model established in chapter 6. As in previous chapters, we call these estimated regression coefficients *total effects*. However, different from the analyses in previous chapters, we are now particularly interested in the interaction between gender and work experience in affecting union formation. This interest is motivated by the idea that the husband is expected to contribute more heavily than the wife to earning money in the labor market. If this gender-specialization model of family division of labor is correct, it should be men's work experience that speeds up marriage

TABLE 11.1 **Total and direct effects of earnings potential and work status by sex on children's rates of entrance into marital and cohabiting unions (as competing destinations)**[a]

	Marriage				Cohabitation			
	Total effects (minimum controls)[b]		Direct effects Model 11.1		Total effects (minimum controls)[b]		Direct effects Model 11.1	
	B[c]	Z[d]	B[c]	Z[d]	B[c]	Z[d]	B[c]	Z[d]
A. Work during prior six months		1.80[e]		0.84[e]		2.36[e]		2.40[e]
Male	1.71	3.11	0.97	2.08	0.98	2.65	1.00	2.60
Female	0.33	1.15	0.40	1.31	−0.11	0.49	−0.15	0.67
B. Current earnings		3.44[e]				0.02[e]		
Male	0.50	4.57			0.04	0.38		
Female	0.08	1.34			0.04	0.60		
C. Earnings over next five years		3.25[e]				0.25[e]		
Male	0.46	4.40			0.01	0.13		
Female	0.08	1.30			0.04	0.59		
D. Future earnings		1.79[e]				0.93[e]		
Male	0.24	3.15			−0.05	0.67		
Female	0.07	1.13			0.04	0.58		
E. Past earnings		4.03[e]				0.80[e]		
Male	0.77	5.24			0.21	1.61		
Female	0.15	1.49			0.11	1.05		
F. Lifetime earnings		2.13[e]				0.82[e]		
Male	0.28	3.50			−0.04	0.53		
Female	0.07	1.08			0.04	0.57		
G. Lifetime earnings through t + 5 years		4.04[e]		3.51[e]		0.37[e]		0.46[e]
Male	0.66	5.34	0.59	4.63	0.11	0.95	0.02	0.16
Female	0.11	1.48	0.10	1.24	0.07	0.77	0.08	0.89
Person-periods			57,886				57,886	
No. of events			341				347	
DF			32				32	
χ^2			180.41				117.90	

Notes: [a] All equations also include the factors from Model 6.6 of chapter 6 (table 6.4).
[b] The total effects with minimum controls were estimated in equations that included only one of the work variables. That is, each was estimated in a separate equation.
[c] Effect coefficient for logit equations transformed by equation: $[\exp(\beta) - 1]$.
[d] Z = ratio of absolute value of coefficient to its standard error.
[e] Denotes a Z-test for gender difference in the estimated coefficient.

and cohabitation. Similarly, women's financial capacity may be associated with nonmarriage, or, according to Oppenheimer (1988, 1994, 1997), late marriage because it supports women's prolonged searches for attractive marriage partners or gives women independence outside of marriage.

The total effects of work status on marriage and cohabitation are reported in panel A of table 11.1. These results are especially powerful in demonstrating the continuing relevance of the historical prerequisite of employment for marriage and of the historical emphasis on the employment of the husband rather than the wife. We find a large, positive, and statistically significant effect of men's work on the rate of marriage. Compared to zero employment experience during the previous six months, full employment experience during the previous six months results in a 171 percent increase in the rate of marriage. This implies a dramatic difference between the marriage rates of men working full time and those with no employment. Interestingly, and consistent with the gendered nature of marriage, we find that women's work status does not have a significant effect on the rate of entering marriage. We conducted formal tests of the differences between the effects for women and men (Z-tests) and found that this gender difference is statistically significant.

Interestingly, the effect of employment on cohabitation is similar to its effect on marriage—that is, male employment substantially increases the rate of cohabitation, but women's employment does not. Also relevant is the fact that for males the effect of full employment (compared to no employment) on cohabitation is less than its effect on marriage (98 percent increase versus 171 percent increase). Thus, although entrance into cohabitation is linked to employment, as expected, this linkage is not as strong as the linkage between marriage and employment.

Earnings Potential

We now expand our attention from work status to a more complicated dimension of economic position—earning capacity. Earning capacity over an entire lifetime—not merely current income—is difficult to measure, particularly for young adults. Most young adults contemplating union formation have either just begun to work or have not worked at all in a career-track job. If long-term financial well-being is indeed an important criterion for union formation, it is also difficult to predict for these largely inexperienced adults making family decisions. To be sure, when selecting future spouses, young people can and do look for certain factors that are likely to signal future career success, but their predictions (like those of social scientists) are fraught with uncertainty.

Previous studies have typically measured economic capacity using factors observed either at, or immediately preceding, marriage or cohabitation. Most prominent among such measures are current earnings, educational attainment, work experience, employment, and parental resources.[3] However, these empirical measures do not closely match the intended theoretical concept of economic capacity as a factor in choosing a mate. Theoretically, researchers should be interested in measuring *perceived* long-term economic potential following marriage, as it is only postmarriage economic well-being that should have any *direct* relevance for marriage behavior. The various concurrently measured variables used in the literature should therefore be viewed as proxies of perceived long-term economic potential.

The use of these proxy measures can be justified by the recognition that evaluation of potential mates in the marriage market is subject to a great deal of uncertainty and information asymmetry (Oppenheimer 1988). It is simply not possible for individuals to accurately assess their own future economic well-being, much less that of potential spouses. For example, current earnings at young ages are often uninformative because they can be artificially low or even zero for some individuals with high future-earnings potential. That is because young people may still invest in human capital accumulation—by receiving formal education in school or undertaking training—for rapid earnings growth in the future. At the same time, individuals base their union-formation decisions not only on their current and past economic well-being, which is observable, but also on their expectations regarding future economic well-being, which is unobservable. This problem is further compounded by the fact that postmarriage economic behaviors of men and women can be substantially altered by marriage itself.

Scholars have used various approaches to overcome the difficulty of measuring potential economic well-being. For example, in an effort to avoid the endogenous influence of marriage on employment, Mare and Winship (1991) use employment potential estimated from work experience and education instead of observed employment status as a predictor of marriage. Similarly, Oppenheimer, Kalmijn, and Lim (1997) focus on "career development" rather than observed earnings, which can be low for young men in good career trajectories. More recently, Sweeney (1999) estimates expected future-earnings trajectories by looking at occupation-specific economic characteristics—mean earnings and trends in occupation-to-occupation transition probabilities. In this study, we propose a new approach to estimating economic capacity by relying on information about education history, work history, and cognitive aptitude.

We approached this measurement problem by focusing on "earnings potential"—a latent, unobservable capacity for generating earned income. Because earnings potential is inherently unobservable, it can affect entry to marriage and cohabitation only through subjective understanding, or perception. Given the inherent uncertainty with which individuals perceive others' earnings potentials, we created six alternative measures to capture earnings potential in six different segments of the life course: predicted current earnings, predicted earnings over the next five years, predicted past earnings, predicted future earnings, predicted lifetime earnings, and predicted lifetime earnings up to five years in the future. We examine and compare the explanatory power of these measures, all of which are estimated from respondents' past and current observed characteristics through a two-step statistical procedure. This two-step procedure creates time-varying indicators of potential earnings that are ascertained at the person-month level. These earnings-potential measures are based upon a person's gender, age, work experience, education, cognitive ability, and, for those who attended college, both college quality and college major. We describe the methodological details concerning the construction of these measures in Appendix D.

We first discuss the total effects of earning capacity presented in columns 1, 2, 5, and 6 of table 11.1. Panels B through G present the total effects of the six key earnings measures, in alternative model specifications, with each effect estimated in a separate equation. We do so separately for marriage and cohabitation and allowing for their interactions with gender. Because meaningful comparisons are made difficult by the fact that the different earnings measures vary greatly in scale, we standardized these coefficients so that they all indicate the multiplicative effects on the odds of union formation for a one-standard-deviation difference in the earnings measures.

Consistent with our theoretical expectations and with empirical results in the literature, we find that potential earnings have a significant positive effect on entry into marriage for men. This is true for all the alternative measures of potential earnings. We observe that, among the different measures of earnings potential, the effect of past earnings is the largest, increasing the odds of marriage by 77 percent per standard deviation, followed by a slightly smaller effect, at 66 percent, of lifetime earnings up to the next five years. The effects of current earnings and earnings in the next five years are estimated around 50 percent. By comparison, future earnings and lifetime earnings have smaller effects, at 24 percent and 28 percent. From these results, it is tempting to conclude that past earnings are the most influential of the earnings-potential measures for men. They are likely to be both known to potential partners and available as resources for marriage. However, given our use of actual labor-force participation histories in constructing our measure of past earnings, this measure was estimated with more accuracy than the other measures (see Equation D.4 in Appendix D). The larger measurement errors for these other earnings measures may have attenuated their estimated effects. Regardless of the relative importance of alternative measures, however, we are confident that economic capacity clearly accelerates the process of marriage for men.

The same earnings measures have no statistically significant effects on women's likelihood of marriage. For all the panels, the tests of the gender differences are statistically significant, meaning that all of the potential-earnings measures affect men's and women's rate of entering marriage differently. These results demonstrate the asymmetric role of economic potential in marriage formation between men and women. However, it is also noteworthy that economic potential has no apparent negative effect on women's marriage. In fact, all the coefficients are estimated to be positive, but not statistically different from zero. Specifically, we do not find support for the idea that greater economic capacity makes marriage less attractive to women by reducing their economic gain from marriage.

The results pertaining to entry into cohabitation (columns 5 and 6) are simple and straightforward: none of the measures of earnings potential has any discernable effect, for either men or women, and none of the interactions between the earnings measures and gender is statistically significant.[4] Recall that earnings potential has large and positive effects on the likelihood of marriage for men but not for women. The results for the transition to cohabitation suggest that, for men, the causal mechanisms leading to marriage are different from those leading to cohabitation—in particular, economic resources hasten marriage but not cohabitation. For women, earnings potential appears to be irrelevant for both types of union formation. Although we know that our estimated earnings potentials are contaminated by measurement error, it is important to note that we have found large and significant effects of earnings potential on entry into marriage among men. That is, our measures of estimated earnings potential are shown to have face validity in yielding a theoretically expected finding.

A comparison of the results for work status (shown in panel A of table 11.1) and earnings potential (shown in panels B–G of table 11.1) indicates an important contrast between the two concerning their effects on cohabitation. Recall from our earlier discussion that employment for men affects entrance into cohabitation while earnings potential does not. This suggests that while a man needs to have some sort of job to have a cohabiting partner, he might need to have a good job (i.e., high earnings) to be married and support a family. For women, economic well-being, however measured, has no influence on the likelihood of entry into either marriage or cohabitation. Together, these results suggest that marriage has a higher threshold than cohabitation, and that the earning capacity of the man is key to surmounting that threshold.

Because work status and potential earnings overlap to some extent, we estimate models that include measures of both in order to partial out their independent contributions in explaining rates of marriage and cohabitation. For this purpose, we define economic potential as lifetime earnings up to five years into the future, a measure that incorporates accurate past-work histories and does not predict too far ahead. Recall that predicted future lifetime earnings is a measure with relatively poor predictive power, presumably because it contains too much measurement error. In Model 11.1 (columns 3, 4, 7, and 8) of table 11.1, we present the coefficients from regressions that include measures of both earnings potential and work status. To differentiate the results from the total effects discussed earlier, we call them *direct effects*.

The direct effects are quite similar to the total effects, with the exception that the direct effect of work status on men's marriage is about half of the total effect. As a result, the gender difference in the net effect of work status is no longer statistically significant. However, the two substantive conclusions that we drew earlier remain unchanged: (1) potential earnings speed up men's, but not women's, rates of marriage and does not affect cohabitation rates; and (2) work status positively speeds up men's, but not women's, rates of marriage *and* cohabitation.

Career Aspirations

We now consider two more dimensions of work that may influence marriage and cohabitation. One is the socioeconomic status (SES) of an occupation (Duncan 1961), and the other is career ambition. Although SES is closely related to earnings (Hauser and Warren 1997), it also represents an individual's standing in the vertical social hierarchy. The SES of current and future jobs could influence entry into marriage and cohabitation negatively or positively. The negative effect may reflect role conflict, with attainment of high social status requiring early investment of time and effort that might otherwise be used to form and maintain a family. The positive effect may work through earnings. As Becker's (1973, 1974, 1991) theory predicts and our earlier findings demonstrate, higher earnings increase the likelihood of marriage among men. However, from both the previous literature and our own work reported earlier, we do not expect occupational SES to have a positive effect on marriage or cohabitation for women.

As in measuring earnings, we encounter a serious problem when attempting to measure occupational SES: the panel study ascertained respondents' occupations at the time of surveys, but did not collect occupational histories in survey intervals. To remedy this problem, we used as a predictor the SES of the "expected occupation at age 30" that was ascertained in 1980, using Hauser and Warren's (1997) scale. This strategy is based on the premise that occupational aspirations predict future occupational status (Hauser, Tsai, and Sewell 1983; Sewell, Haller, and Portes 1969; Sewell et al. 1975). However, our empirical analysis found no evidence that the SES of expected occupation has any influence on marriage and cohabitation (results not shown).[5]

We decided to meet our research needs with responses to other questions about careers that were asked in the 1980 survey. Specifically, we look at career ambition not in terms of attaining a position in the social hierarchy, but in terms of the importance of work relative to family life. To be sure, these items capture respondents' attitudes rather than behaviors, but past research has shown that attainment of high SES is in part determined by such social-psychological factors (Hauser, Tsai, and Sewell 1983; Sewell, Haller, and Portes 1969; Sewell et al. 1975).

These measures of career ambition were examined in chapter 9. From the analysis in chapter 9, we chose to use a composite measure, "attitude toward careers," that is the sum of the values (after rescaling) of the following two items: (1) expectation that work will be a source of satisfaction, and (2) preference for career versus full-time child care for their wives (if male) or themselves (if female). (See table C.5 of Appendix C.) Preliminary analyses (not shown) revealed that the two component variables predict the union-formation outcomes in similar ways.

In chapter 9, we examined the total effect of this composite measure of attitude toward career relative to family life when we added it to our baseline model established in chapter 6, shown in table 9.3. In additional analyses reported in chapter 9, we also examined the direct effect of this measure when we included it with other attitude measures, and found it to exert independent influences on union formation. We drew the conclusion in chapter 9 that high career aspirations relative to family life tend to

TABLE 11.2 **Direct effects of attitudes toward careers, earnings potential, work status, and education on children's rates of entrance into marital and cohabiting unions (as competing destinations)[a]**

	Marriage				Cohabitation			
	Model 11.2		Model 11.3		Model 11.2		Model 11.3	
	B^b	Z^c	B^b	Z^c	B^b	Z^c	B^b	Z^c
Attitude toward careers		1.14[d]		0.97[d]		0.15[d]		0.58[d]
Male	−0.20	1.67	−0.23	1.89	0.09	0.71	0.06	0.50
Female	−0.35	3.77	−0.35	3.82	0.11	0.98	0.16	1.40
Lifetime earnings through $t + 5$ *years*		3.27[d]		2.27[d]		0.42[d]		0.42[d]
Male	0.55	4.35	0.42	3.28	0.03	0.21	0.07	0.53
Female	0.10	1.24	0.06	0.73	0.08	0.91	0.13	1.25
Work during prior six months		0.85[d]				2.38[d]		
Male	0.89	1.95			1.02	2.63		
Female	0.34	1.15			−0.14	0.61		
School enrollment in previous six months								
Full time				1.89[d]				0.30[d]
Male			0.12	0.48			−0.40	1.81
Female			−0.41	2.16			−0.33	1.48
Part time				1.18[d]				1.23[d]
Male			−0.72	4.34			−0.54	3.37
Female			−0.57	3.94			−0.33	1.74
School accumulation				1.24[d]				0.70[d]
Male			0.21	3.10			−0.10	1.75
Female			0.09	1.34			−0.16	2.20
Person-periods	57,886		57,886		57,886		57,886	
No. of events	341		341		347		347	
Df	34		38		34		38	
χ^2	198.59		237.63		119.37		149.72	

Notes: [a] All equations also include the factors from Model 6.6 of chapter 6 (table 6.4).
[b] Effect coefficient for logit equations transformed by equation: $[\exp(\beta) - 1]$.
[c] Z = ratio of absolute value of coefficient to its standard error.
[d] Denotes a Z-test for gender difference in the estimated coefficient.

delay marriage but have little effect on cohabitation. We now consider this measure of attitude toward career, along with the measures of potential earnings, work status, and education in regression models reported in table 11.2. Let us first focus on the results of Model 11.2, which includes attitude toward career, lifetime earnings up to five years into the future, and work status in the past six months, plus their interactions with gender. We find a very large and significant negative effect of work aspirations relative to family life on marriage for women. For each unit increase (on a 4-point scale) in career aspiration, the odds of marriage for women are reduced by 35 percent. The effect of this measure on marriage for men is weaker (at 20 percent) and is only marginally significant. Given that the interaction of career aspiration with gender is not statistically significant, however, we accept the earlier conclusion reached in chapter 9 that having higher work aspirations relative to family life aspirations slows down entry to marriage. We do not, however, find career aspirations to have a significant effect on cohabitation.

After including the career-family life measure in our analysis, the estimates of the positive effects of earnings potential on marriage and of work status on both marriage and cohabitation for men (presented in table 11.1) remain largely unchanged. We are thus led to conclude that the career-aspirations measure does not overlap greatly with the measures of earnings potential and work status. In fact, at least with respect to marriage, they seem to capture seemingly contradictory dimensions of SES: while money and work provide resources to men and facilitate their marriages, career aspirations per se delay marriage. This suggests that those with strong career commitments—either for themselves or for their wives—tend to postpone marriage. This could happen because they want to devote themselves to their careers and postpone marriage until their careers are better established. This delaying effect appears to be more important for women than for men. Furthermore, for men, but not for women, holding a job is important for both marriage and cohabitation, and having a poor job or low earning potential seems to restrict marriage.

Controlling Educational Experiences

We now consider the role of educational experience. From chapter 10 we know that cumulative educational attainment has a positive effect on entry to marriage but a negative effect on entry to cohabitation, whereas school enrollment has negative effects on both. The reason we need to consider educational attainment and school enrollment in this chapter is that they are correlated with our core measures of career attitudes and earnings potential. Thus, it is necessary to see if our earlier findings in this chapter hold true after we control for these two measures of educational experience. However, we do not examine work status and school enrollment in the same equation because early in life and before union formation, these two activities are largely mutually exclusive. Young adults who are not in school are usually working, and those who are not working are usually enrolled in school, making it very difficult to distinguish between the effects of the two. The results for education, career aspiration, and earnings potential in the same equation are reported in Model 11.3 of table 11.2.

These results confirm the earlier findings in chapter 10. School enrollment has negative effects on both marriage and cohabitation, and school accumulation has a positive effect on marriage but a negative effect on co-habitation. As in the case for potential earnings, the positive effect of school accumulation on women's rate of marriage is not statistically significant.[6] We note that the negative effects of career aspirations on marriage are not altered by the inclusion of the education measures in table 11.2, and the positive effect of potential earnings on marriage for men is attenuated (from .55 in Model 11.2 to .42 in Model 11.3), as we expected.

In additional analyses we investigated whether the influences of educational and career factors on marriage were the same for people who were cohabiting as they were for single people. Applying an equation such as Model 11.3 of table 11.2 solely to cohabitors at risk of marriage, rather than singles at risk of marriage, reveals a remarkably similar story (not shown in tables). As with entrance to marriage from being single, full-time school enrollment and career aspirations depress the rate of entry into marriage from cohabitation for both women and men. Also, as before, potential lifetime earnings through the subsequent five years increase the marriage rate for men but not for women. The primary difference for marriage from cohabitation is that the educational completion effect is large and statistically significant for both women and men. Although it is possible that female education has a bigger positive effect on marriage for cohabitors than for single people, the big story is the similarity of education and career effects on marriage for single and cohabiting persons.

We also examined the effects of school enrollment, educational attainment, and earnings on union formation controlling for all factors reported in previous chapters. These additional analyses revealed that even with the full controls of the factors studied here, school enrollment decreases the rates of both marriage and cohabitation; educational attainment increases the rate of marriage and decreases the rate of cohabitation; and earning power increases the rate of marriage for men.

Summary and Conclusion

In this chapter, we have considered a range of factors concerning work and earning capacity and their influence on marriage and cohabitation rates.

Several major findings emerge from our analyses. First, we find working status to be associated with faster entries to marriage and cohabitation for men, but not for women. Second, we find that all the measures of earnings potential strongly and positively influence the likelihood of marriage for men, but not for women. Third, the measures of earnings potential do not affect entry into cohabiting unions for either men or women. Finally, we find persistent negative effects of career ambition on the timing of marriage for men and women.

Our results clearly indicate the connection between employment and household formation for men. A regular job appears to be importantly related to men's, but not women's, entrance into both cohabitation and marriage. This is consistent with the theoretical and empirical observations that male earnings and status are more important than those of women in both actual family life and in the priorities motivating people looking for a partner or spouse (Buss 1994).

Clearly, there is a gender asymmetry concerning the role of economic resources: economic resources are expected from men but not from women in the formation of a union relationship. Given that greater economic resources are expected from men for marriage than for cohabitation, we conclude that marriage exhibits a greater gender asymmetry and is thus more "gendered" than cohabitation.

This chapter adds further evidence to our earlier finding that attitudes affect the likelihood of marriage or cohabitation, independently of actual experiences. Here we showed that career ambition—an individual's preference for career over family life—delays marriage. This is true even though we also found, paradoxically, that career success (as measured by potential earnings) actually speeds up marriage for men. This is analogous to an earlier finding in chapter 10—educational expectation exerts a negative effect on marriage although attained education has a positive effect. Thus, it appears that high career ambition and high educational expectations reflect a psychological state (or attitude) favoring personal achievement over family life, above and beyond what is actually achieved in education and career, and as such they slow down entrance to marriage.

Race Differences

As we note in the previous chapter, less positive employment prospects are often cited as a key reason for lower rates of marriage among the African-American population compared to the White population (Bennett, Bloom, and Craig 1989; Lichter et al. 1992; Oppenheimer, Kalmijn, and Lim 1997; Raley 1996). In this chapter we find that employment and earning are strongly linked to rates of marriage for men. Following from this result, racial or ethnic groups with poor employment and earning prospects are also likely to be characterized by lower rates of marriage. Research on race differences in marriage rates repeatedly identify lower employment and earning prospects of African-American men as a key reason for lower rates of marriage among African Americans (Bennett, Bloom, and Craig 1989; Oppenheimer, Kalmijn, and Lim 1997). To the extent that African-American women search for African-American men with good employment prospects to marry, poorer employment prospects for African-American men translate directly to low marriage rates among African Americans (Lichter et al. 1992).

Conclusion

Employment and higher earning potential accelerate entry into marriage for men, but have no significant effect on marriage rates for women. This is one of the strongest gender differences we have found in our investigation. Earnings do not have significant effects on rates of entering cohabitation, but employment has positive effects on men's, but not women's, rate of cohabitation. Career ambition delays marriage for both men and women, and these effects are independent of employment and earnings. Of course, the observational design in this study means the strong empirical associations we observe may not reflect independent causal forces. Nevertheless, these rich prospective panel measures are consistent with the conclusions that the consequences of employment and earning depend on gender, and that key attitudes have consequences for marital behavior that are independent of educational and employment experiences.

PART IV
Integration and Summary of Effects

CHAPTER TWELVE

Conclusions

Introduction

In this concluding chapter we leave the details of regression coefficients and decompositions of total and indirect effects and discuss the implications of our research for our general understanding of the nature of marriage and cohabitation in the United States today. Although our primary interest concerns the decisions young people make about entrance into marriage and cohabitation, the transformation of cohabitations into marriages, and the intergenerational forces producing these processes, we also consider more generally the place of marriage and cohabitation in American society. We approach this task of summarization and conclusion from a number of different angles. We begin, as we did in chapters 1 and 2, by considering marriage and family life in the world of western Europe during the 1700s, with the confidence that the candle of history can help illuminate understanding of current social relationships. We then move to a picture of marriage, family, and social life in the United States today. As in the earlier chapters, we emphasize both change and continuity in social relationships, being impressed by the remarkable continuities that have accompanied the equally notable changes.

Finally, we will portray the essential elements of American life influencing entrance into cohabitation and marriage. As we have done throughout the book, we take an intergenerational approach to this examination of the influences on the union-formation experience of young adults, considering factors from the lives of both young adults and their parents.

As part of our effort to picture and explain union formation in America today, we consider in some detail the emergence of cohabitation as a common experience in the last few decades of the 1900s. Here we pull together the information we have accumulated on the kinds of families and individuals that participated in the dramatic increase in cohabitation as a form of union during the past few decades. This summary reveals that the recent trend in unmarried cohabitation is linked to some of the centuries-old trends affecting western society and culture, especially those relating to freedom and equality and the decline of religious authority in people's lives.

Of course, as we picture the broad landscape of family life in the past, describe the changes of the past several hundred years, portray the central elements of family life today, and scope out some of the crucial elements of the causal forces influencing family life, we must remember that we can only portray the general picture and must gloss over many of the details. Of central importance here is the necessity to focus on the modal patterns and trends, leaving out the details and exceptions. This approach, of necessity, will provide a picture that is often not applicable to the many important minority groups of the country. This shortcoming of our study is also exacerbated by the fact that the Intergenerational Panel Study of Parents and Children, the data set upon which many of our detailed analyses and conclusions were based, was limited to the majority White population.

Another caveat that we must add concerns the nature of causal analyses. It is impossible in observational studies to make causal conclusions without making important—and often, untestable—assumptions about the nature and direction of certain effects. And, to the extent that these assumptions are violated, the estimates of effects will be too large or too small. Although we have tried to be careful in our assumptions and conclusions—often using multiple alternative assumptions and interpretations—we recognize that our estimates may be off by a substantial amount. Nevertheless, we believe that, given the constraints of data and methods, our estimates and conclusions are reasonable. For this reason, while we have used the language of cause, effect, and consequence in discussing regression coefficients, at the same time we also recognize that our observational data are insufficient to support definitive statements of causation. We have also not provided this caveat at each point we have used causal language, but remind readers of its appropriateness throughout.

Portraying Marriage and Family Life in the Past

We begin this chapter by asking what an artist of the 1500s or 1600s would paint if asked to portray the society of western Europe of that period. The artist would have had to emphasize the rural and agricultural nature of society, with images of farmsteads, the sowing and reaping of crops, and the husbandry of animals. Villages, towns, and even some cities would have been included in the picture as well. The dominance of religion would be evident in the Christian church spires rising above the countryside. And, the role of the government and trade guilds would appear in the municipal and guild buildings of the cities and the activities of the nobles and military.

As the artist moved from the landscape and buildings to the people and their social relationships, the work would have to show how the family unit structured and organized so much of social and economic life—including production, consumption, and living arrangements. The family would be pictured as the primary locus of sexual expression, childbearing, and childrearing. The artist would also show how authority, information, and even the necessities of life were influenced by family roles and relationships.

This monumental painting of life in the western Europe of the 1500s and 1600s would emphasize the importance of marriage in organizing both family life and individual activities and experiences. Marriage would be pictured as a favored status, bringing recognition of adulthood, economic independence, an independent household, the legitimization of sexual relations, and the freedom and responsibility to bear and rear children. Marriage would also be painted as an institution defining the specialization of roles between husbands and wives. The mate-selection system of the western European past would be painted as centering on the young people themselves—with courtship occurring in such places as village festivals, churches, taverns, fields, barns, and homes, and marital union a matter of mutual consent. Yet, the painting of marriage would be woefully incomplete if it did not also show the involvement of parents, the role of the community, the witnessing and blessing of the church, and the incredible celebration involving feasting, drinking, dancing, and making merry.

Portraying Marriage and Family Life Today

Of course, an artist assigned to painting life in the United States today would have to produce a very different masterpiece. This painting would show rural and village life with its farms, fields, and animals in the background and move urban and suburban life and automobiles, communication towers, and dense populations to the foreground. It would also need to show factories, high-rise office buildings, hospitals, and government buildings dominating this landscape, with the spires of religious edifices being difficult to detect.

Today's painting would also have to feature the role of families in social life very differently than in the past. Rather than showing families dominating economic production as they once did, it would show economic activity being conducted by bureaucratic organizations whose primary linkage to families is through the workers they employ. Similarly, today's painting would depict schools and day care centers as important loci for the socialization of children.

Courtship and Marriage

Today's work of art would portray marriage much differently. Rather than depicting marriage as a privileged status signaling adulthood, independent living, and economic self-sufficiency and legitimizing sex and childbearing, today's artist would show that about one-half of today's young adults experience unmarried cohabitation. Both the necessity of marriage and its place as a positive institution in the lives of adults and children would receive less prominence in today's painting than in the one previously described.

Yet as different as these paintings would be, they would also have common elements. Although today's work would show single adults, it would also include numerous images of wedding ceremonies, marriage celebrations, and the lives of wives and husbands and their families. It would show that most of today's young adults still plan to marry.[1]

As in the past, today's painting would show that the focus of the mate-selection process is on the young people themselves—on their meeting, pairing off, falling in love, arranging jobs and residences, and marrying. Although courtship would no longer be portrayed as occurring at village festivals or in fields and barns, it would still be depicted in taverns and homes, as well as in automobiles and movie theaters, and via the Internet. Marriage ceremonies of today would also look similar to those depicted hundreds of years ago, showing a bride and groom standing before a government or religious official with hands clasped and exchanging rings and solemn vows. Today's wedding announcements, marriage licenses, and marriage registrations would also look similar to the wedding banns, licenses, and registrations of past centuries. And wedding celebrations—with their accompanying eating, drinking, dancing, and other merry making—would retain remarkable similarities to those pictured hundreds of years ago. Whereas the artist of the past may have painted such activities among peasants in the barn and village square, the artist today would probably picture these activities in hotel ballrooms and reception halls, but nevertheless, the activities and their fundamental meanings to the participants would undoubtedly be very similar.

Depicting Cohabitation

Today's painter might believe it appropriate to portray cohabitation as an entirely new phenomenon—a way of life quite separate from marriage as it was historically understood. Today's artist also would paint cohabitation in many different forms—as people cohabit in different contexts and for varying reasons—but would show the predominant form of cohabitation sharing many features of the picture of marriage 500 years ago.

Claiming resemblances between some unmarried cohabitations today and marriage in the past will undoubtedly shock many people—especially those who are in the habit of reading the conclusions of books before the introduction and historical setting. Indeed, many people in today's world believe that the entrance into marriage is controlled by the church and state. For these people, marriage typically occurs when an unmarried man and woman enter a church, walk down the aisle, and meet a clergyman in front of the altar. After statements of promise and consent by the bride and groom, the officiator, with the authority of the church and/or state, joins the couple together as husband and wife. It is also likely that this simple and straightforward view of the marriage process and its ultimate authority is believed by most to represent the pattern in history for hundreds and thousands of years.

Yet as the reader of chapter 2 of this book will recognize, this portrayal of the marriage process has little in common with the reality of marriage before 1500. At that time, marriage was a process that required only the consent and vows of two individuals, the bride and groom. Although witnesses could provide useful verification of the marriage, clergy could provide blessings to the couple, and the family and community could provide support and celebration, the authority and act of marriage rested with the young people themselves. Others, including the church and state, were auxiliary to the simple promise of the man and woman.

In this couple-centered marriage system a woman and man could enter marriage in one of two remarkably simple ways. They could exchange vows of marriage and thereby become husband and wife. Or, they could exchange vows promising to become husband and wife sometime in the future; this exchange of vows followed by sexual consummation would turn an unmarried man and woman into a married husband and wife. A third approach evolved and was legitimated in the United States—that of common-law marriage. This required no vows or ceremony, only that the woman and man act like wife and husband and present themselves to the world as such.

For the reasons that we discussed in chapter 2, the church and state worked for hundreds of years to remove the marriage system from the hands of individuals and place it under the rubric of the church and state. Their success in doing so is reflected in two interrelated conditions: (1) the many new laws over the last few hundred years that emphasize the necessity of religious and government authority and formality in contracting marriage; and (2) the strong perception among many of us that it is the authority of the church and state and formal ceremonies that create a wife and husband from the raw materials of unmarried woman and man.

In fact, one of the amazing ironies of the last several decades is that just as the church and state were finally getting the marital system under their control, unmarried cohabitation and its associated elements emerged and changed the system again (Lesthaeghe 1995). One of the central elements of this irony is that this new movement relegated much of the formal aspects of marriage to the church and state while returning the elements of love, commitment, sex, and coresidence to individuals and couples.

This brings us back to the artistic portrayal of cohabitation. An artist today might want to use a series of panels in a still painting or several clips in a film to show the diversity of cohabitors or the movement of cohabitors across categories of cohabitation.

However, today's depiction of cohabitation would use many of the same tones and hues that were used to paint marriage hundreds of years ago. This is true because, as we documented in chapter 3, many unmarried cohabitors today would be married under the definitions and understandings that persisted for hundreds of years. Many of them have pledged to become husband and wife, have consummated that pledge sexually, and have established an independent household—a combination of elements that would have constituted marriage in the distant past. The only thing that separates them from marriage is their own self-definition and the new belief that the authority and blessings of the church or state are required to enter marriage.

Of course, many people enter cohabitation without being engaged to marry. Yet, even for many of them, the connections between cohabitation and marriage are clear and strong. Some cohabiting couples have already decided explicitly to get married, although they might not describe themselves as engaged. Others have less commitment, but may have decided, at least implicitly or privately, that they are going to marry the partner. Yet others enter cohabitation without any plans to marry but consider marriage as a possibility that cohabitation may help realize. Thus, all of these couples make the decision to cohabit in the context of considering marriage—from having a definitive plan to contemplating the possibility. As we discussed in chapter 3, at least in the 1980s and early 1990s, these couples constitute the majority of cohabitors and should have a central place in any portrayal of cohabitation in America.

Nevertheless, some couples enter cohabitation with no thoughts of marriage, at least with their partner, and just slide or drift into cohabitation. Among these are couples who view cohabitation as not much more than an opportunity to enhance the frequency and quality of sex or to capture the economies of scale associated with joint living. These people may go on to marry, perhaps even each other, but at the time of cohabitation initiation they have no such thoughts. In fact, the couple may simply slide or drift from single life into the sharing of living quarters with little explicit discussion or decision-making. This sliding into cohabitation without any connection to marriage may have increased recently as cohabitation became more common.

In addition, a small number couples view cohabitation as a long-term alternative, rather than as a prelude, to marriage. These couples may espouse a marriage-like commitment to and love for each other, but place little or negative stock in the blessings of the church and state and the legalities of a marriage registration and certificate. These cohabitors are especially interesting because they have so many of the characteristics of the married that it is easy for them to be portrayed as married, both socially and legally. In fact, as we saw in chapter 3, some of these people may cross the legal line between cohabitation and marriage without even knowing that they have done so—and be judged by the state to be married under common law. It is this circumstance that has caused some to recommend that cohabitors who do not want to be treated as legally married should sign a document to that effect.

All of this suggests the importance of self-definition in determining one's status as single, cohabiting, or married—an importance that has characterized marriage for centuries. The Catholic Church declared hundreds of years ago that marriage is a sacrament, but as a rite performed by the couple themselves, with the priest acting as only a witness and facilitator in the exchange of marriage vows. It seems that this ancient principal of self-definition has been transmitted down through the years to the present time. Furthermore, as in past times, the state and society seem at least somewhat prepared to support and enforce those self-definitions as they understand them—recognizing, of course, that the fuzziness involved can produce substantial confusion, again as it did in the past.

These conclusions also suggest that a proper portrayal of intimate and family relations in America today requires not only attention to the widespread experience of cohabitation, but recognition that it is frequently a temporary status. Many couples move quickly from cohabitation to marriage; others rapidly dissolve their cohabiting relationship, with little thought of marriage. Very few end up in long-term cohabiting relationships, and among those who do, the relationship often comes to bear a striking resemblance to marriage, and may even come to assume the same social and legal rights and responsibilities as marriage. Thus, unmarried cohabitation today should be pictured as a prevalent, but in most cases relatively short-lived, arrangement.

Sex, Coresidence, and Childbearing

Although a painting of social life today would have more expression of sex, coresidence, and childbearing outside of marriage than would a painting from the 1500s and 1600s, the older painting would not leave out the occurrence of premarital dalliance (even premarital pregnancy), and today's painting would not leave out the central importance of marriage to sexual expression, coresidence, childbearing, and childrearing. Today, young people who begin dating, going steady, and having sexual relationships at young ages enter coresidential unions—both cohabitation and marriage— much more rapidly than those who postpone dating, going steady, and having sexual relationships. Furthermore, the effects of the timing of dating, going steady, and initiating sex are among the strongest we have observed in our analyses, and they remain strong even with controls for numerous other parent and child factors. Clearly, dating and sexual relationships are closely connected to the formation of cohabiting and marital unions.

Interestingly, dating and sexual experience during the teenage years are more closely related to subsequent cohabitation than to marriage. We believe this is because teens with sexual experience are more accepting than their counterparts of having sex outside of marriage. And, because unmarried cohabitation is, among other things, a public statement of this belief and practice, it makes sense that teenage sexuality is more strongly correlated with cohabitation than with marriage. We will return to the connection between teenage sexuality and cohabitation in the following pages when we discuss the people participating in the emergence of cohabitation in the United States in the late 1900s.

Chapter 7 demonstrates that, despite the large proportion of children now born outside of marriage, childbearing is still strongly correlated with marriage. This can be seen in the strong positive effect of nonmarital pregnancy on the marriage rate. Although the practice of marrying to legitimize a birth has decreased in recent decades, many young adults—cohabitors as well as singles—still have a strong marital response to the discovery of a nonmarital pregnancy. Pregnant unmarried women today also have much greater access to abortion than did their maternal ancestors, and unmarried women or couples face less pressure to marry in order to legitimize nonmarital pregnancies or births (Thornton and Young-DeMarco 2001).

One additional connection between marriage and childbearing deserves mention—the influence of fertility in the first generation on union formation in the second. Young people who grow up in families where children are both numerous and desired have higher rates of union formation, especially marriage, than those from families with lower desired and actual fertility. Contrary to our expectations, however, the influence of parental fertility on young-adult marriage is not transmitted through the children's own fertility desires.

The Role of Parents

Just as an artist in the 1500s and 1600s would not depict courtship and marriage as processes controlled by the parents, today's artist would not show these as entirely individualistic processes. As we have documented continuously throughout this book, the role of parents in the lives of their children's marriages and cohabitation experiences is substantial and worthy of emphasis in any picture of contemporary marriage and cohabitation.

In fact, the data from our study clearly support one of the overarching theoretical principles we enunciated in chapters 1 and 5—the existence of strong intergenerational influences on the union-formation process. One can predict a great deal about the marriage and cohabitation experiences of young adults with only the information provided by parents at the time of the child's birth. Young adults' union-formation behavior is influenced by many characteristics of the family they are born into, and this parental family influence extends far beyond the years of infancy into at least the first three decades of life. A range of parental family circumstances during childhood, adolescence, and young adulthood all influence the ways that young adults enter cohabitation and marriage.

For example, the immigration and farm experiences of the family influence the union formation of young adults, as do the socioeconomic experiences and circumstances of the parents. A range of parental marriage and childbearing experiences also have effects—including mother's age at marriage, the number of children she has, her experience with divorce and remarriage, and her experience with premarital pregnancy. Parental religious participation and commitment, parental networks with friends and extended kin, and parental attitudes about a range of family and educational matters also influence young-adult union-formation experiences.

All of this suggests that parents bequeath to their children a rich heritage of cultural and social understandings and meanings. In both word and deed, parents provide children models for dealing with intimate relationships, marriage, and family life. They also embed young people in a system of values and disciplinary patterns that guide the future attitudes and behaviors of the young. Parents also provide resources that permit their children to invest in educations and careers, and that assist them in establishing their own households and families. In addition, any mother or father who has recently been involved in the planning and financing of a child's wedding will certainly know the relevance of parents for the process. Furthermore, with today's lower mortality and greater longevity, grandparents, aunts, and uncles are more likely than in previous generations to participate in the weddings of young adults. And, last but not least, parents provide their children a rich genetic heritage that sets the biological background for the dating, courting, cohabiting, and marital experiences of the young.

It is also important to remember that, as we argued in chapter 6, the parental family is not a static entity, but one that can change—sometimes slowly, sometimes rapidly—across time. Our research indicates that young people are influenced both by the circumstances of the parental family at birth, as well as the evolving situation over time.

Yet, at the same time, there are important continuities in the parental family across time. That is, there are important correlations between parental attributes during the infancy and adolescence of children. These continuities form a strong basis for the transmission of effects from early in the life courses of parents to children's union-formation experiences. Many of the effects of early parental characteristics are indirect, as they operate through the same attributes later in life. These characteristics include: religiosity, family size preferences and behavior, closeness to relatives, and sex-role attitudes. The primary exception is that the effects of early parental financial resources seem to affect children's union-formation experiences independent of later parental resources.

Of importance is the transmission of attitudes, behaviors, and other attributes across generations. Although intergenerational discontinuities are important, young people still tend to be similar in at least some ways to their parents. These intergenerational transmissions can occur through both biological and social mechanisms, and can operate across a wide range of human attributes, including education, earning capacity, religiosity, family attitudes, and union-formation experience itself. Thus, many of the influences of parental attributes on children's union formation operate indirectly as parents influence the education, earning capacity, religiosity, and family attitudes of the children, which in turn influence second-generation union formation.

Despite the rather broad and pervasive influence of parents on their children, we also find that this influence tends to wane as the children age. Many of the parental influences we have documented are stronger during the late teenage years and early twenties than they are in the late twenties. It appears that as children mature they become more independent and less influenced by their experiences in the parental home.

Connections to Friends and Extended Kin

The data we have presented in this book support the importance of the social organization of the family as outlined in chapters 1 and 5. Young adults' union-formation experiences are influenced by the ways their parental family intersects and interacts with other groups to organize the basic social activities of daily life. In particular, the organization of activities around kin or nonkin has important implications for the union-formation experiences of children. Parents who have strong interconnections to their larger kinship system have children with lower cohabitation rates than others. We interpret this association as suggesting that integration within the extended family emphasizes the importance of marriage as a familial institution and inhibits entrance into cohabitation. Interesting in this regard is the fact that some of the negative influence of parental closeness to relatives on cohabitation operates through the marital histories of the parents. Parents who are close to their relatives have lower rates of divorce than others, which in turn decrease young-adult experience with cohabitation. In addition, as we discuss more fully in the following, the religiosity of grandparents is negatively related to the cohabitation experience of young adults.

Parental closeness to relatives also helps us to understand the higher rates of cohabitation for people with farm origins, as discussed in chapter 5. Our research shows that, compared to urban residents who grew up in cities, urban residents who grew up on farms emphasize relatives less than friends. Moving from rural to urban areas tends to separate migrants from their families, which can, in turn, lead to higher cohabitation rates of children whose families came from farm backgrounds.[2]

Mothers who are more gregarious than others (who frequently visit with both relatives and friends) have children who both marry and cohabit more rapidly than others. This suggests that high levels of sociability are transmitted from parents to children through either biological or social mechanisms, and these traits lead to more rapid union formation. More gregarious mothers may also have more interest and skill in helping their children meet and attract partners.

Maternal Marriage and Divorce

As we suggested in chapter 5, any portrayal of the relationships between the parental family and the cohabitation and marriage experiences of young adults requires careful attention to the marriage and divorce experience of the mother. Looking first at parental marriage, we note that young people whose mother married young entered unions substantially more rapidly than others, creating an important positive correlation in union-formation ages across generations. Interestingly, this effect was stronger for cohabitation than for marriage (chapter 5).

As we reported in chapter 5, multiple factors help explain the rapid rates of union formation among those whose mother married young. These include the relatively low financial resources of the mothers who married young—which in turn positively influence both cohabitation and marriage in the second generation. In addition, mothers who married young were more gregarious, which is also related to high rates of union formation among children.

Maternal preferences for children to marry young also lead to more rapid union formation in the second generation, but have a stronger impact on marriage than cohabitation. The explanation of this intergenerational effect is straightforward: mothers who prefer their children to marry at a young age have children who also prefer to marry young, which leads to more rapid marriage behavior. This pattern of results suggests an important intergenerational transmission of union timing preferences and behavior.

Also note that early marriage in the second generation is not only related to a desire for early marriage but to strong negative attitudes against remaining single. This is partly explained by the fact that positive attitudes toward remaining single are also related to older ages at marriage preferences, higher career aspirations, and greater acceptance of premarital sex and cohabitation—all factors that reduce rates of marriage.

Maternal pregnancy at marriage is also strongly related to early union formation in the second generation, with the effect on cohabitation being particularly substantial. The dramatic influence of a premarital pregnancy in the first generation on cohabitation experience in the second generation suggests a clear intergenerational transmission of a willingness to violate the historical proscriptions against sex outside of marriage. The positive effect of a parental premarital pregnancy on young-adult cohabitation is transmitted by some of the same mechanisms we found in the influence of parental early marriage. That is, premaritally pregnant parents tended to have fewer financial resources and to be more gregarious than their counterparts—factors associated with rapid rates of union formation among young-adult children.

Several additional indirect effects help transmit the influence of a parental premarital pregnancy on the high rates of cohabitation in the second generation. Premaritally pregnant parents also tended to attend religious services less frequently, to experience higher levels of marital dissolution, and to hold more egalitarian sex-role attitudes than others—all factors associated with higher rates of cohabitation in the second generation.

Maternal experience with divorce and remarriage also has a strong influence on young-adult union formation. Young people whose mother experienced a marital dissolution and then remarried have substantially higher rates of union formation than others, with the effect on cohabitation being especially significant. The effect is similar whether the maternal marital dissolution and remarriage occurred before or after the birth of the child, suggesting that such marital events may have as much influence on the parents as the children. However, young people whose mothers divorced without remarrying had higher rates of cohabitation, but not marriage.

Love or Money

We have already seen that any reasonably accurate depiction of the past would run counter to the adage that "people in the past married for money while people today marry for love." Our hypothetical paintings from both eras would place considerable emphasis upon the romance and love experienced in the courtship and marriage process. Indeed, actual paintings of the 1500s and 1600s depict just this circumstance (de Jongh 1997; Nevitt 2001; Roberts-Jones and Roberts-Jones 1997; Sluijter 2000; Vergara 2001).

Our contemporary painting would also show that, as in the past, marriages today depend on money and other economic considerations as well as love. This conclusion is drawn from many of our findings presented throughout the book.

To begin with, our research is strongly consistent with the arguments of chapter 5 about the dramatic importance of parental education and financial resources for the union-formation experiences of young adults. A major theme of chapters 5 and 6 is that high levels of parental education and financial resources are negatively related to the speed of entrance into coresidential unions. Furthermore, this negative effect of socioeconomic resources on the speed of union formation operates for both cohabitation and marriage. A key reason that parental education influences young-adult union formation negatively is that it is a primary causal influence on parental financial resources, which also depress the rate of marriage and cohabitation. We had little success in finding any indirect pathways through which parental financial resources slow down young-adult entrance into marriage and cohabitation.

Moving a step further back in the socioeconomic causal process, we have observed important intervening effects of early parental attributes through parental education and financial status. Because parental education and financial resources have such a strong negative influence on the union-formation rates of children, any aspect of the parental family that influences parental education and finances will also influence children's union formation. Both parental farm background and number of siblings meet this criterion, as parents from farms and large families receive significantly less education than others. A premarital pregnancy and young age at marriage also meet this criterion as they are both related to lower economic well-being. This suggests that socioeconomic factors are important elements of the causal processes transmitting the influence of parental attributes to their children's union experience.

Maternal expectations for their children's education are also related to lower rates of union formation among young adults. In fact, maternal educational expectations for children are one of the mechanisms transmitting the influence of parental education on the union-formation experiences of young adults. High young-adult educational and career aspirations are also negatively related to the rate of union formation.

Furthermore, as we saw in chapter 10, enrollment in school is a substantial inhibitor of entrance into both cohabitation and marriage. This is consistent with one of our overarching theoretical principles from chapter 1—the relevance of role compatibility and role conflict. Young people find it difficult to simultaneously attend school and work at a job to establish an independent household. In addition, marriage is often seen normatively as an adult status that is inconsistent with the dependent role of student.

However, as we argue in chapter 10, the same schooling that conflicts with procuring a job that will support a marital household is often undertaken, at least partially, to acquire the skills necessary to obtain a job that will bring a good standard of living and provide the resources for establishing an independent household. The importance of employment was further demonstrated in chapter 11 where we showed it as a key predictor of entrance into both cohabitation and marriage. As in the distant past, a job and the economic resources and stability associated with it are closely tied to union formation and the establishment of an independent household.

Chapters 10 and 11 also show that the accumulation of educational accomplishments and earning potential are strong predictors of entrance into unions. However, they predict marriage and cohabitation differently. While marriage is positively related to school grades and educational attainment, cohabitation is negatively related to school grades and educational attainment. And, while marriage is positively related to earnings potential for men, cohabitation has no significant relationship to earnings potential. These findings indicate that young adults with low grades and little educational accumulation tend to choose cohabitation over marriage, while those with high educational achievements and earnings potential tend to choose marriage over cohabitation. Clearly, economics affect both cohabitation and marriage, but the threshold to marriage seems to be substantially higher than the threshold to cohabitation. That is, many people seem to be willing to cohabit with levels of economic well-being and security that they would judge as insufficient for entering marriage.

The adage that people today marry for love and not for money is inconsistent not only with the empirical picture but with numerous economic and sociological treatises on the subject. In fact, as we discussed in chapter 11, one influential model of marriage and family life compares the contemporary household to an economic system of specialization and trade. In this model husbands specialize in economic production and wives specialize in domestic production and childcare, and the two spouses ensure their overall well-being through trade within the household. Similarly, men are sometimes pictured in academic models of marriage as using their economic resources to purchase or consume marriage and children. Women, on the other hand, are frequently portrayed as specializing in the care of the home and children. Although our data are only partially consistent with this particular economic model, we have clearly demonstrated the importance of economics in any picture of contemporary union formation.

Today's theoretical models and empirical findings would also lend themselves to a portrayal of the gendered nature of marriage—one that would bear many resemblances to the gendered picture of the past. Until recently, it was the husband who specialized in economic production and was considered the head of the household. It was the husband who was generally responsible for the procurement of the economic resources—often from his parents—to support a wife and family. Although the wife often brought economic resources to the marriage, her contributions along these lines were often secondary to those of the husband.

The data and discussion of chapter 11 suggest a similar situation today. It is consistently men's rather than women's employment that predicts both cohabitation and marriage; it is consistently men's rather than women's earnings potential that predicts entrance into marriage. This is not to say that women's employment is irrelevant to a family's economic well-being, for it is clearly not. However, it does suggest that men's employment and earning potential are decisive in making the leap into marriage, and that the lack of a job—even a good job—may be a strong dis-incentive to marry. Women's economic activities may assist the well-being of the family, but those activities do not seem to be decisive in the decision-making process concerning marriage and cohabitation. Thus, al-though the details of this gendered picture differ somewhat from those in the past, the general outlines are similar.

The continuing importance of gender roles in marriage enters the pic-ture in other ways as well. This concerns the incompatibility and conflict that can exist between work and family roles, an issue that—as we argue in chapter 9—is particularly relevant for women. Young people with positive attitudes toward gender equality and women's employment have substan-tially lower rates of marriage than others, perhaps wanting to postpone marriage until the potential wife has finished her schooling and estab-lished her career. In addition, egalitarian sex roles are associated with low levels of religiosity, positive attitudes toward premarital sex and cohabita-tion, high preferred age at marriage, and high career aspirations—factors that themselves lead to low rates of marriage.

Attitudes about work and family roles for men also enter into mar-riage decisions. Young people who believe that men should value family over career marry much more rapidly than others. As expected, the ef-fects of men's priorities for home life were greater for young women than for young men, reconfirming the higher importance of such considerations for women.

Religion

Although an artistic rendition of life 500 years ago would have empha-sized the importance of religion, with church buildings and spires dom-inating much of the landscape, today's landscape would show those reli-gious structures overshadowed by the towers of business and government. However, although today's rendering would reflect the diminished role of religion in the lives of individuals and families, it would not leave it out of the scene entirely. As our findings confirm, many Americans believe in religious teachings, attend religious services frequently, and believe that religion is important in their lives.

The importance of religion in the union-formation process is consis-tent with one of our overarching theoretical principles outlined in chapter 1—the strong role of values and beliefs in the marriage and cohabitation decisions of young adults. Interestingly, the influence of religion does not primarily emanate from religious affiliation, although Catholics tend to marry slower than others once their greater level of attendance at religious services and higher family size preferences are taken into account. Rather, the most significant effect of religion operates through the level of religious participation, commitment, and belief.

In this book we have examined the effect of numerous indicators of religiosity—including grandmother's religiosity, whether the parents had a religious marriage ceremony, parent and child attendance at religious services, the importance of religion to mothers and children, and mother and child belief in religious teachings. Although the influence varies somewhat by the religiosity measure examined, the overall effect is quite similar: religiosity has little effect on the total union-formation rate, but it substantially influences the choice between cohabitation and marriage. In brief, we found that young adults who are from more religious families and are more religious themselves have substantially higher marriage rates and lower cohabitation rates than young adults who are less religious and come from less religious families.

Religiosity affects the union-formation decisions of young adults through a number of pathways. Foremost, religiosity is relatively stable across generations and across time within generations. Children whose parents and grandparents are more religious tend to be more religious themselves, and religious young people often mature into religious older people. These inter- and intra-generational continuities are strong enough that many of the effects of grandparent religiosity work through parental religiosity. Similarly, part of the effect of early religiosity of parents operates through the later religiosity of parents, and parental religious effects are important at least partially because parents influence the religiosity of their children. This chain of indirect influences helps to explain the overall effects of grandparent and parent religiosity on the marriage and cohabitation experiences of young adults.

However, this causal chain does not entirely explain the influence of grandparent and parent religiosity on the union-formation experience of young adults. For example, grandparent religiosity decreases young-adult cohabitation, in part, because it is related to high levels of parental education and older parental age at marriage that, in turn, have a negative influence on entrance into cohabitation. In addition, parental religiosity also influences union-formation experience because it is associated with negative attitudes of mothers toward premarital sex and cohabitation that in turn lead young people away from cohabitation and toward marriage.

Similarly, the children of religious mothers tend to have more negative attitudes toward premarital sex and cohabitation and less sexual experience as teenagers—again factors that are associated with union-formation decisions favoring marriage over cohabitation. Interestingly, although these indirect pathways of influence can explain much of the effect of parental religiosity during the child's adolescent years, they cannot explain the influence of parental religiosity during the childhood years. Apparently, something about childhood religious socialization cannot be explained by the factors examined here.

The effect of religiosity in the second generation is also related to many other dimensions of young adulthood. Among the explanations for religious young people having less experience with cohabitation is that they are substantially less sexually precocious and have less positive attitudes toward abortion, sex, and cohabitation—factors that lead to lower rates of cohabitation. Highly religious young adults also place great value on men's role in the family and prefer a younger age at marriage, two factors that lead to higher rates of marriage. Clearly, religiosity is closely related to many dimensions of family life that are, in turn, related to union formation.

Religion and religiosity are not only important influences on young-adult marriage and cohabitation, but significant intervening mechanisms transmitting the influence of other causal factors on young-adult union formation. For example, parental religiosity helped explain the influence of parental education, age at marriage, and premarital pregnancy on children's union-formation experiences. Parental young age at marriage and premarital pregnancy led to lower levels of parental religiosity that, in turn, influenced both cohabitation and marriage in the children's generation. Also, part of the effect of farm background on children's union-formation experiences is because people from agricultural origins were disproportionately fundamentalist Protestants.

Values and Beliefs

In addition to religiosity, other values and beliefs figure prominently in the union-formation process. Our research findings are consistent with the hypotheses from chapter 9 that values and beliefs held by both young people and their parents are influential in the second generation's marriage and cohabitation behavior. Although representing values and beliefs is a difficult artistic endeavor, it is an essential part of any portrait of union formation today.

We have already mentioned the central importance of religiosity, values concerning marriage and singlehood, and sex-roles attitudes in both generations to young adults' experiences of marriage and cohabitation. Marriage and cohabitation are also influenced by several other important attitudes and values in both the first and second generations. For example, maternal acceptance of premarital sex and cohabitation strongly predicts cohabitation in the second generation, as well as the attitudes of young people toward premarital sex and cohabitation and their sexual experiences as teenagers. Because both the premarital sexual attitudes and behavior of young adults are strong predictors of cohabitation, it should not be surprising that they are indirect pathways transmitting the influence of maternal attitudes toward premarital sex and cohabitation to the cohabitation experience of the young people. In addition, mothers with permissive attitudes also have children who are less religious and have higher preferred ages at marriage, two additional factors related to high rates of cohabitation among young adults.

The attitudes of young adults toward premarital sex and cohabitation influence their union-formation behavior in multiple ways. Perhaps most important is that those who hold more permissive sexual attitudes tend to be more sexually precocious, a behavior that leads to more unmarried cohabitation. In addition, those with more permissive attitudes about premarital sex are less religious and more accepting of abortion, two more factors positively related to unmarried cohabitation. Furthermore, permissive sexual attitudes are associated with positive attitudes toward remaining single, a trait that slows down the rate of marriage.

Thus, there is an important cluster of attitudes and beliefs around sex, abortion, marriage, and single life—transmitted from parents to children—that influences young adults' rate of union formation and their choice between cohabitation and marriage.

Also, as argued in chapter 9, attitudes and aspirations concerning school and work—particularly in relation to family life—are also important predictors of entrance into unions. Whereas positive attitudes and values toward marriage and family life lead to more rapid marriage, educational and career aspirations tend to slow down entrance into marriage.

The Life Course

The research reported in this book is clearly consistent with the life-course perspective, another of the overarching frameworks guiding our analyses. Thus, an artist portraying marriage and cohabitation today would have to capture the various influences on union formation over time. Influences on the individual decisions of young people can be traced back at least to their grandparents—with grandparent religiosity, farm experience, and immigration status being important. We have also documented numerous influences from the parental generation, with many traceable to the early lives of the parents. Early parental life-course experiences affect children's union-formation experiences both directly and indirectly through affecting the later home environment. We also have uncovered numerous influences of parental circumstances during the children's teenage years, influences that operate directly on children's union formation and influences that work through the children's attitudes, values, and behavior.

Our project also indicates that children's own circumstances and experiences in childhood have significant influence on subsequent decisions, with implications for later cohabitation and marriage behavior. We have already emphasized the centrality of dating and sexual experience during the teenage years for subsequent union formation. Early experiences in school also matter as they affect educational aspirations and achievements later in life, factors important for union formation. Here we have emphasized the importance of social processes in these life-course dynamics while also recognizing the relevance of physical and biological influences, both across and within the generations.

Direct and Indirect Effects

As we stated in chapter 1, a central goal of this book has been the explication of the causal pathways of first- and second-generation influences on young-adult union formation. This has led us to pay special attention to the intervening factors and indirect effects explaining any particular causal influence. We believe that we have been successful in identifying many of these indirect pathways.

At the same time that we have identified many indirect pathways of influence on young-adult marriage and cohabitation through the many intervening factors introduced in this analysis, many direct effects remain. Appendix tables A.2, A.3, and A.4 identify the parent and child factors that have statistically significant direct effects on cohabitation and/or marriage net of all other factors considered in this book. The results in these tables show that farm background, mothers returning to school, financial resources, home ownership, family size, and closeness to relatives all retain substantial and statistically significant influence on second-generation union formation, even in our most complete models. Many additional parental factors measured when the child was an adolescent also retain predictive power in our most complete models; these include maternal gregariousness, visiting relatives versus friends, sex-role attitudes, and educational expectations for the child.

A particularly important implication of these last observations is that the parental family has many long-lasting influences on second-generation union formation. Parental influences on young-adult union formation operate through many domains, not just those that are highly similar. That is, parents influence the union formation of their children through mechanisms other than the straightforward transmission of parental traits to the children.

These causal mechanisms, of course, go beyond the factors that we examined empirically in this analysis. They can include additional social, economic, and psychological factors in the lives of the children, as well as genetic and physiological factors. It is possible that genetic forces in the parental generation both influence parental experiences and attitudes and are passed on to the second generation, where they influence cohabitation and marriage experience. Additional research will be required to trace through these complex pathways of influence.

Just as several of the factors from the parental generation maintain strong, direct effects on second-generation union formation independent of all of the factors examined, so do several factors from the children's generation. Perhaps most notable in Appendix tables A.2, A.3, and A.4 is the strong positive influence of early sexual experience on the rapidity of union formation, especially for cohabitation. Religiosity is also a crucial independent factor—increasing marriage and decreasing cohabitation. A preference for higher ages at marriage has a negative effect on rates of both marriage and cohabitation, net of the other factors considered in our analyses, while acceptance of abortion has a positive net effect on both. People who prioritize careers over family enter marriage more slowly than others, while those with positive attitudes toward child-oriented spending enter unions more quickly. School attendance inhibits entry into both cohabitation and marriage. High grades and educational attainment lead to lower rates of cohabitation, but educational attainment and positive earnings prospects increase marriage, net of other factors considered here.

In many ways this group of explanatory factors with direct effects constitutes an agenda for future research about the influences on cohabitation and marriage. This research agenda should examine a host of social, psychological, ideational, economic, and biological dimensions that might help explain the influence of these factors on entrance into marriage and cohabitation.

Participants in the Rise of Cohabitation

Although we have emphasized that cohabitation in America today has much more in common with marriage in the past than is generally recognized, it is also true that cohabitation during the past few decades represents a new phenomenon. Although unmarried cohabitation was practiced in the past, it was relatively rare, and it certainly lacked the widespread acceptance that it has in the United States today.

Unfortunately, it is impossible to use our study to document the causes of the emergence of cohabitation as a common phenomenon in the last part of the twentieth century. Because our study participants were drawn from a single birth cohort of young adults and their families, they cannot provide the historical depth necessary to investigate social change.

However, the young adults in this study came from the generation that participated in the movement toward cohabitation. Most of the parents in the families in our study were born in the years before the end of World War II and all reached adulthood, married, and began childbearing by 1961. The children were all born in 1961, experienced childhood and adolescence in the 1960s and 1970s, and reached adulthood in the 1980s. Thus both the parents and children were born into a very different marriage and family world than the children experienced as they were entering adulthood. Consequently, these families provide a window into the kinds of individuals and families who participated in the emerging trend toward cohabitation in the 1970s, 1980s, and 1990s.

Of course, because our sample of families was limited to Whites and a few Hispanics, our characterization of the groups participating in the trend toward cohabitation applies primarily to the White population. Although we expect that many of our conclusions about recent cohabitors apply to minority populations as well, we limit our conclusions to the population of White Americans. We now turn to a discussion of some of the central characteristics of people participating in the recent increase of cohabitation.

Student Status and Educational Attainment

It would be a mistake for an artist portraying the emergent movement toward cohabitation to follow the common misperception that cohabitation originated among college students and the well-educated segments of the population. In fact, we know of no evidence supporting this impression. In this book we have examined many different dimensions of school attendance, school achievement, financial resources, and home ownership among both parents and children and have found virtually no evidence of a significant positive association between these indicators of socioeconomic status and the rate of entrance into cohabitation.[3] Furthermore, we reported numerous results showing that parental education, parental financial resources, young-adult school attendance, and the amount of school completed were all negatively related to the rate of cohabitation. Clearly, it was not the well-educated and wealthier families in the population that participated in large numbers in the movement toward cohabitation.

Religious Affiliation

The results of our book also suggest that it would be a mistake to paint the new cohabitors as originating among particular religious groups, such as the more mainline Protestant groups. In fact, the data we have examined are consistent in suggesting only modest and statistically insignificant relationships between religious affiliation, as we have defined it, and experience with cohabitation. Of course, a more fine-grained analysis with a much larger data set might have revealed cohabitation to be greater among some groups than others, but our data do not support such an analysis.

Religiosity

Interestingly, although religious affiliation cannot help differentiate the people participating in the movement toward cohabitation, religious commitment and participation can. The young adults cohabiting during the late 1970s through the early 1990s clearly came from the least religious segments of the population. We examined several dimensions of religious participation in our study families—including level of grandmother's religiosity, whether the parents had a religious marriage ceremony, frequency of parent and child attendance at religious services, importance of religion to mothers and children, and degree of mother and child belief in religious teachings—and each one is strongly and negatively associated with the rate of entrance into cohabitation among young adults. This is compelling evidence that cohabitation in these years was concentrated among those from less religious families.

Family Divorce and Premarital Pregnancy

Another factor characterizing the people participating in the movement toward cohabitation is socialization in a family experiencing two events historically proscribed in Western societies—premarital pregnancy and divorce. As we discussed earlier, children growing up in families in which the mother had been premaritally pregnant or divorced had substantially higher rates of cohabitation than children growing up in families in which the mother had not. It appears that the mother's own unorthodoxy in courtship and marital matters provided a fertile source of nonconformity among the second generation. In this regard it is interesting to note that maternal acceptance of premarital sex and cohabitation was also strongly related to cohabitation experience among young adults.

Individual Acceptance of Premarital Sex

Our research also provides, as expected, compelling evidence that the movement toward cohabitation was particularly appealing to young people who rejected in some way the historical rules about the relationship of sex to marriage. As we discussed earlier, young people who had sexual relations frequently as teenagers had substantially higher rates of cohabitation than others. Although this relationship was due in part to the fact that these sexually precocious teenagers entered all unions—both cohabitation and marriage—more rapidly than others, the effect of sexual precociousness was much greater on cohabitation than on marriage. Also as one would expect, the ranks of the cohabitors were disproportionately filled from those with positive attitudes toward premarital sex. These results should not, of course, be surprising because attitudes toward premarital sex and cohabitation were so strongly correlated that we combined them into a scale and analyzed them together (see chapter 9).

Attitudes toward Gender Roles

The correlation of cohabitation with crossing historical boundaries of accepted family and personal behavior in terms of premarital sex, premarital pregnancy, and divorce extends as well to egalitarian attitudes about roles for women and men. In particular, we found that the young people who cohabited during this era were drawn disproportionately from families in which mothers had egalitarian sex-role attitudes. Furthermore, the children of these mothers entered marriage more slowly, suggesting a clear substitution of cohabitation for marriage among the children of mothers with egalitarian attitudes. This pattern was true for maternal attitudes both early and late in the childhoods of the children.[4]

Freedom and Equality

This detailed portrait of the young people who led the new movement into unmarried cohabitation suggests a more general conclusion about them. They seem to come from families that were noncomforming on several dimensions of sexual and family behavior, including premarital sex, premarital pregnancy, divorce, and the equality of male and female roles. Second-generation cohabitors also were nonconformist in that they accepted premarital sex, were sexually precocious as unmarried teenagers, and endorsed the right to abortion. Freedom from historical proscriptions about sexual and family behavior and endorsement of equality seems to be a common theme underlying the movement toward cohabitation in the 1970s, 1980s, and 1990s.

Nonfamily Networks

One more element should be added to the picture of the young adults who participated in the movement toward cohabitation: level of integration into a larger family network. Here we are referring to the observations of chapters 5 and 6 that young people from families that were integrated into larger family networks had substantially lower rates of cohabitation than others. This correlation held true for parental measures of family integration taken both early and late in the childhoods of the young adults. This suggests that the cohabitation innovators were disproportionately pulled from the ranks of families more involved in nonfamily networks than family networks. Perhaps involvement in nonfamily networks gave the children in these families more freedom and opportunity to engage in new and previously prohibited behaviors. Involvement in networks outside the family may also have led to placing less importance on family relationships, which may have led some to choose the nonfamily status of cohabitation as an alternative to marriage, at least for a short period.

Also of relevance in portrayal of early cohabitors is the withdrawal of parental and other social control over the lives of young adults. Recent decades saw a large increase in independent living among young adults, with unmarried young adults increasingly living by themselves or with housemates. And, even when young people live in institutions such as college dormitories where supervision by authorities was historically taken seriously, they no longer have to worry about the rules and prying attention of dorm parents, as most colleges today no longer supervise the nonacademic behaviors of their students. This increase in nonfamily, independent living among young adults has made it much easier for them to implement sexual motivation and drives and to cohabit without negative social sanctions.

This portrayal of the characteristics of the people participating in the dramatic increase in cohabitation in the past several decades suggests that this trend of increasing cohabitation is part of a much larger transformation of American life. It is closely connected with increasing levels of premarital sex, premarital pregnancy, divorce, and egalitarian gender roles. Other elements related to cohabitation include low levels of religiosity, low family connectivity, and great emphasis on freedom and equality. Thus, it should not be surprising that the changes in cohabitation, and the associated changes in marriage, are part of the larger confrontation of cultural values about family and personal issues in the United States. It is likely that marriage and cohabitation will continue to be part of this cultural confrontation, with beliefs, values, and behavior continuing to change in the future.

Appendix A

TECHNICAL EXPLANATION OF ESTIMATION OF TOTAL, DIRECT, AND INDIRECT EFFECTS*

As we explained in chapter 1, a primary goal of this book is the estimation of the total, direct, and indirect influences of a broad range of explanatory factors on rates of entry to marriage and cohabitation. Estimation of such effects requires properly specified models that correctly indicate temporal and causal ordering. By "total effect" we mean the total amount of influence of a factor through all potential causal mechanisms. A total effect can be further decomposed into a "direct effect" component and an "indirect effect" component. An indirect effect operates through a particular intervening factor or set of factors. A direct effect is the residual influence unexplained by all the intervening factors. Because of the ambiguities associated with causal ordering, we estimate these effects in multiple models with different causal assumptions. In doing so we regularly estimate effects with minimum and maximum controls. This provides a method for bounding the sizes of our effect parameters. At the same time, we recognize that the omission of relevant factors and poor assumptions about exogeneity and endogeneity could result in all of our estimates being biased and different from the "true" effects in the "real" world. That is, without experimental data we cannot be sure that extraneous factors have not biased our estimates.

Temporal Ordering of Factors

We utilize a thirty-one-year intergenerational panel study to help us in specifying appropriate causal models. The ordering of attributes by generation and time helps us to get the causal ordering correct. Although we recognize that causal or-

*Li-Shou Yang collaborated in the analysis and writing of this appendix.

dering can sometimes diverge from temporal ordering, we assume that causes generally precede consequences. Thus, we generally use the temporal ordering of the explanatory factors to provide a rough causal ordering of the factors, remaining alert to instances where this assumption may be violated.

We order the intergenerational explanatory factors within a life-course framework, identifying seven periods or phases over the span of both generations: (1) parental youth; (2) parental young adulthood; (3) parent with young child; (4) parent with child age 15; (5) parent with child age 18; (6) children as teenagers; and (7) children as young adults. Given the historical location of our intergenerational panel data set, the information for Periods 1 through 3 generally comes from the 1962 data collection and refers to the period at or before 1962, the year after the children were born. The data for Period 4, parent with child age 15, generally come from the 1977 data collection. The data for Periods 5 and 6 are from, respectively, the parents and their 18-year-old teenagers in 1980. And the data for Period 7, when the children were young adults, generally come from the 1985 and 1993 interviews. Because data from Periods 5 and 6 refer to factors from both generations during the same phase, we faced particularly difficult ordering ambiguities for these two periods in our analysis.

From Period 1—the childhood of the parents—we include the dimensions of immigration status, farm background, number of siblings, and their own parents' religiosity. Among the parental young-adulthood factors considered in Period 2 are religious affiliation, education, age at marriage, premarital pregnancy status, being married by a church official, marital disruption before 1962, and birth order of the child born in 1961. Among the parental factors from the study child's early infancy (Period 3) are financial resources, home ownership, preferred number of children, attendance at religious services, the social organization of activities, and gender-role attitudes. Period 4 focuses on factors from the parental life course from the birth of the study child to the child at age 15. It includes such things as parental social organization of activities, gender-role attitudes, marital dissolution, education, childbearing, religious attendance, and financial resources. Period 5 focuses on parental factors during the period of late adolescence for the study child, including parental attitudes about a range of family issues such as premarital sex, cohabitation, marriage, marital timing, and gender roles. We also introduce at this point parental preferences for the children's school, work, marriage, and trade-offs between family and nonfamily activities.

In Period 6 we shift our focus from parents to factors of the teenage children's lives, including dating and courtship experience, religious commitment, family attitudes and values, school accomplishments and aspirations, and financial expectations. Finally, in Period 7 we include a set of children's attributes occurring during early adulthood—between ages 18 and the time of the first union. These factors include the children's educational, work, and financial experiences and prospects.

We do not identify these periods as developmental stages, but simply as different time points in the lives of parents and children. We assign all the explanatory factors to one of these seven periods, which in some cases involves timing assumptions. We then conduct our analyses of total, direct, and indirect effects in phases corresponding to these seven periods, beginning with the effects of factors from the lives of the parents as youths (Period 1) and moving through effects of factors from each of the subsequent periods.

For this discussion we do not indicate precise parent and child explanatory factors. Instead, we note the parental factors generally as P and the children's factors generally as C. Furthermore, we specify the parental factors from Period 1 as P_j and from Period 2 as P_k. Similarly, the parental factors for Periods 3, 4, and 5 are respectively noted as P_m, P_n, and P_q. The children's factors for Periods 6 and 7 are noted as C_r and C_s. There are respectively J, K, M, N, Q, R, and S factors in Periods 1 through 7. Any of the specific parental factors from Period 1 (P_j) are referred to here as the jth factor. Similarly, a specific parental factor from Period 2 (P_k) is noted as the kth factor.

Estimation Procedures

We gauge the effects of the explanatory factors on children's union formation by estimating a series of hazard models of cohabitation and marriage. However, as noted in Appendix B, we examine the monthly logits (Y) of the probability of generic union formation, where $Y = \ln[H^1/(1-H^1)]$, and H^1 refers to the probability of either cohabitation or marriage.[1] All equations include the children's age and gender because we believe that their effects should be controlled when other dimensions of the lives of parents and children are examined. We now turn to a discussion of the equations used to estimate the total, direct, and indirect effects of interest.

Estimating and Evaluating Total Effects

We follow the principles that models or equations estimating the total effect of a specific explanatory factor should (a) include all other explanatory factors that are exogenous to or simultaneous with that specific explanatory factor, and (b) exclude factors that are endogenous to it. Implementation of these principles is straightforward *across* the life-course phases we have defined. It means, for example, that the total effects of Period 1 factors are estimated in equations that exclude explanatory factors from Periods 2–7. Similarly, the total effects of Period 2 factors are estimated in equations that include Period 1 factors and exclude explanatory factors from Periods 3–7.

In some instances we can use theoretical and/or temporal ordering information to make assumptions about causal ordering *within* a life-course period. The principles just enumerated also apply in these instances. However, in other cases it is difficult to make the appropriate assumptions about causal ordering within time

periods because many of the explanatory factors located within a period are determined simultaneously or the causal ordering is ambiguous. As a result, it is not
always clear what explanatory factors from a particular time period to include in
an equation estimating the total effect of a specified factor from the same period.

We resolve this difficulty of constructing within-period causal priority by calculating two different estimates of total effects for each factor. One estimate, which
assumes the factor of interest is causally exogenous to all other explanatory factors in its period, includes no controls for these other factors. The second estimate
includes controls for all of these factors. By estimating total effects with both minimum and maximum controls, we are able to bound plausibly the magnitudes of
the total effects of each of the explanatory factors.

For some of the factors the two estimates of total effects are very similar, providing additional confidence in the estimates. In these instances no further specification of models is necessary to estimate total effects. However, for other factors,
where the estimates with minimum and maximum controls differ, further specification is useful. This can be done by making further assumptions about causal
ordering for some explanatory factors in a particular period. If, for example, it
could be assumed that an explanatory factor was causally prior to all other factors
in its period, then its total effect is best estimated using an equation with minimum
controls. Or, if it could be assumed that an explanatory factor was causally prior to
none of the other factors in its period, then its total effect is best estimated using
an equation with maximum controls. In other instances, however, it is difficult to
specify a plausible estimate between those provided in models with minimum and
maximum cohorts because the various factors are determined simultaneously, their
causal ordering is ambiguous, or they have reciprocal influence.

More formally, the total effects of the J Period 1 explanatory factors with *minimum* controls are estimated through a series of equations of the form depicted in
equation (1a) of table A.1. Equation (1a) includes, with age and gender, only the
jth explanatory factor (P_j) from Period 1 of the life course, with β_j reflecting the
estimated total effect of that factor. We estimate a separate version of equation
(1a) for each of the J explanatory factors from Period 1.

Estimates of the total effects of the J Period 1 explanatory factors with *maximum* controls are calculated simultaneously in equation (1b) of table A.1. Equation
(1b) includes simultaneously, with child's age and gender, all of the J explanatory
factors from Period 1 (P_j) with their associated effects β_j.

Estimates of the total effects of the K Period 2 explanatory factors with *minimum* controls are estimated through a series of equations of the form depicted in
equation (2a) of table A.1. Equation (2a) adds to equation (1b) (containing age,
gender, and all the Period 1 factors) only the kth explanatory factor (P_k) from
Period 2 of the life course, with β_k reflecting the estimated total effect of that factor. We estimate separate versions of equation (2a) for each of the K explanatory
factors from Period 2.

The equations of the analysis

Period 1—Parental Youth

(1a) $Y = \beta_j P_j$

(1b) $Y = \sum\limits_{j=1}^{J} \beta_j P_j$

Period 2—Adding Parental Young Adult

(2a) $Y = \sum\limits_{j=1}^{J} \beta_j P_j + \beta_k P_k$

(2b) $Y = \sum\limits_{j=1}^{J} \beta_j P_j + \sum\limits_{k=1}^{K} \beta_k P_k$

Period 3—Adding Parent with Young Child

(3a) $Y = \sum\limits_{j=1}^{J} \beta_j P_j + \sum\limits_{k=1}^{K} \beta_k P_k + \beta_m P_m$

(3b) $Y = \sum\limits_{j=1}^{J} \beta_j P_j + \sum\limits_{k=1}^{K} \beta_k P_k + \sum\limits_{m=1}^{M} \beta_m P_m$

Period 4—Adding Parent with Child Age 15

(4a) $Y = \sum\limits_{j=1}^{J} \beta_j P_j + \sum\limits_{k=1}^{K} \beta_k P_k + \sum\limits_{m=1}^{M} \beta_m P_m + \beta_n P_n$

(4b) $Y = \sum\limits_{j=1}^{J} \beta_j P_j + \sum\limits_{k=1}^{K} \beta_k P_k + \sum\limits_{m=1}^{M} \beta_m P_m + \sum\limits_{n=1}^{N} \beta_n P_n$

Period 5—Adding Parent with Child Age 18

(5a) $Y = \sum\limits_{j=1}^{J} \beta_j P_j + \sum\limits_{k=1}^{K} \beta_k P_k + \sum\limits_{m=1}^{M} \beta_m P_m + \sum\limits_{n=1}^{N} \beta_n P_n + \beta_q P_q$

(5b) $Y = \sum\limits_{j=1}^{J} \beta_j P_j + \sum\limits_{k=1}^{K} \beta_k P_k + \sum\limits_{m=1}^{M} \beta_m P_m + \sum\limits_{n=1}^{N} \beta_n P_n + \sum\limits_{q=1}^{Q} \beta_q P_q$

Period 6—Adding Children as Teenagers

(6a) $Y = \sum\limits_{j=1}^{J} \beta_j P_j + \sum\limits_{k=1}^{K} \beta_k P_k + \sum\limits_{m=1}^{M} \beta_m P_m + \sum\limits_{n=1}^{N} \beta_n P_n + \sum\limits_{q=1}^{Q} \beta_q P_q + \beta_r C_r$

(6b) $Y = \sum\limits_{j=1}^{J} \beta_j P_j + \sum\limits_{k=1}^{K} \beta_k P_k + \sum\limits_{m=1}^{M} \beta_m P_m + \sum\limits_{n=1}^{N} \beta_n P_n + \sum\limits_{q=1}^{Q} \beta_q P_q + \sum\limits_{r=1}^{R} \beta_r C_r$

Period 7—Adding Children as Young Adults

(7a) $Y = \sum\limits_{j=1}^{J} \beta_j P_j + \sum\limits_{k=1}^{K} \beta_k P_k + \sum\limits_{m=1}^{M} \beta_m P_m + \sum\limits_{n=1}^{N} \beta_n P_n + \sum\limits_{q=1}^{Q} \beta_q P_q + \sum\limits_{r=1}^{R} \beta_r C_r + \beta_s C_s$

(7b) $Y = \sum\limits_{j=1}^{J} \beta_j P_j + \sum\limits_{k=1}^{K} \beta_k P_k + \sum\limits_{m=1}^{M} \beta_m P_m + \sum\limits_{n=1}^{N} \beta_n P_n + \sum\limits_{q=1}^{Q} \beta_q P_q + \sum\limits_{r=1}^{R} \beta_r C_r + \sum\limits_{s=1}^{S} \beta_s C_s$

Notes: P_j is the jth Period 1 factor where j ranges from 1 to J. P_k is the kth Period 2 factor where k ranges from 1 to K. Similarly, P_m, P_n, P_q, C_r, and C_s are respectively the mth, nth, qth, rth, and sth factors of Periods 3, 4, 5, 6, and 7. Periods 3, 4, 5, 6, and 7 have respectively M, N, Q, R, and S factors each. Thus, there are J versions of equation (1a), K versions of equation (2a), M versions of equation (3a), N versions of equation (4a), Q versions of equation (5a), R versions of equation (6a), and S version of equation (7a). All equations also include gender and age as controls.

Estimates of the total effects of the K Period 2 explanatory factors with *maximum* controls are calculated simultaneously in equation (2b) of table A.1. Equation (2b) includes simultaneously all of the K explanatory factors from Period 2 (P_k), along with child's age and gender and all explanatory factors from Period 1.

We use the procedures just outlined to estimate total effects with minimum and maximum controls for explanatory factors in Periods 3–7. As the series of equations in table A.1 indicates, for each successive period we add into the analysis the explanatory factors from that period. In addition, the analysis equations for each of the phases also include the explanatory factors from previous life-course periods.

Estimating and Evaluating Direct Effects

We now turn to our approach for estimating direct effects of explanatory factors on union formation. Here it is important to note again that a direct effect is the part of the total effect of a factor that does not operate through intervening factors. This means that the estimated direct effect of a factor depends on what other factors are included in the equation.

The addition of new explanatory factors at each period of the analysis provides the opportunity to estimate how much of the effect of a factor from an earlier period operates independently of the factors from later periods of the life course. That is, the effect parameter for a factor from early in the parental or child life course examined in an equation with later factors indicates the direct effect of that factor that does not operate through the later factors. For example, the effect parameter of a particular Period 1 parental youth factor in an equation including Period 1 and 2 factors represents the direct effect of the particular Period 1 factor that does not operate through the intervening factors from Period 2. Similarly, the effect parameter for the same Period 1 factor in an equation with Period 1, 2, and 3 factors represents the direct effect of this factor that does not operate through any of the Period 2 and Period 3 factors. Using this procedure across different periods, factors, and equations provides estimates of direct effects in the context of multiple controls at different points in the life course.

Equations (2b), (3b), (4b), (5b), (6b), and (7b) of table A.1 provide the direct effects for various explanatory factors. Note that this series of equations gives multiple estimates of the effects of factors from early in the life course. This is because each equation controls for different intervening factors, and thus estimates the direct effect of each explanatory factor that does not operate through the intervening factors included. As additional intervening factors are added in successive equations, the estimated direct effects of each explanatory factor can change.

Estimating and Evaluating Indirect Effects

The difference between a total effect with maximum controls estimated in one period of the analysis and a direct effect in a later period provides an estimate of the indirect effect of the early factor through the subsequent factors. For example, the difference between the total effect with maximum controls for a specific Period 1 factor and its direct effect with Period 2 factors controlled provides an estimate of the indirect effect of the Period 1 factor operating through the set of Period 2 factors. This approach provides estimates of indirect effects operating across the two generations, from Periods 1 through 7.

Although this method of identifying indirect effects provides general information about indirect pathways, it does not provide enough detail to identify precise causal mechanisms. The reason is that multiple factors are added at each step, making it impossible to identify exactly which factor added in that step transmits an earlier factor's indirect effect. We, therefore, elaborate on the procedures just described with a more detailed and comprehensive approach to understanding indirect pathways.

We identify the precise factors that transmit an indirect effect of a previous factor by comparing the early factor's effect parameters in two equations: one containing a set of explanatory factors that excludes a particular intervening factor, and a second equation that adds the proposed intervening factor to the first equation (Allison 1995; Clogg, Petkova, and Haritou 1995; Xie and Shauman 1998). The difference between the effect parameters of the early factor in the two equations represents the indirect effect of the early factor operating through the specific intervening factor.

One of the difficulties of estimating indirect effects using this procedure is that the results depend upon the set of factors included in the equation (Xie and Shauman 1998). Just as an estimated total effect depends upon the other factors included in the equation, an estimated indirect effect depends upon the other factors controlled. For this reason we estimate indirect effects in two different contexts: one that includes a minimum set of controls and one that includes a maximum set of controls. This approach allows us to provide plausible bounds for the magnitudes of the indirect effects operating through each intervening factor.

More specifically, to estimate the indirect effects of the Period 1 factors on union formation through a specific Period 2 factor with *minimum* controls we compare the estimated effects of the Period 1 factors in equations (1b) (with no Period 2 controls) with the effects of the same Period 1 factors in the version of equation (2a), which includes the specific Period 2 intervening factor in question. The differences between the estimated effects of the Period 1 factors in equations (1b) and (2a) indicate the indirect effects of the Period 1 factors through the specific Period 2 factor in question. This process is repeated for each of the K Period 2 factors to obtain estimates of the indirect effects of the Period 1 factors through each of the Period 2 factors.

A similar procedure is followed to estimate the indirect effects of the Period 1 and 2 factors through the Period 3 factors with minimum controls. Here we calculate a series of equations in the form of equation (3a) that adds one Period 3 factor to equation (2b), which contains all of the Period 1 and 2 factors but no Period 3 factors. Again, the differences between the effect parameters for the Period 1 and 2 factors in equation (2b) and the effect parameters for the same factors in the new equations (3a) represent the indirect effects of the factors from Periods 1 and 2 through each of the Period 3 factors. This same procedure is used to evaluate minimally controlled indirect effects of factors from each period of the life course through factors from later periods in the life course.

Our estimates of indirect effects with *maximum* controls follow the same general strategy—using maximum rather than minimum controls for other explanatory factors in the same period as the intervening factor in question. Thus, to estimate the indirect effects of Period 1 factors operating through a specific Period 2 factor using maximum controls, we begin with equation (2b) containing all Period 1 and Period 2 factors. We then estimate a new equation that contains all of equation (2b) factors *except* the first intervening factor in Period 2 being examined. The differences between the effect parameters for the Period 1 factors in the new equation and the effect parameters in the original equation (2b) represent our maximally controlled estimates of the indirect effects of the Period 1 factors through the first Period 2 factor (Xie and Shauman 1998). We repeat this process for the second Period 2 factor, and then for each of the remaining Period 2 factors, with the result being a series of estimates of indirect effects of the Period 1 factors through each of the Period 2 factors.

A similar procedure is followed to evaluate with maximum controls the indirect effects of the Period 1 and 2 factors through the Period 3 factors. Here we estimate an equation that contains all of the Period 1, 2, and 3 factors except the first Period 3 factor. Again, the differences between the effect parameters for the Period 1 and 2 factors in the new equations and the effect parameters for the same factors in equation (3b) represent the indirect effects of the factors from Periods 1 and 2 operating through the first Period 3 factor. This process is then repeated for each of the remaining Period 3 factors, with the outcome being a series of estimates of indirect effects of the Period 1 and 2 factors through each of the Period 3 factors. This same procedure is used to evaluate maximally controlled indirect effects of factors from each period of the life course through factors from later periods in the life course.

In some empirical analyses the estimates of indirect effects from the maximally controlled analysis and from the minimally controlled analysis are extremely similar—an outcome that produces both precise estimates and considerable confidence in the estimates. However, in other instances the indirect effects estimated from the two approaches diverge. This occurs because two or more intervening factors are strongly correlated to one another, which makes it difficult to allocate the indirect effect of a prior factor between the collinear intervening factors. The result is ambiguity in the magnitudes of the indirect effects through these intervening factors.

Allocation of the indirect effects among collinear intervening factors can be adjudicated if plausible assumptions can be made about the causal ordering of the collinear factors. If, for example, one of two collinear intervening factors is causally prior to the other, the indirect effects between them can be partitioned more precisely. This can be done by first evaluating the indirect effects through the causally prior intervening factor without controlling for the causally secondary intervening factor. Then, the indirect effects through the causally secondary intervening factor are estimated in the presence of controls for the causally prior intervening factor.

In other instances the causal ordering between the collinear intervening factors is ambiguous, making it difficult to follow this procedure for partitioning indirect effects precisely among them. However, in these instances additional insight can be obtained by estimating the magnitude of the indirect effects through the group of collinear intervening factors. This is done by adding to or subtracting from the appropriate baseline equation the collinear intervening factors as a group—an approach that can be especially valuable when the collinear intervening factors are related conceptually as well as empirically.

One last kind of indirect effect operates within rather than across a life-course phase. In our previous discussion of total effects we noted that we would estimate total effects with minimum and maximum controls. We further noted that the two sets of estimates would sometimes diverge, with this divergence sometimes adjudicated through making assumptions about causal ordering within life-course periods. Here we note that the differences between total effects with minimum and maximum controls are sometimes due to indirect effects operating within the same life-course period. In cases where we can make plausible assumptions about the causal ordering of these factors within a life-course period, it is possible to estimate indirect effects among these factors. The approach for estimating these indirect effects within life-course periods is identical to that outlined previously for indirect effects across periods.

It is important to note that an indirect effect requires two conditions: the exogenous factor must be correlated with the intervening factor, and the intervening factor must have an influence on union formation. Such indirect effects can be either positive or negative, with the sign depending on both the direction of the association between the exogenous and intervening factor and the direction of the effect of the intervening factor on union formation. Indirect effects are positive under either of the following two conditions: (1) the exogenous factor is positively related to the intervening factor and the intervening factor positively influences union formation; or (2) the exogenous factor is negatively related to the intervening factor and the intervening factor negatively affects union formation. Indirect effects are negative under either of the following two conditions: (1) the exogenous factor is positively related to the intervening factor and the intervening factor negatively affects union formation; or (2) the exogenous factor is negatively related to the intervening factor and the intervening factor positively affects union formation.

In our discussion of indirect effects, we denote correlations between exogenous and intervening factors in multiple ways, depending on the measurement properties

of the factors. For two ordinal or interval variables, we report standard pearsonian correlation coefficients that range from −1 to 1. When the exogenous variable
is categorical, we report either the means or proportions on the intervening factor,
with that choice depending on whether the intervening factor is measured inter-
vally (or ordinally) or categorically. The effect of the intervening factor on union
formation is summarized as a direct effect of the factor in question.

Collinearity and the Use of Scales and Indices

Collinearity between the explanatory factors sometimes makes it difficult to estimate precisely total and indirect effects. In the preceding paragraphs we have noted
some approaches to dealing with this issue—through assumptions about causal
ordering and by estimating the effects of collinear factors simultaneously.

Another valuable approach to this issue is to combine individual measures into
scales or indices. We make extensive use of this strategy in our research. In the
many instances that we have multiple indicators for the same underlying construct,
we combine them together into a scale. An example of this includes the aggrega-
tion of several individual sex-role attitude items into a sex-role attitude scale. We
also combine measures for some constructs that are conceptually separate at a
fine-grained level but similar at a more abstract level. For example, we combine
assets and income into a financial resources factor. We also combine some separate information from fathers and mothers into an explanatory factor representing
the parental family more generally. Parental education, number of siblings, and religious service attendance are three examples of this approach.

An added advantage of aggregating related measures into scales is that scales
have higher measurement reliability than the individual items composing them
(Nunnally 1967; Jöreskog and Sörbom 1979; Kim and Mueller 1978; Bollen 1989).
Many of the measures we use in our work are highly reliable single indicators of
objective items that are measured very reliably. Almost all of the other measures
consist of indices or scales measured as aggregates of individual items that also
have high levels of measurement reliability (Thornton and Binstock 2001).

Model Estimates for Chapters 9 through 12

As this description suggests, the estimation of total, direct, and indirect effects
for the later periods of the life course of parents and children involves numerous
factors and estimates. Because of this complexity, we do not present the full tables in the substantive chapters. Instead, for both cohabitation and marriage, we
present in table A.2 the coefficient estimates for four different models: one including parental factors through 1977 (Model 6.6); one including parental factors
through 1980 (Model A.1); one including parent and child factors through 1980

(Model A.2); and one including all parent and child factors (Model A.3). We do a similar approach for the total union-formation rate and marriage ignoring cohabitation in table A.3 and for the choice between marriage and cohabitation in table A.4.

We, thus, begin with Model 6.6 of chapter 6 containing parental factors from parental youth, parental young adulthood, early parenthood, and the adolescence of the children. We then estimate three additional and increasingly complex models. Model A.1 contains all of the parental factors of Model 6.6 plus the parental factors when the young adults were age 18 (Period 5 of table A.1). Model A.2 contains all of the parental factors of Model A.1 plus the behavior, expectations, and attitudes of the young adults during the teenage years through age 18 (Period 6). Model A.3 contains all the factors of Model A.2 plus young adults' experiences with school and work during young adulthood (Period 7).

Because most of the maternal and child factors introduced in these analyses as intervening variables refer to times when the young adults were age 18 or older, we limited the estimation of equations in tables A.2, A.3, and A.4 to the period after the interview when the young adult was 18. Limiting our analysis to the interval from age 18 through 31 helps ensure the correct temporal ordering of the predictors.

Although missing data are relatively scarce in our data set, we do lack information on some predictors for some individuals. Consequently, as we add additional predictors to the equations, the number of cases available for analysis declines, which raises the possibility that the estimates in the various equations change not only because of new predictors, but also because of the case base changing. To eliminate this possibility, we limit our analysis to those individuals who had good data for all of the factors considered in the analysis. That is, anyone with missing data on any parental or child factor was excluded from the entire analysis.[2]

We also made some changes to measures concerning young-adult religiosity and dating/sexual experience (see tables A.2, A.3, and A.4), while retaining the operationalization of all other measures used in previous chapters. Earlier we considered multiple dimensions of both religiosity and dating and sexual experience to study the complex ways they influence union-formation experience. For the sake of parsimony here we use only one indicator each for religiosity and dating/sexual experience. We combine attendance at religious services and the importance of religion at age 18 into a single indicator, with the two components weighted about the same. For dating and sexuality, we created a new set of dummy variables with the following separate categories: no going steady or sexual experience by age 17 (omitted category); went steady but had no sex by age 17; first sex occurred at age 17; first sex occurred at age 16; and first sex occurred before age 16. Preliminary analysis demonstrated that these summary indicators captured most of the power of the multiple measures used in previous chapters.

TABLE A.2 Direct effects estimated from various models of maternal and child factors on the rate of marriage and cohabitation (as competing destinations)[a]

	Marriage								Cohabitation							
	Model 6.6		Model A.1		Model A.2		Model A.3		Model 6.6		Model A.1		Model A.2		Model A.3	
	B[b]	Z[c]	B[b]	Z[c]	B[b]	Z[c]	B[b]	Z[c]	B[b]	Z[c]	B[b]	Z[c]	B[b]	Z[c]	B[b]	Z[c]
Family immigration/Farm background																
Family immigration	-0.09	1.15	-0.06	0.74	-0.08	0.95	-0.06	0.64	-0.14	1.75	-0.13	1.61	-0.16	1.92	-0.14	1.65
Farm background	0.60	2.19	0.56	2.06	0.51	1.88	0.54	1.95	0.27	0.99	0.26	0.95	0.49	1.61	0.48	1.55
Parental socioeconomic standing																
1962 education	-0.01	0.33	0.00	0.06	-0.01	0.27	-0.04	0.88	0.01	0.14	0.03	0.69	0.03	0.76	0.04	0.98
Additional maternal education 1962–1977	-0.18	1.59	-0.16	1.38	-0.13	1.03	-0.10	0.75	-0.24	2.17	-0.26	2.26	-0.30	2.62	-0.30	2.62
1962 financial resources	-0.05	2.04	-0.04	1.56	-0.05	1.91	-0.05	1.98	-0.04	1.49	-0.03	1.38	-0.04	1.52	-0.04	1.40
1976 family income	-0.01	1.86	-0.01	1.62	-0.01	1.18	-0.01	1.50	-0.01	1.98	-0.01	1.99	-0.01	1.79	-0.01	1.81
1962 home ownership	-0.26	2.33	-0.28	2.42	-0.29	2.51	-0.32	2.78	0.12	0.87	0.09	0.62	0.16	1.06	0.17	1.14
Maternal marital experience																
Age at marriage	-0.02	0.68	-0.02	0.85	0.00	0.00	0.00	0.19	0.00	0.02	0.01	0.20	0.03	1.20	0.02	0.95
Premarital pregnancy	0.15	0.86	0.17	0.98	0.18	1.00	0.08	0.48	0.17	0.99	0.15	0.88	0.18	1.03	0.20	1.10
Marital disruption by 1962	0.76	1.99	0.88	2.16	0.69	1.72	0.56	1.47	0.32	0.84	0.39	0.98	0.39	0.95	0.29	0.72
1962–1977 dissolution/remarriage																
Divorce not remarried 1962–1977	-0.26	1.00	-0.20	0.70	-0.23	0.82	-0.20	0.70	0.14	0.57	0.09	0.34	0.05	0.18	0.04	0.15
Divorce remarried 1962–1977	0.08	0.30	0.22	0.69	0.11	0.36	0.15	0.48	0.55	2.08	0.61	2.22	0.46	1.69	0.46	1.68
Widowed 1962–1977	-0.40	1.42	-0.49	1.80	-0.16	0.46	-0.07	0.19	1.04	2.57	0.95	2.36	0.90	2.22	1.11	2.57
Parental childbearing																
1962–1977 children born	0.06	1.53	0.04	0.90	0.14	2.85	0.15	3.06	0.04	0.90	0.05	1.07	0.06	1.28	0.05	1.03
1961 birth unwanted	0.08	0.32	0.18	0.69	0.28	1.01	0.29	1.03	0.27	1.17	0.28	1.20	0.23	0.98	0.18	0.78

Religion

Maternal religious affiliation

	1	2	3	4	5	6	7	8	9	10	11	12	13	14	15	16
Fundamental Protestant	-0.06	0.25	-0.06	0.29	-0.15	0.73	-0.10	0.46	-0.08	0.36	-0.02	0.08	0.18	0.69	0.14	0.55
Catholic	-0.19	1.30	-0.17	1.20	-0.16	1.04	-0.18	1.18	0.13	0.77	0.13	0.80	0.28	1.54	0.27	1.48
Other	0.24	0.59	0.12	0.30	0.54	1.13	0.51	1.05	0.81	2.09	0.91	2.27	0.94	2.28	0.90	2.19
Parental religious attendance	0.10	1.78	0.09	1.67	0.09	1.59	0.10	1.64	-0.06	1.18	-0.06	1.17	-0.05	1.06	-0.05	1.05
1977 maternal religious attendance	0.08	1.77	0.07	1.44	0.05	0.95	0.03	0.63	-0.08	2.06	-0.04	0.98	0.01	0.18	0.01	0.23
Family organization																
Average gregariousness 1962–1977	0.10	1.55	0.10	1.42	0.08	1.16	0.08	1.10	0.24	3.30	0.22	2.97	0.19	2.61	0.19	2.52
1962 closeness to relatives	-0.07	0.40	-0.07	0.40	-0.21	1.26	-0.22	1.31	-0.34	2.24	-0.33	2.10	-0.30	1.84	-0.30	1.84
1977 visiting relatives/friends	-0.07	1.26	-0.05	0.98	-0.04	0.82	-0.04	0.81	-0.09	1.98	-0.10	2.00	-0.13	2.70	-0.13	2.62
1977 sex-role attitudes	-0.25	2.92	-0.17	1.84	-0.19	1.88	-0.17	1.72	0.45	3.62	0.36	2.86	0.45	3.28	0.43	3.17
Maternal attitudes in 1980																
Premarital sex/cohabitation			-0.09	1.17	-0.08	0.99	-0.08	1.00			0.19	2.33	0.08	0.99	0.08	0.90
Preferred age at marriage for child			-0.08	2.53	-0.04	1.05	-0.04	0.95			-0.03	1.01	-0.03	0.86	-0.03	.98
Preferred family size for child			0.16	2.02	0.04	0.50	0.05	0.60			-0.11	1.37	-0.10	1.20	-0.09	1.15
Educational expectations for child			-0.07	1.94	-0.07	1.65	-0.10	2.34			-0.06	1.62	-0.01	0.32	0.00	0.10
Young-adult factors before age 18																
Steady before age 18 but no sex					0.82	3.74	0.89	3.98					0.19	0.94	0.18	0.92
First sex occurring at age 17					1.09	3.61	1.22	3.87					1.44	4.65	1.30	4.30
First sex occurring at age 16					0.27	0.88	0.34	1.10					2.41	5.93	2.16	5.52
First sex occurring before age 16					0.80	2.27	0.88	2.40					4.34	8.09	3.92	7.61
Young-adult factors at age 18																
Religiosity					0.20	2.71	0.19	2.49					-0.16	2.75	-0.15	2.50
Attitude toward premarital sex/cohabitation					-0.06	0.83	-0.05	0.67					0.07	0.84	0.07	0.79

(Continued)

TABLE A.2 (*Continued*)

	Marriage								Cohabitation							
	Model 6.6		Model A.1		Model A.2		Model A.3		Model 6.6		Model A.1		Model A.2		Model A.3	
	B[b]	Z[c]	B[b]	Z[c]	B[b]	Z[c]	B[b]	Z[c]	B[b]	Z[c]	B[b]	Z[c]	B[b]	Z[c]	B[b]	Z[c]
Preferred age at marriage					-0.11	3.48	-0.12	3.64					-0.06	2.07	-0.05	1.84
Attitude toward remaining single					-0.10	1.26	-0.11	1.40					-0.04	0.54	-0.06	0.76
Preferred family size					-0.08	1.64	-0.07	1.59					-0.04	0.75	-0.04	0.84
Attitude toward abortion					0.39	2.37	0.33	2.04					0.18	1.29	0.23	1.60
Educational expectations					0.00	0.12	-0.02	0.37					0.05	1.22	0.08	1.84
Attitude toward careers					-0.24	2.66	-0.21	2.22					-0.06	0.59	-0.05	0.49
Attitude toward child–oriented spending					0.47	2.15	0.39	1.85					0.49	2.23	0.46	2.12
Sex-role attitudes					0.05	0.42	0.01	0.11					0.18	1.34	0.18	1.30
Attitude toward men prioritizing family more highly than career					0.25	2.64	0.28	2.92					0.12	1.28	0.13	1.47
School grades					0.05	0.42	0.00	0.02					-0.21	2.35	-0.19	2.00
School enjoyment					0.01	0.33	0.01	0.25					0.02	0.68	0.02	0.66
Young-adult factors after age 18																
Part-time school enrollment							-0.13	0.71							-0.31	1.85
Full-time school enrollment							-0.61	4.93							-0.34	2.34
School accumulation							0.24	3.59							-0.08	1.17
Predicted earnings over next five years							0.29	3.44							0.06	0.63
No. of periods	52,944		52,944		52,944		52,944		52,944		52,944		52,944		52,944	
No. of events	310		310		310		310		315		315		315		315	
χ²	144.79		166.08		253.64		307.38		98.99		110.36		241.79		254.47	
DF	28		32		49		53		28		32		49		53	

Notes: [a] All equations also control for gender and age. All equations are estimated using data for months after age 18 and for people with good data on all measures.
[b] Effect coefficient for logit equation transformed by equation: [exp(β) – 1].
[c] Z = ratio of absolute value of coefficient to its standard error.

TABLE A.3 Direct effects estimated from various models of maternal and child factors on the rates of total union formation and total marriage[a]

	Total union formation								Total marriage							
	Model 6.6		Model A.1		Model A.2		Model A.3		Model 6.6		Model A.1		Model A.2		Model A.3	
	B[b]	Z[c]	B[b]	Z[c]	B[b]	Z[c]	B[b]	Z[c]	B[b]	Z[c]	B[b]	Z[c]	B[b]	Z[c]	B[b]	Z[c]
Family immigration/Farm background																
Family immigration	-0.12	2.01	-0.10	1.76	-0.11	1.91	-0.09	1.55	-0.09	1.49	-0.06	0.97	-0.05	0.80	-0.03	0.43
Farm background	0.48	2.46	0.45	2.32	0.48	2.39	0.49	2.42	0.42	2.26	0.34	1.85	0.37	1.98	0.37	1.98
Parental socioeconomic standing																
1962 education	0.00	0.08	0.02	0.60	0.02	0.59	0.01	0.33	-0.04	1.65	-0.03	0.95	-0.03	1.17	-0.05	1.79
Additional maternal education 1962–1977	-0.20	2.51	-0.20	2.39	-0.21	2.51	-0.19	2.21	-0.13	1.48	-0.13	1.50	-0.09	1.02	-0.06	0.63
1962 financial resources	-0.04	2.35	-0.04	1.92	-0.04	2.20	-0.04	2.00	-0.05	2.62	-0.04	2.29	-0.04	2.40	-0.04	2.34
1976 family income	-0.01	2.79	-0.01	2.78	-0.01	2.48	-0.01	2.65	0.00	0.85	0.00	0.64	0.00	0.17	0.00	0.45
1962 home ownership	-0.08	0.94	-0.10	1.15	-0.09	0.94	-0.11	1.16	-0.08	0.90	-0.09	0.93	-0.08	0.89	-0.12	1.26
Maternal marital experience																
Age at marriage	0.00	0.33	-0.01	0.39	0.02	0.98	0.01	0.73	-0.01	0.41	-0.01	0.41	0.01	0.61	0.01	0.34
Premarital pregnancy	0.14	1.20	0.15	1.28	0.11	0.94	0.09	0.71	0.07	0.61	0.11	0.86	0.04	0.33	0.01	0.12
Marital disruption by 1962	0.55	2.01	0.58	2.08	0.50	1.78	0.38	1.40	0.50	1.92	0.53	1.95	0.43	1.58	0.32	1.23
1962–1977 dissolution/remarriage																
Divorce not remarried 1962–1977	-0.01	0.07	0.01	0.05	0.05	0.24	0.05	0.26	-0.01	0.07	0.11	0.60	0.03	0.14	0.09	0.46
Divorce remarried 1962–1977	0.33	1.70	0.41	2.01	0.28	1.42	0.26	1.33	0.07	0.38	0.16	0.85	0.12	0.66	0.12	0.62
Widowed 1962–1977	0.15	0.63	0.08	0.36	0.26	1.04	0.38	1.43	-0.10	0.48	-0.14	0.65	-0.09	0.41	-0.09	0.41
Parental childbearing																
1962–1977 children born	0.05	1.78	0.05	1.50	0.10	2.91	0.10	2.84	0.08	2.55	0.07	2.08	0.11	2.98	0.12	3.33
1961 birth unwanted	0.17	1.01	0.21	1.24	0.17	0.98	0.14	0.83	-0.02	0.10	0.00	0.02	0.01	0.06	0.00	0.02

	C1	C2	C3	C4	C5	C6	C7	C8	C9	C10	C11	C12	C13	C14	C15	C16
Religion																
Maternal religious affiliation																
Fundamental Protestant	0.02	0.15	0.00	0.00	0.11	0.62	0.10	0.56	-0.10	0.63	-0.09	0.54	-0.10	0.60	-0.05	0.30
Catholic	-0.04	0.32	-0.03	0.24	0.02	0.17	0.00	0.01	-0.07	0.64	-0.05	0.42	0.00	0.01	0.00	0.04
Other	0.56	1.99	0.60	2.09	0.78	2.55	0.75	2.44	0.48	1.68	0.43	1.50	0.76	2.33	0.71	2.20
Parental religious attendance	0.01	0.38	0.01	0.21	0.01	0.24	0.02	0.45	0.05	1.28	0.05	1.20	0.03	0.81	0.03	0.79
1977 maternal religious attendance	-0.01	0.25	0.01	0.41	0.03	0.95	0.02	0.70	0.01	0.35	0.01	0.16	-0.01	0.16	-0.02	0.52
Family organization																
Average gregariousness 1962–1977	0.18	3.62	0.16	3.28	0.14	2.79	0.14	2.79	0.09	1.89	0.10	2.10	0.09	1.88	0.10	2.01
1962 closeness to relatives	-0.21	1.76	-0.19	1.59	-0.28	2.39	-0.28	2.43	-0.10	0.79	-0.11	0.88	-0.20	1.67	-0.20	1.65
1977 visiting relatives/friends	-0.08	2.40	-0.08	2.28	-0.10	2.69	-0.10	2.65	-0.04	1.22	-0.04	1.20	-0.05	1.26	-0.05	1.33
1977 sex-role attitudes	0.05	0.66	0.05	0.72	0.12	1.43	0.11	1.35	-0.15	2.35	-0.10	1.35	-0.10	1.33	-0.09	1.23
Maternal attitudes in 1980																
Premarital sex/cohabitation			0.06	1.13	0.03	0.45	0.02	0.38			-0.04	0.70	-0.05	0.91	-0.06	1.06
Preferred age at marriage for child			-0.05	2.22	-0.03	1.15	-0.03	1.19			-0.10	4.71	-0.08	3.46	-0.08	3.48
Preferred family size for child			0.03	0.57	-0.03	0.50	-0.03	0.50			0.04	0.64	-0.05	0.93	-0.06	1.09
Educational expectations for child			-0.06	2.43	-0.04	1.21	-0.03	1.05			-0.03	1.29	-0.05	1.69	-0.06	1.78
Young-adult factors before age 18																
Steady before age 18 but no sex					0.54	3.66	0.60	3.96					0.47	3.04	0.57	3.51
First sex occurring at age 17					1.33	6.10	1.34	6.07					1.07	4.97	1.20	5.32
First sex occurring at age 16					1.34	5.32	1.36	5.30					0.60	2.82	0.77	3.35
First sex occurring before age 16					2.52	8.00	2.44	7.73					1.22	4.95	1.43	5.37
Young-adult factors at age 18																
Religiosity					-0.02	0.51	-0.02	0.49					0.08	1.73	0.07	1.48
Attitude toward premarital sex/cohabitation					-0.04	0.70	-0.03	0.62					-0.04	0.75	-0.02	0.46
Preferred age at marriage					-0.07	3.46	-0.07	3.30					-0.09	4.02	-0.09	4.11

(*Continued*)

TABLE A.3 *(Continued)*

	Total union formation								Total marriage							
	Model 6.6		Model A.1		Model A.2		Model A.3		Model 6.6		Model A.1		Model A.2		Model A.3	
	B^b	Z^c	B^b	Z^c	B^b	Z^c	B^b	Z^c	B^b	Z^c	B^b	Z^c	B^b	Z^c	B^b	Z^c
Attitude toward remaining single					−0.06	1.01	−0.07	1.18					−0.14	2.60	−0.14	2.53
Preferred family size					−0.05	1.46	−0.05	1.46					−0.04	1.22	−0.04	1.20
Attitude toward abortion					0.24	2.29	0.25	2.36					0.10	1.07	0.08	0.78
Educational expectations					0.04	1.29	0.04	1.43					0.06	1.91	0.04	1.23
Attitude toward careers					−0.14	2.18	−0.12	1.85					−0.15	2.19	−0.13	1.86
Attitude toward child–oriented spending					0.41	2.76	0.36	2.50					0.29	1.97	0.22	1.54
Sex-role attitudes					0.08	0.98	0.07	0.80					0.02	0.22	−0.02	0.22
Attitude toward men prioritizing family more highly than career					0.19	2.91	0.21	3.23					0.11	1.75	0.13	1.99
School grades					−0.09	1.24	−0.10	1.38					0.06	0.73	0.01	0.14
School enjoyment					0.02	0.72	0.01	0.58					0.00	0.05	0.00	0.05
Young-adult factors after age 18																
Part-time school enrollment							−0.20	1.71							−0.16	1.34
Full-time school enrollment							−0.50	5.46							−0.60	6.20
School accumulation							0.06	1.42							0.16	3.65
Predicted earnings over next five years							0.18	2.88							0.20	3.72
No. of periods	52,944		52,944		52,944		52,944		69,366		69,366		69,336		69,336	
No. of events	625		625		625		625		580		580		580		580	
χ^2	143.92		157.94		284.44		334.22		156.21		188.80		289.56		363.50	
DF	28		32		49		53		28		32		49		53	

Notes: [a] All equations also control for gender and age. All equations are estimated using data for months after age 18 and for people with good data on all measures.
[b] Effect coefficient for logit equation transformed by equation: [exp(β) − 1].
[c] Z = ratio of absolute value of coefficient to its standard error.

TABLE A.4 **Direct effects estimated from various models of maternal and child factors on the choice of cohabitation over marriage[a]**

	Cohabitation over marriage							
	Model 6.6		Model A.1		Model A.2		Model A.3	
	B[b]	Z[c]	B[b]	Z[c]	B[b]	Z[c]	B[b]	Z[c]
Family immigration/Farm background								
Family immigration	−0.10	0.80	−0.11	0.83	−0.12	0.88	−0.10	0.67
Farm background	−0.24	0.86	−0.17	0.58	−0.23	0.75	−0.29	0.97
Parental socioeconomic standing								
1962 education	0.05	0.75	0.06	0.86	0.08	1.12	0.12	1.54
Additional maternal education 1962−1977	−0.16	0.90	−0.20	1.10	−0.28	1.52	−0.26	1.38
1962 financial resources	0.02	0.52	0.02	0.47	0.03	0.79	0.04	0.80
1976 family income	0.00	0.38	0.00	0.36	−0.01	0.62	0.00	0.31
1962 home ownership	0.53	2.10	0.54	2.09	0.52	1.88	0.52	1.85
Maternal marital experience								
Age at marriage	0.02	0.58	0.03	0.77	0.02	0.49	0.02	0.38
Premarital pregnancy	0.05	0.20	0.04	0.16	−0.06	0.25	0.01	0.02
Marital disruption by 1962	−0.36	0.94	−0.42	1.13	−0.39	0.99	−0.42	1.07
1962−1977 dissolution/ remarriage								
Divorce not remarried 1962−1977	0.40	0.83	0.15	0.33	0.14	0.29	0.17	0.33
Divorce remarried 1962−1977	0.52	1.17	0.26	0.63	0.11	0.26	0.13	0.30
Widowed 1962−1977	1.46	1.92	1.16	1.61	0.62	0.97	0.69	1.04
Parental childbearing								
1962−1977 children born	−0.01	0.14	0.03	0.40	−0.01	0.12	−0.02	0.23
1961 birth unwanted	0.06	0.17	0.02	0.04	0.02	0.06	−0.03	0.10
Religion								
Maternal religion affiliation								
Fundamental Protestant	−0.06	0.17	−0.02	0.06	0.26	0.62	0.09	0.22
Catholic	0.34	1.20	0.32	1.14	0.37	1.19	0.30	0.99
Other	0.53	0.86	0.70	1.02	0.34	0.51	0.22	0.35
Parental religious attendance	−0.14	2.02	−0.13	1.80	−0.10	1.31	−0.10	1.25
1977 maternal religious attendance	−0.17	2.93	−0.12	1.93	−0.05	0.69	−0.04	0.50
Family organization								
Average gregariousness 1962−1977	0.06	0.59	0.04	0.41	−0.01	0.06	−0.02	0.16
1962 closeness to relatives	−0.33	1.38	−0.30	1.23	−0.29	1.09	−0.28	1.00
1977 visiting relatives/ friends	−0.04	0.56	−0.02	0.20	−0.02	0.25	−0.01	0.13
1977 sex-role attitudes	1.10	4.58	0.77	3.37	0.76	3.05	0.71	2.82

TABLE A.4 (*Continued*)

	M1	M1	M2	M2	M3	M3	M4	M4
Maternal attitudes in 1980								
Premarital sex/cohabitation			0.31	2.24	0.14	0.95	0.17	1.13
Preferred age at marriage for child			0.06	1.27	0.02	0.30	0.01	0.17
Preferred family size for child			−0.24	2.12	−0.19	1.59	−0.21	1.73
Educational expectations for child			0.02	0.32	0.10	1.29	0.13	1.58
Young-adult factors before age 18								
Steady before age 18 but no sex					−0.35	1.56	−0.42	1.92
First sex occurring at age 17					0.15	0.44	−0.09	0.27
First sex occurring at age 16					1.25	2.18	0.92	1.71
First sex occurring before age 16					1.22	2.13	0.60	1.21
Young-adult factors at age 18								
Religiosity					−0.32	3.52	−0.30	3.24
Attitude toward premarital sex/cohabitation					0.20	1.52	0.17	1.24
Preferred age at marriage					0.06	1.29	0.08	1.50
Attitude toward remaining single					−0.04	0.30	−0.04	0.30
Preferred family size					0.05	0.63	0.06	0.69
Attitude toward abortion					−0.20	1.04	−0.17	0.88
Educational expectations					−0.01	0.21	0.04	0.63
Attitude toward careers					0.39	1.99	0.38	1.94
Attitude toward child-oriented spending					−0.25	0.93	−0.23	0.84
Sex-role attitudes					0.04	0.22	0.05	0.27
Attitude toward men prioritizing family more highly than career					−0.08	0.62	−0.09	0.64
School grades					−0.29	2.02	−0.21	1.32
School enjoyment					0.04	0.78	0.05	0.85
Young-adult factors after age 18								
Part-time school enrollment							−0.16	0.54
Full-time school enrollment							1.00	2.15
School accumulation							−0.27	3.02
Predicted earnings over next five years							−0.18	1.48
No. of unions	625		625		625		625	
No. of cohabitations	315		315		315		315	
χ^2	103.23		118.12		187.90		203.99	
DF	28		32		49		53	

Notes: [a] All equations also control for gender and age. All equations are estimated using data for months after age 18 and for people with good data on all measures.
[b] Effect coefficient for logit equation transformed by equation: $[\exp(\beta) - 1]$.
[c] Z = ratio of absolute value of coefficient to its standard error.

Appendix B

In this appendix, we present the technical details of our strategies for estimating the effects of various parent and young-adult factors on marriage and cohabitation. In this work, our basic phenomenon to be analyzed is the monthly probability of making a union transition (H^1). This transition probability (H^1) can represent any of our conceptualizations of marriage and cohabitation, including marriage as a contrast to both being single and cohabiting; marriage and cohabitation as equivalent contrasts to being single; marriage and cohabitation as independent alternatives (competing destinations) to being single; and marriage as a transition for people already cohabiting. Another phenomenon of interest is the choice between marriage and cohabitation (K) for people entering either marriage or cohabitation.

In our analyses we transform the probability of making a union transition (H^1) with the equation $Y = \ln[H^1/(1 - H^1)]$. We also examine the choice between marriage and cohabitation (K) for those who form a union by the same logit transformation. In our base analysis we estimate the equation

$$Y = \sum_{i=1}^{4} \beta_i A_i + \beta_g G$$

where A_i represents four age factors and G represents the gender of the respondent. β_g represents the effect parameter of gender and β_i represents the effect parameters of the influence of each month of age during each of the four intervals on the log odds of making a union transition or choice. Because of the intuitive difficulty of interpreting effect parameters (β) in the log odds metric, we modify these parameters in our presentation of results by using the following transformation: B equals $[\exp(\beta) - 1]$. These transformed coefficients express the proportionate shift in the union-formation rate associated with each unit of the explanatory factor, and, when multiplied by 100, they represent the percentage increase in the union-formation rate associated with each unit of the explanatory factor.

Gender is entered into the equations as a categorical variable coded zero for male and one for female. Because of the complex association of union-formation rates with age, we use a spline function to estimate the effect of age. In this spline function, we divide the age range into four groups—15–18; 18–22; 22–27; and 27–31—and within each age group estimate the linear effect of each month of age on the union-formation rate.[1] With this flexible spline approach, we are able to model appropriately the shape of the age trajectory of marriage and cohabitation rates because the slope of the age effect can be different for each age group. The effect parameters for all of the marriage and cohabitation rates and choices are summarized in table B.1. For three of these rates we translate these effect parameters into the monthly predicted probabilities of making transitions that are displayed in figures 4.1, 4.2, and 4.3.

All of the equations in the book build upon the base model that includes gender and four age splines. That is, all equations include these five factors as predictor variables. To this basic model we add various combinations of other parent and child factors.

It is important to note that we estimate all standard errors using simple random sample assumptions. This is appropriate because the families were drawn from a systematic listing of birth records, a sample design that is at least as efficient as a simple random sample of birth records. Furthermore, if there is any clustering of characteristics in the original list of births, this systematic sample design is more efficient than a simple random sample of the same size (Kish 1965).

We make two additional comments about analyses using our Conceptualization III (see chapter 4), marriage and cohabitation as independent alternatives to being single. First, we note that some scholars studying union formation argue that many decision makers view cohabitation as primarily an alternative to remaining single and do not consider marriage in the decision to cohabit (Stewart, Manning, and Smock 2003). This perspective is consistent with our Conceptualization III. Moreover, the competing risk models we use to estimate separately the rates of marriage and cohabitation are analytically equivalent to estimating them simultaneously through the multinomial modeling approaches used by Stewart, Manning, and Smock.

Second, note that any treatment of cohabitation and marriage as competing risks, as in Conceptualization III, assumes that these two routes of exiting single life are independent. This occurs because a competing risks analysis of cohabitation treats people who marry as censored at the time of marriage, and a competing risks analysis of marriage treats those who cohabit as censored at the time of cohabitation. This assumption implies that, after all independent variables are included in the analysis, the rate of marriage or cohabitation is unaffected by whether the other outcome is an alternative. This is the independence of irrelevant alternatives

TABLE B.I The effects of age and gender on rates and choices of entrance into marital and cohabiting unions

	Marriage rate ignoring cohabitation (1)		Marriage rate with cohabitation as a competing destination (2)		Cohabitation rate with marriage as a competing destination (3)		Total union-formation rate (4)		Marriage rate resulting from cohabitation (5)		Choice of cohabitation over marriage (6)	
	B^b	Z^c	B^b	Z^c	B^b	Z^c	B^b	Z^c	B^b	Z^c	B^b	Z^c
Age (in years)												
15–18	0.10	7.40	0.10	6.26	0.07	7.70	0.08	10.0	0.01	0.39	−0.04	2.05
18–22	0.02	5.68	0.02	4.89	0.01	1.77	0.01	4.76	0.00	0.78	−0.01	2.37
22–27	0.00	1.46	0.00	0.67	0.00	0.29	0.00	0.29	0.01	1.35	0.00	0.97
27–31	−0.02	3.12	−0.03	2.92	−0.00	0.68	−0.02	2.61	−0.02	1.82	0.02	1.91
Gender (female)	0.54	5.69	0.77	5.50	0.17	1.64	0.42	5.00	0.14	0.97	−0.39	3.37
No. of periods	124,838		103,814		103,814		103,814		8,743		816	
No. of events	709		384		432		816		223		432	
χ^2	496.17		339.16		189.03		494.39		7.91		38.88	
DF	5		5		5		5		5		5	

Notes: [a] All of the variables in columns (1) through (5) are the log odds of union formation. The variable in column (6) is the log odds of a union being cohabitation.
[b] Effect coefficients for logistic regression equations transformed by the equation: $[\exp(\beta) - 1]$.
[c] Z = ratio of absolute value of coefficient to its standard error.

assumption discussed by Luce (1959) and more recently by McFadden (1974) as the "red bus-blue bus" problem. Because both marriage and cohabitation involve the formation of a coresidential union, there is reason to believe that they may not be independent outcomes when compared to remaining single. One approach for addressing this assumption is to estimate models that allow for correlations among competing risks (Hill, Axinn, and Thornton 1993). Unfortunately, these models also require important assumptions about the factors that predict the choice of cohabitation or marriage. Instead we use all five of the conceptualizations previously outlined to construct different types of models that provide a multifaceted insight into the factors affecting transitions from being single to cohabiting or marrying. This approach allows Conceptualizations I, II, IV, and V to inform us about key violations of the assumptions embedded in Conceptualization III.

This interdependence between marriage and cohabitation also has relevance for the way we interpret the effects of explanatory factors. Just because an explanatory factor has no observed effect on marriage (or cohabitation) in this competing risks framework does not mean it has no actual overall effect. For example, a factor could affect marriage rates by its influence on cohabitation rates.

Appendix C

DESCRIPTION OF MEASURES USED IN CHAPTERS 5 THROUGH 11

Table C.1. Description of Parental Factors Included in Chapter 5 Analysis

Family Immigration and Farm Background

FAMILY IMMIGRATION. Mean of recency of migration of maternal and paternal families to the United States. Maternal migration categories coded as: (1) mother, parents, and grandparents born in the United States; (2) mother and parents born in the United States and one or more grandparents born outside the United States; (3) mother born in the United States and one or both parents born outside the United States; and (4) mother born outside the United States. Paternal migration was coded the same. Mean equals 2.08; standard deviation equals .77.

FARM BACKGROUND. Coded one if the place either the mother or father had lived longest before marriage was a farm; otherwise coded zero. Proportion with farm background equals .09.

Parental Socioeconomic Standing

1962 EDUCATION. Mean number of years of education of the mother and father in 1962. Mean equals 12.26; standard deviation equals 1.90.

1962 FINANCIAL RESOURCES. Mean of 1961 income and 1962 assets, measured in thousands of dollars. Liquid assets exclude house value. Mean equals 4.71; standard deviation equals 2.86.

1962 HOME OWNERSHIP. Coded one if the parents owned their own home in 1962; all others are coded zero. Proportion with home ownership equals .63.

Maternal Marital Experience

AGE AT MARRIAGE.   Age of mother in years at time of first marriage. Mean equals 20.52; standard deviation equals 3.09.

PREMARITAL PREGNANCY.   Coded one if mother was pregnant at marriage; otherwise, coded zero. Pregnancy status at marriage was ascertained through a comparison of vital records of birth and marriage (Pratt 1965). Proportion with premarital pregnancy equals .18.

RELIGIOUS MARRIAGE CEREMONY.   Coded one if mother was married by a Protestant clergyman, Catholic priest, rabbi, or other religious official. Otherwise, coded zero. Proportion with religious marriage equals .88.

MARITAL DISRUPTION BY 1962.   Coded one if the mother had been married more than once; otherwise, coded zero. Previous marital dissolution could have been the result of either mortality or marital discord. Proportion with marital disruption equals .05.

Parental Childbearing

NUMBER OF SIBLINGS.   Mean number of brothers and sisters the mother and father had while they were growing up. Mean equals 3.03; standard deviation equals 1.77.

PARITY IN 1961.   Number of children born to the mother by 1961. It is also the birth order of the child participating in the study. Coded as two dummy variables: 2nd parity in 1961; and 4th parity in 1961. The reference group for these two dummy variables is 1st parity in 1961. Proportion with 2nd parity equals .33; proportion with 4th parity equals .32.

1961 BIRTH UNWANTED.   In 1962 the mothers were asked: "Shortly before your (recent) pregnancy began, did you really want to have another child sometime, or would you rather not have had any (more)?" Coded one if mother responded that she "didn't want any/another"; coded zero for all others, including those who were indifferent or fatalistic. Proportion with unwanted birth equals .09.

1962 PREFERRED NUMBER OF CHILDREN.   In 1962 the mothers were asked: "The number of children people expect and want aren't always the same. Now, if you could start life over again, knowing that things would turn out just about the way they have for you and your husband, what number of children would you choose if you could have just the number you want by the time you finish?" Mean equals 3.85 and standard deviation equals 1.38.

Religion

GRANDMOTHER RELIGIOSITY.   In 1962 the mothers were asked: "Now, thinking of your mother at the time when you were growing up, how often did she talk about religious matters, or participate in religious activities with the family? Would it be *quite often, sometimes, almost never,* or *never?*" The answers were coded from 0 for "never" to 3 for "quite often." Mean equals 2.26 and standard deviation equals .89.

MATERNAL RELIGIOUS AFFILIATION.   Religious affiliation of the mother in 1962, coded into three dummy variables: Fundamentalist Protestant, including Baptists (proportion equals .12); Catholic (proportion equals .53); and Other, including Jewish, Muslim, and no affiliation (proportion equals .05). The reference group is nonfundamentalist or mainline Protestants, including such groups as Methodists, Lutherans, and Presbyterians.

PARENTAL RELIGIOUS ATTENDANCE.   Mean attendance of mother and father at religious services since the baby was born in 1961. The frequency of attendance for both mother and father was coded as: (1) never; (2) less than once a month; (3) once a month; (4) a few times a month; (5) once a week; and (6) several times a week. Mean equals 3.59 and standard deviation equals 1.58.

Family Organization

1962 GREGARIOUSNESS.   Frequency of mother getting together with relatives and friends. It is the sum of two 1962 questions: "How often do you get together with relatives and family, either yours or your husband's?"; and "How often do you visit with people other than relatives, to go out, or just get together at your home or theirs?" The identical response categories and codes to these two variables are: (0) never; (1) a few times a year; (2) once or twice a month; (3) once or twice a week; and (4) almost every day. The sum of the two questions ranges from 0 to 8. Mean equals 4.70 and standard deviation equals 1.15.

1962 CLOSENESS TO RELATIVES.   The mean of two indicators of the extent to which the mother included relatives as her closest friends. In 1962 the mother was asked to identify from all of her married friends and relatives the three married women near her own age that she felt the closest to and knew the best. The mother was asked if each woman was a friend or relative. The answers were coded to reflect the proportion (from zero to one) of these friends who were also relatives. The second question was: "When you think of the people you know really well and feel close to—people you can be yourself with and discuss your problems with—are most of them friends or relatives?" Answers were coded as: (0) friends; (0.5) "about the same" or "don't feel close to anyone"; (1) relatives. Mean equals .37 and standard deviation equals .33.

1962 SEX-ROLE ATTITUDES.   The mean of the mother's 1962 responses to the following four statements: "Most of the important decisions in the life of the family should be made by the man of the house"; "It's perfectly all right for women to be very active in clubs, politics, and other outside activities before the children are grown up"; "A wife shouldn't expect her husband to help around the house after he's come home from a hard day's work"; and "There is some work that is men's and some that is women's, and they shouldn't be doing each other's." Responses were coded on a five-point scale: strongly agree, agree, undecided, disagree, or strongly disagree, with the most egalitarian responses coded as five and the least egalitarian coded as one. Mean equals 2.88 and standard deviation equals .68.

Table C.2. Description of Substantive Domains from 1962 Through 1977[1]

Parental Socioeconomic Standing

ADDITIONAL MATERNAL EDUCATION, 1962–1977.   Coded one if the mother obtained any additional education (high school, college, on-the-job training, or technical or specific training course) between 1962 and 1977 interviews. Mean equals .47 and standard deviation equals .50.

1962 MATERNAL EDUCATION.   Years of school completed by the mother by the 1962 interview. Mean equals 12.15 and standard deviation equals 1.86.

1977 MATERNAL EDUCATION.   Years of school completed by the mother by the 1977 interview. Mean equals 12.47 and standard deviation equals 1.93.

1961 FAMILY INCOME.   Income of the family in 1961, in thousands of dollars. Mean equals 6.96 and standard deviation equals 3.30.

1976 FAMILY INCOME.   Income of the family in 1976, in thousands of 1962 dollars. Mean equals 14.54 and standard deviation equals 9.70.

Maternal Marital Experience

1962–1977 DISSOLUTION/REMARRIAGE.   Marital dissolution between 1962 and 1977, coded into three dummy variables: divorced/mother not remarried (proportion equals .09); divorced/mother remarried (.09); and widowed (.04). The reference group is continuously married.

Parental Childbearing

1962–1977 CHILDREN BORN.   Number of children born to the mother between 1962 and 1977. Mean equals 1.49; standard deviation equals 1.29.

1977 PREFERRED NUMBER OF CHILDREN.   Mothers were asked in 1977 the same question about preferred number of children asked in 1962 (and documented in table C.1). If the mother was not married in 1977, no reference to the husband was included in the question. Mean equals 3.12 and standard deviation equals 1.57.

Religion

1962 MATERNAL RELIGIOUS ATTENDANCE.   Frequency of the mother's attendance at religious services in 1962. Coded as: (1) never; (2) less than once a month; (3) once a month; (4) a few times a month; (5) once a week; and (6) several times a week. Mean equals 3.69 and standard deviation equals 1.62.

1977 MATERNAL RELIGIOUS ATTENDANCE.   Frequency of the mother's attendance at religious services in 1977. Coded as 1962 Maternal Service Attendance (previous). Mean equals 3.74 and standard deviation equals 1.62.

Family Organization

1977 GREGARIOUSNESS.   Frequency of getting together with friends and relatives. It is the sum of two 1977 questions identical to those used to measure 1962 gregariousness (documented in table C.1). Each of the two components is measured from zero (never) to four (almost every day), with the range of the scale going from zero to eight. Mean equals 4.40 and standard deviation equals 1.37.

1977 VISITING RELATIVES/FRIENDS.   The 1977 frequency of visiting relatives (measured from zero to four) minus the 1977 frequency of visiting friends (measured from zero to four). Whereas the 1977 gregariousness measure (previous) adds the two visiting measures together, this measure subtracts them. Thus, the possible range is from –4.0 to 4.0. Mean equals –.11 and standard deviation equals 1.19.

1962 VISITING RELATIVES/FRIENDS.   The 1962 frequency of visiting relatives minus the 1962 frequency of visiting friends. Mean equals .39 and standard deviation equals 1.10.

1977 SEX-ROLE ATTITUDES.   The mean of the 1977 responses to eight questions measured on a five-point scale. The first four questions are identical to those used in 1962 and documented in table C.1. The additional four statements are: "A working mother can establish as warm and secure a relationship with her children as a mother who does not work"; "It is much better for everyone if the man earns the main living and the woman takes care of the home and family"; "Women are much happier if they stay at home and take care of their children"; "It is more important for a wife to help her husband's career than to have one herself." Mean equals 3.36 and standard deviation equals .67.

1977 SEX-ROLE ATTITUDES (VERSION 2).   In some analyses we used a reduced version of this index that included only the first four 1977 sex-role attitude questions—the same measures used to construct the 1962 Sex-Role Attitudes (see table C.1). Mean equals 3.51 and standard deviation equals .73.

1962–1977 MATERNAL EMPLOYMENT.   Number of years mother was employed full time between 1962 and 1977. The hours of work between 1962 and 1977 were estimated and then divided by 2,080 to obtain number of years of full-time equivalent work. Mean equals 3.40 and standard deviation equals 3.72.

Table C.3. Description of Children's Adolescent Courtship Factors Included in Chapter 7[2]

AGE AT FIRST DATE.   Children's age at first date, coded into four dummy variables: age 13 or younger (proportion equals .15), age 14 (.18), age 15 (.27), and age 16 (.29). Omitted category is never dated or first dated at age 17 or older (.11).

AGE AT FIRST STEADY.   Children's age at first going steady, coded into five dummy variables: age 13 or younger (proportion equals .09), age 14 (.10), age 15 (.13), age 16 (.20), and age 17 (.18). Omitted category is never went steady or first went steady at age 18 or older (.30).

AGE AT FIRST SEX.   Children's age at first sexual intercourse, coded into three dummy variables: age 15 or younger (proportion equals .16), age 16 (.13), and age 17 (.19). Omitted category is not sexually experienced or had first sex at age 18 or older (.52).

SEX AND STEADY EXPERIENCE BEFORE AGE 18.   Children's overall experience with sexual intercourse and going steady before age 18, coded into two dummy variables: had sex before age 18 (proportion equals .48), and had no sex before age 18 but had gone steady before age 18 (.29). Omitted category is neither had gone steady or had sex before age 18 (.23).

NUMBER OF DATES DURING LAST 4 WEEKS.   Number of times children reported going out on a date in the four weeks prior to the 1980 interview. Coded as an interval variable from zero to 11 (with 11 indicating those who dated 11 or more times). Mean equals 3.96 and standard deviation equals 3.82.

DATING PATTERNS DURING LAST 4 WEEKS (AGE 18).   Children were asked the question: "In the last four weeks when you have gone out, has it usually been with different girls/boys or has it always been the same girl/boy?" Coded as two dummy variables: went out with the same person (proportion equals .54) and went out with different people (.24). Omitted category is no dating in the previous four weeks (.22).

DATING SOMEONE PLAN TO MARRY AT AGE 18.   Coded as one for those dating someone they plan to marry and zero for all others. The proportion dating someone they plan to marry is .32.

DUMBER OF SEXUAL PARTNERS BY AGE 18.   Coded into three dummy variables: one sex partner by age 18 (proportion equals .21); two or three sex partners (.19); and four or more sex partners (.18). The omitted category is no sexual partners by age 18 (.42).

SEXUAL EXPERIENCE BY AGE 18.   Recency of children's sexual experience relative to 1980 interview, when they were 18. Coded into two dummy variables: has had sex within prior four weeks (proportion equals .36); has had sex but not in prior four weeks (.22). Omitted category is had no sex prior to the 1980 interview (.42).

PREGNANCY BEFORE UNION.   Time-varying indicator of the pregnancy status of female respondents or the partners of male respondents during the month immediately preceding each month of risk of cohabitation or marriage. Only pregnancies resulting in live births are included. In this analysis all months from the date of the birth back to seven months prior to the date of the birth are coded as "pregnancy before union."

Table C.4. Description of Religion Factors Included in Chapter 8 Analysis

1962 MATERNAL RELIGIOUS ATTENDANCE.   Frequency of mother's attendance at religious services since the baby was born in 1961. Coded as: (1) never; (2) less than once a month; (3) once a month; (4) a few times a month; (5) once a week; and (6) several times a week. Mean equals 3.67 and standard deviation equals 1.63.

1962 PATERNAL RELIGIOUS ATTENDANCE.   Frequency of father's attendance at religious services since the baby was born in 1961. The categories and coding are the same as for 1962 Maternal Religious Attendance (previous). Mean equals 3.50 and standard deviation equals 1.75.

1962 AVERAGE RELIGIOUS ATTENDANCE. Mean attendance of mother and father at religious services since the baby was born in 1961. The categories and coding are the same as for 1962 Maternal Religious Attendance (previous). Mean equals 3.59 and standard deviation equals 1.58.

1977 MATERNAL RELIGIOUS ATTENDANCE. Frequency of mother's attendance at religious services in 1977. The categories and coding are the same as for 1962 Maternal Religious Attendance (previous). Mean equals 3.96 and standard deviation equals 1.54.

1977 PATERNAL RELIGIOUS ATTENDANCE. Frequency of father's attendance at religious services in 1977. The categories and coding are the same as for 1962 Maternal Religious Attendance (previous). This factor is constructed only for families in which the parents were continuously married between 1962 and 1977. Mean equals 3.50 and standard deviation equals 1.68.

1977 AVERAGE RELIGIOUS ATTENDANCE. Mean attendance of mother and father at religious services in 1977. The categories and coding are the same as for 1962 Average Religious Attendance (previous). This factor is constructed only for families in which the parents were continuously married between 1962 and 1977. Mean equals 3.73 and standard deviation equals 1.50.

1980 MATERNAL RELIGIOUS ATTENDANCE. Frequency of mother's attendance at religious services in 1980. The categories and coding are the same as for 1962 Maternal Religious Attendance (previous). Mean equals 3.73 and standard deviation equals 1.57.

1980 CHILD'S RELIGIOUS ATTENDANCE. Frequency of child's attendance at religious services in 1980. The categories and coding are the same as for 1962 Maternal Religious Attendance (previous). Mean equals 3.20 and standard deviation equals 1.51.

1980 MATERNAL RELIGIOUS IMPORTANCE. In 1980, mothers were asked: "Quite apart from attending religious services, how important would you say religion is to you—very important, somewhat important, or not important?" Responses were coded from 1 for "not important" to 3 for "very important." Mean equals 2.64 and standard deviation equals .58.

1980 CHILD'S RELIGIOUS IMPORTANCE. This factor was ascertained and operationalized in a similar manner as 1980 Maternal Religious Importance (previous). Mean equals 2.22 and standard deviation equals 0.68.

1993 MATERNAL RELIGIOUS BELIEF. In 1993, mothers were asked whether they strongly agree, agree, disagree, or strongly disagree with the following two statements: "The Bible is God's word and everything happened or will happen pretty much as it says"; and "The Bible is the answer to all important human problems." Responses were coded from 1 (strongly disagree) to 5 (strongly agree), with those who indicated they were somehow undecided coded as 3. This factor is the average of the two questions. Mean equals 3.35 and standard deviation equals 1.06.

1993 CHILD RELIGIOUS BELIEF.   This factor was ascertained and operationalized in the same manner as 1993 Maternal Religious Belief (previous). The mean is 3.10 and standard deviation is 1.21.

Table C.5. Description of Maternal and Child Attitudes Used in Chapter 9 Analysis[3]

1980 Maternal Attitudes

MOTHER'S ATTITUDE TOWARD PREMARITAL SEX/COHABITATION.   Mean of mother's responses to the following four statements: "Premarital sex is all right for a young couple planning to get married"; "Young people should not have sex before marriage"; "It's all right for a couple to live together without planning to get married"; and "A young couple should not live together unless they are married". Responses were coded on a five-point scale—strongly agree, agree, undecided, disagree, strongly disagree—with the most negative attitudes toward premarital sex and cohabitation scored lowest. Mean equals 2.40 and standard deviation equals 0.92.

MOTHER'S PREFERRED AGE AT MARRIAGE FOR CHILD.   Coded in years of age from the mother's response to the question: "If your child does get married, and if it were just up to you, what do you think would be the ideal age for (him/her) to get married?" Mean equals 24.46 and standard deviation equals 2.27.

MOTHER'S PREFERRED FAMILY SIZE FOR CHILD.   Coded as the number of children the mother would want the child to have when his/her family is completed. Mean equals 2.38 and standard deviation equals 0.80.

MOTHER'S EDUCATIONAL EXPECTATIONS FOR CHILD.   The minimum amount of years of schooling that the mother would like the child to complete. Those expecting the child to complete high-school education were coded as 12; technical, vocation, trade school, and business and secretarial schools were coded as 14; one or two years of college were coded as 14; three or four years of college were coded as 16; five or six years of college were coded as 18; and seven or more years of college were coded as 20. Mean equals 14.76 and standard deviation equals 1.78.

1980 Young-adult Attitudes

ATTITUDE TOWARD PREMARITAL SEX/COHABITATION.   Mean of the child's responses to the same four statements used for the Mother's Attitude toward Premarital Sex/ Cohabitation (previous), with same response categories and coding. Mean equals 3.29 and standard deviation equals 1.04.

PREFERRED AGE AT MARRIAGE.   Coded in years of age from the child's response to the question: "If you do get married and if it were just up to you, what do you think would be the ideal age for you to get married?" Mean equals 24.07 and standard deviation equals 2.70.

ATTITUDE TOWARD REMAINING SINGLE.   Mean of the child's responses to the following two items: "Suppose that things turn out so that you do not marry, would that bother you a great deal, some, a little, or not at all?" and "All in all, there are more advantages to being single than to being married." Answers to the first question were coded from 4 for "not at all" to 1 for "a great deal." Responses to the second statement were coded from 5 for "strongly agree" to 1 for "strongly disagree." Thus, for both measures, higher scores indicate more positive attitudes toward being single. Mean equals 2.45 and standard deviation equals 0.85.

PREFERRED FAMILY SIZE.   Coded as the number of children the young adult would want to have when his/her family is completed. Mean equals 2.92 and standard deviation equals 1.34.

ATTITUDE TOWARD ABORTION.   Mean of six indicators for attitude toward abortion. The 1980 study listed six possible reasons for abortion, including "the pregnancy seriously endangered the women's health," "the woman was not married," "the couple could not afford to have any more children," "they did not want any more children," "the woman had good reason to believe the child might be deformed," and "the pregnancy was the result of rape." The young adults indicated whether they thought it would be all right for a woman to have an abortion for each of the reasons. Answers were coded as: (1) no, (2) depends, and (3) yes. Therefore, higher scores indicate a more permissive attitude toward abortion. Mean equals 2.10 and standard deviation equals 0.54.

EDUCATIONAL EXPECTATIONS.   The highest level of schooling the children expected to complete. Those who expected no more school were coded as the number of school years completed (minimum of 10); those who expected to complete high school were coded as 12; technical, vocation, trade school, and business and secretarial schools were coded as 14; one or two years of college were coded as 14; three or four years of college were coded as 16; five or six years of college were coded as 18; and seven or more years of college were coded as 20. Mean equals 15.80 and standard deviation equals 2.28.

ATTITUDE TOWARD CAREERS.   Mean of two indicators of the importance placed on having a career by the young adult. The first indicator was the extent to which the young adult agreed or disagreed with the statement: "I do *not* expect work to be a major source of life satisfaction." Responses were coded as: (1) strongly agree, (2) agree, (3) disagree, and (4) strongly disagree. The second indicator was the young adult's ranked preferences of four different postmarriage childbearing and job market combinations. They were asked to choose from among the following four choices the one they would most prefer for their wives (for the male) or themselves (for the female), if they got married: (1) no children, full-time job; (2) one child, $^{3}/_{4}$-time job; (3) two children, half-time job; and (4) three children, no job (assuming that the job was for pay outside the home and that the children were under 10-years-old). If the respondents gave an answer combining both a job and child care, they were asked to indicate a second preference, and some of them a third preference until they answered only a job or only child-care, meaning until they chose either option 1 or 4. The rank orders of attitudes toward career were then "unfolded" to obtain an eight-point scale, with first preferences of entirely job or entirely child-care at the two extremes of the scale—that is, "full-time job, no children" coded as 8 and "three children, no job" coded as 1. The respondents who reached entirely job or child-care at the second preferences were coded as 7 and 2, respectively. The respondents who continuously chose until the third preferences were coded from 6 to 3. The score of 6 was assigned to those who answered "one child and $^{3}/_{4}$-time job," "2 children, $^{1}/_{2}$ time job," and "no children, full time job" for the first to third preferences, respectively. Those who chose the respective preferences as "2 children and $^{1}/_{2}$ time job," "1 child, $^{3}/_{4}$ time job," and "no children, full time job" were coded as 5. The respondents whose respective preferences being "1 child and $^{3}/_{4}$-time job," "two children, half-time job," and "three children, no job" were coded as 4. And those with respective preferences being "two children, helf-time job," "one child, $^{3}/_{4}$-time job," and "three children, no job" were coded as 3. The measure of attitude toward careers was the average of the work satisfaction score (measured by a four-point scale) and the career preference score (measured by an eight-point scale) weighted by 0.5. Mean equals 2.10 and standard deviation equals 0.68.

ATTITUDES TOWARD CHILD-ORIENTED SPENDING.   Mean of the young adult's responses to the following three questions: (1) "How important would it be for you to provide your children with individual lessons in things like music, dance, or sports if your children want them?" (2) "How about making it possible for your children to attend camp or go on organized tours during their summer vacations if they want to?" (3) How important would it be for you to provide your children with a college or technical education if they wanted such an education?" The answers were coded from 4 to 1 for "very important" to "not at all important." Thus, higher scores indicate more positive attitudes toward spending on children. Mean equals 3.63 and standard deviation equals 0.36.

SEX-ROLE ATTITUDES.   Mean of the young adult's responses to the eight questions regarding sex-role attitudes measured on a five-point scale. The eight questions and their scaling are identical to those used in the 1977 Mother's Sex-Role Attitudes documented in table C.2. Mean equals 3.51 and standard deviation equals .64.

ATTITUDE TOWARD MEN PRIORITIZING FAMILY MORE HIGHLY THAN CAREER.   Mean of the young adult's responses to the following two statements: "A man's family should always come before his career" and "It is more important for a man to spend a lot of time with his family than to be successful at his career." Responses were coded on a five-point scale from "strongly agree" to "strongly disagree," with 5 being the most positive attitude toward men giving priority to family than career and 1 being the least positive attitude. Mean equals 3.68 and standard deviation equals .74.

1980 MOTHER-CHILD RELATIONSHIP FROM THE YOUNG ADULT'S PERSPECTIVE.   Mean of young adult's responses to the following seven statements: (1) "My mother's ideas and opinions about the important things in life are ones I can respect." (2) "My mother respects my ideas and opinions about the important things in life." (3) "My mother accepts and understands me as a person." (4) "I enjoy doing things with my mother." (5) "My mother makes it easy for me to confide in her." (6) "My mother gives me the right amount of affection." (7) "When something is bothering me, I am able to talk it over with my mother." Responses were coded as 4 for "always," 3 for "usually," 2 for "sometimes," and 1 for "never." Therefore, higher mean scores indicate a better quality relationship from the young adult's perspective. Mean equals 2.97 and standard deviation equals .62.

1980 FATHER-CHILD RELATIONSHIP FROM THE YOUNG ADULT'S PERSPECTIVE.   Mean of young adult's responses to the seven statements previously listed for the 1980 Mother-Child Relationship, substituting "father" for "mother." The same four-point scale was used to code responses, with higher mean scores indicating a better quality relationship with the father from the young adult's perspective. Mean equals 2.81 and standard deviation equals .68.

1980 MOTHER-CHILD RELATIONSHIP FROM THE MOTHER'S PERSPECTIVE.   Mean of mother's responses to the following five statements: (1) "[Name of child]'s ideas and opinions about the important things in life are ones you can respect"; (2) "[He/She] respects your ideas and opinions about the important things in life";

(3) "You find it easy to understand [him/her]"; (4) "You enjoy doing things with [Name of child]"; (5) "You enjoy talking with [Name of child]." Responses were coded as 4 for "always," 3 for "usually," 2 for "sometimes," and 1 for "never." Therefore, higher mean scores indicate a better quality relationship from the mother's perspective. Mean equals 3.08 and standard deviation equals .56.

Table C.6. Description of Educational Variables for Chapter 10[4]

SCHOOL GRADES.   Grade point average for young adults, based on self-reports made in the 1980 interview on their letter grades from the previous semester. The grade scores were coded as 4 for A, 3 for B, 2 for C, 1 for D, and 0 for E and F. Mean equals 2.99 and standard deviation equals 0.68.

EDUCATIONAL EXPECTATIONS.   This is the same variable used in chapter 9 indicating the highest level of schooling (in years) the young adult expected to ultimately complete. The measure was documented in table C.5. Mean equals 15.80 and standard deviation equals 2.28.

SCHOOL ENJOYMENT.   Mean of how much the children reported that they enjoyed "doing school work" and "going to school" in the 1980 interview. Each enjoyment score ranged from 0 to 10 for "dislike a great deal" to "enjoy a great deal." Mean equals 6.14 and standard deviation equals 2.12.

SCHOOL ENROLLMENT IN PREVIOUS MONTH.   Two dummy variables were created to summarize school enrollment in the previous month—one coding part-time enrollment and the other coding full-time enrollment, with no enrollment being the reference category.

SCHOOL ENROLLMENT IN PREVIOUS SIX MONTHS.   People who enrolled full-time during any of those previous months were coded as a full-time student; those who had no-full-time enrollment during that period but had part-time enrollment were coded as part-time students. All others were coded as being out of school.

SCHOOL ACCUMULATION.   Number of months of school enrollment between age 16 and the beginning of the month in question. Each month of full-time school was assigned a value of 1; each month of part-time school a value of .5; and no school a value of 0. All months, including summer months, were included in these calculations. The school accumulation metric is the number of years.

Appendix D*

CONSTRUCTING MEASURES OF EARNINGS POTENTIAL
FOR USE IN CHAPTER 11

This appendix describes the procedures for constructing the six measures of earnings potential used in chapter 11, which involved combining data from our study with data from the 1990 Census and the High School and Beyond study in the two steps described in the following.

Step 1:

We first used the 1990 Census data to estimate sex- and education-specific earnings equations as functions of potential work experience. Following Mincer (1974), we approximate work experience as the difference between current age and the normative age at which the respondent's highest level of education is attained. Letting j denote education (1 = less than high school, 2 = high school, 3 = some college, and 4 = college+), letting k denote years of experience ($1, 2, \ldots, K$), and assuming all workers permanently exit the labor force (retire) at age 60, we have the following approximations:

$$
\begin{aligned}
&\text{For } j = 1, k = \text{age-16}, k = 1 \ldots 44 \\
&\text{For } j = 2, k = \text{age-18}, k = 1 \ldots 42 \\
&\text{For } j = 3, k = \text{age-20}, k = 1 \ldots 40 \\
&\text{For } j = 4, k = \text{age-22}, k = 1 \ldots 38
\end{aligned}
\tag{D.1}
$$

Letting i denote sex (1 = male and 2 = female), we estimate earnings as a nonparametric function of education, sex, and work experience for the entire $i \times j \times$

---

*Appendix D draws heavily from Xie et al. (2003).

k cross-classification using the 5 percent 1990 PUMS.[1] The dependent variable in these equations is the natural logarithm of total yearly earnings in 1989. We restrict the sample to full-time year-round workers with positive earnings.[2] Regression analysis in this case is tantamount to computing the mean of logged earnings for each $i \times j \times k$ cell. We then take the exponential function of the mean and denote this variable by Y_{ijk}. We call Y_{ijk} the "unmodified" predicted *current earnings* potential. The meaning of "unmodified" will be apparent in Step 2.

Predicted *earnings over the next five years* is calculated as the sum of the predicted earnings at the current level of educational attainment and work experience and the predicted earnings over the following four years. That is,

$$Y\_5_{ijk} = \sum_{x=k}^{k+4} Y_{ijx} \tag{D.2}$$

Calculation of predicted *future earnings* is based on a convenient assumption that retirement occurs at age 60 for men and women of all levels of educational attainment.[3] This variable is thus calculated as:

$$Y\_AF_{ijk} = \sum_{x=k}^{60-\theta_j} Y_{ijx}, \tag{D.3}$$

where θ_j refers to the normative ages of school completion (i.e., $\theta_j = 16, 18, 20, 22$ respectively for $j = 1, 2, 3, 4$). Similarly, we construct an analogous measure for total past earnings. This variable is calculated as the sum of cumulative earnings at all levels of educational attainment:

$$Y\_BF_{ij\bar{k}} = \sum_{j=1}^{4} \sum_{x=0}^{k_j} Y_{ijx}, \tag{D.4}$$

where k_j is the *actual* years of work experience at educational level j constructed from the life-history calendar, and subscript $\bar{k}$ refers to respondents' observed work history. Calculation of this variable proved challenging in that it required the construction of four additional variables representing cumulative past-work experience at each of the four levels of educational attainment. Summing equations (D.3) and (D.4) yields the predicted *lifetime earnings*:

$$Y\_T_{ij\bar{k}} = (Y\_BF_{ij\bar{k}} + Y\_AF_{ijk}). \tag{D.5}$$

Finally, we construct an intermediate summary variable that measures cumulative lifetime earnings potential up to five years into the future. Again, this is a time-varying variable incorporating changes in education and actual work experience at different levels of education. Specifically, we compute

$$Y\_T5_{ijk} = (Y\_BF_{ij\bar{k}} + Y\_5_{ijk}). \tag{D.6}$$

These six variables were then appended to the person-period data in IPS by matching on values of sex, educational attainment, and educational attainment-specific labor force experience.

Step 2:

The measures discussed in Step 1 are crude because they do not take into account other observed attributes in the data that predict earnings. To predict earnings more precisely, we modified the sex-education-experience-specific values of the measures calculated in equations (D.2) through (D.6) according to individual variation in other observable characteristics: cognitive ability assessed when the respondents were age 18, school quality (for college attendants and graduates), and college major (for college attendants and graduates). This modification is accomplished by employing "shift" parameters derived from the estimation of sex- and education-specific wage functions based on data from the sophomore cohort of the High School and Beyond (HS&B) study. To accomplish this, we first estimated the 1992 logged earnings of the HS&B respondents as a function of cognitive ability, college quality, and college major. We approximated cognitive ability by the total scores from math and reading tests provided in HS&B. After collapsing colleges attended by the HS&B respondents into a 17-category classification scheme, we measured college quality as the mean SAT score for entering students in these 17 categories. Similarly, we grouped college majors into 14 categories to capture between-major variation in earnings while maintaining reasonable sample sizes within groups.[4]

We then used the exponentiated coefficients from these regression equations based on the HS&B as shift parameters for the earnings potential measures in the IPS data. To do this, we code college majors in the IPS data using the same classification system as in the HS&B data and append institution-specific mean SAT scores for those respondents who attended college.[5] The IPS survey did not test respondents in any subject matter, but included a 13-item general aptitude test that asked respondents to identify the similarity between pairs of words. Although the test scores from the HS&B and the IPS are not strictly comparable, we assume they are highly correlated. We converted both scores to a standardized scale (with a mean of zero and variance of one) so that the coefficient of test scores from the HS&B data can be used as a shift parameter for the aptitude measure available in the IPS data. Our approach necessitates the assumption that the effects of cognitive ability and school/major characteristics are multiplicative and do not vary by age. For example, we assume that the positive effect of cognitive ability estimated using the HS&B data shifts wages upward by a proportional amount at all levels of work experience. This assumption is tantamount to a noninteractive model with logged earnings as the dependent variable, a common practice in research on earnings (e.g., Mincer and Polachek 1974). These modified earnings measures are then incorporated as covariates in models for the rate of entry into first union. One advantage of our approach is that we are able to estimate earnings potential for all individuals in the sample, regardless of their work status and experience.

Notes

Chapter One

1. Appendix A provides a detailed exposition of our methods for estimating total, direct, and indirect effects.

Chapter Two

1. The opportunities for married children to live together with married parents were also limited by the fact that marriage and childbearing were late by international standards, and mortality and fertility were high (Ruggles 1987, 1994).

2. The belief that love was not part of the calculus of marriage in the Western past originated from two fundamental errors by scholars in the 1700s and 1800s (Thornton 2005). First, these scholars believed that they could know what marriage was like in the Western past by examining marriage at their time outside the West. When they observed that marriages in many contemporary societies outside the West were arranged by parents without the romance and courtship of the marrying couple, they concluded that in the past arranged marriages were common in the West. Second, they assumed that without romance and courtship in the mate-selection process, there could be no love in marriage itself. In recent years historical research has shown substantial amounts of love in both courtship and marriage in the Western past (Brundage 1987; d'Avray 1985; d'Avary and Tausche 1981; Davies 1981; Duggan 1981; Gies and Gies 1987; Gottlieb 1980; Hanawalt 1986, 1993; Hanning 1991; Herlihy 1985; Ingram 1981, 1985; Kooper 1991; Lantz et al. 1968; Leclercq 1982; Macfarlane 1970, 1986; Modell 1985; Noonan 1967, 1973; Norton 1980; O'Hara 1991; Olsen 2001; Outhwaite 1981; Ozment 1983; Pedersen 1998; Pierre 2001; Riley 1991; Rothman 1984; Sarsby 1983; Schama 1997; Shahar 1983; Sheehan 1978, 1991a, 1991b; Smout 1981; Wilson 1984; Wrightson 1982).

3. Although love and affection were seen as important elements of marriage, they were not always achieved in practice. There were also many instances of quarreling, conflict, and violence in domestic life (Shahar 1983).

4. Serving in the army or a religious order was also an alternative for some (Boswell 1988; Gillis 1974; Hrdy 1999; Ozment 1983; Witte 1997).

5. In England, church laws and courts had jurisdiction until the 1800s (Helmholz 1974; Glendon 1977).

6. Fitch and Ruggles (2000), however, suggest that methodological difficulties in the colonial American data make this conclusion about Americans marrying earlier than others from northwestern Europe questionable.

7. Childcare and the quality of relationships between parents and children in the past are complex, multifaceted, and controversial topics that are beyond the scope of this chapter. The literature suggests a wide range of human emotions and behavior of parents toward their children in the past. Although paucity of data make it difficult to specify the distribution of parental care and emotions in the past, they appear to cover the same range as in the present and include everything from infanticide, abandonment, and abuse to love, affection, and concern (Ben-Amos 2000; Boswell 1988; de Mause 1974; Hanawalt 1986, 1993; Hrdy 1999; Kertzer 1993; Ozment 1983, 2001; Pollock 1985; Shahar 1983, 1990; Tilly et al. 1992; Wilson 1984). As young children became integrated into the family and grew to adulthood, most parents devoted considerable material and emotional resources to their rearing (Hrdy 1999; Marvick 1974; Shahar 1983, 1990).

8. For a more complex view of the interactions between religious and secular law in a changing England see Engdahl (1967).

9. Although the limitation of sex to marriage was an ideal, sex outside of marriage was also recognized. Especially relevant here is the toleration of prostitution, which has a long history in human society (Shahar 1983).

10. One exception to this linkage of marriage, economic self-sufficiency, and household headship occurred in the period after World War II in the United States when substantial numbers of young people married while they were still in college and dependent upon their parents (Bailey 1988; Hogan 1981; Modell, Furstenberg, and Hershberg 1976).

11. A substantial body of empirical research in recent years has called into serious question the proposition that marriage is bad for people. Numerous studies have now found that as compared to unmarried people, married people—both women and men—report higher physical and mental health, greater economic accomplishments, more satisfying sex lives, less violence, and higher levels of happiness. Although the causal mechanisms producing such marital-status differences have not been settled, there is growing evidence that these differences reflect the effects of being married on physical, social, economic, and emotional well-being. For recent summaries of much of this literature, see England 2000; Stanton 1997; Waite 1995; Waite and Gallagher 2000; Waite et al. 2000.

12. In both of these questions women were asked about female persons and men were asked about male persons.

13. The remaining one-third said they would be bothered some.

14. This process and outcome are described by McCaa (1994) and Castro Martin (2002) for Spain and Latin America.

15. Gillis (1985) suggests that in England the 1700s and early 1800s saw a simplification of marriage for many people, which was subsequently followed by an increase of ritual and elaboration.

16. Similar trends have also been documented in Europe (Lesthaeghe 1995; van de Kaa 1987).

17. Similar trends in unmarried sexual experience have also been documented in Europe (Kiernan 1989; van de Kaa 1987).

18. Interestingly, there is even growing support for the expanded legal recognition of common-law marriage in the United States in order to protect the rights of individuals living as husband and wife but without the legal formalities of marriage (Ammons 1999; Blumberg 2001; Bowman 1996; Caudill 1982; Estin 2001; Oldham 2001; Vaughn 1991; Westfall 2001).

19. Much less is known about change over time in rates of marriage among Asian-Americans and there is substantial variation in family formation patterns across Asian- and Latino-American subpopulations (McLoyd et al. 2000; some discussion is in Xie and Goyette 2004).

Chapter Three

1. Although the data collections were designed to collect information only about heterosexual unions, it is possible that some respondents may have reported homosexual unions.

2. More information concerning our methods for collecting marriage and cohabitation histories is provided by Freedman et al. (1988), Thornton (1988), and Thornton and Young-DeMarco (1996).

3. Some of these rights and responsibilities associated with marriage in at least some places include: employee fringe benefits such as health insurance and retirement packages for spouses; the right of spouses to inherit property from each other; property and support obligations at marital dissolution; right to immigrate; obligation for debts; legal access to and obligations for children; differential tax treatment; and protection of communications in legal proceedings (Blumberg 2001; Estin 2001; Regan 2001).

4. For a somewhat contrary view, see Jamieson et al. (2002), who report a high degree of permanence and commitment among a group of Scottish cohabitors.

5. These correlations are between the mother's degree of happiness in 1993 about the child's cohabitation and the mother's attitudes about cohabitation in

1980 when her child was age 18 and between the mother's 1993 happiness about the child's cohabitation and the child's perceptions of the mother's attitudes about premarital sex in 1980. The correlations are standard pearsonian correlation coefficients that can range from −1.0 to 1.0, with zero reflecting no association.

6. Of course, these are retrospective reports about a person's state of mind and social relationships at the time of initiating cohabitation rather than reports at the time of initiation of cohabitation. They are, thus subject to recall error, redefinition, and reevaluation designed to match with subsequent events. Although we believe that such measurement errors and biases exist, we also believe that the distributions reported provide a general indication of the relationship between marriage and cohabitation at the time of initiating cohabitation.

7. The precise wording of the question was: "Please think back to just *before* you started to live with (NAME) and tell me how important each of the following reasons was to your decision to live together. You and (NAME) wanted to try out living together before deciding about marriage? Would you say that was *very important, somewhat important, not very important,* or *not at all important*?" In our discussion of these data we dichotomize very and somewhat important in contrast to not very important and not at all important. These answers are, of course, retrospective and subject to recall errors.

8. Of those with private marriage plans who said living together as a trial was important to them, 56 percent actually married, as compared to 65 percent of those with private marriage plans who said a trial was not important. For those with public marriage plans at the time of cohabitation, we found that 65 percent of those who said cohabiting was a trial for marriage went on to marry as compared to 84 percent who said a trial period was not important. Of course, these reports are retrospective and may be influenced by subsequent events.

Chapter Four

1. In the formal language of demography, cohabitation and marriage are treated as competing risks terminating the single status.

2. These trajectories are very similar to those reported in national studies with young people of similar ages in the 1980s and 1990s (Bramlett and Mosher 2002; Gryn, Mott, and Burchette-Patel 2000; Fitch and Ruggles 2000; Kreider and Fields 2002; Raley 2000).

3. These estimates are very similar to those obtained for the national population (Bramlett and Mosher 2002; Bumpass and Sweet 1989; Bumpass and Lu 2000).

4. These figures are again similar to those reported in national studies (Bramlett and Mosher 2002; Bumpass and Lu 2000).

5. These percentages are very similar to those reported for white men and

white women participating in national studies in 1987 and 1995 (Bumpass and Lu 2000; Gryn, Mott, and Burchette-Patel 2000).

6. See Bumpass and Lu 2000 for similar national data.

7. This modest gap between the ever married and the currently married during early adulthood is also evident in national data (Gryn, Mott, and Burchette-Patel 2000).

Chapter Five

1. Because of the relatively small number of people in our sample who identify with religious faiths other than Christianity, our main focus is on differentials within Christianity rather than differences between Christians and other groups. Examination of the full array of religious influences in America today requires larger data sets.

2. In the formal language of demography, marriage and cohabitation in this analysis are treated as competing risks.

3. As described in Appendix B, this Z ratio is more precisely defined as the ratio of the effect parameter in logistic regression to its standard error, testing the hypothesis of no difference in the hazard rate (e.g., that $B = 0$).

4. For parsimony we use the mean recency of immigration of mothers and fathers in our analyses. We specified the relationship between immigration status and marriage and cohabitation as linear because preliminary analysis showed that a categorical specification did not provide a statistically significant improvement of fit to the data. In addition, preliminary analysis showed that an average of the immigration recency of the maternal and paternal families fit the data nearly as well as using separate measures for each side of the family.

5. This 34 percent difference across three units of the immigration scale is calculated by the following formula: $(-.13 + 1)^3 - 1 = (.87)^3 - 1 = .66 - 1 = -.34$.

6. The effect with minimum controls is .06 and the effect with maximum controls is .04.

7. The minimum control estimates are .09 and .08 respectively while the maximum control estimates are .06 and .03 respectively.

8. Parents with farm origins averaged 11.1 years of school and parents with nonfarm origins averaged 12.4 years of school.

9. The negative effect of farm background on education and the negative effect of education on union formation together produce the positive indirect effect through education.

10. Both the maximum and minimum controls produce indirect effect estimates of .08.

11. Several considerations led us to combine the educations of mothers and fathers into a parental education index and to combine income and assets into a

financial resources index. First, the components of each index are highly corre-lated; pearsonian correlations between mother's and father's education and be-tween income and assets are both .50. Second, the components of each index have very similar effects on children's union-formation decisions when examined sep-arately. Finally, combining the components into single indices predicts the chil-dren's union-formation behavior nearly as well as using the two individual vari-ables separately. The variances of income and assets were also very similar, so that the unweighted mean of the two indicators are weighted roughly equally in our financial resources index.

12. Several other socioeconomic dimensions were examined in preliminary analyses. One focused on parental expectations for children to attend college, an-other asked whether parents had already begun to save for their children's ed-ucation, and a third centered on the mothers' ideas about the things that might be important for children to have as they grew older. Contrary to expectations, none of these socioeconomic indicators had statistically significant effects on the marriage or cohabitation experience of the children.

13. Among the most highly educated group, 96 percent had a religious mar-riage and 10 percent were premaritally pregnant, as compared to 77 and 29 per-cent respectively of the least educated group. The correlation between parental education and parental age at marriage is .31.

14. The 31 percent drop across four years of average education is calculated by the following formula: $(-.09 + 1)^4 - 1 = (.91)^4 - 1 = .69 - 1 = -.31$.

15. This is true even though the coefficient for education on marriage is only slightly reduced between Models 5.2 and 5.3.

16. The correlation between gregariousness and maternal age at marriage is $-.17$. Mothers who were premaritally pregnant have mean gregariousness scores of 5.0 compared to 4.6 for those not pregnant at marriage.

17. Interestingly, the indirect effects of a parental premarital pregnancy on rates of union formation do not operate only through parental religiosity when the child is born but through parental religiosity when the child is an adolescent. Between .02 and .03 of the negative effect of a parental premarital pregnancy on marriage and between .03 and .05 of the positive effect on cohabitation operates through parental religiosity when the child is an adolescent. These results are from decompositions associated with analyses in chapter 6.

18. The means of church attendance for the religiously married couples and nonreligiously married couples are 3.7 and 2.5 respectively. The means of being closer to relatives for the religiously married couples and nonreligiously married couples are .37 and .30 respectively.

19. Preliminary analyses showed that paternal and maternal family sizes had similar effects on the children's subsequent union-formation behavior. Therefore, we combined the two family sizes by taking the mean number of siblings in the homes of the two sets of parents.

20. Home ownership ranges from 70 percent for parents with an average sibship of less than two to 56 percent for parents with an average of more than five sibs.

21. The primary factors accounting for the difference between the minimally and maximally controlled estimates of the total effect are preferred number of children, attendance at religious services, and sex-role attitudes. Having an unwanted child is negatively correlated with preferred number of children and attendance at religious services and is positively related to maternal egalitarian sex-role attitudes. Because evaluations of the wantedness of the 1961 birth, preferred number of children, attendance at religious services, and sex-role attitudes were all ascertained as of the 1962 interview, it is difficult to sort out the causal interpretations of these results.

22. Maternal and paternal religious attendance were examined separately in preliminary analyses and are discussed in detail in chapter 8. These preliminary results demonstrated remarkable similarity in the effects of paternal and maternal religiosity. In addition, utilizing the two variables separately in the same equation results in only a trivial improvement of fit over a model utilizing average attendance only. For these reasons, and because maternal and paternal attendance are substantially correlated (pearsonian correlation of .75), the use of average attendance is more parsimonious and less subject to multicollinearity concerns. Preliminary analyses also demonstrated that curvilinear specifications of the religious attendance effect does not significantly improve the prediction of children's marriage and cohabitation over a linear specification.

23. The proportion of parents married by a church official varies from .91 to .67 between those with the highest and lowest grandmother religiosity. The pearsonian correlation between grandmother religiosity and parental attendance at religious services is .22.

24. Preliminary analyses showed that the frequency of seeing relatives and the frequency of seeing friends have similar effects on the children's union-formation experience and little predictive power is lost by summing the two indicators together rather than using the two in the same equation. The pearsonian correlation between the two indicators, however, is only .04.

25. Again, preliminary analyses showed that these indicators could be combined without statistically significant loss of fit as compared to using each of the variables in the same equations. The correlation between the two indicators is .24.

26. Several additional indicators of family organization and interaction were examined in preliminary analyses. One is the frequency of the mother seeing her own mother since the birth of her baby in 1961. This dimension was found to have a statistically significant effect on children's marriage but not cohabitation. We do not, however, present the results for this variable because of the strong overlap between it and the more general indicator of visiting with friends and relatives. Additional family organization and interaction variables were examined, but are not

discussed further because preliminary examination showed that they did not have statistically significant effects on the children's union-formation experience. These include the following dimensions: the extent to which the mother was involved in the home production of food and clothing; whether it was relatives or friends who helped the mother after the 1961 child was born; participation in large family gatherings; social support from relatives; the frequency of going out; preferences for home leisure compared to leisure outside the home; and whether relatives lived in the same area as the mother. Thus, although some of the dimensions of maternal involvement with friends and relatives discussed previously in detail seem to have implications for children's subsequent union-formation behavior, we are unable to demonstrate strong effects of family organization across several other dimensions of that domain.

27. The mothers were asked the extent to which they agreed or disagreed with a series of questions concerning the activities of men and women and the appropriate division of decisionmaking among couples. This series of questions has been analyzed extensively in earlier research and has been shown to scale well with acceptable reliabilities (Thornton, Alwin, and Camburn 1983; Thornton and Binstock 2001). Two other series of questions concerning gender roles were asked in 1962. One asked whether it was the husband or wife who usually performed several different household tasks. These questions were examined in a series of analyses that showed no significant relationship to the children's union-formation behavior. The second additional series of questions asked if it was usually the husband or the wife who made family decisions. Preliminary analyses indicated that an index constructed from these questions was significantly related to marriage but not to cohabitation. However, the explanatory power of this index on marriage overlapped greatly with the explanatory power of the sex-role attitude index. In the spirit of parsimony, no further analyses were conducted using either of these last two series of questions.

Chapter Six

1. For example, as we will discuss later, for the child's age 15 we use parental income as our measure of family financial resources, whereas for the child's infancy we use the average of income and assets. Consequently, both the content and the metric of measurement vary between infancy and adolescence, which makes it difficult to make direct comparisons between the early and late effect parameters in Model 6.2. As we discussed in chapter 5, the financial resources indicator at the child's infancy is the mean of income and assets—or equivalently, the sum of one-half of income and one-half of assets. By dividing the metric of thousands of dollars at infancy by two, we have increased the coefficient of financial resources by two. As noted in Appendix table C.2 and discussed later in this chapter, for the

child's adolescence we use only 1977 family income and do not rescale it by dividing by two. Similarly, at the child's infancy we analyzed mean average religious service attendance of father and mother (or equivalently added together one-half of each of the father's and mother's attendance), but for reasons discussed later, in 1977 we analyze only the wife's attendance, with no adjustment of the scale. As with financial resources in the child's infancy, the division of the original religiosity scale by two results in the coefficients being multiplied by two, an adjustment that does not occur for the data from the child's adolescence.

The issue of scale units and the comparability of coefficients is further complicated by the fact that the estimated coefficients we present are transformations of the original coefficients estimated in the multivariate equations. That is, the coefficients were initially estimated as effects on the log-odds of union formation. These log-odds coefficients were then transformed into coefficients representing the proportional change in union-formation rates associated with a unit change of the explanatory factor. This was done by subtracting one from the exponentiated original log-odds coefficients. It is important to note that it is the original log-odds coefficients that are doubled by the division by two of the original units of financial resources and religious service attendance during the child's infancy. Because the transformation of these log-odds coefficients into the percentage difference coefficients that we present is not linear, the differences between the 1962 financial resources and religious service attendance coefficients in table 6.2 are not transformed exactly by a factor of two.

2. In preliminary analyses we maintained the distinction between formal school-based education and work-related educational programs, but found that the effects of the two kinds of training were very similar. So, in our final analyses we have combined school-based and work-related educational programs.

3. This observation means that parental assets in 1962 were significantly related to children's union-formation decisions, but 1977 assets were not.

4. We did not use average parental education because husband's education was not ascertained in 1977. We also did not estimate the effects of 1962 and 1977 maternal education in the same equation because of the high correlation between the two indicators of maternal education ($r = .85$).

5. Although the effect of income is not statistically significant in all predictions of marriage and cohabitation examined separately, the effect is statistically significant when the two forms of union formation are examined together as a single decrement moving young adults from being single to being in a coresidential union ignoring whether the union is cohabitation or marriage (results are not shown in tables).

6. We use the term divorce to refer to all marital dissolutions due to discord, including separations that do not end in divorce.

7. In preliminary analyses we also distinguished between those who experienced a divorce between 1962 and 1966 (early childhood) and those who experienced

a divorce after 1966 (late childhood and adolescence). We did not maintain this timing distinction in our final analyses because the effects of a divorce during the two periods were similar.

8. Teachman (2003) reports similar results using data from the 1995 National Survey of Family Growth (NSFG).

9. About 20 percent of the nonpremaritally pregnant and 27 percent of the premaritally pregnant experienced a marital disruption between 1962 and 1977.

10. The pearsonian correlation between desired completed family size in 1962 and 1977 is .39. Estimates of the effects of maternal 1962 and 1977 preferred number of children on children's marriage rates are reduced from their levels of .070 and .065 in Model 6.1 and Total Effect respectively to only .024 and .031 in an equation containing the Model 6.1 controls and 1962–1977 children born. These estimates are very close to those observed with the full controls of Model 6.2, .022 and .024 respectively.

11. Between 1962 and 1977 the women of first, second, and fourth parity respectively had, on average, 2.4, 1.4, and 1.0 children.

12. This interpretation of the importance of 1962–1977 children born for the coefficients for 1962 parity is reinforced by an additional equation adding only 1962–1977 children born to Model 6.1. Just the addition of this one variable moves the 1962 parity effects most of the distance from the estimates of Model 6.1 to those in Model 6.2. Although the effects of fourth parity on both cohabitation and marriage just barely miss statistical significance, the effect on the total union-formation rate is solidly significant in Model 6.2 (data not shown in tables).

13. We calculate this one-half figure by assuming the coefficient to be $-.22$ and using the formula $[(1 - .22)^3 - 1]$

14. This effect is not quite statistically significant; $Z = 1.52$.

15. The coefficients for 1962 and 1977 can be directly compared in table 8.1 because the factors are measured identically in the two years.

16. A difference of four points on the scale in *each* of the two years would produce a difference of 72 percent in the union-formation rate. This is calculated as 1.07 to the 8th power.

17. It is not clear why early maternal closeness to relatives is associated with children's cohabitation experience and early maternal visiting patterns is not.

18. In fact, the addition of 1977 sex-role attitudes to Model 6.1 reduces the effects of 1962 sex-role attitudes to levels very similar to those observed in Model 6.2 (results not shown).

Chapter Seven

1. The same series of questions were asked in 1985, but with an expanded set of age categories to reflect that the respondents were then age 23 rather than 18. We

utilized information from the 1985 interview for the small group of respondents who were not interviewed in 1980 but were interviewed in 1985 ($n = 19$). This was done by categorizing these respondents into the 1980 categories based on the 1985 information. In addition, a small number of respondents were not interviewed in 1980 or 1985 ($n = 4$). For these respondents we imputed this information by assigning the means of the respective variables.

2. This was coded as the date of birth minus seven months. Note that alternative time lags were also tried, with minimal influence on the results. Pregnancies that did not result in a live birth were ignored for this analysis.

3. In this chapter we also use the data for all of the families originally included in the study. We are able to do this because we impute missing data for mothers and children who did not provide the relevant information. In addition, we include in the analysis a variable for the mother not being interviewed in 1980 and a variable for the child not being interviewed in 1980. The number of mothers not interviewed in 1980 was 18 and the number of children not interviewed in 1980 was 23. Both of these two numbers are approximately two percent of the sample.

4. A strong positive correlation between the timing of first sex and marriage has also been reported by Miller and Heaton (1991) and by Klassen et al. (1989).

5. These estimates of the effects of sexual experience at age 18 on subsequent union-formation rates are similar to those reported by Laumann et al. (1994) for a national sample.

6. These results are consistent with the findings of Laumann et al. (1994) using a national sample.

7. Bumpass and Lu (2000) found that the percentage of unmarried non-Hispanic white births born to cohabiting women increased from 33 percent in 1980–84 to 39 percent in 1990–94.

8. Although our estimates of the fraction of single pregnant women marrying before the birth of the child closely match those estimated by Manning (1993; also see Manning and Landale 1996) using the National Survey of Families and Households, they are substantially higher than estimates derived from the Current Population Survey. For the time period between 1975 and 1994, Bachu (1999) estimated that between 28 and 40 percent of premaritally pregnant white women aged 15–29 married before the birth of the first child, with the fraction declining over time (also see Ventura and Bachrach 2000 and Morgan and Rindfuss 1999). We have not been able to reconcile the similar estimates from our data and the National Survey of Families and Households with the different ones from the Current Population Survey, although some of the differences may be due to different methods, time periods, ages, and racial classifications used.

9. Nock (1998) reports a similar finding for men using the National Longitudinal Study of Youth.

Chapter Eight

1. All of the mothers in 1962 were married to the child's father, making it possible to include all families in this analysis. However, between 1962 and 1977 many of the mothers separated, divorced, or were widowed from the child's father and could not report on the father's religious service attendance at that time. The description of these measures and their distributions are reported in table C.4 of Appendix C. In a separate analysis we estimated the measurement reliability for maternal frequency of religious attendance at .77 for 1980, 1985, and 1993 observations. This is the proportion of the variance in the observed measures that can be accounted for by their underlying factors or true scores. The reliability for children's attendance during the same years was estimated as .74. We assume that 1962 and 1977 maternal religious attendance reliabilities are of similar magnitude (Thornton and Binstock 2001).

2. It may puzzle some readers that the estimated effect of average parental attendance appears to be greater than the effects of both maternal and paternal attendances. For example, for the 1962 analysis of marriage, the effect of the average parental attendance is .13, whereas those of maternal and paternal attendances are respectively .11 and .09. There are two reasons for this apparent anomaly. First, the average parental attendance has a different scale so that its effect needs to be divided by 2 before being compared to the direct effects of maternal and paternal attendances (i.e., $.13/2 = .065$ in our case). Second, the effect of the average parental attendance should be compared to the direct effects rather than the total effects of maternal and paternal attendances, which are smaller in magnitude (.08 and .05 in the example).

3. Another test of the relative magnitudes of the effects of the 1962 and 1977 parental religious factors on marriage and cohabitation rates is provided in table 6.3 where all families are included in the analysis irrespective of parental marital history. The equations in table 6.3 also include a slightly different set of variables than those in table 8.1. The overall conclusions of the comparisons in table 6.3 are very similar to those of table 8.1.

4. The pearsonian correlation coefficients for the two items were .66 for the mothers and .73 for the children. In addition, the empirical association between the children's union formation and the two separate items are nearly identical for both mothers and children.

5. In order to evaluate the possible impact of this violation on our results we estimated the total effects of service attendance and religious importance measured in 1993 and compared those estimates with the results reported for the comparable 1980 measures. Those comparisons revealed that the results for the 1993 versions of religious attendance and importance are similar to the results for the 1980 indicators of the same factors. This gives added confidence to the belief that a 1980 measure of religious beliefs would have predicated children's union formation similarly

to the 1993 indicator. This test, of course, assumes that the biasing because of improper temporal ordering is the same for all three religiosity indicators.

6. The inter-item correlations for the mothers are of similar magnitude, being respectively .48, .35, and .32.

7. The comparable coefficients for entrance into all types of cohabitation from being single are shown in table 8.2 and equal –.23, –.30, and –.18. All of the coefficients predicting entrance into cohabitation without marriage plans are highly significant while those for entrance into cohabitation with public plans for marriage are only marginally significant (with Z statistics ranging from 1.5 to 1.7).

Chapter Nine

1. Of course, children also influence parents (Axinn and Thornton 1993), and therefore children's experiences and attitudes may affect their parents' attitudes. This suggests a complex and dynamic reciprocal relationship between children's and parents' attitudes. Our treatment of mothers' attitudes as the primary source of these intergenerational links is a simplification.

2. In preliminary analyses using two separate measures, one for attitudes toward premarital sex and a second for attitudes toward cohabitation, we found that these two attitudes have similar effects. For parsimony we have combined them here into a single measure.

3. We also examined the influence of mothers' 1980 sex-role attitudes on the children's cohabitation and marriage behavior. These 1980 measures had no significant impact beyond the impact of the 1977 sex-role attitudes already included in these models, so we do not present those estimates here. We discuss the indirect effects of mothers' 1977 sex-role attitudes via the children's attitudes later.

4. To measure attitudes toward remaining single we averaged an item measuring the extent to which young people were bothered by the possibility that they never married and an item measuring agreement with the idea that there are more advantages to being single than to being married into a single scale. Higher numbers on this scale reflect more positive attitudes toward remaining single. Preliminary separate analyses of these two items demonstrated that they have similar effects on cohabitation and marriage—combining them into a single scale provides greater parsimony.

5. To measure attitudes toward careers with the greatest possible parsimony we also average two different items together into a single scale. One of these items measures the expectation that work will be a source of life satisfaction and the other measures a forced-choice trade-off between full-time work and child care (see table C.5 of Appendix C). In preliminary analyses both of these measures had similar effects on cohabitation and marriage. Responses to the forced-

choice trade-off measure were divided by 2 before the two measures were averaged.

6. We do not know if the lack of an effect at ages older than 23 is the result of there being no effect of consumption aspirations at older ages or if the measurement of aspirations at age 18 is too distal to predict behavior at older ages.

7. Little of the influence of first-generation fertility preferences on second-generation cohabitation is explained by the introduction of second-generation attitudes and experience.

8. The comparisons between the means for the three factors where the mother was divorced and remarried and where the mother was continuously married are: for attitudes toward premarital sex and cohabitation, 3.8 versus 3.2; sex-role attitudes, 3.6 versus 3.5; and attitudes toward abortion, 2.3 versus 2.0.

9. Grade point averages of children of divorced and remarried mothers were 2.8 versus 3.0 for children of continually married mothers.

10. An equivalent way of stating this is that the negative indirect effect of parental family size on marriage through the child's attitude toward child-oriented spending and attitude towards men prioritizing family over career is the result of parental family size being negatively correlated with each of these factors and each of these factors being positively related with marriage.

11. A summary of direct effects of maternal factors net of all other factors is provided in table A.2.

12. Once again, this measure combines two separate measures, one for attitudes toward premarital sex and a second for attitudes toward cohabitation, to provide greater parsimony.

13. The correlations between religiosity and attitudes toward abortion and attitudes toward premarital sex and cohabitation are respectively −.43 and −.49. Similarly, mean levels of religiosity range from 3.9 to 3.2 from the lowest to the highest levels of sexual experience at age 18.

14. Mean levels of acceptance of premarital sex and cohabitation range from 3.1 for those with the lowest levels of sexual experience to 3.8 for those with the highest levels.

Chapter Ten

1. Some of the specific effects of educational expectations were already documented in chapter 9. We revisit those factors here in the context of the overall influence of education on cohabitation and marriage.

2. The only exception is the negative effect of any part-time enrollment during the past six months on rates of marriage, which is not statistically significant. It is however, in the expected direction.

3. All of the maternal factors from Model 6.6 (table 6.4) are also included in these models.

4. The main part of the question introduction read as follows. "I'm going to read a list of activities, and for each activity give me a number from 0 to 10 that tells how much you like or dislike doing it. In answering please keep in mind that we're interested in whether you *like* doing something, *not* whether you think it's important to do."

5. Edin and Kefalas (2005) provide a more complete discussion of the high economic standards required by many before entrance into marriage.

Chapter Eleven

1. Note that many of these (and other) studies show that the relationship between economic resources and union formation is quite different for Blacks and Whites. Because our analysis is based on the experience of a single cohort of White men and women, we do not discuss these differences here.

2. In constructing the summary variable, we made the simplifying assumption that full-time workers worked 40 hours per week, part-time workers reporting 9 through 29 hours worked 20 hours, and part-time workers reporting 1 through 9 hours worked 5 hours.

3. For studies using earnings, see Clarkberg 1999; MacDonald and Rindfuss 1981; Mare and Winship 1991; Oppenheimer, Kalmijn, and Lim 1997; Sweeney 2002. For studies using educational attainment, see Clarkberg 1999; Goldscheider and Waite 1986; Goldstein and Kenney 2001; Mare and Winship 1991; Oppenheimer, Blossfeld, and Wackerow 1995; Oppenheimer, Kalmijn, and Lim 1997; Sweeney 2002; Thornton, Axinn, and Teachman 1995; and Waite and Spitze 1981. For work-experience studies, see Clarkberg 1999; Oppenheimer, Kalmijn, and Lim 1997; and Sweeney 2002. For employment studies, see Goldscheider and Waite 1986; Oppenheimer, Kalmijn, and Lim 1997; and Waite and Spitze 1981. And, for studies using parental resources, see Clarkberg 1999; Goldscheider and Waite 1986; MacDonald and Rindfuss 1981; Oppenheimer and Lew 1995; Sweeney 2002; and Waite and Spitze 1981.

4. Only the coefficient for past earnings is close to statistical significance.

5. It is possible, however, that a large number of missing cases for this item contributed to the nonsignificant results.

6. However, unlike the case for potential earnings, the Z-test statistic testing for the interaction between gender and educational attainment is not statistically significant either.

Chapter Twelve

1. As we have seen in chapter 4, by the age of 31, approximately three-quarters of the young people in our study have married, and these numbers will certainly

expand substantially as additional people marry at more mature ages. In fact, studies today report that approximately nine out of ten people in their forties in the United States have ever married (Bramlett and Mosher 2002; Kreider and Fields 2002). A recent projection suggests that a similar fraction of younger Americans will marry if current marriage rates continue (Casper and Bianchi 2002; Kreider and Fields 2002). This propensity of marriage is very comparable to that of a century ago, although somewhat lower than in the years immediately after World War II.

2. Migration from one city to another may have similar effects, but we have not tested that possibility here.

3. The only statistically significant positive effect of any of these indicators on cohabitation was for past earnings for men. However, none of the other indicators of potential earnings had a statistically significant positive effect on cohabitation.

4. For reasons that we cannot explain, the sex-role attitudes of the young adults was negatively related to their rate of marriage, but had no measurable effect on the rate of cohabitation.

Appendix A

1. We also are using a similar transformation in analyzing the choice between marriage and cohabitation for those entering a union.

2. The analysis of indirect effects across these periods is limited to those with good data on all the factors listed in tables A.2, A.3, and A.4 plus the highest degree of schooling attained. The limitation of the analysis to people without any missing data and to the period of the life course after age 18 can influence estimates of both the direct and indirect effects of various factors. However, as a comparison between the estimates of Model 6.6 with and without the restrictions reveals, the influence of these restrictions on direct effects is not usually very large (compare estimates in table A.2 with those in table 6.4). We will mention important differences for individual factors in the text when we come to them. Also, in preliminary analyses we examined the differences between the estimates in Models 6.6 and A.1 and between Models A.1 and A.2 with different controls for missing data and changing case counts. For comparisons between Models 6.6 and A.1 in this preliminary analysis we limited the sample to people with good data on all parental factors, ignoring whether they had missing data on the children's factors. In comparisons between Models A.1 and A.2 we limited the analysis to people with good data on all parental factors and all children factors at age 18, ignoring children's missing data on factors after age 18. The changes in coefficients between the respective model specifications were very similar in the two approaches, leading us to present the more parsimonious approach of limiting all analyses to individuals with good data on all of the factors in all of the models.

Appendix B

1. Our age groups were defined to correspond roughly to the high-school years, the college years, the years immediately after college, and the late twenties and early thirties. In preliminary analyses we experimented with different age breaks and found that the ones reported here fit the data the closest. We also found that the spline functions provided a reasonable fit to the data relative to using many categorical variables for each age at risk, while using substantially fewer degrees of freedom.

Appendix C

1. The Intergernerational Panel Study of Parents and Children has benefited from high-quality data collection methods and has suffered little attrition during its 31-year lifespan. This resulted in relatively few situations where missing data on independent variables had the potential to reduce the sample size. Since valid dependent variable information was available for these cases, the decision was made to retain them in the sample by imputing any parental factor through the adolescence of the child where missing data was present. This ranged from three cases with missing data concerning whether the sample child's birth was unwanted in 1962, upwards to a maximum of 50 missing data occurrences on 1977 family income. Imputation was done variable-by-variable, and when possible was based on information collected from the family during an earlier wave. Formulas for imputations on complex variables such as family income or assets were constructed using known financial information about the family as well as data derived from other cases with the same demographic characteristics.

2. Individuals with missing data on the dichotomous sex and dating variables were imputed with values corresponding to the proportion of young adults having had that experience at the age in question.

3. Calculated means and standard deviations exclude families where the young adult married or cohabited before the age of 18.

4. Means and standard deviations are calculated excluding young adults who married before the age of 18.

Appendix D

1. This means that we allow full interactions among education, sex, and experience, all of which are represented by dummy variables subject to usual normalization constraints. In preliminary analyses we compared this nonparametric

approach to Mincer's (1974) quadratic function approach and found the nonparametric approach preferable. Note that the 5-percent PUMS is very large, with more than five million cases in our analysis.

2. Full-time work is operationalized as having worked at least 35 hours per week, and year-round work is operationalized as having worked for at least 50 weeks in 1989. We also excluded respondents who turned out to have negative years of experience according to equation (D.1).

3. Changing the retirement age to any other number (such as 62 or 65) would have little effect on the results.

4. The 17 college categories are combinations of visibility (national versus regional), type (public versus private), rank (tier 1 through tier 4), and curriculum (university, liberal arts college, specialty school). The categories for college majors are physical science, math, biological science, engineering, pre-professional, computer science, business, social science, humanities, art and music, education, communications, agriculture, and other.

5. For those respondents who attended schools for which we did not have mean SAT scores, we applied the mean SAT score for the college type using the 17-category classification scheme described in the preceding footnote.

Bibliography

Abma, Joyce C., Anjani Chandra, William D. Mosher, Linda S. Peterson, and Linda J. Piccinino. 1997. Fertility, family planning, and women's health: New data from the 1995 national survey of family growth. *Vital and health statistics.* Washington, DC: U.S. Government Printing Office, U.S. Department of Health and Human Services.

Abma, Joyce C., and Freya L. Sonenstein. 2001. Sexual activity and contraceptive Practices among teenagers in the United States, 1988 and 1995. *National Center for Health Statistics, Vital and Health Statistics* 23 (21): 1–79.

Abray, Jane. 1975. Feminism in the French revolution. *The American Historical Review* 80 (1): 43–62.

Ahlburg, Dennis A., and Carol J. De Vita. 1992. New realities of the American family. *Population Bulletin* 47 (2): 1044.

Ajzen, Icek 1988. *Attitudes, personality, and behavior.* Chicago: Dorsey Press.

Ajzen, Icek, and Martin Fishbein. 1977. Attitude-behavior relations: A theoretical analysis and review of empirical research. *Psychological Bulletin* 84:888–918.

———. 1980. *Understanding attitudes and predicting social behavior.* Englewood Cliffs, NJ: Prentice Hall.

Akerlof, George A., Janet L. Yellen, and Michael L. Katz. 1996. An analysis of out-of-wedlock childbearing in the United States. *The Quarterly Journal of Economics* 111 (2): 277–317.

Allison, Paul D. 1995. The impact of random predictors on comparisons of coefficients between models: Comment on Clogg, Petkova, and Haritou. *American Journal of Sociology* 100 (5): 1294–305.

Alwin, Duane F. 1984. Trends in parental socialization values: Detroit 1958–1983. *American Journal of Sociology* 90 (2): 359–82.

———. 1986. Religion and parental child-rearing orientations: Evidence of a Catholic-Protestant convergence. *American Journal of Sociology* 92 (2): 412–40.

———. 1988. From obedience to autonomy: Changes in traits desired in children, 1924–1978. *Public Opinion Quarterly* 52 (1): 33–52.

———. 1994. Aging, personality, and social change: The stability of individual differences over the adult life span. In *Life-span development and behavior,*

Vol. 12, ed. David L. Featherman, Richard M. Lerner, and Marion Perlmutter, 135–85. Hillsdale, NJ: Lawrence Erlbaum Associates.

Alwin, Duane F., and Robert M. Hauser. 1975. The decomposition of effects in path analysis. *American Sociological Review* 40 (1): 37–47.

Alwin, Duane F., and Arland Thornton. 1984. Family origins and the schooling process: Early versus late influence of parental characteristics. *American Sociological Review* 49 (6): 784–802.

Amato, Paul R. 2000. The consequences of divorce for adults and children. *Journal of Marriage and the Family* 62 (4): 1269–87.

Amato, Paul R., and Alan Booth. 1991. The consequences of divorce for attitudes toward divorce and gender roles. *Journal of Family Issues* 12 (3): 306–22.

Amato, Paul R., and Danelle D. de Boer. 2001. The transmission of marital instability across generations: Relationship skills or commitment to marriage?" *Journal of Marriage and the Family* 63 (4): 1038–51.

Amato, Paul R., and Bruce Keith. 1991. Parental divorce and the well-being of children: A meta-analysis. *Psychological Bulletin* 110 (1): 26–46.

Ammons, Linda L. 1999. What's God got to do with it? Church and state collaboration in the subordination of women and domestic violence. *Rutgers Law Review* 51:1207–289.

Aquilino, William S. 1991. Family structure and home-leaving: A further specification of the relationship. *Journal of Marriage and the Family* 53(4): 999–1010.

Ashcraft, Richard. 1987. *Locke's two treatises on government*. London: Allen and Unwin.

Atkinson, Jeff. 1996. *The American Bar Association: Guide to family law*. New York: Random House.

Axinn, William G. 1992. Family organization and fertility limitation in Nepal. *Demography* 29(4): 503–21.

Axinn, William G., and Jennifer Barber. 1997. Living arrangements and family formation values in early adulthood. *Journal of Marriage and the Family* 59(3): 595–611.

Axinn, William G., Marin E. Clarkberg, and Arland Thornton. 1994. Family influences on family size preferences. *Demography* 31(1): 65–79.

Axinn, William G., Greg J. Duncan, and Arland Thornton. 1997. The effects of parental income, wealth and attitudes on children's completed schooling and self-esteem. In *Growing up poor*, ed. Greg J. Duncan and Jeanne Brooks-Gunn, 518–30. New York: Russell Sage.

Axinn, William G., and Arland Thornton. 1992a. The influence of parental resources on the timing of the transition to marriage. *Social Science Research* 21 (3): 261–85.

———. 1992b. The relationship between cohabitation and divorce: Selectivity or causal influence? *Demography* 29(3): 357–74.

———. 1993. Mothers, children, and cohabitation: The intergenerational effects of attitudes and behavior. *American Sociological Review* 58(2): 233–46.

———. 1996. The influence of parents' marital dissolutions on children's family formation attitudes. *Demography* 33 (1): 66–81.

———. 2000. The transformation in the meaning of marriage. In *Ties that bind:*

Perspectives on marriage and cohabitation, ed. Linda Waite, Christine Bachrach, Michelle Hindin, Elizabeth Thomson, and Arland Thornton, 147–65. Hawthorne, NY: Aldine de Gruyter.

Axinn, William G., and Scott T. Yabiku. 2001. Social change, the social organization of families, and fertility limitation. *American Journal of Sociology* 106 (5): 1219–61.

Bachrach, Christine A. 1987. Cohabitation and reproductive behavior in the U.S. *Demography* 24 (4): 623–37.

Bachrach, Christine A., Kathy S. Stolley, and Kathryn London. 1992. Relinquishment of premarital births: Evidence from national survey data. *Family Planning Perspectives* 24 (1): 27–32.

Bachu, Amara. 1999. Trends in premarital childbearing: 1930–1994. *Current Population Reports*, P23-197, 1–10. Washington, DC: U.S. Census Bureau.

Bahr, Howard M., Colter Mitchell, Xiaomin Li, Alison Walker, and Kisten Sucher. 2004. Trends in family space/time, conflict and solidarity: Middletown 1924–1999. *City and Community* 3 (3): 263–91.

Bailey, Beth L. 1988. *From front porch to back seat: Courtship in twentieth-century America*. Baltimore: Johns Hopkins University Press.

Bailyn, Bernard. 1967. *The ideological origins of the American revolution*. Cambridge, MA: Belknap Press.

Bandura, Albert. 1971. *Psychological modeling: Conflicting theories*. Chicago: Aldine–Atherton.

Barber, Jennifer S. 2000. Intergenerational influences on the entry into parenthood: Mothers' preferences for family and nonfamily behavior. *Social Forces* 79 (1): 319–48.

———. 2001. Ideational influences on the transition period to parenthood: Attitudes toward childbearing and competing alternatives. *Social Psychology Quarterly* 64:101–27.

———. 2004. Community social context and individualistic attitudes toward marriage. *Social Psychology Quarterly* 67 (3): 236–56.

Barber, Jennifer S., and William G. Axinn. 1998. Gender role attitudes and marriage timing among young women. *The Sociological Quarterly* 39 (1): 11–32.

Barber, Jennifer S., William G. Axinn, and Arland Thornton. 1999. Unwanted childbearing, health, and mother-child relationships. *Journal of Health and Social Behavior* 40 (3): 231–57.

Barber, Jennifer S., William G. Axinn, and Arland Thornton. 2002. The influence of attitudes on family formation processes.In *Meaning and choice: Value orientations and life course decisions*, Monograph 38, ed. Ron Lesthaeghe, 45–95. The Hague: Netherlands Interdisciplinary Demographic Institute.

Bartkowski, John P., and Xiaohe Xu. 2000. Distant patriarchs or expressive dads? The discourse and practice of fathering in conservative Protestant families. *The Sociological Quarterly* 41 (3): 465–85.

Bartz, Karen, and Frank Nye. 1970. Early marriage: A propositional formulation. *Journal of Marriage and the Family* 32 (2): 258–68.

Bayer, Alan E. 1969. Life plans and marriage age: An application of path analysis. *Journal of Marriage and the Family* 31 (3): 551–58.

Becker, Gary S. 1973. A theory of marriage: Part I. *Journal of Political Economy* 81 (4): 813–46.

———. 1974. A theory of marriage: Part II. *Journal of Political Economy* 82 (2): S11–S26.

———. 1991. *A treatise on the family.* Cambridge, MA: Harvard University Press.

Bellah, Robert N., Richard Madsen, William M. Sullivan, Ann Swidler, and Steven M. Tipton. 1985. *Habits of the heart.* Berkeley: University of California Press.

Ben-Amos, Ilana K. 2000. Reciprocal bonding: Parents and their offspring in early modern England. *Journal of Family History* 25 (3): 291–312.

Bengston, Vern L. 1975. Generation and family effects in value socialization. *American Sociological Review* 40 (3): 358–71.

Bennett, Neil G., David E. Bloom, and Patricia H. Craig. 1989. The divergence of black and white marriage patterns. *American Journal of Sociology* 95 (3): 692–722.

Bennett, Neil G., David E. Bloom, and Cynthia K. Miller. 1995. The influence of nonmarital childbearing on the formation of first marriages. *Demography* 32 (1): 47–62.

Bennett, Pamela R., and Yu Xie. 2003. Revisiting racial differences in college attendance: The role of historically black colleges and universities. *American Sociological Review* 68 (4): 567–80.

Berg, Barbara J. 1978. *Remembered gate: Origins of American feminism: The woman and the city, 1800–1860.* New York: Oxford University Press.

Berger, Brigitte, and Peter L. Berger. 1984. *The war over the family: Capturing the middle ground.* Garden City, NY: Anchor Books.

Berkner, Lutz K. 1972. The Stem family and the developmental cycle of the peasant household: An eighteenth-century Austrian example. *The American Historical Review* 77 (2): 398–418.

Bernard, Jessie. 1982. *The future of marriage.* New Haven, CT: Yale University Press.

Berrington, Ann, and Ian Diamond. 2000. Marriage or cohabitation: A competing risks analysis of first-partnership formation among the 1958 British birth cohort. *Journal of the Royal Statistical Society, A* 163 (2): 127–51.

Billy, John O. G., Nancy Landale, William R. Grady, and Denise M. Zimmerle. 1988. Effects of sexual activity on adolescent social and psychological development. *Social Psychology Quarterly* 51 (3): 190–212.

Binstock, Georgina. 2001. The transition to marriage and separation from cohabitation during young adulthood. PhD diss., The University of Michigan.

Binstock, Georgina, and Arland Thornton. 2003. Separations reconciliations, and living apart in marital and cohabiting unions. *Journal of Marriage and the Family* 65 (2): 432–43.

Björnsson, Björn. 1971. *The Lutheran doctrine of marriage in modern Icelandic society.* Oslo: Universifetsforlaget.

Blalock, Hubert M. Jr., ed. 1971. *Causal models in the social sciences.* Chicago: Aldine-Atherton.

Blossfeld, Hans-Peter, and Johannes Huinink. 1991. Human capital investment or norms of role transition? How women's schooling affects the process of family formation. *American Journal of Sociology* 97 (1): 143–68.

Blumberg, Grace G. 2001. The regularization of nonmarital cohabitation: Rights and responsibilities in the American welfare state. *Notre Dame Law Review* 76 (5): 1265–310.

Bollen, Kenneth A. 1989. *Structural equations with latent variables*. New York: Wiley.

Book of Common Prayer, Church of England. 1552. The second prayer-book of King Edward VI. Reprinted from a copy in the British Museum, London: Griffith, Farran, Okeden and Welsh.

Boswell, John. 1988. *The kindness of strangers: The abandonment of children in western Europe from late antiquity to the Renaissance*. New York: Pantheon Books.

Bourdieu, Pierre. 1976. Marriage strategies as strategies of social reproduction. In *Family and society: Selections from the annales economies, societies, civilisations*, ed. Robert Forster and Orest Ranum, 117–44. Baltimore: Johns Hopkins University Press.

Bowman, Cynthia G. 1996. A feminist proposal to bring back common law marriage. *Oregon Law Review* 75: 709–80.

Bowman, Henry A. 1942. *Marriage for moderns*. New York: McGraw-Hill.

Bracher, Michael, and Gigi Santow. 1998. Economic independence and union formation in Sweden. *Population Studies* 52 (3): 275–94.

Bradley, David. 1996. *Family law and political culture (Scandinavian laws in comparative perspective)*. London: Sweet and Maxwell.

Bramlett, Matthew D., and William D. Mosher. 2002. Cohabitation, marriage, divorce, and remarriage in the United States. *Vital and Health Statistics* 23 (22): 1–93. Hyattsville, MD: National Center for Health Statistics.

Bramlett, Matthew D., and William D. Mosher. 2001. First marriage dissolution, divorce, and remarriage: United States. Advance Data from *Vital and Health Statistics*, 323: 1–18. Hyattsville, MD: National Center for Health Statistics.

Brines, Julie, and Kara Joyner. 1999. The ties that bind: Principles of cohesion in cohabitation and marriage. *American Sociological Review* 64 (3): 333–55.

Brooke, Christopher N. L. 1981. Marriage and society in the central middle ages. In *Marriage and society: Studies in the social history of marriage*, ed. R. Brian Outhwaite, 17–34. London: Europa Publications Limited.

Broude, Gwen J. 1994. *Marriage, family, and relationships: A cross-cultural encyclopedia*. Santa Barbara, CA: ABC-CLIO, Inc.

Brown, Audrey, and Kathleen Kiernan. 1981. Cohabitation in Great Britain: Evidence From the general household survey. *Population Trends* 25: 4–10.

Brown, Roger L. 1981. The rise and fall of fleet marriages. In *Marriage and society: Studies in the social history of marriage*, ed. R. Brian Outhwaite, 117–36. London: Europa Publications Limited.

Brown, Susan L. 2000. Union transitions among cohabitors: The significance of relationship assessments and expectations. *Journal of Marriage and the Family* 62 (3): 833–46.

Brown, Susan L., and Alan Booth. 1996. Cohabitation versus marriage: A comparison of relationship quality. *Journal of Marriage and the Family* 58 (3): 668–78.

Browning, Don S., Bonnie J. Miller-McLemore, Pamela D. Couture, K. Brynolf Lyon, and Robert M. Franklin. 1997. *From culture wars to common ground*. Louisville, KY: Westminster John Knox Press.

Bruch, Carol S. 1981. Nonmarital cohabitation in the common law countries: A study in judicial-legislative interaction. *American Journal of Comparative Law* 29: 217–45.

Brundage, James A. 1987. *Law, sex, and Christian society in medieval Europe*. Chicago: University of Chicago Press.

———. 1993. Implied consent to intercourse. In *Consent and coercion to sex and marriage in ancient medieval societies*, ed. Angeliki E. Laiou, 245–56. Washington, DC: Dumbarton Oaks Research Library and Collection.

Buck, Nicholas, and Jacqueline Scott. 1993. She's leaving home: But why? An analysis of young people leaving the parental home. *Journal of Marriage and the Family* 55 (4): 863–74.

Bumpass, Larry L. 1990. What's happening to the family? Interactions between demographic and institutional change. *Demography* 27 (4): 483–98.

———. 1998. The changing significance of marriage in the United States. In *The changing family in comparative perspective: Asia and the United States*, ed. Karen O. Mason, Noriko O. Tsuya, and Minja K. Choe, 63–82. Honolulu: The East-West Center.

Bumpass, Larry, and Hsien-Hen Lu. 2000. Trends in cohabitation and implications for children's family contexts in the U.S. *Population Studies* 54 (1): 29–42.

Bumpass, Larry L., and James A. Sweet. 1989. National estimates of cohabitation. *Demography* 26 (4): 615–25.

———. 2001. Marriage, divorce, and intergenerational relationships. In *The well-being of children and families: Research and data needs*, ed. Arland Thornton, 295–313. Ann Arbor: University of Michigan.

Bumpass, Larry L., James A. Sweet, and Andrew Cherlin. 1991. The role of cohabitation in declining rates of marriage. *Journal of Marriage and the Family* 53 (4): 913–27.

Bumpass, Larry, James Sweet, and Teresa C. Martin. 1990. Changing patterns of remarriage. *Journal of Marriage and the Family* 52 (3): 747–56.

Burgess, Ernest W., and Paul Wallin. 1953. *Engagement and marriage*. Philadelphia: Lippincott.

Burguière, Andrè. 1976. From Malthus to Max Weber: Belated marriage and the spirit of enterprise." In *Family and society: Selections from the annales economies, societies, civilisations*, ed. Robert Forster and Orest Ranum, 237–50. Baltimore: Johns Hopkins University Press.

———. 1987. The formation of the couple. *Journal of Family History* 12 (1–3): 39–53.

Burr, Wesley R., Geoffrey Leigh, Randal Day, and Joan Constantine. 1979. Symbolic interaction and the family. In *Contemporary theories about the family*, Vol. 2, ed. Wesley R. Burr, Reuben Hill, F. Ivan Nye, and Ira Reiss, 42–111. New York: Free Press.

Buss, David M. 1994. *The evolution of desire*. New York: BasicBooks.

Buunk, Bram P., Pieternel Dijkstra, Detlef Fetchenhauer, and Douglas T. Kenrick. 2002. Age and gender differences in mate selection criteria for various involvement levels. *Personal Relationships* 9: 271–78.

Call, Vaughn R. A., and Tim B. Heaton. 1997. Religious influence on marital stability. *Journal for the Scientific Study of Religion* 36: 382–92.

Caplow, Theodore, Howard M. Bahr, and Bruce A. Chadwick. 1983. *All faithful people*. Minneapolis: University of Minnesota Press.

Cargan, Leonard, and Matthew Melko. 1982. *Singles: Myths and realities*. Beverly Hills, CA: Sage Publications.

Carmichael, Gordon A. 1984. Living together in New Zealand: Data on coresidence at marriage and on de facto unions. *New Zealand Population Review* 10: 41–53.

———. 1995. Consensual partnering in the more developed countries. *Journal of the Australian Population* 12 (1): 51–86.

———. 1996. From floating brothels to suburban semirespectability: Two centuries of nonmarital pregnancy in Australia. *Journal of Family History* 21 (3): 281–315.

Carr-Saunders, Alexander M. 1922. *The population problem: A study in human evolution*. Oxford: Clarendon Press.

Casper, Lynne M. 1992. Community variations in the rate and type of cohabitation: An evaluation of three explanations with new data. PhD diss., Pennsylvania State University.

Casper, Lynne M., and Suzanne M. Bianchi. 2002. *Continuity and change in the American family*. Thousand Oaks, CA: Sage Publications.

Casper, Lynne M., and Liana C. Sayer. 2000. Cohabitation transitions: Different attitudes and purposes, different paths. Paper Presented at the Annual Meetings of the Population Association of America, Los Angeles, March 23–25.

Castro Martin, Teresa. 2002. Consensual unions in Latin America: Persistence of a dual nuptiality system. *Journal of Comparative Family Studies* 33 (1): 35–55.

Caudill, David S. 1982. Legal recognition of unmarried cohabitation: A proposal to update and reconsider common-law marriage. *Tennessee Law Review* 49:537–75.

Chambers-Schiller, Lee V. 1984. *Liberty, a better husband, single women in America: The generations of 1780–1840*. New Haven, CT: Yale University Press.

Chaytor, Miranda. 1980. Household and kinship: Ryton in the late 16th and early 17th centuries. *History Workshop Journal* 10:25–60.

Cherlin, Andrew. 1980. Postponing marriage: The influencing of young women's work expectations. *Journal of Marriage and the Family* 42 (2): 355–65.

———. 1992. *Marriage, divorce, remarriage*. Cambridge, MA: Harvard University Press.

———. 2000. Toward a new home socioeconomics of union formation. In *Ties that bind: Perspectives on marriage and cohabitation*, ed. Linda Waite, Christine Bachrach, Michelle Hinden, Elizabeth Thomson, and Arland Thornton, 126–44. Hawthorne, NY: Aldine de Gruyter.

———. 2004. The deinstitutionalization of American marriage. *Journal of Marriage and the Family* 66 (4): 848–61.

Cherlin, Andrew J., P. Lindsay Chase-Lansdale, and Christine McRae. 1998. Effects of parental divorce on mental health throughout the life course. *American Sociological Review* 63 (2): 239–49.

Cherlin, Andrew J., Kathleen E. Kiernan, and P. Lindsay Chase-Lansdale. 1995. Parental divorce in childhood and demographic outcomes in young adulthood. *Demography* 32 (3): 299–318.

Chester, Robert. 1977. *Divorce in Europe*. Leiden, Holland: Martinus Nijoff.

Chilman, Catherine S. 1983. Coital behaviors of adolescents in the United States: A summary of research and implication for further studies. Paper presented at Annual Convention of the American Psychological Association, Anaheim, CA, August 26–30.

Clark, Homer H. Jr. 1968. *The law of domestic relations in the United States*. St. Paul, MN: West Publishing Co.

Clarkberg, Marin. 1999. The price of partnering: The role of economic well-being in young adults' first union experiences. *Social Forces* 77 (3): 945–68.

Clarkberg, Marin, Ross M. Stolzenberg, and Linda J. Waite. 1995. Attitudes, values, and entrance into cohabitation versus marital unions. *Social Forces* 74 (2): 609–32.

Clarkwest, Andrew. Forthcoming. Afro-American marital disruption since reconstruction: What's new, what's not? Dissertation in progress at Harvard University, Department of Sociology and Social Policy.

Clogg, Clifford C., Eva Petkova, and Adamantios Haritou. 1995. Statistical methods for comparing regression coefficients between models. *American Journal of Sociology* 100 (5): 1261–93.

Clogg, Clifford C., Eva Petkova, and Edward S. Shihadeh. 1992. Statistical methods for analyzing collapsibility in regression models. *Journal of Educational Statistics* 17:51–74.

Clydesdale, Timothy T. 1997. Family behaviors among early U.S. baby boomers: Exploring the effects of religion and income change, 1965–1982. *Social Forces* 76 (2): 605–35.

Coale, Ansley J., and Melvin Zelnik. 1963. *New estimates of fertility and population in the United States*. Princeton, NJ: Princeton University Press.

Coleman, David. 1992. European demographic systems of the future: Convergence or diversity. In *Human resources in Europe at the dawn of the 21st century*. Eurostat Conference, Luxembourg, 137–79. Luxembourg: Office for Official Publications of the European Communities.

Coleman, James S. 1990. *Foundations of social theory*. Cambridge, MA: Harvard University Press.

Cooksey, Elizabeth C., Frank L. Mott, and Stefanie A. Neubauer. 2002. Friendships and early relationships: Links to sexual initiation among American adolescents born to young mothers. *Perspectives on Sexual and Reproductive Health* 34 (3): 118–26.

Cooney, Teresa M., and Dennis P. Hogan. 1991. Family-building patterns of professional women: A comparison of lawyers, physicians, and postsecondary teachers. *Journal of Marriage and the Family* 51 (3): 749–58.

Crimmins, Eileen M., Richard A. Easterlin, and Yasuhiko Saito. 1991. Preference changes among American youth: Family, work, and goods aspirations, 1976–86. *Population and Development Review* 17 (1): 115–33.

Crissey, S. R. 2005. Race/ethnic differences in the marital expectations of adolescents: The role of romantic relationships. *Family Relations* 3:423–32.

Crittenden, Danielle. 1999. *What our mothers didn't tell us*. New York: Simon & Schuster.

Croog, Sydney H. 1951. Aspects of the cultural background of premarital pregnancies in Denmark. *Social Forces* 30 (2): 215–19.

———. 1952. Premarital pregnancies in Scandinavia and Finland. *American Journal of Sociology* 57 (4): 358–65.

Cunningham, Mick. 2001a. The influence of parental attitudes and behaviors on children's attitudes toward gender and household labor in early adulthood. *Journal of Marriage and the Family* 63 (1): 111–22.

———. 2001b. Parental influences on the gendered division of housework. *American Sociological Review* 66 (2): 184–203.

d'Avray, David L. 1985. The gospel of the marriage feast of Cana and marriage preaching in France. In *The Bible in the medieval world: Essays in memory of Beryl Smalley*, ed. Katherine Walsh and Diana Wood, 207–24. Oxford: Basil Blackwell.

d'Avray, David L., and M. Tausche. 1981. Marriage sermons in ad status collections of the central middle ages. In *Archives d'histoire doctrinale et littéraire du moyen age*, ed. Étienne Gilson, Gabriel Théry, M.-T. d'Alverny, and M.-D. Chenu, 71–119. Paris: Librairee Philosophique J. Vrin.

Daly, Martin, and Margo I. Wilson. 2000. The evolutionary psychology of marriage and divorce. In *Ties that bind: Perspectives on marriage and cohabitation*, ed. Linda Waite, Christine Bachrach, Michelle Hinden, Elizabeth Thomson, and Arland Thornton, 91–110. Hawthorne, NY: Aldine de Gruyter.

DaVanzo, Julie, and Frances Goldscheider. 1990. Returns to the nest in young adulthood. *Population Studies* 44 (2): 241–55.

Davies, Kathleen M. 1981. Continuity and change in literary advice on marriage. In *Marriage and society: Studies in the social history of marriage*, ed. R. Brian Outhwaite, 58–80. London: Europa Publications Limited.

Davis, Kingsley. 1985. The meaning and significance of marriage in contemporary society. In *Contemporary marriage*, ed. Kingsley Davis, 1–21. New York: Russell Sage Foundation.

Davis, Kingsley. 1984. Wives and work: The sex role revolution and its consequences. *Population and Development Review* 10 (3): 397–417.

Dawson, Deborah A., Denise J. Merry, and Jeanne C. Ridley. 1980. Fertility control in the United States before the contraceptive revolution. *Family Planning Perspectives* 12 (2): 76–87.

de Boer, Connie. 1981. The polls: Marriage—a decaying institution? *Public Opinion Quarterly* 45 (2): 265–75.

de Jongh, Eddy. 1997. Realism and seeming realism in seventeenth-century Dutch painting. In *Looking at seventeenth-century Dutch art: Realism reconsidered*, ed. Wayne E. Franits, 21–56. Cambridge: Cambridge University Press.

de Mause, Lloyd, Ed. 1974. *The history of childhood*. New York: The Psychohistory Press.

Deegan, Dorothy Y. 1951. *The stereotype of the single woman in American novels*. New York: King's Crown Press.

DeLamater, John, and Patricia MacCorquodale. 1979. *Premarital sexuality*. Madison: University of Wisconsin Press.

Demo, David H. 1992. Parent-child relations: Assessing recent changes. *Journal of Marriage and the Family* 54 (1): 104–17.

Demos, John. 1970. *A little commonwealth: Family life in Plymouth Colony.* London: Oxford University Press.

Depauw, Jacques. 1976. Illicit sexual activity and society in eighteenth-century Nantes. In *Family and society: Selections from the annales economies, societies, civilisations,* ed. Robert Forster and Orest Ranum, 145–91. Baltimore: Johns Hopkins University Press.

Diamond, Jared M. 1992. *The third chimpanzee: The evolution and future of the human animal.* New York: HarperCollins.

Dixon, Ruth. 1971. Explaining cross-cultural variations in age at marriage and proportions never marrying. *Population Studies* 25 (2): 215–33.

———. 1978. Late marriage and non-marriage as demographic responses: Are they similar? *Population Studies* 32 (3): 449–66.

Donahue, Jr., Charles J. 1976. The policy of Alexander the Third's consent theory of marriage. In *Proceedings of the fourth international congress of medieval canon law,* Vol. 5, ed. Stephan Kuttner, 251–81. Cilta Del Vaticano: Bibliolica Apostolica Volicana.

———. 1983. The canon law on the formation of marriage and social practice in the later middle ages. *Journal of Family History* 8 (2): 144–58.

Drinan, Robert F. 1969. American laws regulating the formation of the marriage contract. *Annals of the American Academy of Political and Social Science* 383: 48–51.

Duby, Georges. 1983/1981. *The knight, the lady and the priest.* Translated by Barbara Bray. New York: Pantheon Books.

Duggan, Charles. 1981. Equity and compassion in papal marriage decretals to England. In *Love and marriage in the twelfth century,* ed. Willy van Hoecke and Andries Welkenhuysen, 59–87. Leuven: Leuven University Press.

Duncan, Greg J., and Saul D. Hoffman. 1985. Economic consequences of marital instability. In *horizontal equity, uncertainty, and well-being,* ed. Martin David and Timothy Smeeding, 427–70. Chicago: University of Chicago Press.

Duncan, Otis D. 1961. A socioeconomic index for all occupations. In *Occupations and social status,* ed. Albert J. Reiss, 109–38. New York: Free Press.

———. 1965. Farm background and differential fertility. *Demography* 2:240–49.

———. 1966. Path analysis: Sociological examples. *American Journal of Sociology* 72 (1): 1–16.

———. 1975. *Introduction to structural equation models.* New York: Academic Press.

Dunifon, Rachel, and Lori Kowaleski-Jones. 2002. Who's in the house? Race differences in cohabitation, single parenthood, and child development. *Child Development* 73 (4): 1249–64.

Durkheim, Emile. 1984. *The division of labor in society.* New York: The Free Press.

Duvall, Evelyn M. 1956. *Facts of life and love for teen-agers.* New York: Association Press.

East, Patricia L. 1998. Racial and ethnic differences in girls' sexual, marital, and birth expectations. *Journal of Marriage and the Family* 60 (1): 150–62.

Easterlin, Richard A. 1980. *Birth and fortune: The impact of numbers on personal welfare.* New York: Basic Books.

Easterlin, Richard A., and Eileen M. Crimmins. 1985. *The fertility revolution: A supply-demand analysis*. Chicago: The University of Chicago Press.

Edin, Kathryn, and Maria J. Kefalas. 2005. *Promises I can keep: Why poor women put motherhood before marriage*. Berkeley, CA: University of California Press.

Edin, Kathryn, Maria J. Kefalas, and Joanna M. Reed. 2004. A peek inside the black box: What marriage means for poor unmarried parents. *Journal of Marriage and the Family* 66 (4): 1007–14.

Ehrenreich, Barbara. 1983. *The hearts of men: American dreams and the flight from commitment*. Garden City, NY: Anchor Press.

Ehrmann, Winston. 1959. *Premarital dating behavior*. New York: Henry Holt and Company.

Elder, Glen H., Jr. 1977. Family history and the life course. *Journal of Family History* 2 (4): 279–304.

———. 1998. The life course as development theory. *Child Development* 69 (1): 1–12.

Elder, Glen H., Jr., Monica K. Johnson, and Robert Crosnoe. 2003. The emergence and development of the life course. In *Handbook of the life course*, ed. Jeylan T. Mortimer and Michael J. Shanahan, 3–19. New York: Kluwer Academic/Plenum Publishers.

Eldridge, Sandra, and Kathleen Kiernan. 1985. Declining first marriage rates in England and Wales: A change in timing or rejection of marriage? *European Journal of Population* 1 (4): 327–45.

Elizabeth, Vivienne. 2000. Cohabitation, marriage, and the unruly consequences of difference. *Gender & Society* 14 (1): 87–110.

Engdahl, David E. 1967. English marriage conflicts law before the time of Bracton. *The American Journal of Comparative Law* 15:109–35.

England, Paula. 2000. Marriage, the costs of children, and gender inequality. In *Ties that bind: Perspectives on marriage and cohabitation*, ed. Linda Waite, Christine Bachrach, Michelle Hindin, Elizabeth Thomson, and Arland Thornton, 320–42. Hawthorne, NY: Aldine de Gruyter.

Ermisch, John, and Marco Francesconi. 2000. Cohabitation in Great Britain: Not for long, but here to stay. *Journal of the Royal Statistical Society A* 163 (2): 153–71.

Espenshade, Thomas J. 1985. Marriage trends in America: Estimates, implications, and underlying causes. *Population and Development Review* 11 (2): 193–245.

Estin, Ann L. 2001. Ordinary cohabitation. *Notre Dame Law Review* 76 (5): 1381–408.

Fass, Paula S. 1977. *The damned and the beautiful: American youth in the 1920's*. New York: Oxford University Press.

Fawcett, Matthew. 1990. Taking the middle path: Recent Swedish legislation grants: Minimal property rights to unmarried cohabitants. *Family Law Quarterly* 24 (2): 179–202.

Feld, Scott L., Katherine B. Rosier, and Amy Manning. 2002. Christian right as civil right: Covenant marriage and a kinder, gentler, moral conservatism. *Review of Religious Research* 44 (2): 173–83.

Fishbein, Martin, and Icek Ajzen. 1974. Attitudes toward objects as predictors of single and multiple behavioral criteria. *Psychological Review* 81:59–74.

———. 1975. *Beliefs, attitude, intention, and behavior: An introduction to theory and research*. Reading, MA: Addison-Wesley.

Fitch, Catherine A., and Steven Ruggles. 2000. Historical trends in marriage formation, United States. In *Ties that bind: Perspectives on marriage and cohabitation*, ed. Linda Waite, Christine Bachrach, Michelle Hindin, Elizabeth Thomson, and Arland Thornton, 58–88. Hawthorne, NY: Aldine de Gruyter.

Flandrin, Jean-Louis. 1980. Repression and change in the sexual life of young people in medieval and early modern times. In *Family and sexuality in French history*, ed. Robert Wheaton and Tamara K. Hareven, 27–48. Philadelphia: University of Pennsylvania.

Flexner, Eleanor. 1975. *Century of struggle: The woman's rights movement in the United States*. Cambridge, MA: Harvard University Press.

Forrest, Jacqueline D., and Susheela Singh. 1990. The sexual and reproductive behavior of American women, 1982–1988. *Family Planning Perspectives* 22 (5): 206–14.

Forste, Renata, and Koray Tanfer. 1996. Sexual exclusivity among dating, cohabiting, and married women. *Journal of Marriage and the Family* 58 (1): 33–47.

Fossett, Mark A., and K. Jill Kiecolt. 1993. Mate availability and family structure among African Americans in U.S. metropolitan areas. *Journal of Marriage and the Family* 55 (2): 288–302.

Foster, Henry H., Jr. 1969. Marriage: A "basic civil right of man." *Fordham Law Review* 37:51–80.

Foyster, Elizabeth. 2001. Parenting was for life, not just for childhood: The roles of parents in the married lives of their children in early modern England. *History* 86:313–27.

Frank, Rainer. 1981. The status of cohabitation in the legal systems of west Germany and other west European countries. *American Journal of Comparative Law* 29:217–45.

Franklin, Benjamin. 1961. Observations concerning the increase of mankind. In *The papers of Benjamin Franklin*, ed. Leonard W. Labaree and Whitfield J. Bell, Jr., 225–34. New Haven, CT: Yale University Press.

Franklin, R. D., and Herman H. Remmers. 1961. Youth's attitudes toward courtship and marriage. *Report of poll of the Purdue opinion panel* 20 (2): 1–9, 1a–16a. West Lafayette, IN: Purdue University.

Freed, Doris J., and Henry H. Foster. 1980. Divorce in the fifty states: An overview as of August 1, 1980. *The Family Law Reporter* 6 (42): 4043–66.

Freedman, Deborah S., and Arland Thornton. 1979. The long-term impact of pregnancy at marriage on the family's economic circumstances. *Family Planning Perspectives* 41 (1): 6–20.

———. 1990. The consumption aspirations of adolescents: Determinants and implications. *Youth and Society* 21 (3): 259–81.

Freedman, Deborah, Arland Thornton, Donald Camburn, Duane Alwin, and Linda Young-DeMarco. 1988. The life history calendar: A technique for collecting retrospective data. In *Sociological methodology*, Vol. 18, ed. Clifford C. Clogg, 37–68. San Francisco: Jossey-Bass.

Freedman, Ronald, Pascal K. Whelpton, and Arthur A. Campbell. 1959. *Family planning, sterility, and population growth*. New York: McGraw-Hill.

Furman, Wyndol, Bradford B. Brown, and Candice Feiring, Eds. 1999. *The development of romantic relations in adolescence*. Cambridge, NY: Cambridge University Press.

Furstenberg, Frank F., Jr., S. Philip Morgan, Kristin A. Moore, and James L. Peterson. 1987. Race differences in the timing of adolescent intercourse. *American Sociological Review* 52 (4): 511–18.

Gaughan, Monica. 2002. The substitution hypothesis: The impact of premarital liasons and human capital on marital timing. *Journal of Marriage and the Family* 64 (2): 407–19.

Gecas, Viktor, and Monica A. Seff. 1990. Families and adolescents: A review of the 1980's. *Journal of Marriage and the Family* 52 (4): 941–58.

Gies, Frances, and Joseph Gies. 1987. *Marriage and the family in the middle ages*. New York: Harper & Row.

Gillis, John R. 1974. *Youth and history: Tradition and change in European age relations, 1770–present*. New York: Academic Press.

———. 1985. *For better, for worse: British marriages, 1600 to the present*. New York: Oxford University Press.

Glendon, Mary A. 1976. Marriage and the state: The withering away of marriage. *Virginia Law Review* 62 (4): 663–720.

———. 1977. *State, law and family: Family law in transition in the United States and western Europe*. Amsterdam: North-Holland Publishing Company.

Glenn, Norval D. 1987. Social trends in the United States: Evidence from sample surveys. *Public Opinion Quarterly* 51:S109–S126.

———. 1996. Values, attitudes, and the state of American marriage. In *Promises to keep: Decline and renewal of marriage in America*, ed. David Popenoe, Jean B. Elshtain, and David Blankenhorn, 15–33. Lanham, MD: Rowman and Littlefield Publishers.

———. 1997. Closed hearts, closed minds: The textbook story of marriage. A report to the nation from the Council on Families. New York: Institute for American Values, September 17.

Glenn, Norval D., and Elizabeth Marquardt. 2001. Hooking up, hanging out, and hoping for Mr. Right: College women on dating and mating today. An Institute for American Values Report to the Independent Women's Forum. New York: Institute for American Values, July 26.

Goffman, Erving. 1959. *The presentation of self in everyday life*. New York: Doubleday.

Goldin, Claudia. 1990. *Understanding the gender gap: An economic history of American women*. New York: Oxford University Press.

Goldin, Claudia, and Lawrence F. Katz. 2000. Career and marriage in the age of the pill. *American Economic Review* 90 (2): 461–65.

Goldscheider, Frances K., Arland Thornton, and Linda Young-DeMarco. 1993. A portrait of the nest-leaving process in early adulthood. *Demography* 30 (4): 683–99.

Goldscheider, Frances K., and Julie DaVanzo. 1985. Living arrangements and the transition to adulthood. *Demography* 22 (4): 545–63.

Goldscheider, Frances K., and Calvin Goldscheider. 1993. *Leaving home before marriage: Ethnicity, familism, and generational relationships*. Madison: University of Wisconsin Press.

———. 1994. Leaving and returning home in 20th century America. *Population Bulletin* 48 (4): 1–35.

Goldscheider, Frances K., and Linda J. Waite. 1986. Sex differences in the entry into marriage. *American Journal of Sociology* 92 (1): 91–109.

———. 1991. *New families, no families? The transformation of the American home.* Berkeley: University of California Press.

Goldstein, Joshua R., and Catherine T. Kenney. 2001. Marriage delayed or marriage forgone? New cohort forecasts of first marriage for U.S. women. *American Sociological Review* 66 (4): 506–19.

Goode, William J. 1960. A theory of role strain. *American Sociological Review* 25 (4): 483–96.

Goody, Jack. 1983. *The development of the family and marriage in Europe.* Cambridge, England: Cambridge University Press.

Gottlieb, Beatrice. 1980. The meaning of clandestine marriage. In *Family and sexuality in French history,* ed. Robert Wheaton and Tamara K. Hareven, 49–83. Philadelphia: University of Pennsylvania Press.

Graefe, Deborah R., and Daniel T. Lichter. 2002. Marriage among unwed mothers: Whites, Blacks, and Hispanics compared. *Perspectives on Sexual and Reproductive Health* 34 (6): 286–93.

Greeley, Andrew M. 1972. *Unsecular man: The persistence of religion.* New York: Schocken Books.

Greeley, Andrew M., William C. McCready, and Kathleen McCourt. 1976. *Catholic schools in a declining Church.* Kansas City, MO: Sheed and Ward.

Greven, Philip J., Jr. 1970. *Four generations.* Ithaca, NY: Cornell University Press.

Gryn, Thomas A., Frank L. Mott, and Diane Burchette-Patel. 2000. Relationship trajectories for a contemporary cohort of men in early middle age: Evidence from the NLSY79. Paper presented at the Annual Meetings of the Population Association of America, New York, March 23–25.

Gutmann, Myron P., Sara M. Pullum-Piñón, and Thomas W. Pullum. 2002. Three eras of young adult home leaving in twentieth-century America." *Journal of Social History* 35 (3): 533–76.

Gwartney-Gibbs, Patricia A. 1986. Institutionalization of premarital cohabitation. *Journal of Marriage and the Family* 48 (2): 423–34.

Hadden, Jeffrey K. 1983. Televangelism and the mobilization of a new Christian right family policy. In *Families and religions: Conflict and change in modern society,* ed. William V. D'Antonio and Joan Aldous, 247–66. Beverly Hills, CA: Sage Publications.

Haigh, Christopher. 1975. *Reformation and resistance in Tudor Lancashire, London.* London: Cambridge University Press.

Haines, Michael R. 1996. Long-term marriage patterns in the United States from colonial times to the present. *The History of the Family* 1 (1): 15–39.

Hajnal, John. 1965. European marriage patterns in perspective. In *Population in history,* ed. David V. Glass and David E. C. Eversley, 101–43. Chicago: Aldine.

———. 1982. Two kinds of preindustrial household formation system. *Population and Development Review* 8 (3): 449–94.

Hanawalt, Barbara A. 1986. *The ties that bound: Peasant families in medieval England.* New York: Oxford University Press.

———. 1993. *Growing up in medieval London: The experience of childhood in history.* New York: Oxford University Press.

Hanning, Robert W. 1991. Love and power in the twelfth century, with special reference to Chrétién De Troyes and Marie De France. In *The olde daunce: Love, friendship, sex, and marriage in the medieval world,* ed. Robert R. Edwards and Stephen Spector, 87–103. Albany: State University of New York Press.

Hargrove, Barbara 1983. Family in the White American Protestant experience. In *Families and religions: Conflict and change in modern society,* ed. William V. D'Antonio and Joan Aldous, 113–40. Beverly Hills, CA: Sage.

Hart, Harold H. 1972. *Marriage: For and against.* New York: Hart.

Haskell, Ann S. 1973. The Paston women on marriage in fifteenth-century England. *Viator: Medieval and Renaissance Studies* 4:459–71.

Hauser, Robert M. 1993. Trends in college entry among Whites, Blacks, and Hispanics. In *Studies of supply and demand in higher education,* ed. C. Clotfelter and M. Rothchild, 61–104. Chicago: University of Chicago Press.

Hauser, Robert M., Shu-Ling Tsai, and William H. Sewell. 1983. A model of stratification with response error in social and psychological variables. *Sociology of Education* 56 (1): 20–46.

Hauser, Robert M., and John R. Warren. 1997. Socioeconomic indexes for occupations: A review, update, and critique. In *Sociological methodology,* ed. Adrian E. Raftery, 177–298. Washington, DC: American Sociological Association.

Hayes, Cheryl D., Ed. 1987. Risking the future: Adolescent sexuality, pregnancy, and childbearing, Vol. 1. Washington, DC: National Academy Press.

Heiss, Jerold S. 1960. Variations in courtship progress among high school students. *Marriage and Family Living* 22 (2): 165–70.

Helmholz, Richard H. 1974. *Marriage litigation in medieval England.* London: Cambridge University Press.

Herlihy, David. 1985. *Medieval households.* Cambridge, MA: Harvard University Press.

Heuveline, P., and J. M. Timberlake. 2004. The role of cohabitation in family formation: The United States in comparative perspective. Journal of Marriage and Family 66:1214–30.

Hill, Daniel H., William G. Axinn, and Arland Thornton. 1993. Competing hazards with correlated unmeasured risk factors. *Sociological Methodology* 23: 245–77.

Himes, Norman E. 1970. *Medical history of contraception.* New York: Schocken Books.

Hochschild, Arlie. 1989. *The second shift: Working parents and the revolution at home.* New York: Viking.

Hofferth, Sandra L., and John Iceland. 1998. Social capital in rural and urban communities. *Rural Sociology* 63 (4): 574–98.

Hofferth, Sandra L., and Cheryl D. Hayes, eds. 1987. *Risking the future: Adolescent sexuality, pregnancy, and childbearing.* Washington, DC: National Academy Press.

Hoffman, Saul D. 1998. Teenage childbearing is not so bad after all ... or is it? A review of the new literature. *Family Planning Perspectives* 30 (5): 236–40.

Hogan, Dennis P. 1981. *Transitions and social change: The early lives of American men.* New York: Academic Press.

Hole, Judith, and Ellen Levine. 1971. *Rebirth of feminism.* New York: Quadrangle/The New York Times Book Company.

———. 1984. The first feminists. In *Women: A feminist perspective*, 3rd ed., ed. Jo Freeman, 543–56. Palo Alto, CA: Mayfield Publishing.

Hollingshead, August B. 1949. *Elmtown's youth: The impact of social classes on adolescents.* New York: Wiley.

Hout, Michael, and Andrew M. Greeley. 1987. Church attendance in the United States. *American Sociological Review* 52 (3): 325–45.

Howard, George E. 1904. *A history of matrimonial institutions.* Chicago: University of Chicago Press.

Howell, Martha C. 1998. *The marriage exchange: Property, social place, and gender in cities of the low countries, 1300–1500.* Chicago: The University of Chicago Press.

Hrdy, Sarah B. 1999. *Mother nature: A history of mothers, infants, and natural selection.* New York: Pantheon Books.

Hufton, Olwen. 1995. *The prospect before her: A history of women in western Europe, vol. one, 1500–1800.* London: HarperCollins.

Hunter, James D. 1991. *Culture wars: The struggle to define America.* United States: BasicBooks.

Hurlock, Elizabeth B. 1968. *Developmental psychology.* New York: McGraw-Hill.

Hurtado, S., K. K. Inkelas, C. Briggs, and B. S. Rhee. 1997. Differences in college access and choice among racial/ethnic groups: Identifying continuing barriers. *Research in Higher Education* 38:43–75.

Ihara, Toni, and Ralph Warner. 1978. *The living together kit.* Berkeley, CA: Nolo Press.

Ihara, Toni, Ralph Warner, and Frederick Hertz. 1999. *The living together kit: A legal guide for unmarried couples.* Berkeley, CA: Nolo Press.

Inazu, Judith K., and Greer L. Fox. 1980. Maternal influence on the sexual behavior of teenage daughters. *Journal of Family Issues* 1 (1): 81–102.

Ingram, Martin. 1981. Spousal litigation in the English ecclesiastical courts, C1350–C1640. In *Marriage and society: Studies in the social history of marriage*, ed. R. Brian Outhwaite, 35–57. London: Europa Publications Limited.

———.1985. The reform of popular culture? Sex and marriage in early modern England. In *Popular culture in seventeenth-century England*, ed. Barry Reay, 129–65. London & Sydney: Croom Helm.

Jacobson, Paul H. 1959. *American marriage and divorce.* New York: Rinehart.

Jamieson, Lynn, Michael Anderson, David McCrone, Frank Bechhofer, Robert Stewart, and Yaojun Li. 2002. Cohabitation and commitment: Partnership plans of young men and women. *The Sociological Review* 50 (3): 356–77.

Jasinski, J. L. 2000. Beyond high school: An examination of hispanic educational attainment. *Social Science Quarterly* 81:276–90.

Jayakody, Rukmalie, Arland Thornton, and William G. Axinn. Forthcoming. Summary and conclusion. In International family change: Ideational perspectives, ed. Rukmalie Jayakody, Arland Thornton, and William G. Axinn. Mahwah, NJ: Lawrence Erlbaum Associates.

Jeaffreson, John C. 1872. *Brides and bridals*. London: Hurst and Blackett.

Jessor, Richard, Frances Costa, Shirley L. Jessor, and John E. Donovan. 1983. Time of first intercourse: A prospective study. *Journal of Personality and Social Psychology* 44 (3): 608–26.

Jessor, Shirley L., and Richard Jessor. 1975. Transition from virginity to non-virginity among youth: A social-psychological study over time. *Developmental Psychology* 11 (4): 473–84.

Jöreskog, Karl G., and Dag Sörbom. 1979. *Advances in factor analysis and structural equation models*, Ed. Jay Magidson. Cambridge, MA: Abt Books.

Kandoian, Ellen. 1987. Cohabitation, common law marriage, and the possibility of a shared moral life. *The Georgetown Law Journal* 75 (6): 1829–73.

Kasarda, John D., John O. Billy, and Kirsten West. 1986. *Status enhancements and fertility*. New York: Academic Press.

Kay, Herma H., and Carol Amyx. 1977. Marvin v. Marvin: Preserving the options. *California Law Review* 65:937–77.

Kelly, Henry A. 1973. Marriage in the middle ages: 2: Clandestine marriage and Chaucer's "Troilus." *Viator: Medieval and Renaissance Studies* 4:435–57.

Kenrick, Douglas T., Edward K. Sadalla, Gary Groth, and Melanie R. Trost. 1990. Evolution, traits, and the stages of human courtship: Qualifying the parental investment model. *Journal of Personality* 58 (1): 97–116.

Kertzer, David I. 1993. *Sacrificed for honor: Italian infant abandonment and the politics of reproductive control*. Boston: Beacon Press.

Kett, Joseph F. 1977. *Rites of passage*. New York: Basic Books.

Kiernan, Kathleen E. 1989. The family: Formation and fission. In *The changing population of Britain*, ed. Heather Joshi, 27–41. Cambridge, MA: Basil Blackwell.

———. 1999. European perspectives on non-marital childbearing." Paper prepared for Conference on Non-Marital Childbearing, Madison, WI, April 29–30.

———. 2000. European perspectives on union formation. In *Ties that bind: Perspectives on marriage and cohabitation*, ed. Linda Waite, Christine Bachrach, Michelle Hindin, Elizabeth Thomson, and Arland Thornton, 40–58. Hawthorne, NY: Aldine de Gruyter.

———. 2004. Redrawing the boundaries of marriage. *Journal of Marriage and the Family* 66 (4): 980–7.

Kiernan, Kathleen E., and John Hobcraft. 1997. Parental divorce during childhood: Age at first intercourse, partnership and parenthood. *Population Studies* 51 (1): 41–55.

Kim, Jae-On, and Charles W. Mueller. 1978. Factor analysis, statistical methods and practical issues. *Quantitative Applications in the Social Sciences No. 14*. Thousand Oaks, CA: Sage Publications.

Kish, Leslie. 1965. *Survey sampling*. New York: Wiley.

Kitch, Sally L. 1989. *Chaste liberation: Celibacy and female cultural status*. Urbana: University of Illinois Press.

Klassen, Albert D., Colin J. Williams, Eugene E. Levitt, Laura Rudkin-Miniot, Heather G. Miller, and Sushama Gunjal. 1989. Trends in premarital sexual behavior. In *AIDS: Sexual behavior and intravenous drug use*, ed. Charles F. Turner, Heather G. Miller, and Lincoln E. Moses, 548–67. Washington, DC: National Academy Press.

Klassen, Albert D., Colin J. Williams, and Eugene E. Levitt. 1989. *Sex and morality in the U.S.* Middletown, CT: Wesleyan University Press.

Klijzing, Erik. 1992. "Weeding in the Netherlands: First-union disruption among men and women born between 1928 and 1965. *European Sociological Review* 8 (1): 53–70.

Kline, Galena H., Scott M. Stanley, Howard J. Markman, P. Antonio Olmos-Gallo, Michelle St. Peters, Sarah W. Whitton, and Lydia M. Prado. 2004. Timing is everything: Pre-engagement cohabitation and increased risk for poor marital outcomes. *Journal of Family Psychology* 18 (2): 311–18.

Knodel, John, and Etienne van de Walle. 1979. Lessons from the past: Policy implications of historical fertility studies. *Population and Development Review* 5 (2): 217–45.

Koball, Heather. 1998. Have African American men become less committed to marriage? Explaining the twentieth century racial cross-over in men's marriage timing. *Demography* 35 (2): 251–58.

Kobrin, Frances E. 1976. The fall of household size and the rise of the primary individual in the United States. *Demography* 13 (1): 127–38.

Koegel, Otto E. 1922. *Common law marriage and its development in the United States*. Washington, DC: John Byrne and Company.

Koehler, Lyle. 1980. *A search for power: The "weaker sex" in seventeenth-century New England*. Urbana: University of Illinois Press.

Kooper, Erik. 1991. Loving the unequal equal: Medieval theologians and marital affection. In *The olde daunce: Love, friendship, sex, and marriage in the medieval world*, ed. Robert R. Edwards and Stephen Spector, 44–56. Albany: State University of New York Press.

Kravdal, Øystein. 1999. Does marriage require a stronger economic underpinning than informal cohabitation? *Population Studies* 53 (1): 63–80.

Kreider, Rose M., and Jason M. Fields. 2002. Number, timing, and duration of marriages and divorces: 1996. *US Census Bureau: Current Population Reports: Household Economic Studies*.

Kuhn, Manford H. 1955a. How mates are sorted. In *Family, marriage, and parenthood*, ed. Howard Becker and Reuben Hill, 246–75. Boston: D. C. Heath and Company.

———. 1955b. The engagement: Thinking about marriage. In *Family, marriage and parenthood*, ed. Howard Becker and Reuben Hill, 276–304. Boston: D. C. Heath and Company.

Kuijsten, Anton C. 1996. Changing family patterns in Europe: A case of divergence? *European Journal of Population* 12 (2): 115–43.

Kussmaul, Ann. 1981. *Servants in husbandry in early-modern England*. Cambridge, England: Cambridge University Press.

Labaree, Leonard W., Whitfield J. Bell, Helen C. Boatfield, and Helene H. Fineman, eds. 1961. *The papers of Benjamin Franklin*, Vol. 3, 30–31. New Haven, CT: Yale University Press.

Lampard, Richard, and Kay Peggs. 1999. Repartnering: The relevance of parenthood and gender to cohabitation and remarriage among the formerly married. *British Journal of Sociology* 50 (3): 443–65.

Landale, Nancy, and Renata Forste. 1991. Patterns of entry into cohabitation and marriage among mainland Puerto Rican women. *Demography* 28 (4): 587–607.

Landale, Nancy S., and Stewart E. Tolnay. 1991. Group differences in economic opportunity and the timing of marriage: Blacks and Whites in the rural South. *American Sociological Review* 56 (1): 33–45.

Landis, Judson T., and Mary G. Landis. 1948. *Building a successful marriage*. New York: Prentice-Hall.

Lantz, Herman R., Raymond Schmitt, Margaret Britton, and Eloise C. Snyder. 1968. Pre-industrial patterns in the colonial family in America: A content analysis of colonial magazines. *American Sociological Review* 33 (3): 413–26.

Lasch, Christopher. 1974. The suppression of clandestine marriage in England: The marriage act of 1753. *Salmagundi* 26:90–109.

Laslett, Peter. 1978. *Family life and illicit love in earlier generations*. Cambridge, England: Cambridge University Press.

———. 1980. Introduction: Comparing illegitimacy over time and between cultures. In *Bastardy and its comparative history*, ed. Peter Laslett, Karla Oosterveen, and Richard M. Smith, 1–64. Cambridge, MA: Harvard University Press.

———.1984. *The world we have lost: England before the industrial age*, 3rd ed. New York: Charles Scribner's Sons.

Laumann, Edward O., John H. Gagnon, Robert T. Michael, and Stuart Michaels. 1994. *The social organization of sexuality: Sexual practices in the United States*. Chicago: University of Chicago Press.

Le Masters, E. E. 1957. *Modern courtship and marriage*. New York: Macmillan.

Leclercq, Jean. 1982. The development of a topic in medieval studies in the eighties: An interdisciplinary perspective on love and marriage. In *Literary and historical perspectives on the middle ages*, ed. Patricia W. Cummins, Patrick W. Conner, and Charles W. Cornell, 20–37. Morgantown, WV: University Press.

Lee, S. 1998. Asian Americans: Diverse and growing. *Population bulletin* 53. Washington, DC: Population Reference Bureau.

Leeuwen, Marco H. D., and Ineke Maas. 2002. Partner choice and homogamy in the nineteenth century: Was there a sexual revolution in Europe?" *Journal of Social History* 36:101–23.

Lehrer, Evelyn L. 2000. "Religion as a determinant of entry into cohabitation and marriage. In *Ties that bind: Perspectives on marriage and cohabitation*, ed. Linda Waite, Christine Bachrach, Michelle Hindin, Elizabeth Thomson, and Arland Thornton, 227–52. Hawthorne, NY: Aldine de Gruyter.

———. 2002. The role of religion in union formation: An economic perspective. Paper presented at the Annual Meetings of the Population Association of America, May 9–11, Atlanta, Georgia.

Leonard, Diana. 1980. *Sex and generation: A study of courtship and weddings*. London: Tavistock Publications.

Leridon, Henri, and Catherine Villeneuve-Gokalp. 1989. The new couples: Number, characteristics and attitudes. *Population* 44 (1): 203–35.

Lesthaeghe, Ron J. 1980. On the social control of human reproduction. *Population and Development Review* 6 (4): 527–48.

———. 1983. A century of demographic and cultural change in western Europe: An exploration of underlying dimensions. *Population and Development Review* 9 (3): 411–35.

———. 1995. The second demographic transition in western countries: An interpretation. In *Gender and family change in industrialized countries*, ed. Karen O. Mason and An-Magritt Jensen, 17–62. Oxford: Clarendon Press.

———. 2000. Europe's demographic issues: Fertility, household formation and replacement migration, United Nations Expert Group Meeting on Policy Responses to Population Decline and Ageing, New York, October 16–18, UN Population Division.

Lesthaeghe, Ron J., and Lisa Neidert. 2006. The "second demographic transition" in the U.S.: Spatial patterns and correlates. PSC Research Report No. 06-592. March.

Lesthaeghe, Ron J., and Johan Surkyn. 1988. Cultural dynamics and economic theories of fertility change. *Population and Development Review* 14 (1): 1–45.

Lesthaeghe, Ron J., and Chris Wilson. 1986. Modes of production, secularization, and the pace of fertility decline in western Europe, 1870–1930. In *The decline of fertility in Europe*, ed. Ansley J. Coale and Susan C. Watkins, 261–92. Princeton, NJ: Princeton University Press.

Lewis, Susan K., and Valerie K. Oppenheimer. 2000. Educational assortative mating across marriage markets: Non-hispanic Whites in the United States. *Demography* 37 (1): 29–40.

Lewontin, Richard C. 1995. Sex, lies, and social science. *The New York Review* April 20, 24–29.

Li, Jiang H., and Roger Wojtkiewicz. 1994. Childhood family structure and entry into first marriage. *The Sociological Quarterly* 35 (2): 247–68.

Lichter, Daniel T., Robert N. Anderson, and Mark D. Hayward. 1995. Marriage markets and marital choice. *Journal of Family Issues* 16 (4): 412–31.

Lichter, Daniel T., Felicia B. LeClere, and Diane K. McLaughlin. 1991. Local marriage markets and the marital behavior of Black and White women. *American Journal of Sociology* 96 (4): 843–67.

Lichter, Daniel T., Diane K. McLaughlin, George Kephart, and David J. Landry. 1992. Race and the retreat from marriage: A shortage of marriageable men. *American Sociological Review* 57 (6): 781–99.

Lichter, Daniel T., Diane K. McLaughlin, and David C. Ribar. 2002. Economic restructuring and the retreat from marriage. *Social Science Research* 31 (2): 230–56.

Liefbroer, Aart C. 1991. The choice between a married or unmarried first union by young adults. *European Journal of Population* 7:273–98.

Liefbroer, Aart C., and Liesbeth Gerritsen. 1994. The influence of intentions and life course factors on union formation behavior of young adults. *Journal of Marriage and the Family* 56 (1): 193–203.

Liefbroer, Aart C., and Jenny de Jong Gierveld. 1993. The impact of rational considerations and perceived opinions on young adults' union formation intentions. *Journal of Family Issues* 14 (2): 213–35.

Light, Audrey, and Wayne Strayer. 2002. From Bakke to Hopwood: Does race affect college attendance and completion. *The Review of Economics and Statistics* 84 (1): 34–44.

Lloyd, Kim M., and Scott J. South. 1996. Contextual influences on young men's transition to first marriage. *Social Forces* 74 (3): 1097–119.

Longmore, Monica A., Wendy D. Manning, and Peggy C. Giordano. 2001. Preadolescent parenting strategies and teens' dating and sexual initiation: A longitudinal analysis. *Journal of Marriage and the Family* 63 (2): 322–35.

Loomis, Laura L., and Nancy S. Landale. 1994. Nonmarital cohabitation and childbearing among Black and White American women. *Journal of Marriage and the Family* 56 (4): 949–62.

Luce, Robert D. 1959. *Individual choice behavior: A theoretical analysis.* New York: Wiley.

Lundberg, Shelly, and Robert A. Pollak. 1993. Separate spheres bargaining and the marriage market. *Journal of Political Economy* 101 (6): 988–1010.

———. 1996. Bargaining and distribution in marriage. *Journal of Economic Perspectives* 10 (4): 139–58.

———. 2001. Bargaining and distribution in families. In *The well-being of children and families: Research and data needs*, ed. Arland Thornton, 314–38. Ann Arbor: University of Michigan.

Lye, Diane N., and Ingrid Waldron. 1993. Correlates of attitudes toward cohabitation, family, and gender roles. Seattle Population Research Center, Working Paper No. 93-10.

Lynch, Katherine. 2003. *Individuals, families, and communities in Europe, 1200–1800: The urban foundations of western society.* Cambridge: Cambridge University Press.

MacDonald, Maurice M., and Ronald R. Rindfuss. 1981. Earnings, relative income, and family formation. *Demography* 18 (2): 123–36.

Macfarlane, Alan. 1970. *The family life of Ralph Josselin, a seventeenth-century clergyman: An essay in historical anthropology.* Cambridge, England: Cambridge University Press.

———. 1979. *The origins of English individualism: The family, property, and social transition.* Cambridge, England: Cambridge University Press.

———. 1986. *Marriage and love in England: Modes of reproduction, 1300–1840.* Oxford: Basil Blackford.

Macklin, Eleanor D. 1978. Review of research on nonmarital cohabitation in the United States. In *Exploring intimate life styles*, ed. Bernard I. Murstein, 197–243. New York: Springer.

Mahoney, Annette, Kenneth I. Pargament, Nalini Tarakeshwar, and Aaron B. Swank. 2001. Religion in the home in the 1980s and 1990s: A meta-analytic review and conceptual analysis of links between religion, marriage, and parenting. *Journal of Family Psychology* 15 (4): 559–96.

Mandelbaum, Maurice. 1971. *History, man, and reason: A study in nineteenth-century thought.* Baltimore: The John Hopkins Press.

Manning, Wendy. 1993. Marriage and cohabitation following premarital concep-
    tion. *Journal of Marriage and the Family* 55 (4): 839–50.
———. 1995. Cohabitation, marriage and entry into motherhood. *Journal of Mar-
    riage and the Family* 57 (1): 191–200.
———. 2001. Childbearing in cohabiting unions: Racial and ethnic differences.
    Family Planning Perspectives 33 (5): 217–23.
Manning, Wendy D., and Nancy S. Landale. 1996. Racial and ethnic differences in
    the role of cohabitation in premarital childbearing. *Journal of Marriage and the
    Family* 58 (1): 63–77.
Manning, Wendy D., and Pamela J. Smock. 1995. Why marry? Race and the tran-
    sition to marriage among cohabitors. *Demography* 32 (4): 509–20.
———. 2002. First comes cohabitation and then comes marriage? A research note.
    Journal of Family Issues 23 (8): 1065–87.
———. 2003. Measuring and modeling cohabitation: New perspectives from qual-
    itative data. Paper Presented at the Annual Meeting of the Population Associ-
    ation of America in Minneapolis, MN, May 3.
Manting, Dorien. 1994. *Dynamics in marriage and cohabitation: An inter-temporal,
    life course analysis of first union formation and dissolution.* Amsterdam: Thesis
    Publishers.
Mare, Robert D. 1991. Five decades of assortative mating. *American Sociological
    Review* 56 (1): 15–32.
Mare, Robert D., and Christopher Winship. 1991. Socioeconomic change and the
    decline of marriage for Blacks and Whites. In *The urban underclass*, ed. Christo-
    pher Jencks and Paul E. Peterson, 175–202. Washington, DC: Urban Institute.
Marini, Margaret M. 1978. The transition to adulthood: Sex differences in educa-
    tional attainment and age at marriage. *American Sociological Review* 43 (4):
    483–507.
———. 1985. Determinants of the timing of adult role entry. *Social Science Re-
    search* 14: 309–50.
Marvick, Elizabeth W. 1974. Nature versus nurture: Patterns and trends in
    seventeenth-century French child-rearing. In *The history of childhood*, ed.
    Lloyd DeMause, 259–301. New York: The Psychohistory Press.
McCaa, Robert. 1994. Marriageways in Mexico and Spain, 1500–1900. *Continuity
    and Change* 9 (1): 11–43.
McFadden, Daniel. 1974. The measurement of urban travel demand. *Journal of
    Public Economics* 3 (4): 303–28.
McLanahan, Sara S., and Larry L. Bumpass. 1988. Intergenerational consequences
    of family disruption. *American Journal of Sociology* 94 (1): 130–52.
McLanahan, Sara S., and Lynne Casper. 1995. Growing diversity and inequality in
    the American family. In *State of the union: America in the 1990s*, Vol. 2, ed. Ren
    Farley, 1–45. New York: Russell Sage Foundation.
McLanahan, Sara S., and Gary Sandefur. 1994. *Growing up with a single parent.*
    Cambridge, MA: Harvard University Press.
McLoyd, V., A. M. Cauce, D. Takeuchi, and L. Wilson. 2000. Marital processes
    and parental socialization in families of color: A decade review of research.
    Journal of Marriage and the Family 62:1070–93.

McSheffrey, Shannon. 1998. "I will never have none ayenst my faders will": Consent and the making of marriage in the late medieval diocese of London. In *Women, marriage, and family in medieval Christendom*, ed. Constance M. Rousseau and Joel T. Rosenthal, 153–74. Kalamazoo: Medieval Institute Publications, Western Michigan University.

Mead, Margaret. 1949. *Male and female: A study of the sexes in a changing world*. New York: William Morrow.

Michael, Robert T., John H. Gagnon, Edward O. Laumann, and Gina Kolata, eds. 1994. *Sex in America: A definitive survey*. Boston: Little, Brown.

Miller, Brent C., and Tim B. Heaton. 1991. Age at first sexual intercourse and the timing of marriage and childbirth. *Journal of Marriage and the Family* 53 (3): 719–32.

Miller, Brent C., J. K. McCoy, and T. D. Olson. 1986. Dating age and stage as correlates of adolescent sexual attitudes and behavior. *Journal of Adolescent Research* 1:361–71.

Miller, Brent C., Maria C. Norton, Thom Curtis, E. J. Hill, Paul Schvaneveldt, and Margaret H. Young. 1997. The timing of sexual intercourse among adolescents: Family, peer, and other antecedents. *Youth and Society* 29 (1): 54–83.

Mincer, Jacob. 1974. *Schooling, experience, and earnings*. New York: National Bureau of Economic Research; distributed by Columbia University Press.

Mincer, Jacob, and Simon Polachek. 1974. Family investments in human capital: Earnings of women. *Journal of Political Economy* 82 (2): S76–S108.

Modell, John. 1983. Dating becomes the way of American youth. In *Essays on the Family and Historical Change*, ed. Leslie P. Moch and Gary D. Stark, 91–126. College Station: Texas A&M University Press.

———. 1985. Historical reflections on American marriage. In *Contemporary marriage: Comparative perspectives on a changing institution*, ed. Kingsley Davis, 181–96. New York: Russell Sage Foundation.

———. 1989. *Into one's own: From youth to adulthood in the United States 1920–1975*. Berkeley: University of California Press.

Modell, John, Frank Furstenberg, and Theodore Hershberg. 1976. Social change and transitions to adulthood in historical perspective. *Journal of Family History* 1 (1): 7–32.

Modell, John, and Tamara K. Hareven. 1973. Urbanization and the malleable household: An examination of boarding and lodging in American families. *Journal of Marriage and the Family* 35 (3): 467–79.

Moore, Kristin A. 1995. Nonmarital childbearing in the United States. In *Report to congress on out-of-wedlock chilbearing*. DHHS Publ. No. (PHS) 95-1257. Washington, DC: U.S. Government Printing office.

Moore, Kristin A., and T. M. Stief. 1991. Changes in marriage and fertility behavior. *Youth and Society* 22 (3): 362–86.

Moore, Kristin A., Brent Miller, Dana Glei, and Donna R. Morrison. 1995. *Adolescent sex, contraception, and childbearing. A review of recent research*. Washington, DC: Child Trends.

Moore, Kristin A., James L. Peterson, and Frank F. Furstenberg, Jr. 1986. Parental attitudes and the occurrence of early sexual activity. *Journal of Marriage and the Family* 48 (4): 777–82.

Morgan, Edmund S. 1966. *The puritan family: Religion and domestic relations in seventeenth-century New England*. New York: Harper & Row.

———. 1978. The puritans and sex. In *The American family in social-historical perspective*, 2nd ed. ed. Michael Gordon, 363–73. New York: St. Martin's Press.

Morgan, S. Philip 1996. Characteristic features of modern American fertility. *Fertility in the United States. Supplement to Population and Development Review* 22: 19–63.

Morgan, S. Philip, A. McDaniel, A. Miller, and S. Preston. 1993. Racial differences in household and family structure at the turn of the century. *American Journal of Sociology* 98:799–828.

Morgan, S. Philip, and Ronald R. Rindfuss. 1999. Reexamining the link of early childbearing to marriage and to subsequent fertility. *Demography* 36 (1): 59–75.

Morgan, Stephen L. 2005. *On the edge of commitment: Educational attainment and race in the United States*. Stanford, CA: Stanford University Press.

Mosher, William D., and William F. Pratt. 1990. Contraceptive use in the United States, 1973–1988. *Advance data from vital and health statistics*, No. 182. Hyattsville, MD: National Center for Health Statistics.

Mount, Ferdinand. 1982. *The subversive family: An alternative history of love & marriage*. London: Jonathan Cape Ltd.

Müller-Freienfels, Wolfram. 1987. Cohabitation and marriage law—a comparative study. *International Journal of Law and the Family* 1:259–94.

Murray, Jacqueline. 1998. Individualism and consensual marriage: Some evidence from medieval England. In *Women, marriage, and family in medieval Christendom*, ed. Constance M. Rousseau and Joel T. Rosenthal, 121–51. Kalamazoo: Medieval Institute Publications, Western Michigan University.

Musick, Kelly. 2002. Planned and unplanned childbearing among unmarried women. *Journal of Marriage and the Family* 64:915–29.

Musick, Kelly, and Larry Bumpass. 1999. How do prior experiences in the family affect transitions to adulthood. In *Transitions to adulthood in a changing economy*, ed. Alan Booth, Ann Crouter, and Michael Shanahan, 69–102. Westport, CT: Praeger Publishers.

Myers, Scott M. 2000. Moving into adulthood: Family residential mobility and first-union transitions. *Social Science Quarterly* 81 (3): 782–97.

Myrdal, Alva. 1941. *Nation and family: The Swedish experiment in democratic family and population policy*. New York: Harper and Brothers Publishers.

Nevitt, H. Rodney, Jr. 2001. Vermeer on the question of love. In *The Cambridge companion to Vermeer*, ed. Wayne E. Franits, 89–110. Cambridge, England: Cambridge University Press.

Newcomb, Theodore M. 1937. Recent changes in attitudes toward sex and marriage. *American Sociological Review* 2 (5): 659–67.

———. 1943. *Personality and social change*. New York: Dryden Press.

Nicholas, David. 1985. *The domestic life of a medieval city: Women, children, and the family in fourteenth-century Ghent*. Lincoln: University of Nebraska Press.

Niemi, Richard G., John Mueller, and Tom W. Smith. 1989. *Trends in public opinion: A compendium of survey data*. New York: Greenwood Press.

Nisbet, Robert A. 1975. *Social change and history.* New York: Oxford University Press.

Nock, Steven L. 1995. A comparison of marriages and cohabiting relationships. *Journal of Family Issues* 16 (1): 53–76.

———. 1998. *Marriage in men's lives.* New York: Oxford University Press.

Nock, Steven L., Laura Sanchez, Julia C. Wilson, and James D. Wright. Forthcoming. Covenant marriage turns five years old. *Michigan Journal of Gender and Law.*

Noonan, John T., Jr. 1967. Marital affection in the canonists. In *Studia Gratiana.* Post octava decreti saecularia collectanea historiae ivris canonici XII. Curantibus. Collectanea Stephan Kuttner II, 497–509. Institutum Gratianum, Bononiae MCMLXVII.

———. 1972. *Power to dissolve: Lawyers and marriages in the courts of the Roman Curia.* Cambridge: Belknap Press.

———. 1973. Marriage in the middle ages: 1: Power to choose. n *Viator: Medieval and Renaissance Studies* 4:419–34. Berkeley: University of California.

Norton, Mary B. 1980. *Liberty's daughters and the revolutionary experience of American women, 1750–1800.* Boston: Little, Brown.

Nunnally, Jum C. 1967. *Psychometric theory.* New York: McGraw-Hill.

O'Donnell, William J., and David A. Jones. 1982. *The law of marriage and marital alternatives.* Lexington, MA: Lexington Books.

Ogburn, William F., and Clark Tibbitts. 1933. "The family and its functions. In *Recent social trends in the United States,* Vol. 1, Report 1, The President's Research Committee of Social Trends, 661–708. New York: Mcgraw Hill.

O'Hara, Diana. 1991. "Ruled by my friends": Aspects of marriage in the diocese of Canterbury, C. 1540–1570. *Continuity and Change* 6 (1): 9–41.

Oldham, J. Thomas. 2001. Lessons from Jerry Hall v. Mick Jagger regarding U.S. regulation of heterosexual cohabitants or, can't get no satisfaction. *Notre Dame Law Review* 76 (5): 1409–34.

Olsen, Glenn W. 2001. Marriage in barbarian kingdom and Christian court: Fifth through eleventh centuries. In *Christian marriage: A historical study,* ed. Glenn W. Olsen, 146–212. New York: Crossroad.

Oppenheimer, Valerie K. 1970. The female labor force in the United States. Population Monograph Series, No. 5, Institute of International Studies, University of California-Berkeley.

———. 1988. A theory of marriage timing. *American Journal of Sociology* 94 (3): 563–91.

———. 1994. Women's rising employment and the future of the family in industrial societies. *Population and Development Review* 20 (2): 293–342.

———. 1997. Women's employment and the gains to marriage: The specialization and training model of marriage. *Annual Review of Sociology* 23:431–53.

———. 2000. The continuing importance of men's economic position in marriage formation. In *Ties that bind: Perspectives on marriage and cohabitation,* ed. Linda Waite, Christine Bachrach, Michelle Hindin, Elizabeth Thomson, and Arland Thornton, 283–301. Hawthorne, NY: Aldine de Gruyter.

———. 2003. Cohabiting and marriage during young men's career-development process. *Demography* 40 (1): 127–49.

Oppenheimer, Valerie K., Hans P. Blossfeld, and Achim Wackerow. 1995. United States of America. In *The new role of women*, ed. Hans P. Blossfeld, 150–73. Boulder, CO: Westview Press.

Oppenheimer, Valerie K., Matthijs Kalmijn, and Nelson Lim. 1997. Men's career development and marriage timing during a period of rising inequality. *Demography* 34 (3): 311–30.

Oppenheimer, Valerie K., and Vivian Lew. 1995. American marriage formation in the 1980s: How important was women's economic independence? In *Gender and family change in industrialized countries*, ed. Karen O. Mason and An-Magritt Jensen, 105–38. Oxford: Clarendon Press.

Oropesa, R. S. 1996. Normative beliefs about marriage and cohabitation: A comparison of non-latino Whites, Mexican Americans, and Puerto Ricans. *Journal of Marriage and the Family* 58 (1): 49–62.

Otto, Luther B. 1979. Antecedents and consequences of marital timing. In *Contemporary theories about the family*, Vol. I, ed. Wesley R. Burr, Reuben Hill, Francis I. Nye, and Ira Reiss, 101–34. New York: The Free Press.

Outhwaite, R. Brian. 1981. Introduction: Problems and perspectives in the history of marriage. In *Marriage and society: Studies in the social history of marriage*, ed. R. Brian Outhwaite, 1–16. London: Europa Publications Limited.

———. 1995. *Clandestine marriage in England, 1500–1850*. Rio Grande, OH: Hambledon Press.

Ozment, Steven E. 1983. *When fathers ruled: Family life in reformation Europe*. Cambridge, MA: Harvard University Press.

———. 2001. *Ancestors: The loving family in old Europe*. Cambridge, MA: Harvard University Press.

Pagnini, Deanna L., and Ron R. Rindfuss. 1993. The divorce of marriage and childbearing: Changing attitudes and behavior in the United States. *Population and Development Review* 19 (2): 331–47.

Parnell, Allan M., Gray Swicegood, and Gillian Stevens. 1994. Nonmarital pregnancies and marriage in the United States. *Social Forces* 73 (1): 263–87.

Parr, Gavin M. 1999. What is a "meretricious relationship"?: An analysis of cohabitant property rights under Connell v. Francisco. *Washington Law Review* 74:1243–73.

Parsons, Talcott, and Robert F. Bales. 1955. *Family, socialization and interaction process*. Glencoe, IL: Free Press.

Pedersen, Frederik. 1998. "Maritalis affectio": Marital affection and property in fourteenth-century York cause papers. In *Women, marriage, and family in medieval Christendom*, ed. Constance M. Rousseau and Joel T. Rosenthal, 175–209. Kalamazoo: Medieval Institute Publications, Western Michigan University.

Peplau, Letitia A., Zick Rubin, and Charles T. Hill. 1977. Sexual intimacy in dating relationships. *Journal of Social Issues* 33 (2): 86–109.

Perkin, Joan. 1989. *Women and marriage in nineteenth-century England*. London: Routledge.

Perna, L. W. 2000. Beyond high school: An examination of Hispanic educational attainment. *Social Science Quarterly* 81:276–90.

Peters, Elizabeth. 1986. Factors affecting remarriage. In *Midlife women at work*, ed. Lois B. Shaw, 99–114. Lexington, MA: D.C. Heath and Company.

Petersen, Larry R., and Gregory V. Donnenwerth. 1997. Secularization and the influence of religion on beliefs about premarital sex. *Social Forces* 75 (3): 1071–89.

Peterson, Richard R. 1996. A re-evaluation of the economic consequences of divorce. *American Sociological Review* 61 (3): 528–36.

Phillips, Roderick. 1988. *Putting asunder: A history of divorce in Western society.* Cambridge, England: Cambridge University Press.

Pierre, Teresa O. 2001. Marriage, body, and sacrament in the age of Hugh of St. Victor. In *Christian marriage: A historical study*, ed. Glenn W. Olsen, 213–68. New York: Crossroad.

Pinchbeck, Ivy. 1969. *Women workers and the industrial revolution, 1750–1850.* London: Virago Press Limited.

Plotnick, Robert. 1992. The effects of attitudes on teenage premarital pregnancy and its resolution. *American Sociological Review* 57 (6): 800–11.

Pollak, Robert A. 1994. For better or worse: The roles of power in models of distribution within marriage. *American Economic Review* 84 (2): 148–52.

———. 2000. Theorizing marriage. In *Ties that bind: Perspectives on marriage and cohabitation*, ed. Linda J. Waite, Christine Bachrach, Michelle Hinden, Elizabeth Thomson, and Arland Thornton, 111–25. Hawthorne, NY: Aldine de Gruyter.

Pollock, Frederick, and Frederick W. Maitland. 1968. The history of English law before the time of Edward I. Cambridge, England: Cambridge University Press.

Pollock, Linda A. 1985. *Forgotten children: Parent-child relations from 1500 to 1900.* Cambridge, England: Cambridge University Press.

Portes, A. and K. L. Wilson. 1976. Black-White differences in educational attainment. *American Sociological Review* 41:414–31.

Pratt, William. 1965. A study of marriage involving premarital pregnancies. PhD diss., The University of Michigan.

Preston, Samuel H. 1986. Changing values and falling birth rates. In *Population and development review*, Supplement: Below-replacement fertility in industrial societies: Causes, consequences, policies. 12:176–96.

———. 1987. The social sciences and the population problem. *Sociological Forum* 2 (4): 619–44.

Preston, Samuel H., and John McDonald. 1979. The incidence of divorce within cohorts of American marriages contracted since the Civil War. *Demography* 16 (1): 1–25.

Preston, Samuel H., and Alan T. Richards. 1975. The influence of women's work opportunities on marriage rates. *Demography* 12 (2): 209–22.

Prinz, Christopher. 1995. *Cohabiting, married, or single.* Aldershot, England: Avebury.

Qian, Z., D. T. Lichter, and L. Mellott. 2005. Out-of-wedlock childbearing, marital prospects and mate selection. *Social Forces* 84:473–91.

Qian, Zhenchao, and Samuel Preston. 1993. Changes in American marriage: 1972–1987. *American Sociological Review* 58 (4): 482–95.

Raley, R. K. 1996. A shortage of marriageable men. A note on the role of cohabitation in BlackWhite differences in marriage rates. *American Sociological Review* 61:973–83.

———. 2000. Recent trends and differentials in marriage and cohabitation: The United States. In *Ties that bind: Perspectives on marriage and cohabitation*, ed. Linda Waite, Christine Bachrach, Michelle Hinden, Elizabeth Thomson, and Arland Thornton, 19–39. Hawthorne, NY: Aldine de Gruyter.

———. 2001. Increasing fertility in cohabiting unions: Evidence for the second demographic transition in the United States? *Demography* 38 (1): 59–66.

Ratcliffe, Barrie M. 1996. Popular classes and cohabitation in mid-nineteenth-century Paris. *Journal of Family History* 21 (3): 316–50.

Regan, Milton C., Jr. 1999. Marriage at the millennium. *Family Law Quarterly* 33 (3): 647–61.

———. 2001. Calibrated commitment: The legal treatment of marriage and cohabitation. *Notre Dame Law Review* 76 (5): 1435–66.

Reiss, Ira L. 1960. *Premarital sexual standards in America*. New York: The Free Press.

———. 1964. The scaling of premarital sexual permissiveness. *Journal of Marriage and the Family* 26 (2): 188–98.

———. 1967. *The social context of premarital sexual permissiveness*. New York: Holt, Reinhart and Winston.

Reiss, Ira L., and Brent C. Miller. 1979. Heterosexual permissiveness: A theoretical analysis. In *Contemporary theories about the family*, ed. Wesley R. Burr, Reuben Hill, Francis I. Nye, and Ira L. Reiss, 57–100. New York: The Free Press.

Rendall, Jane. 1985. *The origins of modern feminism: Women in Britain, France and the United States 1780–1860*. London: Macmillan Publishing.

Reppy, William A., Jr. 1984. Property and support rights of unmarried cohabitants: A proposal for creating a new legal status. *Louisiana Law Review* 44:1677–21.

Rheinstein, Max. 1972. *Marriage stability, divorce, and the law*. Chicago: University of Chicago Press.

Riley, Glenda. 1991. *Divorce: An American tradition*. New York: Oxford University Press.

Rindfuss, Ron R. 1991. The young adult years: Diversity, structural change, and fertility. *Demography* 28 (4): 493–512.

Rindfuss, Ron R., S. Philip Morgan, and C. Gray Swicegood. 1988. *First births in America: Changes in the timing of parenthood*. Berkeley: University of California Press.

Rindfuss, Ron R., C. Gary Swicegood, and Rachel A. Rosenfeld. 1987. Disorder in the life course: How common is it and does it matter? *American Sociological Review* 52 (6): 785–801.

Rindfuss, Ronald R., and Audrey VandenHeuvel. 1990. Cohabitation: A precursor to marriage or an alternative to being single? *Population Development Review* 16 (4): 703–26.

Rivkin, S. G. 1995. Black-White differences in schooling and employment. *Journal of Human Resources* 30:826–52.

Roberts-Jones, Philippe, and Francoise Roberts-Jones. 1997. *Pieter Bruegel*. Paris: Harry N. Adams, Publishers.

Rodgers, Willard L., and Arland Thornton. 1985. Changing patterns of first marriage in the United States. *Demography* 22 (2): 265–79.

Roof, Wade C. 1999. *Spiritual marketplace: Baby boomers and the remaking of American religion.* Princeton, NJ: Princeton University Press.

Roof, Wade C., and William McKinney. 1987. *American mainline religion.* New Brunswick, NJ: Rutgers University Press.

Ross, Catherine E. 1995. Reconceptualizing marital status as a continuum of social attachment. *Journal of Marriage and the Family* 57 (1): 129–40.

Rossi, Alice S., and Peter H. Rossi. 1990. *Of human bonding.* New York: Walter de Gruyter.

Rothman, Ellen K. 1984. *Hands and hearts: A history of courtship in America.* New York: Basic Books.

Ruggles, Steven. 1987. *Prolonged connections: The rise of the extended family in nineteenth-century England and America.* Madison: University of Wisconsin Press.

————. 1994. The transformation of American family structure. *The American Historical Review* 99 (1): 103–28.

Ruitenbeek, Hendrik M., ed. 1966. *Psychoanalysis and male sexuality.* New Haven, CT: College & University Press.

Salts, Connie J., Melisa D. Seismore, Byron W. Lindholm, and Thomas A. Smith. 1994. Attitudes towards marriage and premarital sexual activity of college freshmen. *Adolescence* 29 (116): 775–79.

Sanchez, Laura, Wendy Manning, and Pamela Smock. 1998. Sex-specialized or collaborative mate selection? *Social Science Research* 27:280–304.

Sanderson, Warren C. 1979. Qualitative aspects of marriage, fertility and family limitation in nineteenth century America: Another application of the Coale specifications. *Demography* 16 (3): 339–58.

Santelli, John S., Laura D. Lindberg, Joyce Abma, Clea S. McNeely, and Michael Resnick. 2000. Adolescent sexual behavior: Estimates and trends from four nationally representative surveys. *Family Planning Perspectives* 32 (4): 156–65.

Sarsby, Jacqueline. 1983. *Romantic love and society.* New York: Penguin Books.

Sassler, Sharon. 2004. The process of entering into cohabiting unions. *Journal of Marriage and the Family* 66 (2): 491–505.

Sassler, Sharon, and Frances K. Goldscheider. 2004. Revisiting Jane Austen's theory of marriage timing: Changes in union formation among American men in the late 20th century. *Journal of Family Issues* 25 (2): 139–66.

Sassler, Sharon, and Robert Schoen. 1999. The effect of attitudes and economic activity on marriage. *Journal of Marriage and the Family* 61 (1): 147–59.

Schama, Simon. 1997. *The embarrassment of riches: An interpretation of Dutch culture in the Golden Age.* New York: Vintage Books.

Schneider, Carl E. 1985. Moral discourse and the transformation of American family law. *Michigan Law Review* 83 (8): 1803–79.

Schochet, Gordon J. 1975. *Patriarchalism in political thought.* New York: Basic Books.

Schoen, Robert, and Dawn Owens. 1992. A further look at first unions and first marriages. In *The changing American family. Sociological and demographic perspective,* ed. Scott J. South and Stewart E. Tolnay, 109–17. Boulder, CO: Westview Press.

Schofield, Michael G. 1965. *The sexual behaviour of young people*. Boston: Little, Brown.

Schofield, Roger S. 1985. Through a glass darkly. *Journal of Interdisciplinary History* XV (4): 571–93.

Schulenberg, John, Jerald G. Bachman, Lloyd D. Johnston, and Patrick M. O'Malley. 1995. American adolescents' views on family and work: Historical trends from 1976–1992. In *Psychological responses to social change*, ed. Peter Noack, Manfred Hofer, and James Youniss, 37–64. Berlin: Walter de Gruyter.

Seccombe, Wally. 1992. *A millennium of family change: Feudalism to capitalism in northwestern Europe*. London: Verso.

Seeman, Erik R. 1999. "It Is Better to Marry Than to Burn": Anglo-American attitudes toward celibacy, 1600–1800. *Journal of Family History* 24 (4): 397–419.

Sewell, William H., Robert M. Hauser, Duane F. Alwin, Dorothy M. Ellegaard, Janet A. Fisher, Kenneth G. Lutterman, and Vimal P. Shah. 1975. *Education, occupation, and earnings: Achievement in the early career*. New York: Academic Press.

Sewell, William H., Archibald O. Haller, and Alejandro Portes. 1969. The educational and early occupational attainment process. *American Sociological Review* 34 (1): 82–92.

Shahar, Shulamith. 1983. *The fourth estate: A history of women in the middle ages*. London: Methuen.

———. 1990. *Childhood in the middle ages*. London: Routledge.

Shanley, Mary Lyndon. 2004. Just marriage. In *Just marriage*, ed. Mary Lyndon Shanley, Joshua Cohen, and Deborah Chasman, 3–30. New York: Oxford University Press.

Shanley, Mary Lyndon, Joshua Cohen, and Deborah Chasman. 2004. *Just marriage*. New York: Oxford University Press.

Sheehan, Michael M. 1971. The formation and stability of marriage in fourteenth-century England: Evidence of an Ely Register. *Medieval Studies* 33:228–63.

———. 1978. Choice of marriage partner in the middle ages: Development and mode of application and a theory of marriage. In *Studies in medieval renaissance history*, ed. J. A. S. Evans and R. W. Unger, 1–33. Vancouver: The University of British Columbia.

———. 1991a. "Maritalis affectio revisited. In *The olde daunce: Love, friendship, sex, and marriage in the medieval world*, ed. Robert R. Edwards and Stephen Spector, 32–43. Albany: State University of New York Press.

———. 1991b. The bishop of Rome to a barbarian king on the rituals of marriage. In *Iure veritas: Studies in canon law in memory of Shafer Williams*, ed. Steven B. Bowman and Blanche E. Cody, 187–99. Cincinnati, OH: University of Cincinnati College of Law.

Shorter, Edward. 1977. *The making of the modern family*. New York: Basic Books.

Shorter, Edward, John Knodel, and Etienne van de Walle. 1971. The decline of non-marital fertility in Europe. *Population Studies* 25 (3): 375–93.

Skinner, Burrhus F. 1953. *Science and human behavior*. New York: Macmillan.

———. 1957. *Verbal behavior*. New York: Appleton-Century-Crofts.

Slovenko, Ralph. 1965. A panoramic view: Sexual behavior and the law. In *Sexual behavior and the law*, ed. Ralph Slovenko, 5–146. Springfield, IL: Charles C. Thomas.

Sluijter, Eric Jan. 2000. *Seductress of sight: Studies in Dutch art of the golden age.* Zwolle, The Netherlands: Waanders Publishers.

Smith, Daniel S. 1978. Parental power and marriage patterns: An historical analysis of historical trends in Hingham, Massachusetts. In *The American family in social-historical perspective*, ed. Michael Gordon, 87–100. New York: St. Martin's Press.

———. 1981. Historical change in the household structure of the elderly in economically developed countries. In *Aging: Stability and change in the family*, ed. Robert W. Fogel, Elaine Hatfield, Sara B. Kiesler, and Ethel Shanas, 91–114. New York: Academic Press.

———. 1993. American family and demographic patterns and the northwest European model. *Continuity and Change* 8 (3): 389–415.

Smith, Daniel S., and Michael S. Hindus. 1975. Premarital pregnancy in American 1640–1971: An overview and interpretation. *Journal of Interdisciplinary History* 4:537–70.

Smith, Richard M. 1979. Some reflections on the evidence for the origins of the "European marriage pattern" in England. In *The sociology of the family: New directions for Britain*, ed. Chris Harris, Michael Anderson, Robert Chester, D. H. J. Morgan, and Diana Leonard, 74–112. Chester, England: Bemrose Press.

———. 1981. Fertility, economy, and household formation in England over three centuries. *Population and Development Review* 7 (4): 595–622.

———. 1984. Some issues concerning families and their property in rural England, 1250–1800. In *Land, kinship, and life-cycle*, ed. Richard M. Smith, 1–86. Cambridge, England: Cambridge University Press.

———. 1986. Marriage processes in the English past: Some continuities. In *The world we have gained: Histories of population and social structure*, eds. Lloyd Bonfield, Richard M. Smith, and Keith Wrightson, 43–99. Oxford: Basil Blackwell.

———. 1999. Relative prices, forms of agrarian labour and female marriage patterns in England, 1350–1800. In *Marriage and rural economy: Western Europe since 1400*, eds. Isabelle Devos and Liam Kennedy, 19–48. Belgium: Brepols.

Smith, Thomas E. 1988. Parental control techniques: Relative frequencies and relationships with situational factors. *Journal of Family Issues* 9 (2): 155–76.

Smock, Pamela J. 2000. Cohabitation in the United States: An appraisal of research themes, findings, and implications. *Annual Review of Sociology* 26:1–35.

———. 2004. The wax and wane of marriage: Prospects for marriage in the 21st century. *Journal of Marriage and the Family* 66 (4): 966–73.

Smock, Pamela J., and Wendy D. Manning. 1997. Cohabiting partners' economic circumstances and marriage. *Demography* 34 (3): 331–42.

———. 2004. Living together unmarried in the United States: Demographic perspectives and implications for family policy. *Law and Policy* 26 (1): 87–117.

Smout, T. Christopher 1981. Scottish marriage, regular and irregular 1500–1940. In *Marriage and society: Studies in the social history of marriage*, ed. R. Brian Outhwaite, 204–36. London: Europa Publications Limited.

Snell, Keith D. M. 2002. English rural societies and geographical marital endogamy, 1700–1837. *Economic History Review* 50 (2): 262–98.

South, Scott J. 1991. Sociodemographic differentials in mate selection preferences. *Journal of Marriage and the Family* 53 (4): 928–40.

———. 1993. Racial and ethnic differences in the desire to marry. *Journal of Marriage and the Family* 67:357–70.

———. 2001. The variable effects of family background on the timing of first marriage: United States, 1969–1993. *Social Science Research* 30 (4): 606–26.

Spain, Daphne, and Suzanne M. Bianchi. 1996. *Balancing act: Motherhood, marriage, and employment among American women.* New York: Russell Sage Foundation.

Stanley, Scott M., Galena H. Kline, and Howard J. Markman. 2005. The inertia hypothesis: Sliding vs. deciding in the development of risk for couples in marriage. Paper Presented at the Cohabitation: Advancing Theory and Research Conference, Bowling Green State University, Bowling Green, Ohio, February.

Stanton, Glenn T. 1997. *Why marriage matters.* Colorado Springs, CO: Piñon Press.

Stewart, Susan D., Wendy D. Manning, and Pamela J. Smock. 2003. Union formation among men in the U.S.: Does having prior children matter? *Journal of Marriage and the Family* 65 (1): 90–104.

Stiles, Henry R. 1934. *Bundling: Its origin, progress and decline in America.* New York: Book Collectors Association, Inc.

Stoertz, Fiona H. 2001. Young women in France and England, 1050–1300. *Journal of Women's History* 12 (4): 22–46.

Stolzenberg, Ross M., and Linda J. Waite. 1977. Age, fertility expectations and plans for employment. *American Sociological Review* 42 (5): 769–83.

Surra, Catherine A. 1990. Research and theory on mate selection and premarital relationships in the 1980s. *Journal of Marriage and the Family* 52 (4): 844–65.

Sweeney, Megan M. 1999. Reconsidering the importance of women's economic prospects for marriage: The roles of expected earnings trajectories and uncertainty. Paper presented at the Annual Meetings of the Population Association of America, New York, March 25–27.

———. 2002. Two decades of family change: The shifting economic foundations of marriage. *American Sociological Review* 67 (1): 132–47.

Sweet, James A. 1979. Estimates of levels, trends, and characteristics of the "living together" population from the current population survey. Center for Demography and Ecology Working Paper 79-49. Madison: University of Wisconsin.

Sweet, James A., and Larry L. Bumpass 1990. Religious differentials in marriage behavior and attitudes. *NSFH Working Paper No. 15.* Madison: University of Wisconsin, Center for Demography and Ecology.

———. 1992. Young adults' views of marriage, cohabitation, and family. In *The changing American family: Sociological and demographic perspective,* ed. Scott J. South and Stewart E. Tolnay, 143–70. Boulder, CO: Westview Press.

Tadmor, Naomi. 2001. *Family and friends in eighteenth-century England: Household, kinship, and patronage.* Cambridge, England: Cambridge University Press.

Taglia, Kathryn A. 1998. The cultural construction of childhood: Baptism, communion, and confirmation. In *Women, marriage, and family in medieval christendom,* ed. Constance M. Rousseau and Joel T. Rosenthal, 255–87. Kalamazoo: Medieval Institute Publications, Western Michigan University.

Taylor, R. J., J. S. Jackson, and L. M. Chatters. 1997. *Family life in black America.* Newbury Park, CA: Sage.

Taylor, R. J., M. B. Tucker, L. M. Chatters, and R. Jayakody. 1997. Recent demographic trends in African American family structure. In *Family life in Black America*, ed. R. J. Taylor, J. S. Jackson, and L. M. Chatters, 14–62. Newbury Park, CA: Sage.

Teachman, Jay D. 2003. Childhood living arrangements and the formation of coresidential unions. *Journal of Marriage and the Family* 65 (3): 507–24.

Teachman, Jay D., and Alex Heckert. 1985. The impact of age and children on remarriage. *Journal of Family Issues* 6 (2): 185–203.

Teachman, Jay D., Karen A. Polonko, and Geoffrey K. Leigh. 1987. Marital timing: Race and sex comparisons. *Social Forces* 66 (1): 239–68.

Thomas, Darwin L., and Marie Cornwall. 1990. Religion and family in the 1980s: Discovery and development. *Journal of Marriage and the Family* 52 (4): 983–92.

Thomson, Elizabeth, and Ugo Colella. 1992. Cohabitation and marital stability: Quality or commitment? *Journal of Marriage and the Family* 54 (2): 259–67.

Thornton, Arland. 1977. Decomposing the re-marriage process." *Population Studies* 31 (2): 383–92.

———. 1985a. Changing attitudes toward separation and divorce: Causes and consequences. *The American Journal of Sociology* 90 (4): 856–72.

———. 1985b. Reciprocal influences of family and religion in a changing world. *Journal of Marriage and the Family* 47 (2): 381–94.

———. 1988. Cohabitation and marriage in the 1980s. *Demography* 25 (4): 497–508.

———. 1989. Changing attitudes toward family issues in the United States. *Journal of Marriage and the Family* 51 (4): 873–93.

———. 1990. The courtship process and adolescent sexuality. *Journal of Family Issues* 11 (3): 239–73.

———. 1991. Influence of the marital history of parents on the marital and cohabitational experiences of children. *American Journal of Sociology* 96 (4): 868–94.

———. 1995. Perspectives on changing marriage, sexuality, and family life. *Bulletin of the Center for Regional Studies* (5): 26–35.

———. 2001. The developmental paradigm, reading history sideways, and family change. *Demography* 38 (4): 449–65.

———. 2005. *Reading history sideways: The fallacy and enduring impact of the developmental paradigm on family life.* Chicago: The University of Chicago Press.

Thornton, Arland, Duane Alwin, and Donald Camburn. 1983. Causes and consequences of sex role attitude change. *American Sociological Review* 48 (2): 211–27.

Thornton, Arland, and William G. Axinn. 1996. A review of the advantages and limitations of the intergenerational panel study of parents and children. Unpublished paper. Institute for Social Research, The University of Michigan.

Thornton, Arland, William G. Axinn, and Daniel Hill. 1992. Reciprocal effects of religiosity, cohabitation, and marriage. *American Journal of Sociology* 98 (3): 628–51.

Thornton, Arland, William G. Axinn, and Jay D. Teachman. 1995. The influence of school enrollment and accumulation on cohabitation and marriage in early adulthood. *American Sociological Review* 60 (5): 762–74.

Thornton, Arland, and Georgina Binstock. 2001. The reliability of measurement and the cross-time stability of individual and family variables. *Journal of Marriage and the Family* 63 (3): 881–94.

Thornton, Arland, and Donald Camburn. 1987. The influence of the family on premarital sexual attitudes and behavior. *Demography* 24 (3): 323–40.

———. 1989. Religious participation and adolescent sexual behavior and attitudes. *Journal of Marriage and the Family* 51:641–53.

Thornton, Arland, and Deborah S. Freedman. 1979. Changes in the sex role attitudes of women, 1962–1977: Evidence from a panel study. *American Sociological Review* 44 (5): 831–42.

———. 1982. Changing attitudes toward marriage and single life. *Family Planning Perspectives* 14 (6): 297–303.

———. 1983. The changing American family. *Population Bulletin* 38 (4): 85–90.

Thornton, Arland, Ronald Freedman, and William G. Axinn. 2002. Intergenerational panel study of parents and children. In *Landmark studies of the twentieth century*, ed. Anne Colby, Frank F. Furstenburg, and Erin Phelps, 315–44. New York: Russell Sage Foundation.

Thornton, Arland, and Thomas Fricke. 1987. Social change and the family: Comparative perspectives from the West, China, and South Asia. *Sociological Forum* 2 (4): 746–72.

Thornton, Arland, and Hui-Sheng Lin. 1994. *Social change and the family in Taiwan.* Chicago: University of Chicago Press.

Thornton, Arland, Terri L. Orbuch, and William G. Axinn. 1995. Parent-child relationships during the transition to adulthood. *Journal of Family Issues* 16 (5): 538–64.

Thornton, Arland, and Willard L. Rodgers. 1983. Changing patterns of marriage and divorce in the United States. *Final report to the National Institute of Child Health and Human Development.* Ann Arbor, MI: Institute for Social Research.

Thornton, Arland, and Linda Young-DeMarco. 1996. Measuring union formation and dissolution in surveys. Paper presented to the Interagency Forum on Data Needs for Children and Families, Washington, DC, May 22.

———. 2001. Four decades of trends in attitudes toward family issues in the United States: The 1960s through the 1990s. *Journal of Marriage and the Family* 63 (4): 1009–37.

Tilly, Louise A., Rachel G. Fuchs, David I. Kertzer, and David L. Ransel. 1992. Child abandonment in European history: A symposium. *Journal of Family History* 17 (1): 1–23.

Tilly, Louise A., and Joan W. Scott. 1978. *Women, work, and family.* New York: Hold, Rinehart, and Winston.

Toulemon, L. 1997. The fertility of step-families: The impact of childbearing before the current union. Paper for the Annual Meeting of the Population Association of America, Washington, DC, March 27–29.

Traer, John F. 1980. *Marriage and the family in eighteenth-century France*. Ithaca, NY: Cornell University Press.

Treas, Judith, and Deirdre Giesen. 2000. Sexual infidelity among married and cohabiting Americans. *Journal of Marriage and the Family* 62 (1): 48–60.

Trost, Jan. 1978. Attitudes toward and occurrence of cohabitation without marriage. *Journal of Marriage and the Family* 40 (1): 393–400.

———. 1979. *Unmarried cohabitation*. Vasteras, Sweden: International Library.

———. 1981. Cohabitation in the Nordic countries. *Alternative Lifestyles* 4 (4): 401–27.

———. 1988. Cohabitation and marriage: Transitional pattern, different lifestyle, or just another legal form. In *Lifestyles, contraception and parenthood*, eds. Hein Moors and Jeannette Schoorl, 3–14. The Hague: NIDI CBGS Publications.

U.S. Catholic Conference. 1977. *Declaration on sexual ethics: Sacred congregation for the doctrine of faith*. Washington, DC: Holy See: Persona Humana.

Udry, J. Richard. 1995. Sociology and biology: What biology do sociologists need to know? *Social Forces* 73 (4): 1267–78.

Ulrich, Laurel T. 1982. *Good wives: Image and reality in the lives of women in northern New England 1650–1750*. New York: Alfred A. Knopf.

van de Kaa, Dirk J. 1987. Europe's second demographic transition. *Population Bulletin* 42 (1): 1–59.

———. 1994. The second demographic transition revisited: Theories and expectations. In *Population and family in the low countries 1993: Late fertility and other current issues*, ed. Gijs Beets, Hans van den Brekel, Robert Cliquet, Gilbert Dooghe, and Jenny de Jong Gierveld, 81–126. Netherlands: Krips repro Meppel.

van de Walle, Etienne, and J. Knodel. 1980. Europe's fertility transition: New evidence and lessons for today's developing world. *Population Bulletin* 34 (6): 1–44.

Vaughn, Kathryn S. 1991. The recent changes to the Texas informal marriage statute: Limitation or abolition of common-law marriage? *Houston Law Review* 28 (5): 1131–69.

Ventura, Stephanie J. and Christine A. Bachrach. 2000. Nonmarital childbearing in the United States, 1940–99. *National Vital Statistics Reports* 48 (16): 1–40. Hyattsville, MD: National Center for Health Statistics.

Ventura, Stephanie J., Christine A. Bachrach, Laura Hill, Kelleen Kaye, Pamela Holcomb, and Elisa Koff. 1995. The demography of out-of-wedlock childbearing. In *Report to Congress on out-of-wedlock childbearing, DHHS Pub. No. (PHS) 95-1257*, 1–133. Washington, DC: U.S. Government Printing Office.

Vergara, Lisa. 2001. Perspectives on women in the art of Vermeer. In *The Cambridge companion to Vermeer*, ed. Wayne E Franits, 54–72. Cambridge, England: Cambridge University Press.

Vernier, Chester G. 1931. *American family laws vol. I. Introductory survey and marriage*. Stanford, CA: Stanford University Press.

Veroff, Joseph, Elizabeth A. M. Douvan, and Richard A. Kulka. 1981. *The inner American: A self-portrait from 1957 to 1976*. New York: Basic Books.

Viazzo, Pier P. 1986. Illegitimacy and the European marriage pattern: Comparative evidence from the Alpine area. In *The world we have gained: Histories of population and social structure*, ed. Lloyd Bonfield, Richard M. Smith, and Keith Wrightson, 100–21. Oxford: Basil Blackwell.

Vinokur-Kaplan, Diane 1978. To have—or not to have—another child: Family planning attitudes, intentions, and behavior. *Journal of Applied Social Psychology* 8: 29–46.

Waite, Linda J. 1995. Does marriage matter? *Demography* 32 (4): 483–507.

Waite, Linda J., Christine Bachrach, Michelle Hinden, Elizabeth Thomson, and Arland Thornton, eds. 2000. *Ties that bind: Perspectives on marriage and cohabitation*. Hawthorne, NY: Aldine de Gruyter.

Waite, Linda J., Frances Goldscheider, and Christina Witsberger. 1986. Nonfamily living and the erosion of traditional family orientations among young adults. *American Sociological Review* 51 (4): 541–54.

Waite, Linda J., and Maggie Gallagher. 2000. *The case for marriage*. Cambridge, MA: Harvard University Press.

Waite, Linda J., and Glenna D. Spitze. 1981. Young women's transition to marriage. *Demography* 18 (4): 681–94.

Waite, Linda J., and Ross M. Stolzenberg. 1976. Intended childbearing and labor force participation of young women: Insights from nonrecursive models. *American Sociological Review* 41 (2): 235–51.

Waldfogel, Jane. 1997. Working mothers then and now: A cross-cohort analysis of the effects of maternity leave on women's pay. In *Gender and family issues in the workplace*, ed. Francine D. Blau and Ronald G. Ehrenberg, 92–126. New York: Russell Sage.

Wardle, Lynn D. 1999. Divorce reform at the turn of the millennium: Certainties and possibilities. *Family Law Quarterly* 33 (3): 783–900.

Weinstein, Maxine, and Arland Thornton. 1989. Mother-child relations and adolescent sexual attitudes and behavior. *Demography* 26 (4): 563–77.

Weir, David R. 1984. Rather never than late: Celibacy and age at marriage in English cohort fertility, 1541–1871. *Journal of Family History* 9 (4): 340–54.

Weiss, Robert S. 1979. Growing up a little faster: The experience of growing up in a single-parent household. *Journal of Social Issues* 35 (4): 97–111.

Weitzman, Lenore J. 1981. *The marriage contract: Spouses, lovers, and the law*. New York: The Free Press.

———. 1985. *The divorce revolution*. New York: Free Press.

Westfall, David. 2001. Forcing incidents of marriage on unmarried cohabitants: The American law institute's *principles of family dissolution*. *Notre Dame Law Review* 76 (5): 1467–90.

Westoff, Charles F., and Norman B. Ryder. 1977. *The contraceptive revolution*. Princeton, NJ: Princeton University Press.

Weyrauch, Walter O. 1965. Informal marriage and common law marriage. In *Sexual behavior and the law*, ed. Robert Slovenko, 297–340. Springfield, IL: Charles C. Thomas.

———. 1980. Metamorphoses of marriage. *Family Law Quarterly* 13 (4): 415–40.

Weyrauch, Walter O., Sanford N. Katz, and Frances Olsen. 1994. *Cases and materials on family law: Legal concepts and changing human relationships*. St. Paul, MN: West Publishing Company.

Whitbeck, Les B., Ronald L. Simons, and Meei-ying Kao. 1994. The effects of divorced mothers' dating behaviors and sexual attitudes on the sexual attitudes and behaviors of their adolescent children. *Journal of Marriage and the Family* 56 (3): 615–21.

Whitehead, Barbara D., and David Popenoe. 2001. *The state of our unions: The social health of marriage in America, 2001.* New Brunswick, NJ: National Marriage Project.

———. 1999. Why wed? Young adults talk about sex, love, and first unions. Rutgers University: The National Marriage Project. A focus group report from The Next Generation Series.

Whitelock, Dorothy. 1952. *The beginnings of English society.* Baltimore: Penguin Books.

Whyte, Martin K. 1990. *Dating, mating, and marriage.* New York: Aldine de Gruyter.

Wilcox, W. Bradford. 1998. Conservative Protestant childrearing: Authoritarian or authoritative. *American Sociological Review* 63 (6): 796–809.

———. 2002. Religion, convention, and parental involvement. *Journal of Marriage and the Family* 64 (3): 780–92.

Wildsmith, Elizabeth, and R. Kelly Raley. 2006. Race-ethnic differences in non-marital fertility: A focus on Mexican American women. *Journal of Marriage and the Family* 68 (2): 491–508.

Wilkie, Jane R. 1993. Changes in U.S. men's attitudes toward the family provider role, 1972–1989. *Gender and Society* 7 (2): 261–279.

Willcox, Walter F. 1897/1891. *The divorce problem: A study in statistics.* New York: Columbia University Press.

Willis, Robert J. 1973. A new approach to the economic theory of fertility behavior. *Journal of Political Economy* 81 (2): S14–S64.

Wilson, James Q. 2002. *The marriage problem.* New York: HarperCollins Publishers.

Wilson, Stephen. 1984. The myth of motherhood a myth: The historical view of European child-rearing. *Social History* 9 (2): 181–98.

Wilson, William J. 1987. *The truly disadvantaged: The inner city, the underclass, and public policy.* Chicago: University of Chicago Press.

Witte, John, Jr. 1997. *From sacrament to contract: Marriage, religion and law in the western tradition.* Louisville, KY: Westminster John Knox Press.

Wolfinger, Nicholas H. 2001. The effects of family structure of origin on offspring cohabitation duration. *Sociological Inquiry* 71 (3): 293–313.

Wolfle, L. 1985. Post-secondary educational attainment among Whites and Blacks. *American Educational Research Journal* 22:501–25.

Wrightson, Keith. 1982. *English society, 1580–1680.* London: Hutchinson & Co. Ltd.

Wrigley, Edward A. 1981. Marriage, fertility, and population growth in eighteenth-century England. In *Marriage and society: Studies in the social history of marriage,* ed. R. Brian Outhwaite, 137–85. London: Europa Publications Limited.

Wrigley, Edward A., and Roger S. Schofield. 1981. *The population history of England 1541–1871: A reconstruction.* Cambridge, MA: Harvard University Press.

Wu, Lawrence. 1996. Effects of family instability, income, and income instability on the risk of premarital birth. *American Sociological Review* 61 (3): 386–406.

Wu, Lawrence, and Brian Martinson. 1993. Family structure and the risk of a pre-marital birth. *American Sociological Review* 58 (2): 210–32.

Wu, Zheng, and T. R. Balkrishnan. 1995. Dissolution of premarital cohabitation in Canada. *Demography* 32:521–32.

Wuthnow, Robert. 1998. *After heaven: Spirituality in America since the 1950s.* Berkeley: University of California Press.

Xie, Yu, and Kimberly Goyette. 2004. *A demographic portrait of Asian Americans.* New York: Russell Sage Foundation and Population Reference Bureau.

Xie, Yu, James M. Raymo, Kimberly Goyette, and Arland Thornton. 2003. Economic potential and entry into marriage and cohabitation. *Demography* 40 (2): 351–67.

Xie, Yu, and Kimberlee A. Shauman. 1998. Sex differences in research productivity: New evidence about an old puzzle. *American Sociological Review* 63 (6): 847–70.

Zelnik, Melvin, and John F. Kantner. 1980. Sexual activity, contraceptive use and pregnancy among metropolitan area teenagers: 1971–1979." *Family Planning Perspectives* 12 (5): 30–36.

Zelnik, Melvin, John F. Kanter, and Kathleen Ford. 1981. *Sex and pregnancy in adolescence.* Beverly Hills, CA: Sage Publications.

Zumthor, Paul. 1994. *Daily life in Rembrandt's Holland.* Translated by Simon Watson Taylor. Stanford, CA: Stanford University Press.

Index

Note: 1962 refers to events when the child was an infant; 1977 refers to events when the child was an adolescent; 1980 refers to events when the child was 18 years of age.